BERLITZ®

DISCOVER
PYRENEES

Edited and Designed by
D & N Publishing,
Lambourn, Berkshire.

Cartography by
Hardlines, Charlbury, Oxfordshire.

2nd Edition (1994/1995)

Printed by C.S. Graphics, Singapore.

Although we have made every effort to ensure the accuracy of all the information in this book, changes occur incessantly. We cannot therefore take responsibility for facts, addresses and circumstances in general that are constantly subject to alteration.

All photographs by the authors.

Front cover photograph: view of the Pyrenees by A. James, courtesy of the Daily Telegraph Colour Library.

Back cover photograph: Pyrenean landscape by the authors.

 The Berlitz tick is used to indicate places or events of particular interest.

Acknowledgements
We would like to thank Chantal Corbineau for translation.

BERLITZ®

DISCOVER
PYRENEES

Paul Jenner

Christine Smith

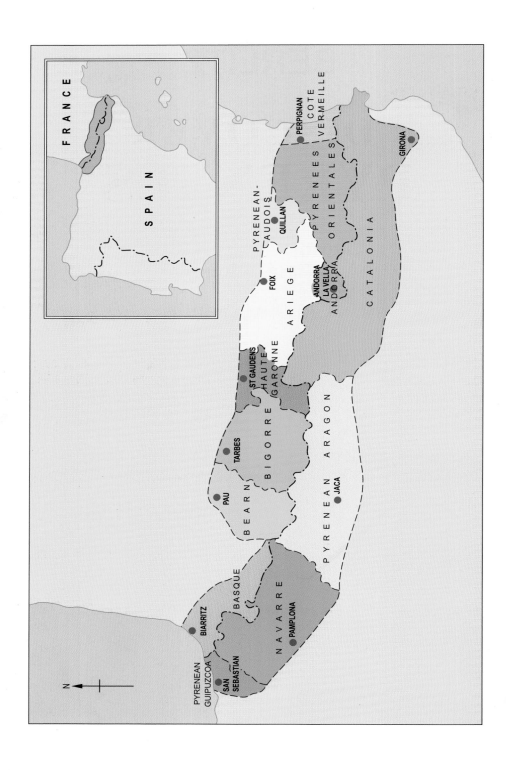

FRANCE

SPAIN

PERPIGNAN

CÔTE VERMEILLE

GIRONA

PYRENEAN-AUDOIS

PYRÉNÉES ORIENTALES

QUILLAN

FOIX

ARIEGE

ANDORRA LA VELLA

ANDORRA

CATALONIA

ST GAUDENS

HAUTE-GARONNE

TARBES

BIGORRE

PYRENEAN ARAGON

PAU

JACA

BEARN

BASQUE

PYRENEAN GUIPUZCOA

BIARRITZ

NAVARRE

PAMPLONA

SAN SEBASTIAN

N

Contents

The Practicalities and Pre-planning

This chapter is designed to help you work out the most suitable time of the year to visit the Pyrenees, to decide which of the main centres interest you most, to sort out transport considerations, and to plan the essentials of accommodation and eating. Every month in the Pyrenees there is something special to offer the visitor. Travel freely, ignoring frontiers, and you will have a wonderful time.

When to Go

The Pyrenees have plenty to offer at all times of the year. The traditional main season of July and August has as much to do with the timing of school holidays as with the weather. If you can avoid the two peak months you will find accommodation easier, the roads quieter and the mountains more tranquil. In fact, the Pyrenees in July and August are not merely crowded but

*A*tlantic breakers attract surfers to the Basque coast every summer, but they are beautiful to watch too.

can be unbearably hot, especially on the eastern side, when all enthusiasm for hiking is drained. Moreover, these are the thunderstorm months, when clouds build up around the high peaks during the day, climaxing in the early afternoon with lightning flashes and rolling thunder. It can be spectacular from the valleys but it is actually dangerous for high-mountain walkers (who should start early and be off the summits by lunchtime). That is not to say a visit to the Pyrenees in high summer will not be enchanting. The meadows will be covered with flowers and flickering butterflies, tourist attractions will be in full swing and, for those who seek solitude, there are always quiet corners to be found away from the more famous beauty spots.

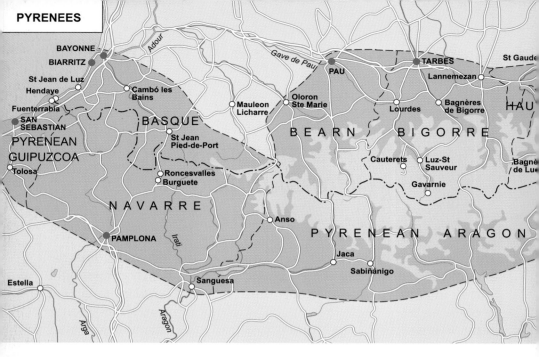

M *ap of the whole Pyrenees region.*

But early summer and early autumn will be better still, when the crowds have receded. If you are at all interested in high-mountain walking, you should aim to arrive in the early autumn because all but the highest passes will then be clear of snow and ice; before summer the snow will still be on the upper slopes, making hiking difficult and even dangerous. If you also plan to swim in the Atlantic or Mediterranean (or to plunge into mountain streams) the water will be at its warmest in early autumn. But those who intend to remain more in the valleys and along the low-level walks will

S *pring is a magical time in the Pyrenees, with mountainsides covered in flowers, like these wild roses.*

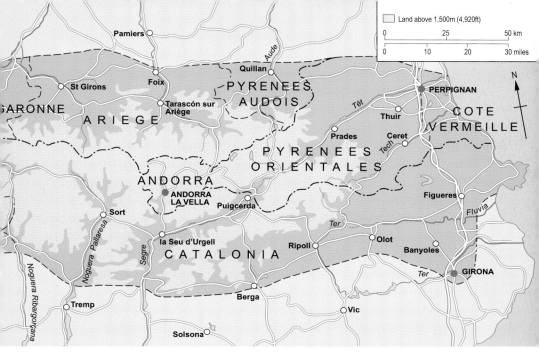

Pamiers

St Girons

Foix

Quillan

PYRENEES
AUDOIS

Tarascón sur
Ariège

A R I E G E

Aude

Têt

PERPIGNAN

Thuir

Prades

Ceret

COTE
VERMEILLE

Tech

GARONNE

PYRENEES
ORIENTALES

ANDORRA

ANDORRA
LA VELLA

Puigcerda

Sort

la Seu d'Urgell

Ripoll

Olot

Banyoles

Figueres

Fluvia

Ter

GIRONA

C A T A L O N I A

Ter

Noguera Pallaresa

Segre

Noguera Ribargorçana

Tremp

Berga

Vic

Solsona

Land above 1,500m (4,920ft)

0   25   50 km

0   10   20   30 miles

N

enjoy May and June, when the hillsides are dotted with flowers like an Impressionist painting. These are also the months for canoeing, because the rivers are full with melt-water.

Winter is the ski season in the high mountains but it can also be a marvellous time at slightly lower altitudes, especially in the eastern Pyrenees where Mediterranean influences prevail. Rainfall is then a matter of luck but, as a rule of thumb, it is better to be at altitude and above the cloud mass which covers the plains and valleys frequently in winter. The western Pyrenees, however, should be avoided by non-skiers in winter, having higher rainfall and less winter sun than the east.

*T*hunderstorms can build up very quickly in the high mountains in July and August—aim to be off summits by early afternoon.

9

Travel Documents

All tourists require a passport for stays of up to 90 days in each country. No EU citizens require visas.

For stays in excess of 90 days, a *permanencia* is necessary in Spain or a *Carte de Séjour* in France. In either case, evidence of financial soundness is required.

Insurance

Spain and France have reciprocal health agreements with Britain and travellers should order form E111 from the DSS two weeks before departure. Motorists are also protected by the EU regulation that a driver properly insured in his own country will automatically enjoy the minimum legally

Snow can cut off mountain villages even in late spring. This one is having to be supplied by helicopter in May.

Either motor insurance can be extended to the Continent for a specific period or, for frequent travellers, it is now possible to take out a policy covering all of Europe. Health and theft can both be dealt with under a normal travel insurance policy and this should additionally cover such matters as cancellation of travel arrangements due to ill health, repatriation by air ambulance and injury to third parties whilst taking part in sports activities. Note that for participation in dangerous sports such as skiing, diving and *parapente*, an additional premium may be payable. It is vital that you inform your insurers at the outset of any intention to take part in activity sports, otherwise, should an accident occur, the financial repercussions may not be covered. If you should need to be rescued from the site of a high-mountain accident then this can be enormously expensive; one of the cheapest ways of obtaining this cover, if not included in the travel policy, is to join the outdoor association known as *Randonnées Pyrénéennes*. Membership with insurance cover for recovery costs throughout western Europe, as well as injury to third parties costs about 100F. The address is: Randonnées Pyrénéennes, 29 rue Marcel Lamarque, 65000 Tarbes, France. Similarly, France has an excellent system of ski insurance which will cover British skiers on both sides of the Pyrenees. Known

required motor insurance of any EU country travelled in. There is no legal requirement to obtain travel insurance and a good household policy will, indeed, give a measure of protection against theft. However, while additional insurance for a holiday in the Pyrenees is not strictly necessary, it is strongly advised that you obtain additional specific cover.

as *Carte Neige* it can be bought very reasonably at any French Pyrenean ski station and many ski-equipment shops and gives cover for an entire year. The policy does not cover loss of equipment, however, only personal injury and damage to third parties. Travellers to the Pyrenees need have no fears about the quality of medical services available in the region, especially on the French side of the range. Experience with mountain injuries, in particular, is great.

In both France and Spain you will have to pay for prescriptions and treatment at the time, except in emergencies. You will receive a stamped receipt with which the costs may be reclaimed.

Rail Concessions

Both French and Spanish railways operate the recently introduced Freedom Pass system of flexible budget-price travel coupons. These are available for individuals or families travelling together, and allow free rail travel on any 3, 5 or 10 days within a one-month period, in the country or countries of your choice. The coupons must be purchased outside the country or countries in which they are to be used—in other words, for travel to the Pyrenees, they should be purchased in the UK.

For those who wish to travel across several countries of Europe the Inter-rail pass is currently available in two forms; the under 26 version is valid for 4 weeks and allows free rail travel in 26 countries, including Morocco. There is also an inter-rail pass available for those aged over 26, which is valid for either 2 or 4 weeks, covering fewer countries at higher cost.

The Spanish railway company RENFE has its own special offers, especially on the so-called "Blue Days" when discounts of up to 50 per cent are available. SNCF, the French railway company, has a similar three-tier system of blue days (highest discount), white days (medium discount) and red days (full price). The French TGV (high-speed train) from Paris to Bordeaux and Biarritz offers substantial discounts for advance booking.

Health

There are no particular risks to health involved in travelling in the Pyrenees. Water is fit to drink everywhere in the range, rabies is not a threat and the malarial mosquito that plagued the marshes of Roussillon and Emporda has now been eradicated. There is a slight risk to health from sea bathing in certain areas, however. Some beaches at St Maries de la Mer, St Nazaire, St Cyprien, Port Vendres and Cerbère on the French Mediterranean coast; Anglet, Biarritz and Cibourne on the French Atlantic coast; and at San Sebastian on the Spanish Atlantic coast, have in the past failed to meet minimum EU standards for bathing water quality. Efforts are being made, however, to bring all French and Spanish beaches up to standard and if you are particularly concerned about the health risks of sea bathing you should ask for an up-to-date list of safe beaches from the nearest tourist office. Remember that mountain sunshine is stronger than on the plain, both summer and winter, so sunglasses, hats and good protection creams are essential.

Where to Go

Whatever your taste, for beaches or mountains, cosmopolitan towns or remote hamlets, sophisticated hotels or friendly inns, vigorous outdoor sports or fascinating historical sites, the Pyrenees have something to offer.

Biarritz

With its luxury hotels, promenades, golf courses and wide beaches (washed by an Atlantic swell that attracts surf enthusiasts from all over Europe), Biarritz is one of the most sophisticated resorts of the Pyrenees. If style, comfort, gourmet eating, up-market shops, swimming, sunbathing and only occasional excursions into the mountains are the essential ingredients of your ideal holiday then Biarritz is the base for you.

St Jean Pied-de-Port

An immensely picturesque small town of half-timbered houses, St Jean Pied-de-Port was an important halt on the fa-

Catalonia, like all the regions of the Pyrenees, is fiercely proud of its culture, but happily embraces the European Union. Travel across Pyrenean frontiers is easy—but remember to have your passport with you all the same.

mous Santiago de Compostela pilgrim route. It sits at the foot of the Ibañeta pass where Charlemagne's rearguard was wiped out on its retreat from Spain. The battle was made famous by the medieval French epic poem *Chanson de Roland* (although the portrayal was highly inaccurate). Intimate and colourful, St Jean Pied-de-Port has plenty of cultural and folkloric entertainments, fine Basque restaurants (including one of the best in the Pyrenees) and marvellous scenery.

Pau

13

Pau

Pau is a prosperous university town with shops that are chic by Pyrenean standards. It makes an excellent centre for touring the **Aspe** and **Ossau** valleys to the south, where lush emerald-green pastures produce some of the best cheeses in the range. Higher, in the dense woodlands, a few surviving brown bear still roam, especially close to the exquisite **Cirque of Lescun**, one of the most enchanting beauty spots in the Pyrenees. Pau itself has a fine château, the earliest part built by Gaston Fébus, and in which Henri IV of France was born in 1553. It is also a town with strong British connections, beginning in the 12th century and strongly revived with the arrival of Wellington's troops during the Peninsular War.

Lourdes and the Pyrenees National Park

In season, thousands of pilgrims flood to the daily services in Lourdes in the hope of a miracle, or simply to be part of one of the world's great religious events. Lourdes is also the gateway to the central part of the Pyrenees National Park which boasts the opportunity to see izards, marmots and lammergeiers (Europe's largest vulture) plus the dramatic **Cirque of Gavarnie**. Do not miss this natural rock ampitheatre that is unquestionably one of the great natural wonders of the world. If you would like to combine human and natural spectacle then Lourdes and its surroundings are essential.

Luchon

If your taste is catholic then the mountain town of Luchon is for you. A spa since the mid-18th century, soon becoming the fashionable base for exploration of the highest part of the chain, Luchon has something for all the family, all tastes and all pockets. While none are in the luxury or gourmet class, its hotels and restaurants range from the good to the inexpensive and the surrounding mountains provide plenty of variety. You can drive, stroll, picnic and visit ancient sites or, if you want to be more active, experience the full range of mountain pursuits from hiking and climbing to horse-riding and even hang-gliding.

Foix

Foix is the main town of the Ariège, one of the most satisfying regions of all the Pyrenees for the tremendous diversity of things to see and do. It was here, for example, that prehistoric man left his greatest artworks, in the marvellous caves at Niaux, La Vache, Bédeilhac and Mas d'Azil. Here too stand the sad ruins of the Cathar religion, such as the castle at Montségur, a monument to human intolerance. For hikers this is the most demanding part of the range with deep, dank valleys rising with heart-thumping steepness through dense woods to high plateaux and savage peaks.

Quillan

Quillan is the principal town of the Pyrenean part of the *département* of the Aude, where the river of the same name cuts through the mountains in a series of superb and dramatic gorges. As an ingredient of your holiday, it is wonderful car-touring country with an endless succession of exhilarating

The Pyrenees are not all the Great Outdoors but have played an important rôle in the history of art. Hyacinthe-Rigaud was a society painter born in Perpignan in 1659.

scenes unfolding on the other side of the windscreen. For the active there are walks of all categories, horse-riding and canoeing, and even the Grotte l'Aguzou, the most superb cave system in the Pyrenees that is open to the general public.

Perpignan

With its benign climate and position close to the Spanish frontier, Perpignan has attracted immigration from other parts of France, from Catalan Spain and from North Africa. It is therefore the most cosmopolitan town of all the Pyrenees, with a tremendous diversity and vitality. There are colourful street markets with goods from Algeria and Morocco and boutiques with the latest Paris fashions. There are gipsy buskers and concert evenings of Franck and Debussy; there are pavement artists and there are art galleries. Moreover, Perpignan has access to the aromatic scenery of the Mediterranean Pyrenees where the huge number of Romanesque churches underlines the almost spiritual luminance of the landscape.

Collioure

Once an important fishing port, Collioure is now a relaxed artists' haven where the old lateen-rigged *barques*, colourfully restored, float complacently in front of the harbourside cafés. The most atmospheric of the Côte Vermeille resorts (the French counterpart of the Spanish Costa Brava), Collioure is literally surrounded by vermilion sea cliffs resulting not only in a dramatic coastline of inlets and islets but also in an underwater habitat of immense beauty and importance. Just to the south, the alternative base of Banyuls-sur-Mer, set among the vineyards that produce the famous dessert wine, was the home of the sculptor Maillol.

Andorra la Vella

Remaining outside the European Community, Andorra la Vella—and all of the principality of Andorra of which it is capital—has become synonymous with tax—and duty-free spending. The shops are packed with the latest

Under the hot sun of the Mediterranean Pyrenees all kinds of exotic plants explode into growth—like these wild vines near Collioure.

consumer goods, especially electrical products, cameras, sports equipment, jewellery, watches, fashions, tobacco and alcohol. Prices are undeniably cheap by Spanish, and especially by French standards; but they are not necessarily cheaper than in Britain. Although the hotels are amazingly inexpensive, Andorra la Vella is a place to visit rather than to linger (unless you really love shopping). If you do stay, take the time to discover the traditional Andorra that still exists high in the unspoilt mountains, aloof from the commercialism of the valleys below. In winter, Andorra has the most reliable skiing in the Pyrenees.

San Sebastián

San Sebastián is the Spanish counterpart to Biarritz, with the same resort ambience of sophistication and grandeur, but laced with the earthy sounds, sights and smells of a south-of-the border working city. If you like to shop late into the evening, dine even later, stay out until the small hours and catch up with your sleep on the beach, then San Sebastián rather than Biarritz is the base for you.

Pamplona and the Navarre Nature Park

Made famous by Ernest Hemingway in his novel *Fiesta*, Pamplona is the quintessential bullfight town of the world. But bullfighting is not what it was in Hemingway's age of innocence when animal suffering was ignored and "green" thinking was unknown. Bullfighting aside, Pamplona is the only great town of the Navarrese Pyrenees from which to make tours into the Navarre Nature Park to the north. Here lie the last great forests of the range and tiny villages where Basque culture and language are kept alive.

Jaca

Boasting the finest Romanesque cathedral south of the Franco-Spanish border, Jaca is the obvious town base for excursions into the eastern end of the Navarre Nature Park which stretches from Roncesvalles (northeast of Pamplona) to the Belagoa valley. The griffon vultures which inevitably float above the town emphasize the remoteness of the region, which is also the final sanctuary for the Pyrenean brown bear. If you are a bird lover you will also be able to see black and Egyptian vultures and lammergeiers (bearded vultures). Here, too, around the peak of Trés Reyes, is some of the most bizarre scenery in all the Pyrenees, where naked limestone has been tortured into fantastic shapes.

*P*igeon shooting, from wooden platforms built on hillsides, is a way of life in the Basque country.

Torla and the Ordesa National Park

Torla is only a tiny village but it is the gateway to the exhilarating Ordesa National Park. The mighty **Ordesa Canyon** truly rivals America's Grand Canyon and, along with the Cirque of Gavarnie, ranks as the most important natural spectacle of the range. This is an experience not to be missed.

Benasque

Everyone should also visit Benasque and the surrounding mountains which contain the two highest peaks of the range, **Aneto** (3,404 metres/11,170 ft) and **Posets** (3,375 metres/11,073 ft). And, indeed, if you are a real mountain enthusiast for whom shops and gourmet eating are of minor significance, then this attractive and lively village could be the place to spend your entire holiday. For everyone else, Benasque is an indispensable part of the high Pyrenees car tour.

The Boí Valley and the Aigües Tortes National Park

The Boí Valley, on the western side of the Aigües Tortes National Park, is famous for its collection of Romanesque churches. **Caldas de Boí** is a luxurious spa complex in the valley, which is both a good base for exploring or to spend idle days unwinding. The park, the only national park in Catalonia, is famous for its hundreds of lakes and streams, from which it derives its name meaning "twisted waters".

Girona

With its long history of sieges, all of which have left their mark on its architecture, Girona is unique in the Pyrenees. It is the complete town of the range, not merely on account of its hotels, restaurants and shops but also for its marvellous museums and historic sites, ranging from the medieval to *modernisme*. And when all that has been explored, there is the scenery of Emporda, which includes the rugged Costa Brava coastline, the weird volcanic Garrotxa region and the resin-scented mountains to the north.

Cadaqués

Cadaqués simply oozes art. Salvador Dalí lived nearby and the white-painted houses and cobbled streets of Cadaqués have ever since been a mecca for painters and for anyone with artistic pretensions. The surrounding coastline is also the least spoiled along the Costa Brava; if you have a strong pair of legs, or have brought your own inflatable boat, you can seek out the tranquil and often unpeopled coves that are the real Costa Brava—literally, the "wild coast".

Getting There

There are plenty of flights from most major airports in Europe, the U.S.A. and Canada, and it is possible to pre-arrange car rental from Perpignan, Toulouse, Tarbes/Lourdes, Bordeaux, Girona or Barcelona airports. France has a marvellous rail network along main routes and the Spanish rail services are being fully modernized. There are a number of special fares available. Finally there are the long-distance coach services which may not appeal to everyone, but which are a direct and cheap option.

By Car

For a speedy journey, the good long-distance motorways through France could hardly be bettered. They are monotonous, but easy for driving, and the service areas are of a high standard. But for a more stimulating journey there is a vast network of minor and not so minor roads which, with a detailed map, will take you across country, often in a more direct line than the motorway. By motorway it is possible to complete the journey from Britain with one overnight stop, whereas taking the slower roads will add at least one extra night. It is worth bearing in mind that the motorway tolls north to south will amount to the equivalent of a modest overnight stop with dinner.

There are two main motorways serving the Pyrenees. One is the A10, western route, the other the A6 eastern route (becoming the A7 at Lyons). Both lead off the Paris ring-road system (which is to be avoided at all costs at rush hours and holiday times). From

The Mérens are the authentic horse-power of the eastern Pyrenees. From Mérens-les-Vals in the Ariège, they are closely related to the wild horses of European prehistory.

19

Dunkirk, Calais or Boulogne, Paris is most rapidly reached by the A1 motorway; passengers to Dieppe, Le Havre, Caen and Cherbourg can pick up the A13 motorway to Paris.

Almost all motorway service areas offer meals, toilets (usually pretty clean) and a wide range of motorist facilities. The experts recommend a maximum of two hours non-stop motorway driving, with rest and refreshment to keep the driver at maximum alertness. If you do not want petrol or a meal choose one of the many *aires* or rest areas. These are more frequent than service areas and usually consist of just a toilet block and some shaded parking. For overnights, motorway service areas do not often have pleasing accommodation and are expensive. If you have the time it is better to turn off the motorway and find something more sympathetic in one of the towns or villages close by. The top speed on motorways is 80 mph (130 kph) and you should not travel in the fast lane any slower than 50 mph (80 kph). Continental drivers tend to keep the indicator flashing while in the fast lane. This lets the driver coming up fast behind know you are still overtaking. Indicate to the right when you are ready to pull in once more.

Choosing a route along more minor roads requires skilful navigation. It seems that many important signposts are positioned so that only drivers coming from the other direction can read them. At complicated town junctions it is often worth looking behind to see if the sign you seek is there. Petrol stations are frequent on main roads, close to towns, but much less so on the minor ones. Many villages have one or two pumps attached to the local garage or even shop. These will invariably look closed, but a single hoot tends to bring the attendant from within. These smaller garages rarely take credit cards and many are closed on Sundays and holidays.

There is always plenty of choice of wayside hotels and restaurants. Shops start closing for lunch at about midday, so stocking up for picnics should be done before this time. As lay-bys are inevitably dirty and not much fun, pull into a quiet lane and make the most of a short break. Wherever you stop, it is very important that you take all your rubbish away with you.

A minor road will double journey time compared to a motorway, so many regular tourers combine motorway and route national or D-road itineraries for variety and efficiency. The idea is to clock up as many kilometres as possible each morning and at lunchtime turn off for some country hostelry. The rest of the day is spent on minor roads and finding suitable accommodation for the night. It is advisable to start looking for a hotel quite early, from about 5 p.m., to give time for a couple of disappointments and then a shower and aperitif before dinner. In the country last orders can be as early as 9 p.m.

It is important that the car log book and insurance documents are carried. Any accident or infringement of driving regulations may lead to documents being checked and spot fines.

Ferry Services

If coming from Britain, the choice of Channel crossing depends largely on the itinerary. The ferry routes that go closest to the Pyrenees are the Brittany Ferries Plymouth–Santander service (from Portsmouth during the winter months) and the P & O European Ferries service from Portsmouth to Bilbao. Average journey times are a little over 24 hours, but you will be travelling aboard a luxurious ship. From Santander or Bilbao you can drive to San Sebastián, where the Pyrenees begin, in about three hours. The demand in mid-summer is extremely heavy and reservations should therefore be made well in advance.

The so-called short sea Dover–Calais and Dover–Boulogne crossings, by both P & O European Ferries and Stena Sealink, are under 90 minutes on the latest ferries and even less by hovercraft or Seacat (Hoverspeed). Both Calais and Boulogne are within easy reach of the motorway. Other alternatives are: Sally Line, Ramsgate to Dunkirk; P & O European Ferries, Portsmouth to Le Havre and Cherbourg; Stena Sealink, Newhaven to Dieppe, Southampton to Cherbourg; Brittany Ferries, Portsmouth to Caen and St Malo, Poole to Cherbourg and Plymouth to Roscoff. For travellers from Ireland, Brittany Ferries also operates services from Cork to Roscoff and St Malo. For an early start on the Continent an overnight crossing on one of the longer routes is recommended. In peak season these can be fully booked and early reservation is necessary. Even on day journeys a cabin is a worthwhile and an inexpensive luxury on these longer routes.

In general, 90 minutes should be added to the arrival time of the ferry—one hour to take account of Continental time and the other thirty minutes to allow for unloading, Customs and port traffic delays.

By Plane

For direct flights from Britain, the most convenient airports for the Pyrenees are Biarritz (Air France), Bordeaux (Air France and British Airways), Tarbes/Lourdes (British Airways and charters), Toulouse (Air France and British Airways), Perpignan (British Airways), Girona (charters) and Barcelona (Iberia, British Airways and charters). It is also possible (but more expensive) to fly to Paris and catch a domestic connection (Air Inter or Air France). Charter flights are normally the cheapest (but note that for children, the 50 per cent discount on scheduled flights generally undercuts the charter price). Booking a package holiday may sometimes prove the cheapest way of buying a flight; on arrival you can ignore the hotel reservations and follow your own itinerary.

By Train

Rail used to be *the* method of travel through Europe before the coming of cheap jet travel, but now it has considerably waned in popularity. The Continental rail services, however, are trying to win back customers with much faster, more luxurious facilities. The bugbear of taking the train to the Pyrenees remains the necessity, with rare exceptions, of having to change from Gare du Nord to Gare Austerlitz in Paris, but it is possible to check bags right through in advance. The food in the restaurant cars can be surprisingly good. There are special senior citizen (over-65s) and youth (under 26) fares available.

Many motorists like to break the back of the journey south by taking the Motorail service which carries both passengers and cars from Boulogne, Calais, Dieppe and Paris to Narbonne. The fares are relatively expensive but you save on overnight hotel accommodation as well as tolls, petrol and wear and tear both on the car and on yourself.

Getting About

Driving

A car enormously enhances enjoyment of the Pyrenees since many of the most spectacular areas are inaccessible by public transport. If you are arriving by air or train you should therefore consider hiring a car for at least part of the stay. Costs are slightly lower on the Spanish side of the range.

Driving in the Pyrenees is hugely enjoyable. Tiny roads climb in steep hairpins to high passes and precarious viewpoints and there are still areas on both sides of the range that are served by track. Unfortunately or fortunately, depending upon your point of view, many of the narrow roads are being widened and many unsurfaced roads surfaced, all as part of the EU programme to bring infrastructure to a common standard. For the moment, however, the adventurous motorist has plenty of scope.

Naturally the important connecting routes are wide and well-engineered but high average speeds are only possible well away from the crestline. The fastest west–east traverse lies on the French side of the range which is skirted by the excellent Bayonne–Toulouse–Perpignan motorway system. Motorways also run along the coast at both extremities of the range. Inevitably it is quicker to make a long journey by motorway rather than cut across country; from Toulouse, for example, it would be quicker to reach the Canigou massif by taking the motorway to Perpignan, rather than heading directly towards the massif on minor roads.

Drink-driving limits in France are the same as in Britain and there are random breath tests. The on-the-spot fine for exceeding the drink drive limit is from 2,000F to 30,000F. The minimum fine for speeding is 1,300F. In Spain the police also have the power to make on-the-spot fines and the level is almost as high.

In France yellow-tinted headlights are not compulsory for tourists (and, in fact, to conform with the rest of the EU, France will have to change to white headlamps). Beams should be adjusted for right-hand driving, however, for either France or Spain—the black plastic adhesive strips available from car accessory shops will do. You should also be equipped with a warning triangle (although this is not a legal requirement in France for cars fitted with hazard warning lights) and a set of spare bulbs.

Extension of insurance cover for Continental motoring (as proven by possession of a green card) is no longer necessary, but is still highly advisable, since otherwise you will only have the minimum level of compulsory insurance applicable to the country you are travelling in.

First-time motorists in France and Spain are often unnerved by the give-way-to-the-right rule, but in reality this only applies to towns and generally not even then to major roads passing through. It is vital to be alert for the rule, however, where minor roads intersect in a town. The rule has now been abolished on French roundabouts so that you give way to traffic already on the roundabout.

From the beginning of winter to late spring certain passes in the Pyrenees may be closed due to snow. The state of the passes is generally announced by road signs well in advance. Driving on snow need present no particular problem. Front-wheel drive cars cope best and require only one set of snow chains, on the driving wheels. Rear-wheel drive cars may require chains on all four wheels if the conditions are particularly severe.

Chains are widely available in garages and supermarkets in the Pyrenees. They can also be hired in garages but anyone touring the high Pyrenees in winter or early spring would be better to buy. The fitting of snow chains is very simple and takes only a few minutes. Usually one end of each chain is fixed to the tyre with the temporary clamp provided, and the rest of the chain stretched out on the ground in front; the car is then driven forward over the chain until the wheel is encased and the chain fixed in place with hooks.

More difficult is knowing when to put the chains on. If fitted when there is insufficient snow, both car and road will be damaged. On the other hand, it is no good waiting until the car begins to slide backwards into the vehicles behind; too often the approaches to passes are blocked by inexperienced motorists trying to fit chains to cars stranded in the middle of the road. On an ascending route, fit chains as soon as there is snow on the road.

Petrol in the French Pyrenees varies enormously in price. It is usually cheapest to buy at supermarket garages, which can be 10 per cent to 15 per cent cheaper than other garages. Unleaded and diesel are available everywhere. The price of petrol in Spain and Andorra is low, but unleaded fuel is not yet widely available in the Spanish Pyrenees.

Taxis, Trains and Buses

For travellers without either their own car or a hire car, taxis are available throughout the range. In several regions, such as the Aigües Tortes and the Cadi, these take the form of jeeps which can either be booked on a personal basis or which can be used like minibuses. A jeep excursion to Canigou in the French Pyrénées-Orientales is a classic day out.

Some parts of the Pyrenees are well served by public transport, others not at all. Along both the Atlantic and Mediterranean coasts there are frequent trains while the north side of the range is served by the line linking Bayonne with Perpignan via Pau, Lourdes, Tarbes, Toulouse and Carcassonne. In addition, there are services (on the French side) to St Jean Pied-de-Port, Oloron Ste Marie, Luchon, Latour-de-Carol (the only point away from the coast at which the frontier can be crossed by train), Quillan and Villefranche-de-Conflent. On top of these mainline services, the Cerdagne and the western part of the Têt valley are served by the tourist train which is known as the *Petit Train Jaune*, a tourist attraction in its own right •

Walking in the mountains brings you close to the raw forces of nature, like this gathering storm, coloured yellow by sand from the Sahara.

which connects Villefranche de Conflent with Latour-de-Carol.

In Spain, the coastal services connect with those in France. Inland, the Spanish Pyrenees are badly served by train. In the west there are services to Pamplona in Navarre, Jaca in Aragon, and as far as Canfranc just to the north of Jaca (which is connected by bus with the French railway system at Oloron Ste Marie). No trains approach the central Spanish Pyrenees. In the east there is a service from Barcelona via Ripoll and Ribes de Freser to Puigcerdá; a few trains continue from there into France via Latour-de-Carol.

There are no trains in Andorra.

Bus services tend to be better in Spain than in France where huge areas have either a service too infrequent to be of much use to tourists or no service at all. The most difficult areas are the French Basque country, the eastern part of the Couserans and the Pays de Sault. In Spain the most difficult area is the Ordesa National Park. On its western side the park is served only by daily minibus to Torla, close by the park boundary; on the eastern side there is an ordinary bus to Ainsa, but that falls a day's hiking short of the park itself.

Walking and Cycling

The Pyrenees are criss-crossed by walking routes of all degrees of difficulty, and by minor roads and tracks which provide excellent itineraries for both touring and mountain bikers. All of these are detailed in the Further Information section at the rear of the book (*see* HIKING AND RAMBLING and CYCLING.)

The Disabled Visitor

The Pyrenees are particularly demanding for people with disabilities, for whom few concessions are made. Enquire at the local *Syndicat d'Initiative* or *Turismo* for details of hotels, restaurants and tourist sights with appropriate facilities. One of the few specialist companies is Au Fil des Pyrenees which arranges hiking tours for the blind. The company's address is BP 14, 65120 Luz-St-Sauveur, Hautes-Pyrénées (Tel. 62-92-85-84).

Where to Stay, Eat and Shop

The Pyrenees are not all wilderness—there are all kinds of hotels and restaurants, from the grandest to the rustic, and all kinds of shopping, from the latest fashions to traditional folklore.

Accommodation

All hotel prices quoted in this book are in local currency for 1991, based on the best double rooms.

The Pyrenees is very much for the independent traveller with no international hotel companies and few large hotels at all, except on the coast and in a few of the modern ski developments. An infrastructure such as the one which exists in the Alps has yet to develop and consequently there is little package tourism. There is no lack of comfort though, and in place of the large and impersonal there is the intimate and welcoming.

Hotels

There are very few hotels in the grand style of the Palais or Miramar at Biarritz where a double room can cost over 2,500F a night. In the majority of towns, even if you go straight to the best available hotel you will seldom have to pay more than 475F for a double room and in many cases, especially on the Spanish side of the range where prices are on average about one-third less than in France, hotels of a good standard can be considerably cheaper. In the French villages there are excellent inns where a double room costs no more than 335F and there are Spanish villages where 4,500 ptas will be enough. For budget travellers it is still possible to find double rooms at as little as 130F or 2,500 ptas.

In addition to the standard classifications, there are a few terms that may require explanation. *Logis et Auberges de France* is a national organization with more than 4,000 members. *Logis* are one- or two-star hotels with good ambience, while *auberges* have a more rural flavour and are usually cheaper. *Chambres d'hôte* in France may be translated as "guest rooms"—accommodation in farms, village houses and occasionally in small towns. *Chambres d'hôte* in farmhouses are particularly recommended as an unusual travel experience, particularly where meals from the farm are provided; Spain has a similar system known as *Residencias-casa de payés* (*Residécies-casa de pagés* in Catalonia).

Gîtes d'Etape and Refuges

Gîtes d'étape are common in the mountains of the French Pyrenees. *Gîte* means "shelter" and *étape* implies a stage or section of a route. Thus the *gîte d'étape* is a rustic roof over the head for anyone walking (or riding) the Pyrenean footpaths. Unlike a refuge, though, a *gîte* is always in a town or village. The standard varies.

Normally accommodation is in small dormitories, an experience of camaraderie that the French seem to love; sleeping bags are required—or, at least, a sleeping bag liner or sheet that can be used in conjunction with blankets provided. Charges are around 60F per person. But many *gîtes* now also have private rooms, ranging from the basic up to the equivalent of a well-appointed room in a country hotel,

where the cost of a double room is as little as 130F. The programme for the creation of *gîtes* has been developing for little more than a decade and up-grading is a constant process. A *gîte* normally has a restaurant with good regional cuisine, as well as the facilities for hikers to prepare their own food. The budget-conscious should note that dinner can cost as much as the room. Travellers concerned about the ac-commodation that awaits them should telephone. It would be a pity for the uninitiated to ignore *gîtes* entirely since many of them are in superb locations and with attractive facilities. They of-fer an opportunity to have dinner in a jolly and intimate atmosphere with others enthusiastic and often knowl-edgable about the mountains.

Gîtes ruraux are quite different and are simply another term for Self-Cater-ing accommodation (*see* below). Many of them are owned by the local *com-mune* and are usually good value.

Mountain refuges vary, enormously. At their most extreme they are nothing more than basic shelters about which the best that can be said is that they might save someone from death by ex-posure. At the other end of the scale, they are large with good, communal fa-cilities and staffed by one or two people who provide basic meals, and who will

have the skills to advise on routes and dangers. But sleeping is always in dor-mitories and conditions are basic. At the height of the season, refuges also be-come crowded.

Gîtes de France, Cléconfort and Other Self-catering

If you are staying as a couple, family or group in one location for a week or more you should consider self-catering. There are two organizations in France which inspect and market properties, the now well-known *Gîtes de France* and the lesser known, but in the Pyre-nees better established, *Cléconfort*. Booking a Gîte de France is usually through a central or regional office but the Cléconfort system relies on direct booking; either drive around a village looking for bright yellow Cléconfort signs or ask for a list at the local tourist office. Cléconfort-registered properties are in three categories, from one to three "keys"; a three-key (luxury) prop-erty would be decorated and appointed to a high standard with some sort of garden or terrace, and possibly access to a swimming pool, while a one-key prop-erty would be clean and comfortable but more basic. Prices vary enormously, depending on size of property and time of year, but as a guide prices could be as little as 800F a week in the low season for a two-bedroom property up to 3,500F for an eight-bed house at the height of the season.

Self-catering is not well developed in the Spanish Pyrenees but there is an ac-tive rental market along the Costa Brava in season, mainly based on for-eign-owned apartments and villas. Enquire at the tourist office, one of the international agencies such as

*E*very hotel in the *Pyrenees has its individual and very special character. This one is in Fuenterrabia.*

*There are all kinds of delightful self-catering residences.
This flower-decked village house is in the Cadí region.*

Interhome which has offices in several of the resorts, or at the local letting agencies retained by holiday home owners to rent their properties when they are away.

Youth Hostels

There are so few youth hostels in the Pyrenees that they can all be listed here. In France they are known as *Auberges de Jeunesse*:

Biarritz-Anglet, 19 Route des Vignes, Quartier Chiberta, Anglet (Tel. 59-63-86-49).
Pau-Gelos, Base de Plein Air, Gelos (Tel. 59-06-53-02).
Montrejeau, Route de Tarbes.
Axat, Terrain des Sports, Route de Montlouis (Tel. 68-20-53-27).
Perpignan, Parc de la Pépinière, Avenue de Grande-Bretagne (Tel. 68-34-63-32).

In Spain they are known as *Albergues Juveniles*:

Fuenterrabia (Hondarribia), Centra Faro (Tel. 941/64-15-50).
San Sebastián, Ciudad Deportiva Anoeta (Tel. 943/45-29-70) and at Parque Ulia (Tel. 943/29-37-51).
Roncesvalles, Real Colegiata-Roncesvalles (Tel. 948/76-00-00).
Jaca, Avda Perimetral (Tel. 974/36-05-36).
Canfranc, Lés, "Matacabos", Sant Jaume (Tel. 973/64-80-48).
Salardú, Centra de Viella (Tel. 973/64-52-71).
Planoles, Centra de Neva, Prat Cap Riu (Tel. 972/73-61-77).
Nuria, Pic de L'Aliga (Tel. 972/73-00-48).

Olot, Passeig de Barcelona (Tel. 972/26-42-00).
Girona, Ciutadans 9 (Tel. 972/20-15-54).
Figueres, Anicet Pages 2 (Tel. 972/50-12-13).

Caravanning and Camping

There are hundreds of official campsites throughout the Pyrenees, both private and municipal, and with a wide range of facilities. It is most unlikely that you will be unable to find a pitch in an area in which you wish to stop, even in the high season, but if you are anxious to stay in a particular campsite that you know of, especially for a long period, a reservation is advisable. In France the range of sites has recently been extended by camping *à la ferme*, which are small sites with only basic facilities but with considerable tranquillity. In the high mountains, wild camping is normally permitted or tolerated, except: where the local authority has specifically forbidden it (in which case there will be signs along the road and along the walking trails); inside the Spanish national parks (except at specific designated "bivouac" areas); within 1 km (⅝ mile) of a road if within the Pyrenees National Park.

Payment

Credit Cards

The credit card has transformed travel in the Pyrenees. No longer is it necessary to carry even travellers' cheques and certainly not large sums in cash. The most widely accepted card is Visa which is known as *Carte Bleue* in France and as *Visa* (pronounced bisa) in Spain; Mastercard and American

*H*ow about this for a tent! Tipis are increasingly popular in the Pyrenees, especially in the Ariège where some visitors pass the entire summer.

Express are accepted in fewer outlets and Diners' Club in fewer still.

For several years it has been possible to draw cash from automatic dispensers in Spain, using either Visa or Mastercard, and this facility is now being extended throughout the French Pyrenees.

Petrol is one of the major expenses while touring and the credit card is the most convenient way of settling the bill in France, as it is in most large supermarkets, shops, restaurants and hotels. In the Spanish Pyrenees, credit cards are still only accepted by a minority of garages and considerably fewer other outlets than in France. Many French outlets, especially garages, are now equipped with electronic card readers which means the transaction is immediate.

Eurocheques

As a second source of funds, Eurocheques are also more convenient than travellers' cheques. Travellers' cheques have to be paid for at the start of the holiday, with consequent loss of interest, whereas Eurocheques are only debited to your account after they have been used and gone through the bank processing system. Eurocheques can be used to make withdrawals at most banks and also to settle bills in outlets which bear the Eurocheque symbol. Note that the high cost of cashing Eurocheques for the recipient makes them unacceptable for small sums of money.

Currency

As a rule of thumb, it is generally better to change currency in its issuing country. Therefore the rate of exchange to convert sterling into francs or pesetas is generally better in Britain than in France or in Spain. Similarly, it is normally better to change francs into pesetas in France. Have some local currency available before arriving. Travelling on the motorway, for example, there may be a toll to be paid before an exchange is reached (but note that credit cards can now be used to settle motorway tolls on the way to the Pyrenees).

Banks and Exchanges

Banking hours in the French Pyrenees are generally 9 a.m. to 12.30 p.m. and 2 to 5 p.m. Monday to Saturday but in many villages there are only sub-branches open one or two days a week. In the Spanish Pyrenees, banking hours are generally from 9 a.m. to 2 p.m. Monday to Friday and from 9 a.m. to 1 p.m. on Saturdays but, as in the French Pyrenees, village opening hours may be much shorter and confined to only one or two days a week. On the Costa Brava, however, there are always money exchanges open seven days a week and able to cash both Eurocheques and travellers' cheques; compare commissions as well as exchange rates before doing business.

Security

The relatively gentle nature of tourism in most of the Pyrenees means that the range is very safe for the traveller in terms of theft but vigilance is necessary in large towns and on the coast, especially the Costa Brava. Organized gangs work all along the Costa Brava in summer and a foreign car parked with valuables in sight will be broken into. No money, passports, documents or valuables should be left in cars and expensive radios should, if possible, be removed or hidden. Car alarms are a proven deterrent and worth installing. Thefts or malicious damage should be reported at once to the nearest *Gendarmerie* or, in Spain, the *Guardia Civil* and you will be provided with insurance documentation and, if necessary, paperwork acknowledging passport theft sufficient to get you back home.

Restaurants

France, and to a lesser extent Spain, have marvellous restaurants, internationally renowned and often filled to bursting point. The Pyrenees has its share and details of very many different types of establishment are given throughout the guide. However, it is worth remembering that restaurants do best what they know best and therefore it is the small, perhaps remote, mountain restaurants which will serve mountain food at its most authentic—plain, filling and inexpensive. Wherever possible always choose from the set menu of the house. This is invariably the freshest food, prepared that day and made from ingredients bought from markets and local suppliers. To choose à la carte, while absolutely fine in an international-class restaurant, can mean a long and eventually disappointing wait.

If, however, you have special dietary requirements, vegetarian or, say, diabetic, you are in for a tougher time. Country restaurateurs (again with some very notable exceptions) have little time for, or experience of, special diets. Vegetarians must expect plenty of omelettes, while vegans will have to put up with a succession of *crudités*, salads and chips. Wherever possible try to warn the restaurant in advance and have some suggestions. Given enough time, chefs often love to rise to a challenge.

There are three leading restaurant guides which between them assure a fair choice of reputable restaurants. These are the *Michelin,* which categorizes with rosettes, the *Gault-Millau,* which uses chefs' hats, and the *Guide Hubert,* which uses plates and, to indicate exception, a crown. In addition there are a number of specialist eating guides printed in Britain. These include: *France for the Gourmet Traveller*, Vandyke Price/Harrap (£7.95), *French Food in France*, Bins/Waymark (£2.95) or Eperon's *French Wine Tour*, Eperon/Pan (£6.95). For some insight into Spanish food, recipes and wine, and restaurant recommendations, read *The Spanish Table* by Marimar Torres (published by Ebury Press).

For snacks you can patronize cafés and bars, though generally the choice is not extensive. Except for places specializing in food, you will have to settle for a sandwich or a reheated pizza or maybe some dried sausage. Sadly, even in the Spanish Pyrenees the bar is a disappointment, with much less of the *tapas* or wonderful assortment of titbits to be found in the south of Spain. The towns and cities are different. Here competition and availability of produce means the choice is better. Omelettes, *oeufs plat* (fried eggs) and even more complex dishes may be available—but at meal times (usually lunch time only) and under no circumstances out of hours. Exceptions are the huge supermarkets which have marvellous cafeterias with a full hot and cold choice, and which are open long hours.

Markets

Markets are still very much a way of life in many mountain areas, the main valley towns holding regular livestock and general markets. For the visitor, the livestock markets are worth visiting, not necessarily to buy, but to take part in what is often a fascinating tradition. Best of all, follow the farmers into the local cafés and bars for their late breakfast and enjoy the convivial atmosphere, becoming ever more animated with each successive bottle of dark local wine. This is the social event of the month when farmers, who tend to lead solitary lives, gather to discuss politics, prices and the weather.

The general markets, by contrast, tend to be disappointing. Even in the mountains, the same tired and cheaply manufactured goods you can find all over northern Europe reappear once more. However local fresh produce is worth considering, especially if you are self-catering. Prices will be cheaper on the market stalls and quality often better. Keep an eye on those stalls doing the best business from the locals. Tourist offices will have details of market days and many towns in France give their market days along with the other signs at the entrance to the town. Where a town has a particularly noteworthy market, information is given in this guide.

Shopping

Andorra is the duty-free crowd puller of the Pyrenees. A small principality squeezed into the high mountains between France and Spain, it is a hell of crowds, noise and endless traffic jams to some. To others it is a heaven, where undreamed of bargains are to be found.

It principally attracts those in search of hi-fi equipment, cameras, videos, household gadgetry, perfume, cigarettes and alcohol. But thrifty French housewives also search out cut-price butter, olive oil and sugar which can cost up to five times less than in French shops. For these and other goods you would be wise to bone up on prices back home—not all Andorran prices are cheaper.

Other popular shopping expedition destinations are Le Perthus on the French/Spanish border close to the Costa Brava resorts and Col d'Ibardin on the French/Spanish border just behind the Côte Basque resorts. These two are not duty free. They are no more than concentrated shopping zones where Spanish goods can be bought cheaply, often with special offers on certain items and, particularly appealing to the French.

Prices generally throughout the Pyrenees are not cheap, since transportation costs have to be taken into account. Neither is fresh produce of much use to the visitor unless self-catering. If this is the case then the Roussillon Valley, in particular, is overwhelmed by fresh peaches, nectarines, kiwis and other fruit and vegetables all summer, and whole trays can be bought for next to nothing.

All the shops you would expect to find can be found in the major Spanish and French centres in the Pyrenees; however, villages may only have a small grocery shop, if that. Many villages actually have bread and general grocery deliveries, so if you coincide with these you may be able to stock up. Opening hours are variable and there are numerous public holidays, when most shops will be closed all day. Otherwise expect shops in France to open 8.30 a.m. to 12.30 p.m. and 2–6 p.m. (supermarkets 7 a.m. to 7.30 p.m.). In Spain, shop hours are 9.30 a.m. to 2 .p.m. and 4/4.30–8/9 p.m.

The Chemist

Large towns have a duty chemist (*pharmacie* in French, *farmacia* in Spanish); in an emergency check with the police. Chemists in France and Spain also deal with some minor complaints. Finally, on the subject of chemists, there is much more active interest in homeopathic remedies and treatments in France and Spain. Many chemists have full homeopathic stocks and, if it is necessary to obtain homeopathic products while in the Pyrenees, there should be no problem. Check the dosage as this may differ.

Post Offices

In the Spanish Pyrenees, post offices (*correos*) are generally open 8 a.m. to noon and 4/5–7 p.m. (Saturday 8 a.m. to noon). In the French Pyrenees, post offices (PTT) are generally open 8 a.m. to noon and 2–5/5.30 p.m. (Saturday 8.a.m. to noon). Post offices in small towns and resorts off season may have much shorter hours whereas in large towns they may be open earlier in the afternoon. If you only need stamps, buy them in Spain at the *tabac*, and in France at any *tabac* or *libraire* (newsagent).

Three Mountain Countries Between the Atlantic and Mediterranean

The visitor, particularly if travelling by car, can discover a land of rich rewards. There are spectacular cave systems, dramatic canyons and glaciers, extinct volcanoes and three national parks with rare species of wildlife. Also historic towns and villages, with their abbeys, castles and monasteries, where smuggling was a way of life and where, in World War II, the French Resistance flourished.

Geology and Geography

Stretching for more than 400 km (250 miles) between the Bay of Biscay and the Mediterranean, the Pyrenees lie within three countries. The greater part is in Spain, which has the three highest peaks—Aneto (3,404 metres/ 11,169 ft), Posets (3,375 metres/11,073 ft) and Monte Perdidio (3, 355 metres/ 11,008 ft). Vignemale (3, 298 metres/

10,791 ft), fourth in the range, lies on the border but its glacier is decisively in France.

You will see a huge amount of grey, cream or white limestone as you tour the range. This once lay below the sea. Monte Perdido in the Ordesa National Park is, in fact, the highest limestone mountain in Europe and the permanently iced caves to the west of the massif are the highest ice caves in the world. Limestone also means extensive cave systems and, whether you want to visit organized "show" caves or are an experienced speleologist, you will not be disappointed. The Pyrenees have several exquisite managed caves and one of the deepest potholes in the world (Gouffre Pierre St Martin in the Basque country).

*H*unting is a way of life in all of the Pyrenees.

35

*T*here are some 30 glaciers in the Pyrenees. This rock, beautifully coated in rime, was photographed on the Glacier de la Brèche.

Glaciers

There are some 30 surviving glaciers, of which a score are worth the name. The Ossoue is now the only one of any length, stretching for more than a kilometre from close by the summit of Vignemale. But during the last glaciation, over 15,000 years ago, there was permanent ice even in the foothills of the Pyrenees and the glacier on the site of Lourdes is estimated to have been 500 metres (1,640 ft) thick. It was this glaciation which was responsible for some of the Pyrenees' most spectacular features, scouring out the huge cirque at Gavarnie (the number one natural tourist attraction in the range), the neighbouring cirques of Estaubé and Troumouse and many others. It also created hanging valleys, carved out lake beds and dumped a huge quantity of material, known as *moraines*, like that at Arudy. Since the beginning of the century, the glaciers have been receding rapidly. In 1882, the mountaineer Henry Russell had three caves cut near the head of the Ossoue glacier to spend his summers in. Five years later he had to abandon them because the glacier was rising. Today, the glacier is 8 metres *below* the caves.

The glaciers of the Pyrenees have claimed their victims in the past—one of the most famous, the guide Pierre Barrau who fell into the Maladeta glacier and emerged at the bottom a century later. But nowadays they are fairly safe for mountaineers. One of the easiest to visit, and with no danger except that of slipping over, is the narrow *Glacier de la Brèche de Roland* above Gavarnie.

The crestline generally forms the frontier between France and Spain and, naturally, the watershed. The southern, Spanish, side of the range tends to be more arid, enjoying greater sunshine. But it is just as possible to leave a cloud-covered Spain and enter France with a clear sky as it is the other way round.

Vegetation

The most dramatic contrast, though, is between the relatively high rainfall of the west (up to 1,500 mm/60 in) and the dry Mediterranean climate of the east and the consequent change in vegetation. On the Atlantic side the forests are of beech and oak (and, formerly, before the extensive clearances, of ash and chestnut); the Irati forest to the east of St Jean Pied-de-Port is the largest in the range. In the central area the beech of the lower slopes gives way higher up to fir, larch and pine, especially the mountain pine which the French know as *pin à crochet* because the cones have tiny hooks on them. In the east the mountain pine keeps the high ground but the valleys are full of evergreen oak, including cork oak. If you drive in the part of the Pyrenees near the Mediterranean known as the Albères, you will see the naked trunks where the cork has been cut away—a harvest that is taken once every ten years without killing the tree. Where Mediterranean foothills have been cleared of trees there is instead the typical scrub known as *maquis* and *garrigue*. *Maquis* consists of evergreen shrubs like myrtle, laurel, oleander and rosemary, whereas *garrigue* is typical of poor limestone soil, as in parts of the Fenouillèdes, where the flora includes lavender, sage and other herbs and prickly plants. So favourable is the eastern climate that in the valleys it is possible to grow exotic fruits, including almonds, pomegranates, oranges, apricots, peaches, vines, olives and cherries.

Terrain and Roads
In the central area all the passes are high, tortuous and snowed in in winter, which is why a tunnel is now under construction at Puymorens. This will connect the French Ariège with the Spanish Cerdanya, via French Cerdagne. It is really only possible to pass rapidly between France and Spain via the coastal motorways. Thus the motorway towns, such as Perpignan in the east and Bayonne in the west, are poised to reap the benefits of European integration. In the eastern Pyrenees travel along the line of the range is relatively easy, but in the central and western area, the valleys tend to run north–south which either means crossing some quite high passes (often closed in winter) or moving away from the crestline.

Contrasting Regions
There is no doubt that the Pyrenees makes a wonderful car-touring region and in a fortnight it is possible to sample a great deal of it. On the other hand, you may prefer to concentrate on a specific region and there are, indeed, significant geographical differences between different parts of the range.

Western Pyrenees
Apart from its Atlantic climate, which tends to make it wetter, more misty and cooler than the rest of the range, the **western Pyrenees** are notable for their remote uplands, their extraordinary limestone formations and, on the Spanish side of the frontier, their forests. The mountains descend far more gradually to the coast than in the east, leaving a wide coastal plain and generous beaches onto which the Atlantic breakers can hurl themselves with ferocity. Given the cuisine of the Basque country, the standard of the hotels and the colourful folklore, this adds up to a holiday both for those who enjoy the good things of life and for those who crave solitude and the chance to see some rare wildlife.

Pyrenees and Ordesa National Parks
East of **Pic d'Anie** (2,504 metres/8,216 ft) the high peaks begin and the wonderful **Pyrenees National Park** stretches out along the border on the French side to just beyond Gavarnie. Within its boundary lie **Pic Midi d'Ossau** (2,884 metres/9,462 ft), the remote **Balaïtous** (3,144 metres/10,315 ft), Vignemale and the famous Cirque of Gavarnie. The eastern area of the park adjoins the Spanish **Ordesa National Park**, so that the two together form a continuous protected area of more than 600 km² (232 miles²). The Ordesa is particularly dramatic, carved into spectacular canyons reminiscent of Arizona. There are easy paths through

some of these, notably the **Ordesa Canyon** itself and the **Añisclo**, but others call for climbing skills. This is the prime region of the new sport of canyoning, which means descending the actual watercourses, sliding down as on a water chute.

Central Pyrenees
The really big peaks, **Aneto** and **Posets**, lie in Spain to the east of the Ordesa, accessed from the village of Benasque or, on the French side of the border, from Bagnères de Luchon. The summit of Aneto, a full day round trip from Benasque (slightly less from the Renclusa base hut), requires fitness (and the use of crampons on the glacier) but no special climbing skills.

Aigües Tortes National Park and Andorra
Moving east again, the third national park in the Pyrenees (and the only national park in Catalonia) is the **Aigües Tortes**. The name means "twisted waters" and this is, indeed, a beautiful region of streams and lakes, though many sadly dammed for hydroelectricity (in contravention of the internationally agreed regulations for national park status). Beyond the Aigües Tortes lie the last two 3,000 metre (10,000 ft) peaks of the Pyrenees, **Estats** (3,143 metres/10,312 ft) and **Montcalm** (3,077 metres/10,096 ft), approximately where the

*The gorgeous yellow Turk's cap lily (*Lilium pyrenaicum*) flowers from June to August on rocky slopes up to 2,200 metres (7,218 ft).*

borders of France, Spain and Andorra meet. In terms of relief, Andorra is indeed a kind of Shangri-La, totally surrounded by tall peaks and with only two road accesses, one of them over the highest road pass in the range (**Port d'Envalira**, 2,408 metres/7,900 ft).

The Ariège
To the north of Andorra lies **Ariège**, for walkers perhaps the most difficult region in all the Pyrenees because its valleys are so deep. This is an excellent base if you want a holiday with plenty of variety. Not only does Ariège have some fabulous scenery but also a fascinating history, as evidenced by prehistoric **caves**, like **Niaux** and **Bédeilhac**, and ruined castles, of which the most important is Montségur.

Other Areas
Not all of the terrain of this central Pyrenean area is difficult, though. **The Baronnies**, to the north of the Pyrenees National Park, the **Cadí**, to the south of Andorra, and the **Plateau de Sault**, a little to the east of the Ariège, are just three areas of Pyrenean foothill and plateau that combine relaxed walking with plenty of tranquillity.

Eastern Pyrenees
In the Mediterranean Pyrenees, the geographical highlights include the Garrotxa, an area of extinct volcanoes, now lush with vegetation, lying between Olot and Banyoles in Spain. In France, Canigou—the sacred mountain of Catalonia—is one of the most picturesque in all the range. And to the north of Canigou lies the wine-growing area of the Fenouillèdes, an arid region of broken schist. The Mediterranean light is

*T*he mountains are a paradise for the geologist. The rocks make pretty patterns for the rest of us to enjoy, too.

particularly luminous and for those who would like to combine mountain and sea, there can be no finer place, the last ridges of the range descending steeply into the blue to create the little bays and dramatic contours of the French Côte Vermeille and the Spanish Costa Brava.

History

There have been many attempts to create kingdoms straddling the Pyrenees and even some to create a "kingdom of

The eastern Pyrenees is a region of dazzling sun and romantic sunsets.

the Pyrenees" itself but it was almost inevitable, given the geography, that they would all be doomed and that the Pyrenees would become, as they are now, the border between two countries.

Early Times

The first definite evidence of human habitation in the range comes from Tautavel, a little village to the north of Perpignan, where in 1971 part of the skull of *Homo erectus* was found in a cave where it had lain for 455,000 years. This "Tautavel Man" with his protruding cranial ridge, lying on the evolutionary scale between *Homo habilis* and *Homo sapiens* (modern man), rates along with the oldest human finds in Europe. There is little more evidence until the art and artefacts of cave life dating from the Upper Palaeolithic (35,000–10,000 BC), such as those found at Mas d'Azil and Niaux in the Ariège, which can both be visited. Dolmens or stone burial chambers, dating from about 5,000–2,000 BC, are found throughout the Pyrenees but with a particular concentration around the Albères, close to the Mediterranean.

The Romans and After

The first empire incorporating the Pyrenees was that of the Romans who expelled the Carthaginians from Spain after the Second Punic War (218–201 BC). After the various "Barbarian" invasions, the next great kingdom was that of the Visigoths in the 5th century. In AD 711 the Moors landed in Spain, defeated the Visigoth King Roderic and, aided by the Jewish communities in Spain who had latterly been persecuted by the Visigoths, rapidly swept north. It is unlikely that the Moors ever controlled the high Pyrenees, though, and their defeat by the tough Charles Martel at Poitiers in France, in 732, marked the beginning of their expulsion from the Pyrenean foothills, a process not completed until the 10th century. The grandson of Charles Martel was Charlemagne (768–814), a man whose enormous energy matched his ambition and who, between 771 and 814, extended his empire to include all of the Pyrenees as far south as Barcelona in the east and Pamplona in the west.

40

The Kingdom of Navarre

Upon the death of Charlemagne, his empire began to break up and, in 987, Hughes Capet became the first of a new Paris-based dynasty of French kings. In the Pyrenees, it was the turn of the "Spanish" to control vast chunks of the range. The most stable transpyrenean kingdom was that of Navarre, which from the 9th century until the 16th included that part of south-western France which is nowadays known as Basse-Navarre. Further east, in 1137, Count Ramon Berenguer IV of Catalonia was betrothed to the two-year-old daughter of the king of Aragón, thus uniting the two kingdoms. His son Alfonso I won Roussillon and became the "Emperor of the Pyrenees".

The Cathars

The opportunity for the Capetian monarchs of Paris to extend their rule in the eastern Pyrenees came with the arrival of the Cathar "heresy". This was a Christian religion which believed the material world to be the work of the Devil, and which had taken a strong grip in the eastern Pyrenees. The Pope was determined to crush it and enlisted the help of Philippe Auguste (1180–1223), the seventh Capetian monarch who was attracted by the rule of Crusading, which gave the victors the territories of the vanquished. Pere I of Catalonia was killed fighting on the Cathar side at the siege of Muret in 1213. This, together with the defeat of the local French *seigneurs* (lords), virtually incorporated Languedoc into France and signalled the eventual incorporation of the north-eastern Pyrenees as well. The Cathar religion was effectively extinguished at the siege of Montségur in 1244. James the Conqueror (1208–76) the successor to Pere, although expanding his territory south and east to include the Balearics, gave up much of his claim inside France by the Treaty of Corbeil in 1258—but he held on to Roussillon and the Cerdagne.

Attempt at a Kingdom
Another attempt to form a kingdom of the Pyrenees was made by Gaston Fébus (1331–91), the count of Foix. He set out to exploit the divisions of the Hundred Years' War (1338–1453) between England and France to enlarge his inheritance by acquisition in Gascony. He extended as far as Soule in the Basque country but his vision of a united Pyrenees died with him. The French won the Hundred Years' War and control of Aquitaine went to Paris but the north-western Pyrenean areas of Basse-Navarre and Béarn and the more central region of Foix remained independent until Henri of Navarre and Foix-Béarn annexed them to the crown on becoming Henri IV of France in 1589.

Catalan Rebellion
Roussillon was seized from Catalonia by Louis XI of France in 1463 but was given back by Charles VIII in 1493. The next chance for France came in 1640 when Catalonia rebelled against Spain over taxation and conscription, a Catalan misjudgement which resulted in partition. France, Catalonia's ally, won the siege of Perpignan in 1642 but Spain won the siege of Barcelona in 1652. Under the **Treaty of the Pyrenees** of 1659, France kept Roussillon and half of Cerdanya (the French part is now known as Cerdagne).

Louis XIV and Napoleon
After 1659, France built new defences, as at Mont Louis, and strengthened existing ones, such as Villefranche de Conflent, all to the designs of the famous military engineer Sébastien le Prestre de Vauban (1633–1707). There was yet another attempt to create a *de facto* transpyrenean kingdom when Louis XIV engineered his grandson, Philippe d'Anjou, on to the throne of Spain, left vacant by the death of Charles II in 1700. However, although Philippe d'Anjou retained the throne, Louis' more ambitious plans were blocked by Britain and others after his defeat in the War of Spanish Succession (1701–14). The final chance for France and Spain to be linked came with Napoleon who installed his brother Joseph as king of Spain. Britain intervened as it had before and, allied with Spain and Portugal, drove the French troops out in the Peninsular War (1808–14). Wellington pursued the troops of Marshall Soult along the north Pyrenees from the Ibañeta pass near Roncesvalles as far as Toulouse. The British were well received by French royalists, particularly at Pau, which consequently developed a large British community.

The Carlists
In 1814, Fernando VII, whom Napoleon had deposed, was restored to the Spanish throne and on his death in

1833, both his daughter, Isabella II and his brother, the ultra-conservative Carlos, laid claim to the crown. The more liberal faction prevailed but the dispute led to two "Carlist" wars, separated by a doomed attempt to create a republic, and still goes on today. The heartland of Carlist support is Navarre. There was a second attempt to form a republic in 1931, in which year Catalonia also declared itself independent.

Spanish Civil War

All of these pressures, coupled with the new ideas of anarchism and communism given prominence by the Russian Revolution, exploded. The army, under the direction of the nationalistic Spanish Military Union, staged a rebellion against the Republican Government and unleashed the Spanish Civil War (1936–39). Aragón had taken to the new ideologies with particular zeal. All wood was collectivized and, in many villages, all money was confiscated and replaced by a barter system. Catalonia, on the other hand, formed few cooperatives. The Civil War was the ultimate proof that violence can never be a way of achieving ideals.

In the Pyrenees, only Navarre supported the Nationalists, but that was enough to create the bridgehead that allowed the Nationalists to advance eastwards through the Aragonese foothills and from there finally into Catalonia. The defeated Republicans fled north over the mountains into France, secretly at first, along smuggling trails, and then as the numbers of defeated swelled into thousands, quite openly. France, unable to cope with the numbers, sent them to internment camps (the main ones were at Argelès, St Cyprien and Barcarès on the *Côte Radieuse* near Perpignan).

World War II

With the collapse of France in World War II, the country was divided between the occupied north and the collaborationist Vichy-governed south. French refugees were soon following the same smuggling trails that had been taken by the Republicans, but this time south from France. Franco, who had been assisted during the Civil War by both Germany and Italy, was nevertheless maintaining a neutral stance. There was a flood across the range and onwards by sea to Britain, following General de Gaulle's 1940 appeal for men to join the Free French army. Another wave of refugees came with the German occupation of the Vichy zone in November 1942, prodded by the Anglo-American landings in North Africa. Altogether, about 35,000 people are estimated to have escaped over the Pyrenees into Spain. Their numbers included 5,000 Jews. Many others, unable to escape, were held in French-run transit camps one of which, ironically, was on the fringe of the Pyrenees, at Noé, some 50 km (30 miles) south-west of Toulouse; from the transit camps they went to their deaths at Auschwitz.

Towards the end of the war, the Germans determined to break the Resistance in the Pyrenees, which included Jews and large numbers of Spanish Republicans. The inhabitants were driven from many mountain villages and the houses burned—as at Mantet and Valmanya on the Canigou massif—a process which accelerated the depopulation of the high valleys.

After World War II

When the war was over, many French remained in the towns to which they had been sent and the villages lay abandoned. On the Spanish side there was a similar depopulation, though in this case caused by the search for work in the desperate economic conditions of the 1950s.

Smuggling across the Pyrenees became even more a way of life than it had been before the war, particularly *into* Spain which, under Franco, was starved of luxuries. At the western end of the range, the escape routes also remained in use for Basque separatists. ETA (*Euskad Ta Azkatasurra*, meaning "Basque Homeland and Freedom") was set up in the early 1950s, dedicated to violent action. In 1973, ETA assassinated Admiral Carrero Blanco, Franco's likely successor and in 1975 Franco himself died. But even with the democracy and devolution that followed, the issue of Basque separatism, at least for a handful of violent activists, remains unresolved.

Calendar

January

16th Festival, Gerri de la Sal.
17th Festival of Saint Anthony, Sant Llorenç, de Morunys.
20th Festival, El Pont de Suert.
24th Leather Fair, Sort.

February

Carnivals at Sort, Rialb, Pobleta de Bellvei, La Molina, Arles sur Tech (the *Fête de l'Ours*), Prats de Mollo

(the *Dia des Ossos*) and Amélie les Bains (the *Mascarade des Grégoires*).

Easter

Festival of Sacred Art and Music, Lourdes; *Procession de la Sanch*, Perpignan; *Procession Nocturne des Pénitents Noirs*, Arles sur Tech and Collioure; *Procession du Réssuscité*, Arles sur Tech and Ceret; *Procession de l'Angelet*, Villefranche de Conflent; other festivals at Alins, La Pobla de Segur, Llivia and Tallo.

May

First Friday, Folklore, Jaca.
First Sunday and last Sunday, *Fiesta*, Gerri de la Sal.
Fourth Sunday after Easter, *Fiesta de la Lana*, Ripoll.
3rd *Fires i Festes de la Santa Creu*, Figueres.
8th Festival, St Miquel d'Engolasters.
Last Sunday, Procession to *Virgen de la Cueva*, Jaca.
Pentecost Monday, Processions at various places including Gorges de Galamus, Villefranche-de-Conflent and Serrabone.

June

During month, *Festival du Chant Pyrénéen* at Bagnères de Luchon.
12th Wool fair, Rialb; sheep-shearing, Llessui.
24th St John's Day (St Jean in France and St Joan in Catalonia), but celebrated the *night before* by bonfires and fireworks, especially on Canigou, the sacred mountain of Catalans, by the *Feux de la Saint Jean* at Bagnères de Luchon, by fireworks at Montségur and by festivals at Arties, Lés and Boi.

24th–30th *Fiestas* at Jaca, Alins and Tor.

25th *Bonfires and pelota*, St Jean de Luz and Hasparren; *Fiesta* at Montgarri; *Fête de la St Eloi*, Amélie les Bains.

29th *Fiestas*, Guingueta d'Aneu and Espot.

Corpus Christi. *Festa de la Patum*, Berga.

July

The summer music festivals begin, including San Sebastián, Pau, Bagnères de Bigorre, Escaladieu, St Bertrand de Comminges, Escaldes, Meritxell, Ordino, Llivia, Prades, Besalú, Cadaqués, Camprodon, Castellfollit de la Roca, Girona, Llança, Ripoll and Roses. The month also includes the outdoor theatrical spectacle at Gavarnie, the International Folklore Festival at Jaca (odd years), the International Canoe Rally at Sort and Rialb, *Son et Lumière* at Puivert, *Les Journées Mediévales de Gaston Fébus* at Foix, the Country Fair at Lavelanet, the *Salon des Arts* at Quillan, and *Sardanas* at Perpignan, Ceret, Ripoll, Camprodon and all along Costa Brava.

First Sunday, *Raiers* Festival, La Pobla de Segur; Rose Festival, Puigcerdá.

6th–14th *Fiesta de San Firmin*, Pamplona.

8th–22nd *Son et Lumière*, Caudies de Fenouillèdes.

10th *Sant Cristobal*, Olot.

13th *Tributo de las Tres Vacas*, near Arette la Pierre St Martin and later in the day at Roncal.

14th–18th Folklore and fireworks, Bayonne.

18th *Fiesta*, Canfranc.

Third Sunday, *Fiesta Major*, Canillo.

23th–24th Folklore, pelota and dancing at Ustaritz.

24th–25th *Fiesta*, La Pobla de Segur.

25th *Fiesta*, Sabiñanigo.

25th–27th *Fiesta Major*, St Juliá de Lória.

August

During the month: Medieval fair, Axles-Thermes.

Continuation of music festivals and *Son et Lumière* at Puivert.

First weekend, *Festival de la Montagne*, Luz St Sauveur; *Fiesta Major*, Andorra la Vella; *Festa Major*, Saint Laurent de Cerdans.

First week, *Fiesta*, Bayonne; International Folklore Festival, Oloron Ste Marie.

1st Canoe races, Sort.

5th *Fiesta*, Sallent de Gállego.

6th–8th Basque sports and folklore, Cambo and St Etienne de Baïgorry.

11th *Semana Grande*, San Sebastián.

15th Basque sports and folklore, St Jean Pied-de-Port; procession of the *Ermita Virgen de las Nieves*, Ochagavia; *Fiestas* at Biescas, Panticosa, Valle d'Aran, Santa Pau, Ribes de Freser, Collioure; Canoe races, Rialb.

15th–17th *Fiesta Major*, Encamp and Massana.

23th–25th *Fête de St Louis*, Le Perthus.

29th *Fête Folklorique*, Banyuls-sur-Mer.

Third Sunday, Flower festival, Bagnères de Luchon.

Penultimate Sunday, Festival of the Lake, Puigcerdá.

Last Sunday, *Fête Foraine*, La Seu d'Urgell.

Festivals

February
The festival year really begins in February with carnivals throughout the range, one of the most entertaining being the Dia des Ossos at Prats de Mollo, when young men dressed as bears (in sheepskins and with their faces blackened) are chased through the village by "hunters".

Easter
The next big festival period is Easter, at its most spectacular at Perpignan's Procession de la Sanch. On the afternoon of Good Friday, in a ceremony dating back to the 15th century, red and black-robed members of the *Confrèrie de la Sanch*, in masks and pointed hats, carry a figure of Christ through the streets from the church of St Jacques.

Summer
June sees some major celebrations, notably the Festa de la Patum at Berga on Corpus Christi, probably the most important festival in all Catalonia. It lasts three days and includes processions of *capgrossos*, grotesque figures with huge heads, accompanied through the town to the sound of the *gralla* (hornpipe). The climax comes on the Saturday night with dancing in the streets and a huge dragon called Patum, spitting fire from its mouth. St John's Day is also celebrated throughout the eastern Pyrenees on 24 June (Sant Joan in Catalonia, St Jean in Roussillon); on the night before (23 June) shepherds carry flames from a bonfire on Mount Canigou to bonfires all over the old kingdom of Catalonia, that is, modern Catalonia plus Roussillon. The accompanying fireworks are often at their most memorable at Montségur, where

the last of the major figures of the Cathar religion were burnt to death in 1244.

July and August is the summer music festival season. One of the best is in Prades, founded by the great Catalan cellist Pablo Casals (1876–1973) and held in the abbey of St Michel de Cuxa. In Catalonia and Roussillon summer means the eerie sound of *La Cobla*, the 11-man band that accompanies the *Sardana*. The *Sardana* is Catalonia's national dance and is danced everywhere, but particularly along the coast, generally on Sunday mornings. The circles with clasped hands are very Greek-looking and the dance almost certainly has its origins with the Greek colonists of Roses. Anyone can join in, but be sure you know what to do first. The biggest spectacle of *Sardana* is held at Ceret, where hundreds of dancers circle the arena.

At the opposite end of the range, the Basque country has an even more visible folklore, with Basque sports such as pelota, feats of strength and a style of dancing reminiscent of the English Morris tradition. St Jean Pied de Port has more festivities than any other Basque villages or towns but there are also important events at Cambo, St Etienne de Baïgorry and Ochagavia.

Three specific summer events have to be mentioned. The raft races on the Noguera Pallaresa river near La Pobla de Segur, held the first Sunday in July, are particularly fascinating as a celebration of the way logs used to be floated down to the sawmills on Catalonia's greatest river. The Tributo de las Tres Vacas, when three white heifers are given to the villagers of the Spanish Roncal valley by the villagers of the French Barétous valley, recalls a 14th-century agreement on grazing rights; the ceremony is held on the frontier every 13 July. And at Gavarnie, close to the famous cirque, there is an outdoor theatrical spectacle, different each year.

As regards the various bullfight festivals, like San Fermin in Pamplona, it is worth bearing in mind that bullfighting is an entertainment illegal in Britain. In Catalonia, bullfighting is not a significant part of popular culture. It is tourism which helps perpetuate it.

In July and August, principally in Catalonia, the Cobla bands accompany dancers in the Sardana, Catalonia's national dance which is mainly performed on Sunday mornings.

THE REGION, ITS HISTORY AND ITS PEOPLE

September

First Monday, Fireworks, Foix.

7th–9th *Fiesta de la Natividad de la Virgen*, Ochagavia; *Fiesta de la Virgen de Guadalupe*, Fuenterrabia.

8th *Son et Lumière*, Javier; *Fiesta del Pimiento*, Espelette; Festivals at Sort, Esterri d'Aneu, Ribera de Cardós, Viella, Les Bordes, Meritxell (the National Day in Andorra), Font-Romeu.

11th *La Diada* all over Catalonia.

14th *Fiesta*, Sallent de Gállego.

16th–17th *Fiesta*, Ordino.

Last Sunday, Festival at Llessui.

October

7th *Grand Fête Patronale*, Thuir and Amélie les Bains.

Last week, Festival of *St Narcis*, Girona.

November

11th *Foire de la St-Martin*, Perpignan.

December

17th *Fiesta de Santo Tomás*, San Sebastián.

24th Festival at La Guingueta; *La Faia-Faia*, Baga.

Travel Tips

Touring in the Pyrenees poses no particular problems but there are a few "tips" that are worth passing on.

Passports

When motoring, always carry your passport. You may not intend to cross a frontier but an over-the-border route may nevertheless prove too enticing.

Similarly, have your passport with you on walks near the frontier.

Petrol

Leaded petrol and diesel are widely available but always fill up on a Saturday evening since many petrol stations are closed on Sundays. If you use unleaded petrol and are touring the Spanish Pyrenees, fill up whenever you can—unleaded petrol is not yet as widely available in Spain as it is in France. Remember that fuel is cheaper in both Spain and Andorra than it is in France.

Security

Keep valuables out of sight when your car is parked. If you have an expensive radio or cassette player, either remove it at night or disguise it. Theft from cars is a particularly serious problem in large Spanish towns and on the Costa Brava. Car parking areas at major tourist attractions are also favourite targets for thieves. Beware if passengers in an overtaking car wave to indicate that you have some kind of mechanical problem. This is one of the tricks used by organized gangs—while you are looking for the "problem", one of the gang will be helping himself to the contents of your car. However, if oncoming drivers "flash" you, this is probably to indicate an oncoming police "speed trap" or some other problem ahead. Slow down.

Keeping Cool

On hot days park your car in the shade and cover the windscreen; cheap windscreen covers are widely available and significantly reduce the temperature inside a car parked in the sun.

People of the Pyrenees

The people of the Pyrenees are of three nationalities—French, Spanish and Andorran—but there are four main languages—French, Castilian, Catalan and Basque—plus Aranese, which the people of the Aran Valley claim as a separate language. You will also come across numerous dialects. No single racial thread unites these people but those who live near the frontiers have at least one thing in common and that is their indifference to them. They have always lived their lives as if frontiers did not exist, anticipating 1992 by centuries. They have moved their herds wherever the grazing was best, moved goods to take advantage of different prices and taxes, and moved themselves in time of war.

Of course, the frontier as it is today, dictated by the tactical significance of relief in modern warfare, has been elsewhere in the past. There have been several transpyrenean kingdoms. Catalonia, for example, once included modern Roussillon. The Spanish Cerdanya and the French Cerdagne were once united. Navarre once included the region north of the range known as Basse-Navarre. It is these divisions of kingdoms and movements of the border that have given the Pyrenees its cultural quirks. It was Catalan custom, for example, that a woman looked after her own financial affairs, a freedom that, after northern Catalonia was incorporated into France, was to rub uneasily against the Napoleonic code of obedience to a husband.

During the time of Franco, French Catalans were joined by as many as 200,000 Spanish Catalans who were refugees from the Nationalists and many of them, together with their descendants, still live in France today. It was a similar story in the Basque country, where a distinct culture was eventually partitioned between Spain and France; after the Spanish Civil War French Basques were joined by tens of thousands from Spain. During World War II these Spanish refugees played a major role in the Pyrenean Resistance and, after the war, in French Pyrenean reconstruction and politics. Even so, there is no serious movement in either region to create a transpyrenean Catalan or Basque state. It is almost certain, though, that the freedoms that follow 1992 will see a renewed sense of community.

Generally, the people of the Pyrenees are extremely friendly, although they tend to be formal, especially on the French side. It is normal on entering a restaurant, for example, to bid everyone "Bonjour Messieurs, 'Dames". Friends shake hands and, of course, kiss on the cheeks. Two kisses are normal; three kisses are given only to close friends and relations.

Depopulation... and Repopulation

The traditional life of the high mountains has changed drastically with the coming of mechanized agriculture on the plains. As mountain agriculture became less and less profitable, so younger people moved away to the towns. In much of the central Pyrenees in particular the population is only half what it was a century ago. There are entire villages standing empty and decaying. Now there is a move back to some of these villages. There are those who buy the shells to reconstruct as holiday homes. And there are those who come in search of a new kind of life. They are often the "greens" from the towns who have never experienced rural life before; they learn how to keep rabbits, goats, sheep and cows and how to cultivate organically.

The number of dilapidated and ruined houses, especially in the eastern Pyrenees, is symptomatic of the reluctance to part with family property. In medieval times the house (the *domus* in much of the Pyrenees, or the *casa* in Andorra) was almost animate, given life by the spirits of ancestors. To sell it was unthinkable. Nowadays, particularly in the French Pyrenees where the system of inheritance means that a dozen or more people could have an interest in a property, it is also difficult to purchase an old village house on practical grounds. Not all the interested parties can be found, or will agree. Instead, squatters, particularly from Holland and Belgium, often move in to run-down homes.

Village Economics

The old way of life, though, is still apparent. The custom of gifts within the village, for example, has its roots in the barter system. If you live in a Pyrenean village for any length of time, and are accepted, then you will receive presents of vegetables from neighbours and be expected to give something, produce or perhaps labour, in return.

It is typical of mountain areas that people have several ways of earning a living. Even tourism seldom provides a year-round income. A man might run a restaurant in summer and work as a stonemason in the winter. Your hotel manager might also run the ski school. A mountain guide might keep a flock of sheep or let rooms. And a shepherd might make baskets of woven hazel twigs as he sits in the pasture.

Tourism in the Pyrenees has reached nothing like the degree of sophistication of the Alps, where it has been the sole force for repopulation. The Pyrenees now count around 40 fairly serious ski

The occasionally harsh climate brings village people together, here to share out bread dropped by helicopter.

resorts, mostly on the French side and in Andorra, but hopes of creating more have been dashed by a succession of poor snow winters. Indeed, on the best available forecasts, many existing ski resorts will be forced to close. This loss of winter business will pose severe problems for the tourism industry and all those who depend on it. In Gavarnie, for example, many villagers work as *muletiers* in the summer, taking visitors to the cirque on horseback, and depend on the ski business in winter, working as *pisteurs* or instructors.

Apart from employment related to tourism, forestry and agriculture, there is little else. Mining and associated industry (iron ore, aluminium smelting, lignite, talc, marble) has been on a long decline, with activity now confined to small pockets in regions like the Ariège, the Aure valley, the Cadí and the the Valle de Aran. Hydro-electric construction has been a big source of employment but almost every suitable river on both sides of the range has now been dammed, leaving only maintenance work. Without year-round employment, many, especially younger people, continue to leave the villages.

Andorra

Andorra has found its own solution, with its duty-free trade which keeps going, summer and winter, whatever the weather. On average, 50,000 tourists a day flood into Andorra by its two road entrances. The 7,500 locals are outnumbered more than four to one by non-Andorran residents, most of whom come from Spain to service the tourist influx. The main road through the principality is one long traffic jam all summer and the beauty of the valley bottom has been permanently destroyed. The Andorrans themselves regret the damage to their country but keep on counting the money from the terraces of their chalets on the mountainsides, well above the duty-free mayhem. Despite this willingness to sell out to materialism, Andorrans remain an otherwise conservative people, Catalan-speaking, and proud of it. They have consistently refused to allow a casino, for example. Furthermore, there was no universal male suffrage until 1933 and women did not get the vote until 1970; in the old days, everything was decided by the heads of the 300 richest families.

Village Life

Coupled with conservatism there is a parochialism and introversion that extends right along both sides of the range. Only dire necessity has forced villages to cooperate over ski development. It used to be impossible to buy a lift pass to cover adjoining ski stations, for example. Only recently has Barèges—La Mongie become a single-ski domaine and at St-Pierre-dels-Forcats in the Pyrénées Orientales, a wall was once actually built to stop skiers straying onto the runs of neighbouring Eyne, though the two villages now cooperate in a single pass. The mountain village of Mantet once tried to have a new road built through a gorge to the main valley so that the villagers could avoid their traditional enemies along the existing road in the neighbouring *commune* of Py. In France, these hostilities between villages are known as *guerres des clochers*.

The traditionalism, a wisdom handed down from generation to generation, expresses itself even in simple things like the wild mushrooms someone from a particular village will eat. One village will have four or five types that are prized and collected; in another village it will be a different assortment. And numerous other edible species will be ignored by both, according to the traditions. This conservatism also has its negative side. In Ariège, shepherds still illegally burn the mountainsides to improve the next year's pasture, as they always have done, even though modern agronomists have shown that this spoils the pasture for several years. And where people of the Pyrenees are in contact with immigrants, as around Perpignan, where many North Africans have settled, there has been unpleasant and often violent racism and growing support for the neo-Fascist policies of the *Front National*.

Just the Essentials

On a first-time visit to the Pyrenees, you may be overwhelmed by the sheer wealth of choices you have wherever you start, from the sun-drenched beaches of the Mediterranean to the icy glaciers of the high peaks. The major landmarks and places to see and visit are proposed here to help you establish your priorities.

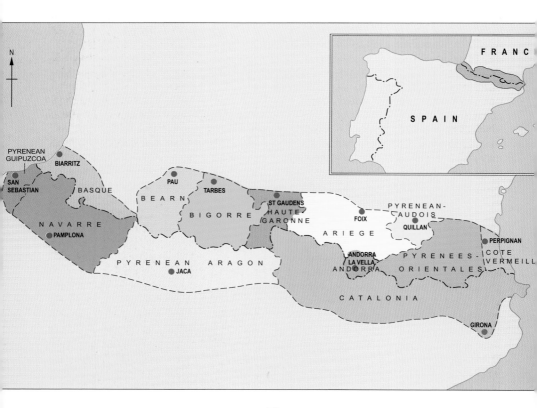

Biarritz and the Basque
Biarritz: Plage de la Côte Basque
Bayonne: museums, chocolate
Biriatou: hill-top village, church
St Jean Pied-de-Port
Iparla Ridge Walk
Gorges de Kakouéta

Pau and the Béarn
Pau: château
Lescun: one of the prettiest places
Petit Train d'Artouste: highest railway

Lourdes and the Bigorre
Lourdes: château-fort, museum
Argelès-Gazost: falconry
Cirque de Gavarnie, Brèche de Roland
Barèges: Pic du Midi de Bigorre
Bagnères: Médous caves—"orchid" wall

Luchon and the Haute-Garonne
St Bertrand de Comminges: popular
   historical site
Gargas caves: superb hand images

Foix and the Ariège
Foix: château-fort
Mas d'Azil: prehistoric cave
Montségur: last refuge of the Cathars
Niaux: prehistoric cave art
Bédeilhac: paintings, engravings, three-
   dimensional carvings
Lombrives: underground train ride,
   largest show caves in Europe

Quillan and Pyrénées-Audois
South of Quillan: Aude river gorges
Lapradelle: Puilaurens castle
Puivert castle: troubadour culture

Perpignan and the Pyrénées-Orientales
Perpignan: Rigaud museum
Casteil: St Martin du Canigou
Villefranche de Conflent
Bouleternère: 11th-century priory
Carlit and Canigou Massifs: hiking
Céret: summer home of *Fauves*
Tautavel: Europe's oldest man

Collioure and the Côte Vermeille
Collioure: heavily fortified 17-century
   church of St Vincent
Banyuls sur Mer: home of sculptor
   Aristide Maillol

Andorra
Andorra la Vella: Barri Antic
Canillo: sanctuary of Meritxell
Tristana: lakes in mountain landscape

San Sebastián and Guipúzcoa
La Concha: best beach
Pasajes: photogenic area
Fuenterrabía: frontier town
Irún: Peñas de Haya mountains—
   wonderful viewpoint for region

Pamplona and Navarre
Pamplona: cathedral
Roncesvalles: Royal Collegiate Church
Sangüesa: church of St Maria
Javier: castle—birthplace of St Francis
   Xavier
Yesa: Leyre monastery

Jaca and Pyrenean Aragón
Jaca: early 9th-century cathedral
near Jaca: San Juan de la Peña—first
   Roman Catholic mass in Spain, 1071
Ordesa National Park
Añisclo Canyon: second great canyon
   of Monte Perdido
Pineta Valley

Girona and Catalonia
Girona: cathedral and Jewish quarter
Besalú: beautiful medieval village
La Seu d'Urgell: Diocesan Museum
Aigües Tortes National Park
Taüll: two romanesque churches and
   medieval village centre
Gerri de la Sal: romantic setting

Roses and Pyrenean Costa Brava
Selva: ruined monastery and castle
Figueres: theatre museum designed by
   Dalí

Planning your Itinerary around your Interests

People who have special interests often appreciate exploring in their own way when on holiday instead of following prescribed routes which try to please everybody. The lists given here are suggestions to help you to get to know some of the recreational and cultural riches of the region.

Beaches

Atlantic Coast
1 ANGLET
Plage de la Chambre d'Amour. Good beach but often with powerful surf.

2 BIARRITZ
Grande Plage and Plage de la Côte Basque—fine golden sand and huge breakers for surfing. Old port—sheltered swimming beach.

With a car you can tour freely in the Pyrenees, easily reaching otherwise awkward places, like the village of Tuxient in the Cadí region.

3 HENDAYE PLAGE
An excellent wide beach, popular with French families.

4 SAN SEBASTIAN
La Concha Beach—famous beach recalling Rio de Janeiro, sheltered by hilly promontories on both sides.

Atlantic coast beaches.

Castles and houses of the Pyrenees.

Ondarreta beach—the westward extension.

Mediterranean Coast

The Mediterranean end of the Pyrenees is characterized by rocky headlands and tiny coves—for big beaches try Banyuls on the Côte Vermeille or Roses on the Costa Brava.

Castles and Houses

The whole range of the Pyrenees is studded with castles and hill forts—many of them now in picturesque ruin—a reminder of the days when frontier country was always in dispute.

1 ANDORRA

Casa d'Areny de Plandolit in Ordino is a wonderful example of traditional Andorran architecture.

2 CAMBO LES BAINS

Villa Arnaga is open to the public in the summer. Marvellous gardens.

3 CASTELNOU

The castle above the town is now a museum.

4 COLLIOURE

The Château Royal was built in the 12th century by the Templars and now contains an art gallery and museum. Open March to November 9 a.m.– 12.30 p.m. and 2.30–6 p.m.

5 FOIX

Château Foix, open daily. Museum of the Ariège housed in 15th-century round tower.

6 JAVIER

16th-century birth place of St Francis Xavier. Daily guided tours in season and weekend *son et lumière*. Immaculately restored.

7 LOURDES

The Château-Fort towers above the town and houses the excellent Pyrenean museum.

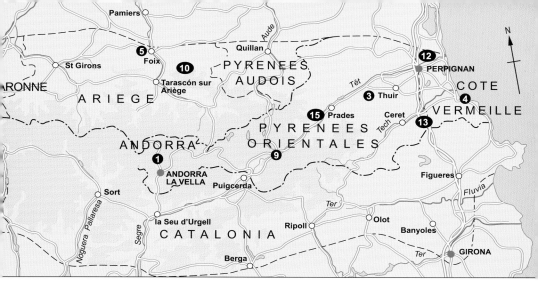

8 MAUVEZIN

The castle is open daily mid-June to mid-October. The rest of the year, afternoons only. The state rooms are a museum dedicated to Gaston Fébus.

9 MONT LOUIS

The citadel is the work of Vauban, military engineer to Louis XIV.

10 MONTSEGUR

Now a ruined castle. Sheltered 500 besieged Cathars in the Middle Ages.

11 PAU

The château is the most important site in the town. Summer exhibition of Henry IV memorabilia. Second Empire state rooms. Exhibition of local crafts in the Musée Béarnais on top floor.

12 PERPIGNAN

Palais des Rois de Majorque. Largest site in Perpignan with long history.

13 PERTHUS

Fort de Bellegarde on the frontier south of Perpignan is another *tour de force* by Vauban. Museum open July–September.

14 ST JEAN DE LUZ

Maison Louis XIV, a great merchant house with period furniture and extravagant decoration.

15 VILLEFRANCHE

Fort Liberia, high on the hill above the town. Access by underground stairway, minibus or horse.

Cathedrals

Romanesque, the style of the Christian reconquest, is the predominant architecture of Pyrenean cathedrals (c. 800–c. 1200). Gothic became the major style from the late 13th–early 14th centuries.

1 BAYONNE

Cathedral of St Mary (northern Gothic). Some magnificent stained glass.

2 ELNE

Fortified cathedral with both Romanesque and Gothic influences. Cloister with beautifully carved capitals. Small museum.

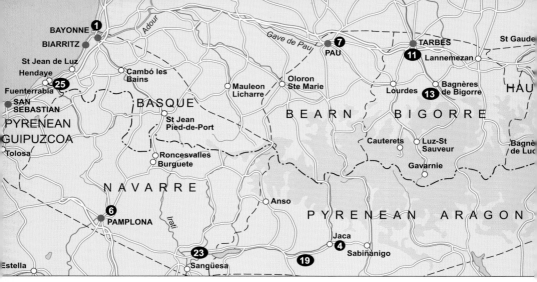

3 GIRONA
Widest Gothic nave in the world. Romanesque cloister of twinned columns. Capitular Museum with 12th-century tapestry. Art Museum in Bishop's Palace.

4 JACA
Romanesque building, most of which dates from the mid-11th century. Cloisters are 12th century. Diocesan Museum contains paintings and frescos from churches all over the region.

5 LA SEU D'URGELL
12th-century, twin-towered cathedral. Restored in the Romanesque manner. 13th-century cloisters. Diocesan Museum containing 10th-century illuminated manuscript.

6 PAMPLONA
Mixture of different styles with peppermill towers. Cloisters and Diocesan Museum in old cathedral refectory.

7 PAU
12th-century cathedral, heavily restored. Many of the original sculptures and mosaics though.

8 PERPIGNAN
Gothic cathedral with Romanesque Chapel of Notre Dame dels Correchs.

9 ST BERTRAND DE COMMINGES
Romanesque, Gothic and Renaissance. Cathedral and medieval village.

10 ST LIZIER
Romanesque cathedral. Magnificent vaulting and two-storey cloister. Cathedral museum.

11 TARBES
12th-century cathedral of Notre Dame de la Sède.

Monasteries, Priories and Abbeys

Mountains have always been considered mystical places, hence the large number of beautifully situated religious buildings in the Pyrenees.

12 BERGA
Our Lady of Queralt is on the mountainside behind the town. Noted for

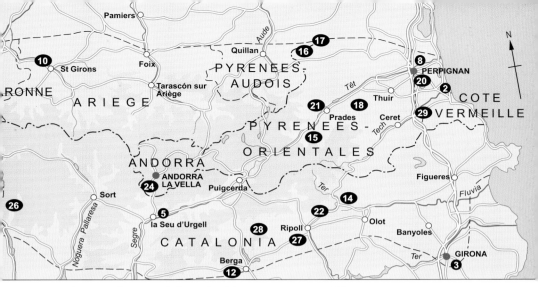

attractive gardens and breathtaking views.

13 BAGNERES DE BIGORRE
Escaladieu Abbey is open to the public from June to mid-September from 10 a.m.–1 p.m. and 2-6 p.m. In winter, weekends only. Now a cultural centre.

14 CAMPRODON
The Romanesque monastery of San Père, with square bell-tower.

15 CASTEIL
St Martin du Canigou is hidden in the mountains above the village of Casteil, near Vernet les Bains. Abbey building, cloisters and two churches.

16 CAUDIES DE FENOUILLEDES
Notre Dame de Laval is a hermitage situated above Caudiès de Fenouillèdes.

17 GALAMUS GORGE
St Antoine de Galamus: another hermitage near Caudiès de Fenouillèdes.

18 ILLE SUR TET
Serrabone Priory, near Ille sur Têt, one

Cathedrals, monasteries, priories, abbeys and churches of the Pyrenees.

of the best Romanesque monuments in the eastern Pyrenees.

19 JACA
Near Jaca, San Juan de la Peña has a 12th-century cloister, extensively restored with original capitals.

20 PERPIGNAN
Notre Dame de Pene is situated at Cases de Pène, Perpignan. Perched on a high ridge with marvellous views.

21 PRADES
St Michel de Cuxa. Extensively renovated. Music festival in July and August.

22 RIPOLL
St Joan les Abadesses is a 9th-century foundation, operated as a parish church from the 12th-century. Pleasing architecture.

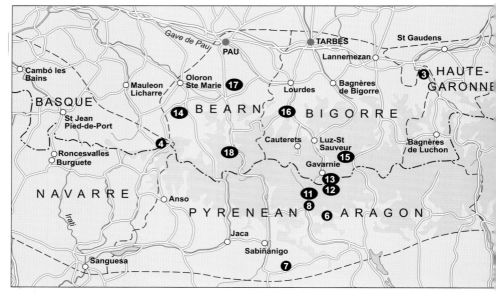

23 YESA
Near Yesa, Navarre, is the 11th-century Leyre Monastery built under dramatic cliffs. Immaculately restored. Massively constructed crypt.

Churches

Here is just a small selection of the churches of the region which will delight the interested visitor.

24 ANDORRA
Santa Coloma church is one of the most unusual Romanesque buildings of the Pyrenees.

25 BIRIATOU
Hill-top Basque village church, designated as a site of interest.

26 BOI VALLEY
There are several very fine Romanesque churches to be found in this small area. At Coll, the church of Santa Maria; at Barruera, San Feliu; the church at Durro has a large bell-tower; Erill la Vall church has a six-storey tower; at Taüll there are two Romanesque churches: Santa Maria and San Climent de Taüll, the latter a perfect example of Romanesque architecture, with a six-storey bell-tower.

27 BORREDA
Ten kilometres (6 miles) north of Borredá, San Jaume de Frontanya is one of the best Romanesque churches in Catalonia.

28 LA POBLA DE LILLET
San Miguel is a circular church, containing a rare 12th-century Christ in Majesty.

29 LE BOULOU
St Martin de Fenouillar near le Boulou is a church with some of the finest Romanesque frescos in Roussillon.

Caves

Much of the Pyrenees is limestone, eroded over the millenia to create spectacular cave systems which are decorated with wonderful stalactites and stalagmites. A few have also been decorated by prehistoric man such as those at Niaux. Here is a selection of caves that are open to the general public.

1 AGUZOU CAVES

Near Axat in the Aude gorge. Open to the more adventurous for day-long visits, guided by an experienced caver. Reserve a place by phone (Tel. 68-20-45-38). Cost 200F per person but worth every centime.

2 BEDEILHAC

Near Tarascon sur Ariège. Prehistoric art and three-dimensional carvings. Open daily in July and August from 10 a.m.–6 p.m.

Natural features of the Pyrenees.

3 GARGAS CAVES

St Bertrand de Comminges. Mysterious prehistoric hand outlines. Open 2.30–4.30 p.m. and some mornings in high season. 45-minute tours.

4 GOUFFRE PIERRE ST MARTIN

Basque region. One of the largest underground caverns in the world.

5 NIAUX AND LA VACHE CAVES

Near Tarascon sur Ariège. Internationally important site. Essential to book in advance to join small guided parties to visit the Niaux caves which open daily July–September, 8.30–11.30 a.m. and 1.20–5.15 p.m. The nearby site of La Vache is open daily in July and August, 10 a.m.–6 p.m.

Canyons

6 ANISCLO

Second only to the Ordesa canyon in drama but with a more intimate character.

7 GUATIZALEMA AND PILLERA

The area to the south of the Ordesa is dissected by at least a score of beautiful and often remote canyons. The two most accessible are Guatizalema and Pillera between Ainsa and Sabiñanigo.

8 ORDESA

A great spectacle—one of the natural wonders of the world.

Gorges

9 CARANCA GORGE

Near Thuès Les Bains. The route through the gorge is one of the most exciting hikes of the Pyrenees.

10 COLLEGATS GORGE

Near La Pobla in Catalonia. Spectacular "Wild West" cliffs, bluffs and gulleys.

11 LAS CAMBRAS GORGE

In the Ordesa National Park. One of the narrowest and most exciting road gorges in the Pyrenees.

Other Natural Spectacles

Cirques are curved vertical walls of rock, scoured by glaciation—the visual effect is dramatic. A *brèche* is a point where some of the wall has collapsed after thousands of years of weathering.

12 BRECHE DE ROLAND

A way through the cirque of Gavarnie (*see* below) where the top of the wall has collapsed to leave a natural gateway between France and Spain.

13 CIRQUE OF GAVARNIE

An hour's walk from the village of Gavarnie, some 20 km (13 miles) south of Luz St Sauveur. The waterfall is one of the longest in the world.

14 CIRQUE OF LESCUN

The highlight of the Aspe Valley, approximately 60 km (40 miles) south of Pau and north of the Pyrenees National Park.

15 CIRQUE OF TROUMOUSE

Near Luz St Sauveur. A 10-km (6-mile) cirque, more remote but not as dramatic as Gavarnie.

Wildlife Centres

16 ARGELES-GAZOST

At Beaucens Castle, 20 km (13 miles) south of Lourdes, the Donjon des Aigles is a centre of birds of prey.

17 ARUDY

Some 25 km (15 miles) south of Pau, the Maison d'Ossau has an exhibition of Pyrenean flora and fauna.

18 GABAS

On the edge of the Pyrenees National Park in the Ossau valley, the Centre d'Ecologie Montagnarde is open in summer, 9 a.m.–12 p.m. and 2 p.m.–6 p.m.

National Parks and Reserves

AIGUES TORTES NATIONAL PARK

In the north-west corner of Catalonia where there are over 200 lakes, but somewhat marred by hydro-electric projects. Access from Espot in the east or the Boí valley in the west. Wildlife includes izard, brown bear, griffon vulture and golden eagle.

CADI-MOIXERO

This park which lies south of Andorra and the Cerdanya inspired young Picasso with its often startling scenery. Part is accessible by car on dirt tracks.

The wildlife includes izard, red and roe deer, black woodpecker, capercaillie, partridge, golden eagle.

GARROXTA
A volcanic park extending over a wide area behind the Costa Brava. Some 30 extinct volcanoes. Mammals include wild boar, beech marten, wild cat and genets. Birds include goshawk, reregrine falcon, short-toed eagle.

NAVARRE NATURE PARK
Established in 1990. Irati Beach Forest and *Karst* area. Brown bears survive here—the only protected area of the Pyrenees where they still do.

ORDESA NATIONAL PARK
Most spectacular national park in the range, with the Ordesa canyon accessible to motorists and a wide, easy trail for walkers. This is the most rewarding of the Pyrenean parks with a total of 32 mammal species, including ibex, izard, roe deer, wild boar, fox, wild cat, genet, otter and desman. Birds to be seen are lammergeier, griffon vulture and Egyptian vulture.

PYRENEES NATIONAL PARK
The national park of the French side of the range, running along the frontier from the Ossau valley in the west to the cirque of Troumouse in the east. Adjoins the Ordesa at the cirque of Gavarnie and has a similar wildlife—but no ibex.

NEOUVIELLE NATURAL RESERVE
Includes the highest forest in the Pyrenees. Easily accessible from Fabian in the Aure valley.

ORLU NATURE RESERVE
Beautiful landscape near Ax-les-Thermes where there are izard, marmot, fox, deer and wild boar.

Art Galleries

1 BAYONNE
Bonnat Museum. Art collection which includes works by Rubens, Murillo, Constable and Degas.

2 CADAQUES
Municipal art museum—local artists and local themes. Perrot-Moore Museum—Dalí collection of memorabilia and other artists with local connections.

3 CERET
Modern art museum. In summer open 10 a.m.–12 p.m. and 2–7 p.m. Picasso, Matisse, Manolo, Maillol, Gris, Chagall and Dalí.

4 ESCALDES
Andorran exhibition of sculpture by Catalan artist Josep Viladomati Massanes.

5 FIGUERES
Dalí Theatre Museum and Empordá Museum. Paintings by artists with local connections—Picasso, Miró, Dalí. Also a toy museum.

6 ILLE SUR TET
Musem of Sacred Art. Open May–September 10 a.m.–12 p.m. and 4–7 p.m.

7 OLOT
Garrotxa Comarcal Museum. There

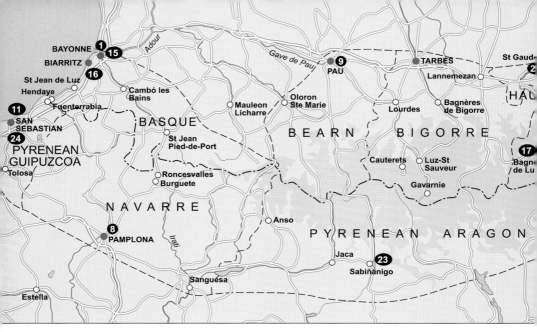

Art galleries and museums of the Pyrenees.

are paintings by the Olot School. There is also a museum housed in a Palladian Palace, Casal des Volcans, surrounded by botanical gardens. Interesting information about the volcanic region of the Garrotxa.

8 PAMPLONA
Navarre Museum. In the remains of the 16th-century civil hospital building. Comprehensive collection of early art.

9 PAU
Beaux-Arts Museum. Wide selection of European art and works of local interest.

10 PERPIGNAN
Rigaud Museum. Early Catalan paintings and modern works, including Maillol and Picasso.

11 SAN SEBASTIAN
St Telmo Museum. Art gallery which has a small selection of Spanish painting.

Museums

There are many museums in the area, some of them are small and concentrate on local history and crafts. Here are a few of the extra-rewarding ones.

12 ARGELES SUR MER
Catalan Museum. Open June –September 9 a.m.–12 p.m. and 3.30–6 p.m. Closed Sundays.

13 AUGIREIN
Museum of Couserans Arts and Traditions. Exhibits relating to the history and folklore of the Bethmale Valley. July–mid-September 2–6.30 p.m.

14 BANYOLES
Archaeological museum in the shell of a restored 14th-century palace. The Darder Natural History Museum is nearby.

15 BAYONNE
Basque Museum. One of the finest folk museums in the world.

16 BIARRITZ
Museum of the Sea. Huge aquarium and exhibits detailing fishing through the ages.

17 LUCHON
Eccentric local collection. Pyrenean room depicting the history of climbing. Summer weekdays 9 a.m.–12 p.m. and 2–6 p.m.

18 MAS D'AZIL
Near Foix. Museum of Prehistory contains finds from the caves.

19 MONTSEGUR
Museum devoted to the Cathars.

20 PERPIGNAN
Casa Pairal, Museum for the arts and crafts of Roussillon.

21 RIPOLL
Folk museum in church of San Pedro.

22 ST GAUDENS
Comminges Museum. Good display of prehistoric finds.

23 SABINANIGO
Aragón. Museum of traditional Aragonese style arts. Open 11 a.m.–1 p.m. and 4.30–7 p.m., daily, except Sunday afternoons and on Mondays.

24 SAN SEBASTIAN
St Telmo Museum. Folk museum ranging from dress to ancient Basque gravestones.

25 TAUTAVEL
Museum dedicated to "Tautavel Man"—some of the most ancient human remains found in Europe, half-a-million years old.

Relax on the Coast or Explore the Mountains

The Basque coastal region includes sophisticated Biarritz as well as St Jean de Luz, which still has the air of a fishing village. Inland, the busy town of Bayonne can supply pelota equipment for the Basque national game. The gorges of the Haute Soule and also the Irati Forest can be visited from the picturesque small town of St Jean Pied-de-Port.

Biarritz

To its many faithful fans, Biarritz is undoubtedly Queen of the Côte Basque coastal resorts. Long patronized by the rich, and the famous, it remains uncompromising in its quest for today's jet-set elegance, and only slightly battered by the frequent onslaught of huge Atlantic breakers which it turns to good effect by offering top-quality surfing.

The Cathedral of St Mary at Bayonne is northern Gothic in style, rather than the Pyrenean Romanesque more usually seen in the range.

It is the unreliability of sociable weather on the west coast which has kept Biarritz relatively pure of packaged tourism and safe from the would-be developers of the concrete playgrounds of the Mediterranean. That is not to say that Biarritz is under developed. Far from it, but it lacks the brashness of the Côte d'Azur. It sits at the top end of the southern Côte Basque which offers all types of accommodation, including acre after acre of luxury campsites.

History
You will find an arrogance about Biarritz that the centuries have failed to subdue. This was the favoured resort of Napoleon III and his wife Eugénie who, as a young Spanish noble of the de

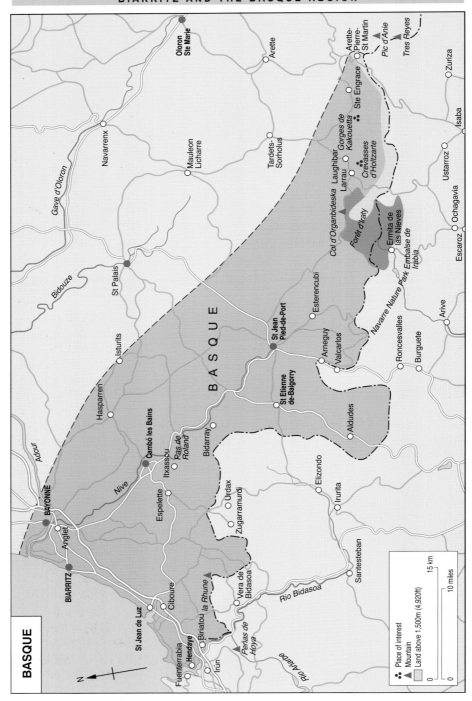

BASQUE

Oloron Ste Marie

Navarrenx

Arette

Arette-
Pierre-
St Martin

Pic d'Anie

Tres Reyes

Zuriza

Mauleon
Licharre

Tardets-
Sorholus

Ste Engrace

Isaba

Gave d'Oloron

Gorges de
Kakouetta

Crevasses
d'Holtzarte

Laughibar

Larrau

Col d'Organbideska

Forêt d'Iraty

Ustarroz

Ochagavia

Escaroz

Bidouze

St Palais

Ermita de
las Nieves

Embalse de
Irabia

Navarre Nature Park

Esterencubi

Arive

BASQUE

St Jean
Pied-de-Port

Arneguy

Valcarlos

Roncesvalles

Burguete

Isturits

Hasparren

St Etienne
de-Baigorry

Aldudes

Cambo les Bains

Pas de
Roland

Bidarray

Itxassou

Espelette

Urdax

Elizondo

Irurita

Zugarramurdi

Adour

Nive

BAYONNE

Anglet

BIARRITZ

Ciboure

Biriatou

la Rhune

Vera de
Bidasoa

Santesteban

St Jean de Luz

Fuenterrabia

Hendaye

Irún

Peñas de
Hoya

Rio Bidasoa

Rio Aritabe

BASQUE

N

Key

• Place of interest

Mountain

Land above 1,500m (4,920ft)

0 15 km

0 10 miles

Montijo family, spent happy childhood summers here through the 1830s, and it soon developed an up-market image which it has striven hard not to lose. It certainly succeeded in attracting a wealthy British clientele during the late 19th and early 20th centuries. Queen Victoria came in 1889, provoking quite a political storm by visiting Spain as well, and the Duke and Duchess of Windsor were frequent visitors. Only two world wars and currency restrictions succeeded in diminishing its appeal. The town is dominated by a number of impressive old buildings. Look out for the old Résidence Impériale, one-time holiday home of the Napoleon clan and now the sumptous **Hôtel du Palais**. Like the Municipal Casino it is on the southern curve of La Grande Plage. Several other Regency-style buildings were once great hotels, though most are now converted into more convenient apartments.

Before its fame as a resort, Biarritz was admired along with St Jean de Luz down the coast, as a great whaling centre. The *Atalaye*, a tall watch-tower with its signal chimney, would send up smoke signals to announce the approach of a school of whales. You can still see the remains of the tower in the Old Port—all that is left of the once-flourishing industry. Local whales were mostly hunted out by the mid-16th century and the whale boats were forced to take to further-flung fishing grounds.

The Basque region.

Sightseeing and Beaches

The **Old Port** is an interesting part of Biarritz, offering one of the few sheltered swimming beaches. Its **Museum of the Sea** has a huge aquarium and comprehensive exhibits detailing fishing through the ages. A short stroll to the north, there is a causeway to the mammoth statue of the Virgin, from where you can share her view out to open sea. The causeway had formed part of Napoleon's plan to create a mega-harbour, though the scheme was soon abandoned.

The other beaches of the town are less tranquil. **Grande Plage** is to the north of the huge rocky promontory presided over by the Virgin. **Plage de la Côte Basque** is to the south. Both offer fine golden sand and huge breakers. The lack of protection from the ocean rollers conspires to make Biarritz the surfing capital of Europe, and certainly many visitors are in possession of a traditional or wind-surfing board. When the sea is too rough you can try the lake at nearby La Négresse, where there is also dinghy sailing and water-skiing. If you prefer your sport on dry land there are five 18-hole golf courses in the area.

Shopping

This is predictably up-market. Set only a short distance back from the beaches, especially around the **Rocher de la Vierge**, you will find the best shops in place du Port-Vieux, avenue Edouard VII and rue Gambetta. For the fine chocolate for which Biarritz is famous visit Daranatz, 12 avenue du Maréchal-Foch; Dodin, boulevard Clemenceau; or Henriet, place Georges-Clemenceau.

Festivals

There are many festivals in Biarritz during the summer. These begin in early July with the festivities for *Gant d'Or*, with pelota, traditional Basque plays and dancing. On 15 August every year there is a huge firework display and on the third Sunday in August there is the important Festival of the Sea, with fishing competitions, parades and a Grand Ball. For one week either at the end of August or the beginning of September, Biarritz together with the other resorts along the coast, hosts an international festival of music.

Anglet

If you cannot find accommodation in Biarritz, try Anglet, a couple of kilometres to the north on the way to Bayonne. Its **Plage de la Chambre d'Amour** is a good beach but often with powerful surf. Visit the **Grotte de la Chambre d'Amour**, in which two young lovers were said to have drowned. You can pick up the Chemin Piétonnier Littoral footpath here. It offers well-marked easy walking all along the coast from the mouth of the River Adour down to Hendaye.

A Food Tour of the Basque Region

If you are interested in gourmet food, try the following circular tour from Biarritz. Covering 200 km (124 miles), it could be completed in a day, but your enjoyment will be improved if you spend at least one night on the road. (You will find the detailed entries for Espelette, St Etienne de Baïgory, St Jean Pied-de-Port and Bayonne below.)

Basque Cuisine

The cuisine of the Côte Basque naturally relies heavily on what is being pulled out of the nearby sea. Coupled with the Basque liking for heavy textures, strong flavours, and above all, generous helpings, favourite local dishes include the inevitable fish stew, known elsewhere in France as *bouillabaisse* but in the Basque country as *Ttoro*. It is made from a base of conger eel and monkfish. Other fish specialities are anchovies, salt cod served in a huge variety of ways, whiting and tuna, and plates of mixed seafood (*assiette des fruits de mer*).

Biarritz restaurants serving local specialities include the Michelin one-rosette Café de Paris in place Bellevue, just opposite the casino.

Starting from Biarritz, with its famous chocolate head south towards Bidart from where, by following the D455 in the direction of Arbonne, you will find the working windmill of **Bassilour**, which has produced flour since the 18th century. Behind the windmill is a bakery with a wide variety of different breads as well as a good version of the Gâteau Basque. Continue a short distance south to **Ahèize** and you will find an *épicerie* in the place du Fronton which has a wondrous assortment of charcuterie and cheeses. To the east, **Espelette** is a centre for pimento growing and, during late summer, you will see colourful strings of drying red peppers hanging from houses and barns. If it is lunch time, dine at the **Hôtel Euzkadi** which specializes in Basque cuisine; specialities include Ttoro and almost every imaginable kind of sausage. Into **Les Aldudes** and the premises of master

conserver, Pierre Oteiza, whose speciality is a wild pigeon paté, known as *Perkaïn*. At the next stop, St Etienne de Baïgorry, wine is the quarry. This is the **Irouléguy wine-growing region**, one of the best in the Pays Basque, and you can sample the reds and rosés at the Cave Coopérative. Half-an-hour further on, St Jean Pied-de-Port is an excellent place to spend the night, especially at the Hôtel des Pyrénées, one of the finest restaurants in the range. In the morning, buy some fruits bottled in *eau de vie* from Eienne Brana at 23 rue du 11 Novembre and some local sheep's cheese, *Ardi-Gasna*, which can be found all over the town. (The best *Ardi-Gasna* is farm produced and very strong tasting.) Now make your way back towards the coast via **St Palais**, famous for its lamb, and Guiche, where Maison Montauzer is the acknowledged expert in the authentic Bayonne ham known as *Ibaïona*. At least 1,000

Not a golf ball but a puffball, one of the most distinctive of all the mushrooms found in the Pyrenees.

hams at any one time hang for up to a year in their gauze bags, tended lovingly by Jaques Montauzer. They are salted but not treated in any other way. Last stop before the coast is Auberge Galupe at Urt on the left bank of the great Adour, a highly regarded restaurant, famous for its river fish, particularly salmon and sturgeon brought in at the port of Urt. Return to Biarritz via Bayonne, itself home to many great restaurants and food shops.

A Cultural Tour Inland

From Anglet, the D932 heads inland 8 km (5 miles) to **Ustaritz** which for 600 years was capital of the Basque province of Labourd. Its 35 parish representatives would meet at Ustaritz to form a people's government or *Bilcar*. Built on the left bank of the River Nive, the village has recently grown very rapidly into a town, the lifeblood of which is the large catholic seminary of **St François de Larresore**. The seminary was founded in 1753 and is known to Roman Catholics internationally as a major venue of learning and multi-nation debate—its summer school giving the town an air of contemplation. If you should arrive around lunch or dinner time, go to the

M isty days in the Basque country have a magic all their own but take your waterproofs with you.

three-star **Hôtel La Patoula**. Its restaurant is highly recommended for its delicate cuisine.

Just under 8 km (5 miles) further inland along the same road is Cambo les Bains, a spa town, on the outskirts of which is the fabulous Villa Arnaga, former home of Edmund Rostand, author of *Cyrano de Bergerac*. He used the large house and marvellous gardens as a haven from the rigours of Parisian theatre society during the early 20th century. The house is filled with personal effects and theatrical memorabilia and the gardens continue to delight. Both are open to visitors during the summer months.

You will find Cambo itself well whitewashed and decked with flowers throughout the summer. It too has expanded considerably, most rapidly in the upper part of the

The Basques

Within Europe, no people are more mysterious than the one million Basques. For centuries their existence has been a challenge to anthropologists but no theory of their origins has ever gained acceptance.

Their language of Euskara, for example, spoken at least partially by half a million people and almost unpronounceable to visitors, has no known relative. A once popular theory held that Basque was related to the long-extinct Iberian language, another that it is derived from the Afro-Asiatic group. But all such theories have been overturned.

The most popular explanation of the origin of the Basques is that they were Europe's original people, established long before the arrival of the Eastern cultures which gave much of Europe its present languages. Certainly at the beginning of the Christian era, Basque was spoken along both sides of the Pyrenees as far east as the Val d'Aran. Less plausible theories have held Basques to be the refugees of Atlantis, or descendants of the Scots. Scholarship is not helped by the absence of early Basque texts—the first printed Basque book dates only from 1545. From before that, only a few inscriptions, names and sentences have been unearthed.

Basque is not a uniform language but has some eight dialects. Similarly, not all Basques consider themselves part of a homogeneous race. Many French Basques, in particular, see themselves as close but not identical to Spanish Basques and give little support to the idea of an independent Basque country. Few would support the violence of nationalist organizations such as ETA over the border, and refuge in France is no sort of guarantee of safety for ETA activists.

In France some 200,000 Basques live within the official *département* of the Pyrénées-Atlantique, made up specifically of the ancient divisions of Labourd (capital Bayonne); Basse–Navarre (capital St Jean Pied-de-Port); and Soule (capital Tardets). In Spain the Pyrenees run through the Basque provinces of Guipúzcoa (capital San Sebastián) and Navarre (capital Pamplona).

Although violence continues sporadically, there is very little danger to tourists either in France or Spain. Occasionally you will suffer the inconvenience of a car search at the frontier. Otherwise Basque nationalist feeling is overwhelmingly positive for tourism. Nowhere else in western Europe can you enjoy such a rich and excitingly different folk culture, embracing dance, song, sport, costume and cuisine. It is hard to travel far through the Basque country without encountering a folk museum, or, in summer, some sort of fête dedicated to Basque tradition.

But there is one popular myth that has to be dispelled—the Basque house. The white-walled Basque home, half timbered in browny-red originated in Labourd and has gained popularity in the rest of the Basque country only recently. Look out for the even more spectacular "true" Basque houses which survive in the interior, the solid stone-built mini-fortresses, often with overhanging upper storeys and picturesque wooden galleries.

village which functions as a minor spa, used by locals and long-established visitors. The lower part, less vigorous and older, clusters around the river. There are places to stay and eat well in either part.

About 4 km (2½ miles) south-west is the truly Basque village of

Espelette, famous for its stubby, hard-working and hairy *Pottock* ponies which were once imported into England as pit-ponies. Espelette's other claim to fame is as prime grower of the pimento, the glossy red pepper much used in Basque cooking. There is an annual **Pimento Festival** in the first week of September, during which much wine is drunk and pepper eaten—all to a colourful backdrop of sun-dried pimentos. A special holiday dish called *axoa* (pronounced hachua) is cooked by both residents and restaurants at this time—main ingredients are veal, onions, potatoes, fresh red and green peppers and dried ground pimento.

About 4 km (2½ miles) along the main road from Cambo towards St Jean Pied-de-Port, the village of **Itxassou**. This is no less Basque, with a central church complete with three galleries and some good interior decoration. The graveyard is a fine example of Basque styling, with its round-topped gravestones, very typical of the region.

From the village it is a short, well-signposted walk or drive to the *Pas de Roland* where a small hole in the rock alongside both the river and road is said to have been created by the great hoofs of Roland's mighty horse. Roland was the commander of Charlemagne's rearguard which was ambushed and wiped out at Roncesvalles in AD 778 (*see* RONCESVALLES, below).

Finally, to the north-east of Cambo lies the tiny village of **Isturitz**, close to which are the cave systems of Isturitz and Oxocelhaya, decorated both with prehistoric paintings and carvings, and festooned with stalagmites and stalactites. There is a small museum in the village itself.

Returning westwards, you should pick up the D22 at Hasparren rather than continue to the main road at Cambo. The D22 is known as the Imperial Route of the Peaks because it was planned by Napoleon I and on the proverbial clear day gives a wonderful view south to the high peaks of the Pyrenees. It thus makes a suitable end to a day's touring.

Bayonne

Ten kilometres inland of Biarritz, the key to Bayonne is its two rivers. One, the Nive, comes straight down from the mountains, turbulent and passionate. This is Basque Bayonne, full of berets, white houses half timbered in browny-red, and frontons—those curved-topped walls against which the ball game **pelota** is endlessly played. The other is the wide and sedate Adour from the pragmatic heart of Gascony.

The rivers give the city its character—the bridges, the quays, the reflection of warehouses and merchant homes and the water traffic are as important to the exploration of the city as the fine old streets, the museums and the military history.

History
Bayonne grew up on the site of the Roman fort of Lapurdum and has been strategic ever since. In the mid-12th century it became English as part of the dowry of Eleanor of Aquitaine upon her marriage to Henry of

Basque Sports

Traditional Basque sports, involving staggering speed, strength and agility, are tremendous fun to watch.

Your best opportunity to see some exciting action and soak up the atmosphere (or even have a go) is at the village *fronton*, a huge round-topped blank wall, usually painted pink, peach or salmon, at the back end of a marked court. During weekdays the court may function as the car park or market, but its area is sacred during evenings and weekends, when villagers gather to play pelota—or one of the 20 or so variations of it. The basic concept is that teams of one or more people hit a ball alternately against one or more walls. Some larger towns have a *trinquet* or indoor court in which the game is more like royal Tennis, and there is a professional version known as Jaï Alaï.

It is thought pelota was first played by the Romans. Certainly, a game much like it was played throughout the Middle Ages against village church or barn walls with the bare hand or a wooden bat, and using a ball made from wool covered in dog or goat skin.

Nowadays the type of pelota played is a question of local choice. Some opt for the "slow" traditional game, played with a leather scoop-shaped glove called a *lachua*, a wooden bat called a *pala* or even (despite the agonizing power of the modern rubber ball) with the bare hand. Outside of the professional game, the most exciting version uses a long, thin basket called a *chistera*, which was first introduced in the 1860s. This is strapped to the arm and used as both a scoop for catching the ball and as a launching device. The ball moves so fast that, as with the puck in ice-hockey, you hardly see it go and the players' ability to position themselves borders on the extra-sensory.

For maximum enjoyment it helps to know a little about the rules. The fronton is up to 10 metres (30 ft) high and 17 metres (50 ft) wide, with a playing area or *cancha* between 60 metres and 90 metres (65 yd–100 yd) long, and about 20 metres (60 ft) wide. Across the fronton, about one metre from the ground, there is a metal bar which makes a noise if it is hit. On or below this line a ball is out. Teams can be one, two or three players. A serve is made from a fixed distance and the other team must return the ball or lose a point.

There is nothing to beat the ambience of the village game as a travel experience, but for sheer sporting excitement you must get along to watch at least one professional jaï alaï match. Two teams of two players use long, heavy chisteras for electrifying speed. The ball must hit two walls and the ground before being returned.

Other Basque sports can only be seen during summer festivals, resembling the Scottish Highland Games in their feats of chopping, lifting, throwing and dragging tree trunks. The most skilled are the lumberjacks, known in Basque as *aizkolaris*, but for out and out muscle the prize has to go to the professional stone lifters, known as *harrijasotzailes*, the sort of men who could put hydraulic excavators out of business.

Among the more conventional sports in the Basque country, football, rugby and rowing are also very popular.

Normandy, who shortly became Henry II of England. A flourishing trade was established, especially in wine. So useful was this alliance with the English crown that Bayonne did not succumb to the French until 1453.

Breaks in maritime activities were caused intermittently by the inclination of the Adour to silt and change course, which it did several times, bypassing Bayonne altogether until the present route was permanently engineered by

Charles IX in 1578. Nowadays the situation is commercially rather than militarily strategic, given Bayonne's key position close to the Spanish frontier. The aeronautical and chemical industries are the big employers.

Bayonne Today

The city is divided into three parts by the T-junction of its rivers. On the north bank of the Adour is the St Esprit district where the citadel stands and also where chocolate has been manufactured for 300 years, ever since the Jewish sweet-makers fled persecution in 17th-century Spain. The area to the south of the Adour is then itself divided by the Nive—the Vielle Ville (old town) to the west and Petit Bayonne to the east.

The Old Town

For shopping, you shoul.d seek out the pedestrianized, cobbled streets of **Vielle Ville**, flanked by vaulted arcades, which run down from the cathedral

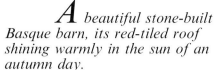

A beautiful stone-built Basque barn, its red-tiled roof shining warmly in the sun of an autumn day.

For the truly specialist shopper there is a chance to buy hand-made pelota equipment. The elongated basket-weave thrower (*chistera*) and the goat-skin ball (*pelote*) are available at souvenir shops, but the best place to buy is the workshop of M. Lucugaray (one of the few remaining pelota craftsmen) at 53 rue d'Espagne, not far from the cathedral (Tel. 59-25-51-79).

The workshop of **Gérard Léoncini** at 31 rue de la Vielle Boucherie (Tel. 59-59-18-20) is even more unusual. Here are made the traditional Basque walking-cum-swordsticks known as *makhilas* which have evolved over the centuries from simple tools into symbols of family honour. A Basque would no more part with his *makhila* than he would sell his mother. *Makhilas* are always enigmatically carved, the finest with intricate silver-work on the handle incorporating the family "coat of arms". If you do not have time to visit the workshops you can see some superb examples at the Basque Museum.

The most famous product of the town, however, is the bayonet, created by armourers here and first used by the French infantry in 1703.

Strolling around Bayonne is always a delight. On Tuesdays, Thursdays and Saturdays there are general markets along the quays (for fruit and vegetables quai de Galuperie), after which you can slip into one of the many cafés—the best are around **place de la Liberté** close to the Town Hall and

to the river Nive. When the strong smell of chocolate hangs over the city no one can resist buying, either from **Casenave** at 19 rue Pont-Neuf, or from **Daranatz** two doors along at number 13, styled more like an exclusive jewellery store than a confectioner. You should also try some authentic Bayonne ham, slowly wind-dried to be cut and eaten wafer thin (there is plenty of opportunity to sample this speciality during the annual Ham Fair held each Easter).

Bayonne is famous for its chocolate, the smell of which often hangs over the city. Daranatz, in the old town, looks more like a jewellery shop than a confectioner.

municipal theatre. Or you could cross the Adour by Pont St Esprit to sample the fiery local liqueur at the Izarra distillery at 9 quai Bergeret (Tel. 59-59-18-20). Window shopping is best done around the cathedral, especially in rues Pont-Neuf, Victor Hugo and Thiers; opposite the town walls, by the cathedral, there is also the Galeries Lafayette department store.

Little Bayonne

When you have spent enough, continue your stroll across the Nive, through **Petit Bayonne** and into the **Mousserolles Park**, right up against the eastern walls of the town. Petit Bayonne is the centre of the annual Bayonne Fête, a huge, raucous affair in which exotic parades during the day give way to drinking and making merry virtually all night. This event is held either at the end of July or the first week in August.

Bayonne has four major tourist sites which you should not miss—the citadel, the cathedral and the Bonnat and Basque museums.

St Esprit

High in the St Esprit quarter, **the citadel** was built by Vauban, favourite military engineer of Louis XIV, in 1680. The legend that Vauban's fortresses could never be taken was proved in 1814 when it held out against the British for three months—until after Napoleon's abdication, in fact. Today it is possible to visit the massive ramparts, but only on prior arrangement with the tourist office—

located across the Adour in place de la Liberté.

The **Cathedral of St Mary**, in the old town, is northern Gothic rather than Pyrenean Romanesque, possibly because it was begun in the early 13th century, under English rule. You will see some magnificent stained glass, of which the best is in St Jerome's chapel, depicting a woman of Canaan pleading with Jesus to cure her daughter. There is also a series of substantial paintings by the Steinheils, father and son. The graceful cloister, dating from the 14th century, makes a superb haven from the hubbub of the streets.

The two museums are a short stroll apart on the east bank of the River Nive. The **Bonnat Museum** in rue Jacques Lafitte is named after Léon Bonnat (1833–1922), a son of the city who became a successful society portrait painter in Paris, and who even more successfully amassed his own art collection which he then dedicated to his home town. In addition to a gallery of his own work, there are sculptures, drawings and paintings from classical to modern times. Particularly important are a sketch of Napoleon by David, a self-portrait by Goya, a crayon by Leonardo da Vinci and an Ingres. There are also works by Rubens, Murillo, Constable and Degas.

Just round the corner in rue Marengo, on the quay, is the **Basque Museum**. It was substantially reorganized in 1990 and is now one of the finest folk museums in the world. If you intend to spend much time in the Basque region this is essential. There are tableaux and exhibits concerning everything Basque—pelota and other games, the makhila, sorcery, architecture, the sea and the input of Jewish tradition.

The best eating in Bayonne tends to be Basque rather than Gascon. Be sure to try Bayonne ham (cut thin, like Parma); at least one of the many dishes with locally grown pimento (most famous, *piperade* a tender mix of peppers, onions and oil, served with or without egg); the spicy (and very garlicky) sausages known as *loukinkos*; the heavily seasoned black pudding (*tripotcha*); and the almond-flavoured *Gâteau Basque*.

St Jean de Luz

Even when it is packed to the hilt with summer holidaymakers, St Jean de Luz, 15 km (10 miles) south along the coast from Biarritz still retains more of the air of a fishing village than that of a tourist town. Much of its popularity is due to a good natural harbour, protecting the beach and port—unusual for this stretch of coast.

A Nautical History

It was from here in the 11th century that the whaling fleets set out. As at Biarritz, almost the whole town would turn out to deal with the carcasses which were towed in by tiny boats. When the whales were hunted out of local waters—an environmental message that went unheeded—the boats became larger and searched as far as Newfoundland. It was a St Jean fisherman who invented a process of rendering blubber which enabled the boats to stay out at sea for extended periods.

St Jean de Luz still has the air of a traditional fishing village. Once, the boats went as far as Newfoundland.

Hand-in-hand with the increasing success of the port came the growth in the wealthy managerial and merchant classes who built the many towering flat-fronted town houses. These give the town its only real architectural heritage since little survived the arrival of a Spanish invasion force in 1558. The Spanish reduced the town to ashes, so there are few buildings pre-dating the mid-16th century. More were destroyed by a freak tidal wave in 1749.

Many of the finest streets, like rue République and rue Gambetta, have been pedestrianized. The sea front is comparatively modern with apartments and villas and promenades decorated with hydrangeas and pink tamarind. To the north-east of the beach is the newer part of the town, well-designed and harmonious, full of whitewashed houses.

St Jean's main historical claim to fame was as host to the prolonged marriage formalities between Louis XIV and the then Infanta Maria Theresa of Spain, an event which filled an entire month in 1660 with extravagant celebration. The official signing of the contract, an important political alliance of two great powers, took place on the Ile des Faisans, in the centre of the River Bidasoa, which marks the frontier between France and Spain, some 14 km (9 miles) south. The glamorous mass, took place in **St Jean's church**, St John the Baptist in rue Gambetta. A party followed in one of the great merchant houses, Château Lohobiague, now called **Maison Louis XIV**. You can see the period furniture and decoration of the interior in place Louis XIV. A little way off in rue de l'Infante is **Maison Joanoenia** where the young Spaniard stayed before her wedding.

You should not miss the church, which is a fine, rare example of pure Basque styling with a dark wooden interior, three sides of which are lined with balconies accessed by wrought iron stairs. The balconies were added to boost capacity and in practice separated the men who sat in the galleries from the women and children who sat in the main body of the church.

The oldest house in St Jean de Luz (1540) stands on the stylish rue de la République which runs from place Louis XIV down to the beach. It also happens to be one of the best restaurants in the area, with a wonderfully atmospheric decor to match.

Inland of St Jean de Luz

An easy trip from St Jean is to **La Rhune** (900 metres/3,000 ft), standing out as a solitary peak visible from most of the Côte Basque resorts.

Steeped in legend, it is said to be a meeting place for witches. Nowadays there is a cog railway up the mountain from the Col de St Ignace on the D4 between the typical Basque villages of Sare and Ascain. On foot the ascent takes about three hours. The views from the top are superb; the Bay of Biscay to the west, the forests of Les Landes to the north and the Pyrenees to the east.

Sare also claims hauntings and there are tales of a particularly famous sorceress called Marie Dindard. It is an amazingly pretty village with lots of trees and a square-towered Basque church which has the characteristic wooden galleries. Sare is also worth visiting for the Michelin-recommended

restaurant **Arraya**, where specialities include locally caught wild pigeon. Menus are from 130F—if you would like to stay in one of the 21 rooms, the cost is about 400F for a double.

Ciboure

Just across the wide River Nivelle from St Jean the quayside houses of Ciboure are even grander and the streets are narrower and steeper. One typical example, right on the sea front, at what was 12 (now 27) **quai Maurice Ravel** was the birthplace of the French composer in 1875. He lived most of his creative life close to Paris, but childhood in Ciboure left its indelible mark. The Basque and Spanish influences are unmistakeable in *Bolero* and *Rapsodie Espagnole* while *Une Barque Sur L'Ocean* recalls the young Ravel looking out across the sea from his harbourside home.

The **Church of Saint Vincent** in Ciboure is in the same Basque style as St John the Baptist with its balconies and panelling. But it also has an enigmatic "Cagot door", a special entrance reserved for the unfortunate Cagots, who, shunned by the general population, were forced to worship separately (*see* THE CAGOTS below).

From Ciboure the road runs west to Socoa at the mouth of the bay where there is an ancient fortified port, originally built as a strategic lookout by Henry IV and later renovated by Vauban. You can make this a stimulating walk from either St Jean or Ciboure—it takes about two hours. Continuing south from Socoa the road soon becomes a spectacular corniche cresting up-tilted cliffs and offering staggering views along the coast.

Hendaye

Hendaye, 14 km (9 miles) south of St Jean, is the last town in France before the Spanish border which is formed by the River Bidasoa. Right in the middle of the river, the flat and unimportant looking Ile des Faisans is an historic chunk of shared Spanish and French territory. Louis XI of France negotiated with Henry IV of Castile on the island in 1469, the hostage Francis I was exchanged for his two sons here in 1526 and the Treaty of the Pyrénées (1659) was signed here, as was the following year the marriage treaty between Louis XIV of France and the Infanta, Maria Theresa of Spain.

To long-distance walkers especially it has a magic and excitement as the starting place for two classic trans-Pyrenean footpaths, the GR10 and the HRP.

Hendaye is divided into two parts—"Ville" which is on the river, and "Plage" which is on the sea. Hendaye-Ville is not very attractive (unlike Spanish Fuenterrabía on the opposite bank) but it is cheaper than the beach resort.

Hendaye-Plage lacks the chic of St Jean or Biarritz but it has an excellent wide beach and is very popular with French families.

Inland from Hendaye

You can experience the excitement of setting off on the HRP *Haute Randonnée Pyrénéenne* or GR10 (*Grande Randonnée Pyrénéenne*) by following the red-and-white-striped marks through the town. Both footpaths follow the same route to begin with. But it is more enjoyable to join the path at the tiny hill-top village of Biriatou, a few kilometres upstream on the River Bidasoa. This village is a gem. The Basque church is designated *site classé* and to reach the town hall you have to climb up the tiered seating of the village *fronton*, which doubles as steps. The most picturesque hotel and restaurant is the Auberge Hirribarren, which adjoins the *fronton*. When a game is in progress you can sit outside with a drink at the barrel tables and watch (but a weekend lie-in may prove impossible as the thud of the high-speed ball resonates through the building).

From the road on the south side of the church, the GR10/HRP footpath is well marked with red and white paint stripes. From Biriatou half-an-hour's walking is enough to leave civilization far below as the path crosses rock-strewn heath, flowered plateau, barren crest, lake and forest. A complete circle, incorporating a visit to the Bayonnette Redoubt (a defensive earthwork on the frontier) and returning on one of the local marked footpaths, takes a full day. Other hikers on the path out of Biriatou may be contemplating the full transpyrenean itinerary—which takes 45 days at least.

If you stay on the footpath as far as Col d'Ibardin (a half-day from Biriatou), you can enjoy a very different kind of experience. Amazingly the pass, right on the frontier, has become a "mini-Andorra" of shopping bargains, between French and Spanish customs. There are plenty of bargains here for French shoppers, plus the additional attraction of Spanish snacks. Of course, you can also drive. Best route is to take the Urrugne road out of Hendaye and then the road to Herboure where you turn south for the pass.

Cycle Tours

You can enjoy idyllic cycle touring in the French Basque country, except that the most tranquil and scenic routes are often the most strenuous as well. Consult the *Carte Randonnée: Pays Basque Ouest* in the *Randonnées Pyrénéenne* series, on which the suggested *piste cyclable* is clearly shown in yellow. The following are just suggestions. Most major towns in France have cycle rental outlets, as do many stations (Gare SNCF). Expect to pay about 45–70F a day, slightly more for a specialist mountain bike.

Bayonne (near the cathedral)—west on the D5 along the left bank of the river Adour to the campsite at La Barre (almost at the river mouth)—south on the D5 behind the beaches—pass the campsite at La Chambre d'Amout—Pointe St Martin—Biarritz (30 km/20 miles return).

Biarritz (old port)—slightly inland of the Plage de la Côte Basques—Ilbarritz on the N10b—east at Bourrountz crossing the Autoroute de la Côte Basque—join the D255 north-east—Arangues—Bertbeder—cross the D932—join the left bank of the River Nive at Bellegarde—follow the river to Bayonne—return as above (47 km/30 miles).

Biarritz to Ilbarritz and Bourrountz as above—right onto D255 to Arbonne —east through Chenchinenea—Araneceta—turn right onto D3—left onto D250—Ustaritz—south onto D137—Souraïde—right onto D20 (optional detour to Espelette)—right on to D14 via Ainhoa—Sare—Col de St Ignace (La Rhune)—Ascain—St Jean de Luz—Biarritz (86 km/54 miles—one or two days depending on ability).

Walking Tours

One of the main attractions of the Pyrenees is its walking. There are itineraries varied enough to suit both the dedicated trekker and the casual stroller. On the west coast it is surprising how soon a walk can take you from the hurly-burly of the coastal strip to the tranquility of the hills and mountains above. Within half-an-hour you can be deep in the real Pays Basque. The following are only suggestions. Most tourist offices will be able to recommend other local marked walks.

The *Randonnée Pyrénéenne Pays Basque Ouest* map marks some of the local walks and all the GR (Grandes Randonnées) footpaths. For long-distance walking, plan your shopping and overnight stops carefully because the Pays Basque contains some of the most remote country in the Pyrenees. If you are fit you should be able to cover about 4 km (2½ miles) in an hour on the flat, but you must allow another hour for every 300 metres/1,000 ft of ascent. Make a further allowance if you have to carry heavy camping equipment. In much of the region it is essential to carry water.

If you are following a marked route and lose your way, retrace your steps to the last mark and begin a search. The red and white stripes of GRs are rarely more than a couple of hundred metres apart.

Sentier de Piétonnier Littoral—Bayonne (Tour des Signaux on the mouth of the River Adour)—follow the path behind Plage de la Chambre d'Amour—Biarritz; Pointe St Martin—Grande Plage—around Rocher de la Vierge—Plage de la Côte Basques—Bidart—Guéthary—St Jean de Luz; Pointe de Ste-Barbe—

The famous GR10 footpath, marked by red and white stripes, begins at Hendaye and traverses the length of the Pyrenees to Banyuls sur Mer, a distance of some 700km (450 miles).

Ciboure—Socoa—Hendaye; Pointe Ste-Anne—Hendaye-Plage (32 km/21 miles one-way; allow 2 days).

Biriatou (6 km/4 miles inland of Hendaye)—GR10/HRP Rocher des Perdrix—Col d'Osin—Col de Poiriers—Col des Joncs (optional 30 minute round-trip detour to Redoute de la Bayonnette)—frontier stone 11 and follow frontier to Col d'Ibardin—return the same way (18 km/11 miles; 5–6 hour round trip).

Biriatou—follow same itinerary to ridge above Col des Joncs and with optional visit to the Redoute de la Bayonette—now descend along the frontier ridge into the Bidasoa Valley down to the river—follow River Bidasoa ascending into Biriatou (16 km/10 miles; 4½ hours).

Sare (GR10)—summit of La Rhune (round trip 12 km; 8hour). An alternative would be to drive to Col de St Ignace and ascend La Rhune from there (about 4½–5hours).

St Jean Pied-de-Port

St Jean Pied-de-Port is one of the most picturesque small Basque towns, self-consciously touristic in season with its wide range of hotels, restaurants, gift shops and almost continuously festive ambience. Set at the foot of the mountains which rise gently to the south, it makes an excellent base for motorists, just over 50 km (30 miles) from the sea, whilst for those staying on the coast without transport it is easily accesssible as a day trip by train via Bayonne.

History

In the Middle Ages, it was an important stop on the famous pilgrim path to Santiago de Compostela, that leads from Ostabat 20 km (13 miles) to the north where the three main routes through France converged. As soon as a group of pilgrims was spotted coming from Ostabat, the church bells at St Jean Pied-de-Port would be rung and the pilgrims would sing in reply. The symbol of the Compostela pilgrim is the scallop shell or *coquille St Jacques*, still worn by pilgrims passing through the town today.

The Town Today

The **Citadel** stands at the top of the town (now a college and closed to the public) and makes a convenient landmark, with the River Nive to the south and the River Laurhibar to the north. The **Tourist Office** is on place Général de Gaulle, the main square, which lies immediately to the west of the citadel, at the foot of the old town walls. Most of the shops are in the old streets to the south of the citadel.

In season **folklore festivals** and **Basque sports** take place every week. These are held either in the Jaï-Alaï arena, north of the citadel, the Fronton Municipal to the south, close to the town campsite, or in one of the squares. No visitor should miss watching one of the many forms of pelota (see BASQUE SPORTS) nor the folk-dancing which in the Basque country, more than any other parts of the Pyrenees, is a living part of the culture. In July there is usually a celebration of the Chemin de St Jacques pilgrimage, held in the citadel itself, while the climax of the season is a week-long *fête*, usually in the middle of August, with Basque games, dancing in the streets, the *Noce Basque* (re-enactment of a traditional Basque wedding), folk-dancing and fireworks. For food lovers there are *foires gastronomique* in the market by the town walls to the south of place Général de Gaulle, conducted with the usual French enthusiasm for eating and drinking; visitors can taste *gâteau basque* (an almond flavoured tart), *ardi-gasna* (sheep's cheese), other regional specialities and the local wine and *eaux de vie*. Poire William by St Jean Pied-de-Port's Etienne Brana is especially recommended for its natural aroma and elegance—the address is 23 rue du 11 Novembre.

Sights

The best way of seeing the old part of St Jean Pied-de-Port is to walk through as the pilgrims used to, entering by the Porte de St Jacques on the north side of the walls by the citadel and following rue de la Citadelle down to the river. On the way you can visit the **Prison des**

The Cagots

The Cagots were mysterious outcasts who inhabited the area around St Jean Pied-de-Port and other parts of the Pyrenees from the 13th to the 18th centuries. No historians have positively unravelled the truth about their origins nor the reasons for the discrimination against them, but their persecution was undoubtedly linked to the fear of leprosy. Cagots were condemned to live apart from the society of other people, could not marry outside the Cagot community, could not serve in any army, were banned from living in the centre of St Jean Pied-de-Port and other towns, and were refused entry both to mills and to the church. But it is in the design and decoration of churches that some possible clues to the Cagots are to be found. The church at St Savin in the Bigorre, for example, has a low-arched window known as the *Fenêtre des Cagots* where it is said the outcasts could listen to Mass from outside the church, and the church at Arras en Lavedan has a low, now blocked-up, doorway that is called the *Porte des Cagots*. From this many have deduced that the Cagots were short people, which seems to be confirmed by at least one 14th-century account which describes them as dwarfish and dark skinned. Another 14th-century account, however, contradicts that and likens the Cagots to Nordic races, tall and fair with blue eyes.

The name "Cagots" is equally covered in confusion. One suggestion is that it derives from *can goth*, meaning dog of the Visigoths, but the Visigoths moved into the Pyrenees in the 6th century after defeat by the Frankish king Clovis, while the first documented mention of Cagots does not occur for another 700 years.

Whatever the original origin of the persecution, the fear of leprosy was undoubtedly a component and for 67 years between 1560 and 1627 the court at Toulouse intermittently heard representations and subjected Cagots to medical examination. Doctors pronounced them free of leprosy. In 1683 Louis XIV ordered that Cagots should enjoy the same rights as other citizens and not be segregated. But none of this did any good and the discrimination continued right up to the French Revolution. Only by the 19th century had the Cagot communities disappeared although the word persisted as a term of abuse.

Around St Jean Pied-de-Port, the Cagot villages were those to the west side of the town in the hills to the north and south of the road to St Etienne de Baïgorry, and close to Baïgorry itself at the hamlet of Michelene.

Evêques, a jail not for Bishops, as the name implies, but for those found guilty of crimes against the pilgrims—the thieves, fraudulent beggars and the like, of which there were many. The **church**, Notre Dame du Bout du Pont is right by the bridge, the view from which is the subject of many postcards, the timbered and shuttered houses with their flowered balconies reflected in the lazy waters of the River Nive.

The rue d'Espagne then leads out of the city walls again, through Porte d'Espagne, with various enticing shopping streets off to the side. There are shops selling espadrilles (42 rue d'Espagne), local watercolours (**Galerie Labia**, 36 rue de la Citadelle), regional foods (**Laurent Petricorena**, 1 rue de la Citadelle), jewellery (**Martocq Etcheverry**, 18 rue d'Espagne), Basque linen, woollens and sheepskins (**Maison Garicoix**, rue d'Uhart off rue d'Espagne), *gâteau basque* (Primo and Artizarra, both in rue d'Espagne) and general souvenir shops are all around.

Self-catering opportunities abound in the countryside, many of them in traditional Basque farmhouses; either collect a list from the tourist office or drive around watching for "Gîte de France" signs.

Following the Pilgrim Route

After his beheading by Herod Agrippa, the legend of Santiago de Compostela claims that the body of St James was taken to Spain for burial. There it lay forgotten until it was discovered some 750 years later by a hermit attracted to the spot by a vision of stars. Hence the name. Santiago is Spanish for Saint James (St Jacques in French) while Compostela comes from the Latin *campus stellae* meaning "field of stars". The truth is rather different (St James was buried in the Nile Delta) and the legend was nothing more than the invention of the church at a time when the Moorish invasion was sweeping all of Spain. Soon, according to the Church, St James was appearing on the battlefield to assist the Christians.

The pilgrim trail on from St Jean Pied-de-Port has followed different routes at different times. The main road that runs via the Spanish frontier at Arnéguy is one of them but by far the most enjoyable is the so-called *Route des Crêtes*. It follows tiny lanes through the rolling Basque countryside, well away from the main road traffic, and continues into Spain as an easy and highly recommended footpath.

The Start

For walkers, the route is known as the **GR65** and is well signposted from the town, beginning at the **Porte d'Espagne**, sometimes following tarmac but also taking short cuts through the fields. Motorists should begin by following the signposts for St Michel and Estérençuby from the main road just south of place Général de Gaulle; after 200 metres turn off right into route du Maréchal Harispe, also marked "GR65" and "Chemin de St Jacques". The lane climbs steadily up between fields, farms and copses with occasionally spectacular views to right and left.

After some 14 km (9 miles) the remains of **Château-Pignon** can be seen above to the left. The fortress was built by King Ferdinand the Catholic at the beginning of the 16th century to mark the limit of his lands. Close by is the spot known locally as **Karrosa-Uzkali**, which means "overturned coach" a reference to the procession of Elisabeth de Valois in the winter of 1560 whose coach turned over in the snow on her way to marry Philip II of Spain.

After 16 km (or 1½ km after the right-hand turning to Arnéguy) the red and white stripes indicate that the pilgrim route is leaving the road behind. (Measure the distance on the speedometer so that there is no confusion with other places where the footpath temporarily diverges from the road— the correct position is recognizable by the two rocky hillocks between which the footpath passes.) If you would like to follow the pilgrim route for a short distance on foot, park the car here; it takes about one hour to reach the frontier at marker stone 199, which, according to some authorities, was the site of the defeat of Charlemagne's

Leaves of the sweet chestnut in early autumn—the nuts can be roasted or boiled.

rearguard by the Basques; the more popular choice for the battle site is the nearby Ibañeta Pass (for more on the history, see the entry under RONCESVALLES). Keen hikers (with their passports) can walk as far as the **monastery** at Roncesvalles in 4–5hours.

After stretching your legs along the GR65, you can continue by car to the **Arnostéguy Pass** where, just under the summit of **Pic d'Urculu**, stands a strange low tower known as the **Monument d'Urculu**. At one time this was believed to be a fort but modern scholarship leans towards it being a funeral monument dating from around 1500 BC. From the pass, the road swings north and then east to descend through the Orion forest to Estérençuby and back to St Jean Pied-de-Port along the right bank of the Béhérobie river.

Irouléguy Wines and St Etienne de Baïgorry

Wine and food lovers should take the D15 road west from St Jean Pied-de-Port the 11 km (7 miles) to St Etienne de Baïgorry. Soon the road is surrounded by vineyards and about half way the village of **Irouléguy** is passed, which has given its name to the best of the Basque country wines. None of them are great but Irouléguy is the only *vin d'Appellation* of the Pays Basque and comes either red or rosé. The place to taste Irouléguy is in St Etienne de Baïgorry itself, either at the **Cave Coopérative**, or at the **Hôtel Arcé**.

Baïgorry (as it is locally known for short) is a large village, less touristic than St Jean Pied-de-Port, on the banks of the Nive des Aldudes river and under the impressive sweep of the Iparla Ridge.

The Iparla Ridge Walk

The Iparla Ridge is justly one of the most famous walks of the Basque country because of the exhilarating sense of height created by the sheer drop to the east. From Irouléguy and Baïgorry it appears as a long steep-sided wall softened by green sheep pasture on which the effects of sun and cloud play continuously. As an additional attraction it is usually possible to see griffon vultures spread out in the sky as they search for carrion. The ridge forms part of the route of the two long distance footpaths, the GR10 and the HRP, but the ascent is well within the capabilities of most walkers and is marked with red-and-white painted stripes at regular intervals.

The ridge can be tackled from the Baïgorry direction but the opposite end is preferable. Non-motorists can take the train either from St Jean Pied-de-Port or from the direction of Bayonne, alighting at Pont Noblia, the part of the village of Bidarray that is beside the River Nive. From the station, cross the river by the new bridge, turn left and climb up through Bidarray village following signs to the *Mairie* beside which is the pink-painted *fronton* that is the standard feature of French Basque villages. Motorists should leave their cars here.

From the *mairie*, follow the red and white paint markings, taking the left-hand fork at the first junction and the right-hand fork at the second. The tarmac ends at a farm some 15 minutes from the parking area where the serious hiking starts. The really spectacular views begin after about 90 minutes of effort and it would be a pity to turn back before then.

The ridge forms the border between a particularly remote part of Spain, where smuggling still goes on today, and an only slightly more populous part of France. Keen hikers can enjoy the immense panorama throughout the day, as the ridge is followed beyond the high point of Pic d'Iparla (1,044 metres/3,400 ft) to the Col de Buztanzelhay. From the col it is possible to walk down to St Etienne de Baïgorry on the GR10 footpath and catch a bus to the train station at Ossès St Martin d'Arossa, between Pont Noblia and St Jean Pied-de-Port.

Smuggling

Smuggling still goes on in the Basque country, as it does all along the Pyrenees, but the strange contours of the Basque frontier probably make it easier here than in any other part of the range. The Regata Urrizate valley, for example, immediately to the west of the Iparla Ridge, has its entrance in France yet lies mostly in Spain. In these parts it is often impossible to take a country hike without crossing the frontier several times.

East of St Jean Pied-de-Port

To the east of St Jean Pied-de-Port lies some of the most remote scenery in all of the French Pyrenees, climbing steadily to the summit of **Pic d'Anie** (2,504 metres/8,140 ft), the western slopes of which mark the boundary between the Pays Basque and Béarn. There is no public transport and few hotels, but you can easily drive to **Arette la Pierre St Martin** close to the foot of Pic d'Anie (80 km/50 miles approx.) and return the same day, still having time to take a stroll in the Irati

The Iparla Ridge walk is one of the classic hikes of the Basque country, but you don't have to walk all the way to enjoy yourself.

Scotland, until the Col de Burdincurutcheta (1,135 metres/3,690 ft). From the col there is a new vista eastwards, over the tiny lake in the valley below and over the immense **Irati Forest** (also spelt Iraty). Mostly beech, the Irati is the greatest forest of the Pyrenees, with two-thirds of its 12,000 hectares/30,000 acres on the Spanish side of the frontier and one-third on the French. Descending to the lake at Plateau Irati, there is a choice of forestry tracks for walking, while the main road continues towards the village of Larrau.

Walking in the Irati Forest

The tourist office at St Jean Pied-de-Port has published walking itineraries, *Circuits Pédestres en Irati* of which one of the most interesting is that to the prehistoric circle of standing stones on the western side of Sommet d'Occabé (1,466 metres/4,765 ft). You can take your car south from the lake and leave it near Chalet Pedro (about 1 km/½ mile) from where the GR10 footpath climbs fairly easily westwards through beech dotted with the fir trees that used to supply the French and Spanish navies, and then descends on the far side of Occabé where the standing stones are easily spotted, a circle of irregular boulders on the bare ground dating from some 2–3,000 years ago (about two hours from Chalet Pedro). From here, you can retrace your steps or take the trail that passes around the

Forest or one of the four famous gorges of Haute Soule. Those who wish to linger will find only a very few small hotels and would be advised to book ahead. The Basque country is renowned for its concealing mists and rain so that if you plan any serious hiking you should bring waterproofs, compass and map.

From St Jean Pied-de-Port, follow the main D933 eastwards some 4 km (2½ miles) to St Jean le Vieux and there turn off on the D18, signposted "Irati". The road now begins to climb upwards below bare crests, very reminiscent of the most denuded parts of south side of Occabé and regains the parking area after about six hours' walking.

It is worth lingering for there are red and roe deer in the woods as well as wild boar, although all are difficult to see. Among the birds, the white-backed woodpecker has recently been rediscovered in the Irati. The male has a red crown, the female black, and in flight the white lower back and upper rump are clearly visible The trailing edges of the wings are dotted white.

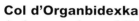

Col d'Organbidexka

A short way beyond Plateau Irati, the road reaches the holiday development at the Col d'Organbidexka. For bird lovers, Col d'Organbidexka is the most famous pass in the Pyrenees because of its importance in the autumn migration, which extends from August until October. It is difficult to appreciate the hundreds of thousands of birds that cross this single pass (millions for the Pyrenees as a whole) since vast numbers use the safety of darkness, but even the daytime spectacle is considerable.

Birdlife

Among the largest birds to be seen are the cranes, their jagged wings set well to the rear; the white storks, which, despite the name have black trailing edges to their wings; and the greylag geese, all of which cross in thrilling V-formations. Another beautiful migrant is the honey buzzard. The best time to see it is around the end of August or the beginning of September.

Conservationists have been brought into bitter conflict with Pyrenean hunters, who take to the passes every October and shoot around one-and-a-half million woodpigeons and some four-and-a-half million other birds, some of them protected species. Since 1979 a group of conservationists known as *Organbidexka-Vol libre-Pertuis pyrénéens* has rented Col d'Organbidexka, specifically to keep the hunters off and this has led to angry and sometimes violent scenes.

Larrau and Logibar

From the col, the road descends gradually at first but then with a rare steepness to the tiny village of **Larrau**, set amidst rolling green hillocks and thickets of beech. A road climbs from the entrance to the village to the Port de Larrau, which is the border with Spain, while eastwards the road continues descending to the hamlet of **Logibar** at the entrance to the first of the famous gorges of that part of the French Basque country known as Haute Soule. There is only a **gîte d'étape** at Logibar, but the **gérant Félix Quihilirry** does serve excellent local food to passing travellers.

The Gorges

The **Gorges d'Holzarté**, which is reached by a clear footpath running south from Logibar, is famous for its suspension bridge, reached after about three-quarters-of-an-hour's walking. No visit would be complete without at least getting that far. The bridge is hung from cables, swings alarmingly over a 200 metres (650 ft) drop and takes several minutes to cross, but being both tourist attraction and the traditional route for shepherds and their *troupeaux*, it is always in reliable condition. From the centre of the

*B*eautiful and delicate
flowers like these pinks cling
tenaciously to life on the rocks.

(4 miles) turn right, following signposts for Ste Engrâce. The narrow road climbs steadily beside the Ste Engrâce stream, into what was until recently the furthest and least visited recess of the Basque country. Until 1987 it was a cul-de-sac for cars but the road (D113) has now been pushed through to Arette la Pierre St Martin, admitting a steady flow of tourist traffic between the lush tiny green fields with their regular hedgerows and conical haystacks. The famous **Gorges de Kakouéta** is 7 km (4½ miles) from the junction, the only one of the Haute Soule gorges to be provided with a boardwalk, for the privilege of which there is an entrance charge of 15F (open every day Easter to October from 8 a.m. until dusk—the rest of the year free at the hiker's own risk).

Unlike the previous gorges, the footpath allows you to trace the course of the canyon bottom, the walls as much as 300 metres (1,000 ft) high and the distance between them as little as 5 metres (16 ft). The moist air has little chance to escape, creating an almost tropical micro-climate in which the walls are draped in a dense green curtain of shrubs and moss. The path continues for approximately 40 minutes, ending at picnic tables beside a 20 metre (65 ft) waterfall; if you do not have your own picnic, there is a café at the gorge entrance.

The entrance to the last of the Haute Soule gorges, **Ehujarré**, is at the hamlet of Calla, little more than a kilometre (half-a-mile) beyond the Kakouéta. It is wider than Kakouéta and therefore less dramatic but it has the advantage of more sunshine. If you are a keen hiker, take the path that begins

bridge there is a marvellous view eastwards along the sheer white rock of the interconnecting **Gorges D'Olhadubi**. Serious walkers can make a circuit by continuing from the far end of the bridge to the very head of the Olhadubi gorge and then returning by the path above the east side, which finally returns to Logibar after some six hours' walking.

Beyond Logibar, the road penetrates deeper into Haute Soule and the Gave (stream) de Larrau becomes a torrent popular with canoeists. After 6 km immediately beyond the bridge at Calla, dropping south-east into the gorge entrance, where it follows the left bank at first. It is possible to make a circuit, lasting some six or seven hours, continuing right along the gorge, climbing out through woods at the far end, and returning in a broad sweep along well-trodden paths, either to the east or west of the defile.

Ste Engrâce

Ste Engrâce is not a single village but a collection of hamlets, and it is at the one called Senta, just beyond Ehujarré, that the **Ste Engrâce** *commune* has its idiosyncratic church, its sloping-roofed nave set to one side of the bell-tower. The crosses in the graveyard are interspersed with the traditional disc-shaped headstones of the Basque country and inside there is a rough wooden gallery that is another essential feature of Basque design.

There is no very comfortable accommodation in the valley but there is a **restaurant** and a **gîte d'étape** (Tel. 59-37-42-39).

Arette la Pierre St Martin

Beyond Senta, the scenery changes dramatically as the road climbs up towards the modern ski resort of Arette la Pierre St Martin. Where there was lush grassland there is instead bare greyish rock, dotted with stunted mountain pines, against which the ski development stands out as an unsympathetic collection of apartment blocks, with the tiny green pyramid of Pic d'Arlas (2,044 metres/6,650 ft) immediately behind and the more famous Pic d'Anie (2,504 metres/8,140 ft), a huge white pyramid to the south-west.

Enjoying the Landscape

The strange formations of the *karst* landscape can be seen all around the apartment blocks of Arette la Pierre St Martin but to enjoy them fully it is better to park the car and walk a little way on the GR10 footpath. From the development the GR10, marked by the usual red and white stripes, heads south along a lane which passes under the Pescamou chairlift. In under an hour the lane peters out and the footpath swings eastwards across the naked grey fissures of the Arre de Soumcouye. If you wish, you can continue towards the Osque Pass (about 3 hours from Arette la Pierre St Martin), swinging to the north of the rounded lump of Pic de Soum Couy (2,315 metres/7,525 ft) for the sumptuous views eastwards into the Aspe and Lescun valleys.

An ascent of Pic d'Anie, the sharp peak to the south of Soum Couy is possible by following instead the HRP footpath. It begins as for the GR10 but from the lane swings west rather than east into the Col de Pescamou before turning back in a south-easterly direction towards the summit. Once at the Col des Anies, a red-marked trail leads south to the summit (about 4 hours from Arette la Pierre St Martin).

Accomodation in the development, the most westerly downhill ski station in the Pyrenees, is almost entirely in self-catering apartments and chalets.

Walking in Limestone Country

The bizarre scenery around Arette la Pierre St Martin is known as *karst* and is the most memorable and unusual in all of the Pyrenees. The weird rock formations are entirely due to the unique way that limestone—formed from the skeletal remains of sea creatures—is eroded by the elements.

One of the features of limestone is that it fractures easily along the bedding-planes, where one layer is separated from another by a vein of shale. The frequent faults that run at right angles to the bedding plane are known as *joints*. Although it is not porous, limestone is soluble in rainwater and the more acid it is, the more rapid the erosion. On the surface, therefore, bare limestone often has the appearance of a giant pavement, the slabs being known as *clints* and the eroded joints between them known as *grikes*. Other surface features are the *dolines* or bowl-shaped depressions, and the *sinks*, where water disappears underground.

The French and Spanish both call this range of bare limestone features *lapiaz*. Cliff faces are often traversed by natural ledges, where softer limestone has broken away along the fault lines as a result of the contraction and expansion caused by sun and ice. These ledges, particularly useful for mountaineers, are a notable feature of the limestone terrain further east, around Monte Perdido (the highest limestone mountain in Europe), where the Spanish call them *fajas*.

Under the surface, the water entering the joints accumulates in the widest cracks which become even more enlarged through erosion to form potholes, known in French as *gouffres*.

Gouffre Pierre St Martin

The Gouffre Pierre St Martin, which has its entrance on the frontier beside the road that runs from Arette la Pierre St Martin to Isaba, is one of the largest-known cave systems in the world, with an entrance shaft 346 metres (1,125 ft) straight down. When water erodes horizontal passageways these are known as *phreatic* tunnels and are often high enough for a man to walk through and so smooth as to seem man-made.

Gouffre Pierre St Martin can be visited by contacting Pyrénées Aventures Nouvelles at 15 allée des Myrtilles in Arette la Pierre St Martin or one of the other operators listed at the tourist office. The cave system was once only the preserve of Europe's most skilled speleologists but since Electricité de France cut an exploratory tunnel to test the flow for hydro-electric purposes it has become easy to reach the **Salle de la Verna**, one of the largest underground caverns in the world, at the foot of one of the longest-known vertical shafts. Today the entrance is a horizontal man-made tunnel but before it involved a vertical descent of 346 metres (1,125 ft) which could only be accomplished by a mechanical hoist. The visit is very worthwhile, for the Salle de la Verna is so huge (270 metres x 230 metres x 180 metres/880 ft x 750 ft x 585 ft) that with the stream running through it and the ground littered with huge boulders, it recalls Jules Vernes' *Journey to the Centre of the Earth*.

Those who prefer to stay above ground can visit the old entrance, now grilled over, beside the road a few metres beyond the Spanish frontier.

To return to St Jean Pied-de-Port either retrace your route or follow the itinerary through the Spanish Basque country detailed below.

Walking Tours in the Mountains of the Pays Basque

The main walking routes through the Pays Basque mountains are the **Haute Randonnée Pyrénéenne** (HRP), the **Grande Randonnée 10** (GR10) and the **Piémont**, all of which traverse the Pyrenees to the Mediterranean in descending order of difficulty, plus the GR65, the old pilgrim route. Casual walkers can make use of all of these to construct some not over-demanding itineraries. The footpaths are marked on the Carte de Randonnées 1:50,000 Pays Basque Est published by Randonnées Pyrénéennes and available from most bookshops and newsagents.

Drive or train to Bidarray—Iparla Ridge (see description above)—St Etienne de Baïgorry—bus and train back to Bidarray (about 10 hours).

St Jean Pied-de-Port—Lasse—Monhoa (1,021 metres/3,320 ft)—Col de Leizarze—Col d'Aharza—St Etienne de Baïgorry—bus or taxi back to St Jean Pied-de-Port (about 7 hours).

St Jean Pied-de-Port—taxi to Col d'Arnostéguy and the Monument d'Urculu, returning on foot along the GR65 via Pic Urdanarre—Elhursaro—Pic d'Hostatéguy—Honto—St Jean Pied-de-Port (6 hours plus taxi ride).

Col de Burdincurutcheta—Pic Mendibel (1,411 metres/4,585 ft)—Pic Chardéca (1,440 metres/4,680 ft)—Pic des Escaliers (1,472 metres/4,785 ft)—Chalets d'Irati—Col d'Organ-bidexka—Plateau Irati—and then along the road to Col de Burdincu-rutcheta (about 7 hours).

Fontaine d'Otxolatzé (by car from St Jean Pied-de-Port via Mendive)—Col d'Egurcé—Col Haritxarte—Mendive (about 5 hours plus taxi back to retrieve car at Fontaine d'Otxolatzé).

Walks in the Irati Forest—see description above and also the itineraries provided by the tourist office in St Jean Pied-de-Port.

Col d'Organbidexka—Pic des Escaliers (1,472 metres/4,785 ft)—Cayolar Mendikotziague—Bois d'Etchelu—Logibar (about 10 hours).

Logibar—Gorges d'Holzarté—Gorges d'Olhadubi—Bois de Saratzé—Gorges de Kakoúeta—Ste Engrâce (about 10 hours)

Cycling Tours in the Mountains of the Pays Basque

If you are cycling east, you are in for some magnificent scenery and exciting descents—but some very tough climbs. The most scenic route is:

St Jean Pied-de-Port—Col de Burdincurutcheta—Plateau Irati—Col Organbidexka—Larrau—Logibar—Ste Engrâce—Arette la Pierre St Martin (one–two days, depending on ability).

For day tours the tourist office at St Etienne de Baïgorry has published a leaflet decribing five cycling circuits.

A Centre for the Western Pyrenees

The Aspe and Ossau valleys lead south into the mountains where brown bears still survive. An ideal place for horse-riding, cycling, canoeing and rafting on the rivers, as well as exploring on foot. For the less active, the mountain train, *Le Petit Train d'Artouste*, is the highest railway in Europe.

Pau

There is an elegantly British ambience to Pau (pronounced *po*), reminiscent of Mayfair and Bond Street. In the mid-19th century nearly one-fifth of the population was composed of British army officers and minor aristocracy and their families and even today the

Shepherds watch their flocks carefully in the Lescun area—a handful of magnificent brown bears survive in this region, but before they hibernate for the winter each one seeks out a sheep or two to keep starvation at bay.

Cercle anglais still meets for its monthly dinners. The British connection goes back to the time before the English loss of Gascony and Aquitaine after the Hundred Years' War (1338–1453). But most of all the British came to stay after the Duke of Wellington had defeated Napoleon's Marshal Soult at nearby Orthez. The Pau royalists were delighted, celebrating the defeat of their own army with a ball for Wellington and his officers. Those who drifted back after Napoleon's defeat at Waterloo began to talk of Pau as "Old England"—a name that has now been taken by a boutique in place Royale.

For anyone exploring the western part of the French Pyrenees, **Pau** makes an excellent town base, just over

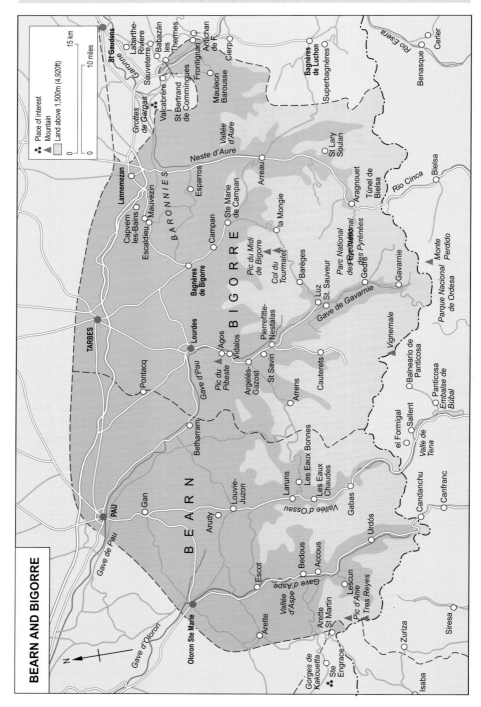

BEARN AND BIGORRE

Place of interest
Mountain
Land above 1,500m (4,920ft)

15 km
10 miles

N

St Gaudens
Labarthe-Rivière
Sauveterre
Babazán
Thermes
Frontignan
Antichan de F.
Cierp
Bagnères de Luchon
Superbagnères
Benasque
Cefer
Rio Esera

Grottes de Gargas
Valcabrère
St Bertrand de Comminges
Mauleon Barousse

Lannemezan
Vallée d'Aure
St Lary Soulan

Esparros
Neste d'Aure
Arreau
Aragnouet
Tunel de Bielsa
Rio Cinca
Bielsa

Capvern les-Bains
Escaldieu
Mauvezin
Ste Marie de Campan
la Mongie

BARONNIES
Campan
Pic du Midi de Bigorre
Col du Tourmalet
Bareges
Parc National des Pyrénées
Pyrénées
Gedre
Parque Nacional de Ordesa
Monte Perdido

TARBES
Bagnères de Bigorre
BIGORRE
Luz
St. Sauveur
Gavarnie

Pontacq
Lourdes
Agos
Vidalos
Pierrefitte-Nestalias
Gave de Gavarnie
Vignemale

Gave d'Pau
Pic du Pibeste
Argelès-Gazost
St Savin
Cauterets
Balneario de Panticosa

Betharram
Arrens
Panticosa
Embalse de Búbal
Valle de Tena

BEARN
Louvie-Juzon
Laruns
Les Eaux Bonnes
Les Eaux Chaudes
el Formigal
Sallent
Candanchu
Canfranc

Gan
Arudy
Vallée d'Ossau
Gabas
Urdós

PAU
Gave de Pau
Escot
Bedous
Accous
Lescun
Tres Reyes
Zuriza
Siresa

Oloron Ste Marie
Vallée d'Aspe
Gave d'Aspe
Arette
St Martin
Pic d'Anie
Isaba

Gorges de Kakouetta
Ste Engrace
Gave d'Oloron

100 km (65 miles) from the coast, with plenty of good hotels and restaurants. For non-motorists, its frequent rail services from Bayonne and Toulouse and its choice of bus routes onwards into the mountains make it ideal.

The central part of the town, containing the most interesting sights, shops, hotels and restaurants, stands on the north bank of the River Pau, bounded by the château to the west and the Beaumont Park to the east. Undoubtedly the most important site to visit is the **château**, a rather olive-coloured mansion with a slate roof, at the eastern end of boulevard des Pyrénées. From early times, the only local crossing place on the river was guarded by simple defences, known in Béarnais as "*pau*", hence the name of the town. Over the years the castle grew and was remodelled in the 14th century for Gaston Fébus (1331–91) by his military architect Sicard de Lordat (*see* ARIEGE).

The château was next improved by Gaston IV in the mid-15th century and then by the d'Albrets, who for a time ruled both French and Spanish Navarre. It was here in 1553 that Jeanne d'Albret gave birth to the future Henry IV of France. The château at Pau was little used until restoration by Louis-Philippe in the mid-19th century and afterwards by Napoleon III.

The first floor is normally devoted to a **summer exhibition** of Henry IV memorabilia. The second floor contains the **state rooms**, mainly furnished

The Béarn and Bigorre regions.

during the Second Empire (though in medieval style), but also containing Henry's tortoise-shell cradle and a marvellous series of 17th- and early-18th-century **tapestries** from the famous Gobelin workshop in Paris. (The business was founded as a dyeworks by Gilles and Jean Gobelin in the 15th century and continues today.) There is also a set of early 17th-century tapestries of the story of Psyche by Flemish weavers working in Paris. The third floor is the Musée Béarnais, which has exhibits devoted to local crafts (including cheese-making and beret manufacture), dress, architecture, fauna and people, including the Pyrenean poet Francis Jammes.

Two Museums

There are two other worthwhile museums in Pau, the Beaux-Arts and the Bernadotte. The **Beaux-Arts** is situated at the junction of Cours Bosquet and rue Mathieu Lalanne just to the north of Parc Beaumont. It contains works from much of Europe from the 14th century onwards, of which the most notable is a painting by Degas *Bureau du coton à la Nouvelle-Orléans*; regional interest comes from the works of Eugène Devéria (1805–65), particularly his Pyrenean landscapes. The curious tale of Jean-Baptiste Jules Bernadotte (1764–1844) is told at the Bernadotte museum at his birthplace five minutes walk to the north-east of the château in rue Tran. Bernadotte became one of Napoleon's Marshals but in 1818 accepted the vacant throne of Sweden under the name Charles XIV, establishing a dynasty which still continues.

There are two campsites, the Municipal on the north side of town, in the same street as the Mecure hotel, boulevard du Cami Salié; and Le Coy, in the Bizanos suburb, on the south side of Pau.

Walking around Pau

Any stroll around Pau must include the boulevard des Pyrénées, connecting the château and Parc Beaumont along the south side of the city. About half way, close to where the funicular from the station arrives, there is a *table d'orientation* giving the direction and names of the various mountains that can be seen—on a clear day you can see about a quarter of the range from Pic d'Anie in the south-west to Pic du Midi de Bigorre in the south-east. Near the *table d'orientation* there is a car park.

The Environs of Pau

Jurançon, no more than 2 km (1¼ miles) south of Pau on the D934, has two excellent restaurants worth making the journey for. On a hot day there is nothing better than to get out of town to the quiet terrace of **Castel du Pont d'Oly** which is also a small three-star hotel, or to the traditional Béarnaise cuisine of **Ruffet**.

This is, of course, the centre of one of the most important wine-growing areas in the Pyrenees, in the rolling green foothills to the south of the Pau river. The *cave coopérative* for Jurançon is actually at **Gan**, some 6 km (4 miles) further on. You can sample the wines here. The cheap ones are to be avoided but the dry whites "Clos de la Vierge '88", "Domaine Cauhapé '88" and "Clos Uroulat, Cuvée Marie '88" and the sweet whites "Domaine Lapeyre '87", "Domaine Bru Baché, Cuvée Les Casterrasses '87", "Clos Uroulat '87" and "Domaine Cauhapé '87" are all recommended. According to tradition, Jurançon was the first liquid put to the lips of the newly born Henry of Navarre, the future Henry IV of France. Gan also has a worthy rustic restaurant **Le Tucq** to complete a gastronomic tour.

Some 5 km (3 miles) to the west of Pau, **Lescar** was formerly the Roman town of Beneharnum, from which the regional name Béarn probably derives. Sacked by the Moors and the Vikings it became Lescar in the 11th century and was the old capital of Béarn. The citadel and the **12th-century cathedral** inside it are worth the journey. The cathedral has been heavily restored, having been pillaged by the Protestants during the Wars of Religion and, again, during the French Revolution, but many of the **sculptures** and **mosaics** have survived.

The Aspe and Ossau Valleys

From Oloron Ste Marie, some 35 km (22 miles) south-west of Pau, the parallel Aspe and Ossau valleys lead south into the mountains, passing either side of the famous isolated summit of **Pic Midi d'Ossau**, a popular picnic spot in the **Pyrenees National Park**. The scenic highlight, however, is unquestionably the **Cirque of Lescun** to the north of the park and reached from the Aspe valley. Both valleys are served by bus from either Pau or Oloron. In the high mountains there is no connecting road between the two so that a circular car tour is impossible without crossing the

The cirque of Lescun is one of the most exquisite beauty spots in all the Pyrenees.

frontier into Spain, an itinerary of some 250 km (160 miles), best spread over two days or more. On the French side of the frontier, the last opportunity to pass between the valleys is the D294 running between Escot and Bielle.

Oloron Ste Marie is a pleasant small town at the confluence of the Aspe and Ossau rivers, famous for the manufacture of the standard French beret. It is said a Frenchman can be judged by the way he wears it: the *bon viveur* has it back on the neck, the taciturn shepherd forward to shade his eyes, the snappy dresser tilted a little to the side and the military man sharply raked. A second beret, often the larger Basque pattern, is reserved for Sunday-best. You can buy a Béarn beret in the main shopping area, which encompasses rue Louis Barthou and the two squares beyond the eastern end of the street, place Gambetta and place de la Résistance (where the tourist office is situated).

There is little to see in Oloron except its **two churches**. The 13th-century **Ste Croix**, in the Quartier Ste Croix between the two rivers, is distinctive for its Moorish-style vaulting, recreated by Spanish craftsmen. **Ste Marie**, to the west of place de Jaca, has a marvellously carved portal of Pyrenean and biblical scenes and, inside, a so-called Cagot stoup (*see* ST JEAN PIED-DE-PORT).

Aspe Valley

The early part of the **Aspe Valley** is not particularly scenic and those with time to indulge the whimsical may prefer to detour along the D919 to **Aramits**. Alexandre Dumas borrowed and slightly altered the name to Aramis for one of his Three Musketeers; Portos, another of the famous trio, was named after the Portau family who lived in the chateau in the neighbouring village of Lanne. From Aramits you can return to the Aspe at Lurbe St Christau or via the convoluted but highly scenic D132 and the marvellous **Issaux Forest** to meet the Aspe further south at Bedous.

Escot, 13 km (8 miles) south of Oloron, is the last chance to change valleys (into the **Ossau** via the woods and pastures of the Col de Marie-Blanque) before the mountains close in and the road climbs slowly to the Lescun turning. If you are travelling by bus, get off at Lescun Cette Eygun from which the village of **Lescun** itself is a 6 km (4 mile) walk along a road which climbs in steep hairpins. It is one of the prettiest places to stay in all the Pyrenees but it only has one hotel and this should be booked well in advance—**Hôtel Pic d'Anie**.

The village faces south across wide and lush green pastures to the dramatic pine-clad peaks of the Pyrenees National Park, while, further west, lies the arid *karst* scenery of Pic d'Anie (2,504 metres/8,140 ft), the Table des Trois Rois (2,421 metres/7,870 ft) and the cirque itself. Here, and in the adjoining Spanish forests, is the last Pyrenean stronghold of the brown bear.

Walks

The pastures in front of the cirque are criss-crossed by narrow tarmac lanes and jeep tracks, serving the various hamlets and pastures. Exploring the valley by car is a delight and it is actually possible to drive right on to the Sanchèse plateau at the foot of the cirque (the last bit along easy track). The plateau is an attractive picnic area, dissected by two streams and with a waterfall as a backdrop.

The **HRP footpath** climbs up beside the waterfall and passes around the north side of Pic d'Anie to Arette la Pierre St Martin, while a variant crosses into Spain to the Belagoa refuge. The HRP is a generally unmarked trail for mountaineers and those without experience or equipment should go no further than the wood

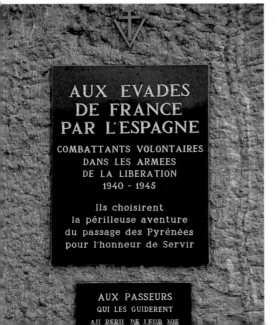

*T*his roadside memorial in the Aspe valley reads: "For those who escaped from France into Spain. Volunteers in the armies of liberation 1940–45. They chose the perilous crossing of the Pyrenees for the honour of serving. To the guides who risked their lives to lead them."

AUX EVADES
DE FRANCE
PAR L'ESPAGNE

COMBATTANTS VOLONTAIRES
DANS LES ARMEES
DE LA LIBERATION
1940 - 1945

Ils choisirent
la périlleuse aventure
du passage des Pyrénées
pour l'honneur de Servir

AUX PASSEURS
QUI LES GUIDERENT
AU PERIL DE LEUR VIE

above the waterfall. An easier walk lies along the GR10 to the Orgues (organ pipes) de Camplong. These are rocks which have been eroded into bizarre, sharp shapes and which lie a little to the north of the cirque. You can drive as far as the Labérouat refuge, from where the GR10, well marked with red and white stripes, climbs gently through the Braca d'Azuns beech wood, the "organ pipes" glimpsed through the trees to the north and, more clearly, for those with the energy, from the Pas d'Azuns (1,873 metres/6,090 ft) about two hours walking from the refuge.

The summit of **Pic d'Anie** can be reached in about 4 hours from the refuge by a path that cuts off south before the steep climb into the Pas d'Azuns.

Ossau Valley

The Ossau Valley is a little more tranquil than the Aspe because the road is narrower and the pass at its end, the Pourtalet, is closed in winter, diverting commercial traffic into the Aspe. The valley is particularly famous for its cheese.

Before setting off it is a good idea to plan for lunch. There are three particularly interesting restaurants, of which **Les Bains de Secours** at Sévignac–Meyracq, just under 25 km (15 miles) from Pau, is definitely the best. Here the young chef Jean-Pierre Paroix is making a name for himself.

An alternative would be to picnic either at the Bious-Artigues lake at the foot of Pic du Midi d'Ossau, or at the Artouste lake reached by the high-mountain railway *Petit Train d'Artouste*.

There is little actually to visit in the valley, except the **Maison d'Ossau** at **Arudy**, with an exhibition of Pyrenean flora and fauna (open daily in summer from 8.30 a.m. to 6 p.m.), and the **Centre d'Ecologie Montagnarde** at **Gabas** (open daily in summer from 9 a.m. to noon and from 2 p.m. to 6 p.m.). Between the two lie the spas of **Eaux-Chaudes**, just to the south of Laruns in the Ossau valley, and **Eaux Bonnes**, a short distance along the Valentin valley to the east of Laruns, on the way to the ski station of Gourette. *Thermalisme*, as the French call it, has a long history in the Pyrenees, certainly stretching back to Roman times when the properties of the springs were responsible for the foundation of several towns. There are more than 500 thermal springs along the Pyrenees, the vast majority on the French side, where there are some 40 spas towns, as against only two of consequence in Spain (Panticosa and Caldes de Boí). Around 150 springs have actually been exploited, ranging from waters up to 45°C (113°F), to those prized for their radioactivity, sulphur content or other properties. The Eaux-Chaudes spa, a long line of dramatically-situated white-painted buildings, has five sources, and Eaux-Bonnes three, both spas considered good for the treatment of rheumatism.

Despite the absence of man-made sights, there is plenty to see in the landscape and opportunities to stop and buy local produce, especially honey and *brebis* (sheep) cheese which is a speciality of the tiny village of **Gabas**. Situated on the north side of Pic du Midi d'Ossau (2,884 metres/13,500 ft), Gabas is the last

Borce and the Brown Bear

Some 6 km (4 miles) beyond the Lescun turning, the little village of Borce would have been touristically unknown had a group of schoolchildren and teachers not returned from a picnic one day in 1971 carrying a bear cub. The cub was alone, the mother presumed shot by poachers. Jojo, as the cub was known, became a huge tourist attraction. In 1990 an appeal was launched to rescue Jojo from his tiny cage and provide an enclosure more suited to his 200 kg (440lb) frame. He moved in the following year, but died within weeks.

Beyond Borce the road climbs to the Spanish frontier at the Col du Somport (19 km/12 miles; 1,632 metres/5,356 ft; open all year).

Brown bears still survive in the Pyrenees but their numbers have been falling steadily towards extinction. In the 1930s there were as many as 200 in the range but by 1954 their numbers were estimated to be only 70, by 1960 40 and, by 1987, 20. Numbers have undoubtedly fallen even lower since and there have been periods of several years when no cub footprints have been seen. Fortunately, cub prints were discovered in 1990, together with those of their mother. Almost all the survivors live in the area bounded, on the French side of the frontier, by the Ossau and Aspe valleys and the cirque of Lescun and, on the Spanish side, by the eastern part of the Parque Natural Pirenaico en Navarra.

The reasons for the decline include hunting, which was not banned until 1962 and which still goes on illegally, and poisoning by shepherds to protect their flocks. However, the bear is 70 per cent herbivorous and each bear is estimated to kill only one to two sheep a year, for which compensation is paid. In addition to this, forestry, tourism, skiing and hunting for other species such as the wild boar, have all had an indirect effect by disturbing the bear, which is exceedingly timid. In 1984 the "Plan Ours" (Bear Plan) was launched to save the species but the action has been inadequate and in all probability, the numbers have for some time been too small for successful reproduction. The introduction of bears from elsewhere in Europe is technically possible but would mean the loss of a distinct, shy and, to man, harmless sub-species that was unique to the Pyrenees.

The chances of actually seeing a brown bear are remote, but there is always the possibility of seeing a track, dropping or other sign. The brown bear is an animal of the forest, and lives at an altitude of around 1,500 metres (4,920 ft). Its track is quite unmistakable, roughly similar in size and appearance to that left by a large bare-footed man, except that the five toes are longer and the track more rounded; in addition there is a distinct difference between the mark left by the fore foot, which shows only the front part of the sole, and the hind foot, which shows the whole sole. The droppings, too, on account of their size could not be confused with those of smaller mammals and differ from those of farm animals by the insect and plant remains that are clearly seen in them.

Only tourists can now give the bear any financial value and thus save it from extinction by coming to see it—once the numbers have been restored to a viable level. If you would like to help the bear, get in touch with Groupe Ours National, FFSPN, 57 rue Cuvier, 75231, Paris cedex 05.

There are delightful and scenic walks of all standards in the Aspe valley.

village before the road climbs to the Spanish border at the Col du Pourtalet (1,794 metres/5,830 ft)

Pic du Midi d'Ossau is one of the most distinctive peaks of the Pyrenees, standing isolated from the surrounding summits. Lake Bious-Artigues is at the foot of its northern slopes, reached by a pretty lane from the village of Gabas, and very popular as a picnic spot. An ascent of the mountain by the normal route is within the capabilities of the determined walker, amounting to a tough scramble rather than a climb. But most walkers will prefer either a tour of the mountain or a visit to the other lakes lying above Bious-Artigues to the west. To walk all round Pic du Midi d'Ossau is a rewarding day-long itinerary on marked trails. The route begins south-west from the lake along the Bious stream (which is crossed after about 30 minutes by a bridge to the south bank). The trail then climbs under the south of the summit to the Pombie refuge from which the return trail to the lake lies amost due north. Rather than cross the bridge over the Bious stream, an alternative walk is to continue along the north bank to the Ayous lakes, set above the trees (about 3 hours from the parking).

Petit Train d'Artouste

The **Petit Train d'Artouste** is the highest railway in Europe, climbing to over 2,000 metres (6,500 ft) in a 10 km (6 mile) journey which takes about one hour. It is even smaller than the *Petit Train Jaune* of the Cerdagne and all its four carriages are open. The line operates from the beginning of June until the end of September. Those wishing to spend the whole day in the mountains should arrive early and buy the special *randonnée* ticket which is for the 8.30 a.m. departure and guarantees a seat on the train returning at 7.18 p.m.

Park on Lake Fabrèges and take the *télécabine* (cable car) to the *gare d'Artouste*. From there the little red-and-white carriages climb south through magnificent wild scenery, often on a specially excavated ledge, finally arriving at the austere setting of the Artouste lake. Refreshments are available at the Arrémoulit refuge, which is reached in about 90 minutes walking around the western side of the lake, and then by the footpath that climbs south to the smaller Arrémoulit lake. If you would like a meal at the refuge, it is advisable to telephone ahead (tel. 59-05-31-79).

The Spanish border is close by and those with the energy can climb up to it at the Col de Palas for a magnificent view of Balaïtous.

Rather than return by train it is possible to walk down from the Artouste lake. The descent involves first an ascent into the Arrious pass to the southwest of the lake. The pass can be reached either directly from the southern end of the lake, or from the refuge—but note that the path from the refuge includes a difficult section along an unprotected ledge with a steep drop. From the pass the path descends fairly directly to the road, from where the parking at the cable-car station is a good hour's marching away (total four hours from the end of the train ride).

Exploring the Béarn

Walking Tours

In addition to the three long-distance footpaths, *Haute Randonnée Pyrénéenne* (HRP), *Grande Randonnée 10* (GR10), and *Sentier de Piémont*, the Aspe and Ossau valleys have their own circular tours, taking five days to a week depending on stamina. For dedicated walkers the *Tour de la Haute Vallée d'Ossau* is strongly recommended, passing round **Pic du Midi d'Ossau** and within sight of **Balaïtous** (3,144 metres/10,220 ft), one of the most remote and difficult Pyrenean peaks. Hikers on this route can make use of five staffed refuges, Gabas, Bious-Artigue, Pombie, Arrémoulit and the Migouélou.

A less-demanding full-day walk through wonderful countryside would be to follow the *Piémont* between Sarrance in the Aspe valley and Louvie–Juzon in the Ossau valley. Sarrance can be reached on one of the morning buses from Pau via Oloron Ste Marie; the last bus back from Louvie–Juzon is around 6.25 p.m. Both routes are shown on *Carte de Randonnéees No. 3* (Béarn) published by Randonnées Pyrénéennes.

Horse-Riding

An extensive network of riding trails exists in Béarn. Those who prefer the going easier should contact Chevauchée Pyrénéenne at Sévignac Meyracq in the Ossau valley, about 25 km (15 miles) south of Pau (Tel. 59-05-63-11). For riding in the mountains, try Auberge Cavalière on the main Aspe valley road, just north of the Lescun turning; this is also a *gîte d'étape* (Tel. 59-34-72-30). The ride from Auberge Cavalière to Arette la Pierre St Martin (see above) is particularly recommended for its spectacle. Several good trails connect the Aspe and Ossau valleys and these can be used to construct a circuit. They run from Sarrance to Bielle, from Accous to either Laruns or Eaux-Chaudes and from Borce to Gabas.

Cycling

Any cyclists having reached Arette la Pierre St Martin in the mountains of the Pays Basque (*see* above), should take the descent through the Issaux Forest and then follow the Issaux river north through the Lourdios gorge to Lurbe St Christau in the Aspe Valley. The Ossau valley is then reached over the Col de Marie Blanque on the D294 which connects Escot, to the south of Lurbe St Christau, with Bielle. To move on into the Bigorre, you can then either take the D35 from Louvie–Juzon, to the north of Bielle, or the much tougher N618 which climbs over the Col d'Aubisque (1,709 metres/5,555 ft).

The Rivers

In spring especially, there is a unique view of Béarn from its many rivers. The Gave (River) d'Oloron is particularly famous both for canoeing and rafting; instruction and craft are available in Sauveterre de Béarn, on the river about 40 km (25 miles) to the west of Oloron Ste Marie (Tel. 59-38-93-75).

High Peaks, Impressive Scenery and Spa Towns

The central area of the French Pyrenees is a beautiful mountain landscape with a fascinating history and folklore (*see* map on page 98). The Brèche de Roland is the most popular high-mountain objective in the Pyrenees and the Cirques of Gavarnie and Troumouse are worth a mountain trek to see. The town of Cauterets is an elegant mountain resort.

Lourdes

Every year five million visitors make the pilgrimage to Lourdes, a small mountain town at the heart of the Bigorre. For many it is the culmination of years of planning, hope and high expectations. The centre of attraction is the cave, the Grotte Massabielle, where in the mid-19th century Bernadette Soubirous is said to have encountered the Virgin Mary 18 times. During one

T he Brèche de Roland is one of the most famous places in all the Pyrenees, a natural breach in the rock wall dividing France from Spain in the mountains of the Bigorre.

vision a miraculous spring is said to have appeared. Every year people claim to have been cured by it and there is usually a queue to collect the water—now rationed due to drought.

Fame has not left Lourdes a prettier place than it was before Bernadette but it is an astonishing one. On summer evenings you will be amazed at the spectacle of thousands of pilgrims joining the torch-lit processions, many in wheelchairs. You will almost certainly feel humbled by the sight of so intense a devotion during the packed open-air masses, given in seven languages. And you will perhaps be saddened by the commercial exploitation so rife in the streets around the holy sites.

You will find the **religous sector** quite self-contained, filling the right-angled

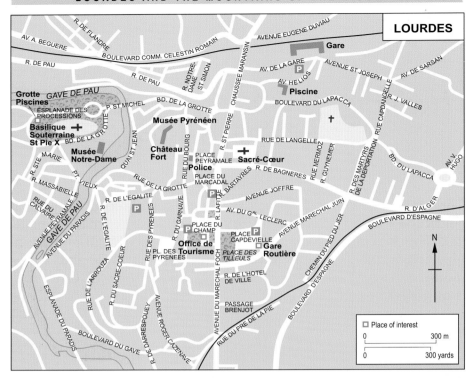

*T*own plan of Lourdes.

bend of the wide Gave de Pau with fringe developments such as reception centres, car parks, and shops spread along the banks. Back from the river, the narrow streets are crammed with souvenir shops, small hotels and restaurants, mostly doing a roaring trade. In winter this entire area virtually shuts down. But although it is one of the most important religious centres in Europe, Lourdes is not just about religion. Take away the *cité religieuse* for a moment, close your eyes to the shanty town of souvenir stalls and traffic-snarled main shopping streets and you have an old market town which makes an excellent touring base.

The Legend of Bernadette

There are still a few tall and ramshackle houses dating from 1858, the year of the visions which were to change the entire shape of the town. Number 2 rue Bernadette-Soubirous, whitewashed and blue-shuttered, is typical of Bigourdan homes of the time. Now called the Maison Paternelle it was for a time the Soubirous family home and is now a museum with authentically furnished rooms.

Bernadette had tuberculosis and was rather a frail girl of 14 when she encountered the Virgin Mary. Despite being told to keep away from the cave by both her mother and the local magistrate—on pain of imprisonment—she continued to keep her appointments with the vision. For all her fame,

Bernadette remained retiring and spent most of her life in a convent, where she died aged 37.

The Church, meanwhile, was less bashful and the Bishop of Tarbes confirmed the apparitions in 1861. The Pope added his endorsement in 1869. Bernadette was beatified in 1925 and canonized in 1933. New official miracles and a row of discarded crutches at the cave chapel testify that the lure of Lourdes is not diminishing.

The Cave and Religious Sector

Follow the crowds down to the river bank to find the cave itself, a small disappointing place, crammed with candles and fenced off by wooden benches where pilgrims queue up to pray.

At the heart of the *cité religieuse* are three cathedral-sized churches. Two are above ground, the **Church of the Immaculate Conception** built in 1854, and the **Church of the Rosary** built as an overflow some 30 years after the apparitions. The third, **St Pie X**, resembling an underground aircraft hangar, is an engineering marvel accommodating up to 25,000 pilgrims and supported without central pillars. This was opened in 1958 to mark the centenary of Bernadette's visions. In all three you will see thousands of engraved prayer stones, marked with the names of hopeful, or grateful, visitors.

Several other sites are associated with Bernadette—**Boly Mill**, in the same road as the Maison Paternelle, where Bernadette was born; the **Cachot Museum** in rue des Petits Fossés, where the pressured Soubirous family stayed during the apparitions; and the audio-visual show at 38 rue de la Grotte, depicting the life and times of Bernadette.

Other religious attractions include the **Grevin Museum** in rue de la Grotte with tableaux of more than 100 Madame Tussaud-style wax figures; and at 21 quai St Jean, the **Nativity Museum**.

The Château-Fort

From just about anywhere in Lourdes you can see the *Château-Fort*, a glamorous castle towering above the town in true turreted style and housing the excellent **Pyrenean Museum**. Home to the Counts of Bigorre, it was "donated" to the English by the Treaty of Brétigny in 1360 and only regained by the French after two difficult sieges, in 1393 and 1406, when the English defenders used the revolutionary device of pouring boiling oil over the enemy. It has several times served as a prison, one of its most famous inmates being Lord Elgin, who was captured during the Revolutionary Wars.

From the top (by steep stone steps or the lift) the views out across the city and over to the Pyrenees are enormous, while within the the ramparts there are well-tended gardens with miniature models of Bigourdan buildings. Inside, the **museum** has rooms depicting the geology of the region (important for its variety of marble), prehistory, Bigourdan life in the 19th century and Bigourdan dress throughout the ages. But if you are at all interested in mountain walking you will probably find the room of the *Pyrénéistes* the most moving, containing the climbing equipment used by Henry Russell and other famous explorers. The **library**, which you can visit by special arrangement, holds an important collection of documents,

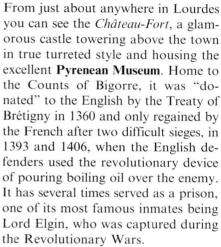

maps, photographs and paintings, as well as books.

Museums and Sights

There are two museums dedicated to the town of Lourdes, the **Model Village** of Lourdes at 65 avenue Peyramale, a well-researched mock-up of what the town looked like in 1858; and **Lourdes Museum** at Parking de l'Egalité, an animated re-creation of old Lourdes.

When you have had enough of indoor pursuits, enjoy some fresh air and sumptuous views with a cable car excursion up **Pic Béout** (12 avenue Francis-Lagardère—four minutes to the top). At the same time, visit Gouffre Béout, a small cave discovered by master speleologist Norbert Casteret and containing prehistoric bones and tools.

An alternative mountain ride is the funicular up **Pic du Jer**, also from avenue Francis-Lagardère, while two further caves worth visiting are **Grottes des Loup** and **Grottes des Sarrasins**, both within easy reach of the town.

Lourdes is not a great shopping town but you can buy good mountain souvenirs, particularly sheepskin and woollen clothing ranging from waistcoats and bulky oiled-wool cardigans to delicate shawls. There is an excellent fortnightly Thursday market in an area known as *Les Halles* close to the Palais des Congrès in the town centre. A huge covered section traps all the odours and bustle of a good French market and on busy days stalls also spill out into the car park. Local cheeses are a speciality, but best of the lot is a stall selling all manner of traditional berets, from the restrained Bigourdan version to the vast Basque hat.

Religious Activities

During the summer (end of March to 1 November) the procession leaves the Grotte Massabielle at 4.30 p.m. Masses are held at the Grotte at 9.30 a.m.; at the upper church at 7 a.m., 8 a.m. and 4 p.m.; at the Church of the Rosary at 10 a.m., 11.30 a.m. and 8 p.m.; and in the underground church of St Pie X at 9 a.m. on Wednesdays Saturdays and Sundays.

Around Lourdes

Just under 3 km (2 miles) west of Lourdes, **Lac du Lourdes** is a popular excursion, accessible by regular bus if you do not have your own car. During the Ice Age the region was engulfed in glaciers

Within a few minutes from the centre of Lourdes, by the Pic du Jer funicular or the Pic Béout cable-car, you can be in the countryside.

as high as the Pic du Jer and the lake is a legacy of that period. Myths abound. According to one legend, a drowned village, whose church bells can sometimes be heard ringing, lies at the bottom of the lake. The lake is also the subject of a real-life drama in which Lourdes residents are trying to block developments which would ruin its beauty.

If you feel slightly energetic you can hire pedaloes, learn wind-surfing or fish. Afterwards, there are plenty of refreshments available around the lake, including restaurants **L'Embarcadere** and **Le Frelon**.

Just over 12 km (7 miles) west of Lourdes, the **Betharram Caves** claim to be the most visited in the Pyrenees. But it is worth the crush to see the spectacular limestone formations, and children in particular will relish the cable-car approach and the underground rides by boat and train through the vast caverns.

After Betharram, you can visit nearby **St Pé de Bigorre**, a riverside village with an abbey which was once more important as a religious site than Lourdes itself. Built by the Cluniacs as a stop-over on the Santiago de Compostella pilgrim route, at its height it would have been perhaps the biggest Romanesque site in the Pyrenees. Ruined both by the Wars of Religion and an earthquake in 1661, you can visit the picturesque remains and the later church with its 14th-century statue of Our Lady of Miracles.

Some 3 km (2 miles) north of Lourdes, Bernadette spent much of her childhood at the village of **Bartres**. Her former home, **Maison Lagues**, is a compelling excursion for

Bigourdan Cuisine

If you are lucky you may still encounter a Pele-Porc, a kind of village fête for which the farmers get together and sacrifice pigs. The villagers turn them into preserved meats and sausages, as they had to in winters long ago. The ceremony and accompanying eating and drinking can last for several days.

Pastry is important—short-crust or puff, but sometimes deep fried, flavoured with honey or anis and usually eaten hot with coffee. Special pastries made with pigs' blood are known as *miques* or *micoles*.

Bigourdan cuisine naturally belongs to the rhythm of the seasons in the mountains and the ingredients of dishes can vary. Thus *garbure* can be a hearty mix of many vegetables and meat, including cabbage, peas, beans, pork, sausage or goose. Small dumplings, made from wheat or corn flour and known as *truses* are sometimes cooked in with the *garbure*, but they can also be sugared and eaten later in the meal.

The famous dessert *gâteau à la broche* can be found all over the central Pyrenees, though it is most at home around Arreau in the Bigorre. It is based on an egg batter and cooked very slowly on a spit turned over a wood fire. It can be flavoured with many ingredients, though it is most commonly plain. Other desserts include nougat from around the Tarbes area and candied chestnuts.

The local wine is Madiran, grown on the plains of Bigorre, and introduced by a Benedictine monk who brought the vines from Burgundy. The red is best. Recommended are: Château Laffitte Teston Vieilles, 1987; Château Montus, 1987; Domaine Bouscasse, 1987; Domaine Pichard, 1985 and Collection Plaimont, 1988.

The path to Vignemale, trodden by so many Pyrenean explorers—Henri Brulle, La Boulinière, Henry Russell, Ann Lister—and maybe you!

believers and even for sceptics is interesting for its furniture of the era.

Argelès–Gazost

Birds of prey at the Donjon des Aigles, and a rare fortified church are two of the sights close to **Argelès-Gazost**, a small town some 13 km (8 miles) south of Lourdes, which makes a good alternative valley base for those who find Lourdes too hectic.

If you have lunch at **Le Viscos** in St Savin you will then have time to visit the **church**, the stones weathered almost to ochre, of which the walls have very obviously been raised (in the 14th century) to permit gun slits to be added. Here, as elsewhere in France, the local *seigneurs* spent much of their time raiding one another's fields and villages. The situation was so extreme that the church eventually introduced an interdiction on fighting between Wednesday evening and Monday

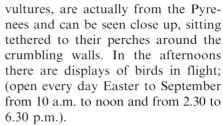

morning. This was known as the *trêve de Dieu* (God's truce). To enforce it, and to make good its offer of sanctuary to the persecuted (particularly by Aragonese raiding parties), the church also had to be ready to defend itself. But the church at St Savin is also interesting for its connection with the Cagots (*see* ST JEAN PIED-DE-PORT). To the left of the multi-lobed entrance is a low window known as the "*fenêtre des Cagots*", where the outcasts are said to have stood to hear mass. Inside the church is a stoup supported by two rather crudely carved figures said to represent Cagots—if true, then this is perhaps the only surviving representation.

Just across the Pau river from St Savin is the ruined **Beaucens Castle** which affords a suitable backdrop for the falconry of the **Donjon des Aigles**. Many of the birds, such as the griffon

---

The Enchanted Mountain

Some 7 km (4½ miles) south of Lourdes on the N21 and just to the west of the village of Agos-Vidalos, Pic du Pibeste (1,349 metres/ 4,050 ft) is nicknamed the "enchanted mountain" because of its almost Mediterranean microclimate. It supports dazzling butterflies and an introduced herd of mouflon. With its handsome scimitar-shaped horns the mouflon is the ancestor of the domestic sheep, the woolly undercoat hidden under a layer of straight hair. The animals are sometimes quite close to the road, near the quarry to the north of the village. For a better view take the path towards the summit from the hamlet of Viger, just before Agos-Vidalos is reached. There are excellent self-catering apartments in Agos-Vidalos at Residence Belle Vue (Tel. 62-97-05-05).

---

vultures, are actually from the Pyrenees and can be seen close up, sitting tethered to their perches around the crumbling walls. In the afternoons there are displays of birds in flight; (open every day Easter to September from 10 a.m. to noon and from 2.30 to 6.30 p.m.).

About 6 km (4 miles) south of Argelès-Gazost the road divides, the right-hand D920 climbing to Cauterets and the left-hand D921 continuing south towards Gavarnie.

Cauterets

Cauterets is one of the most elegant French resorts of the central Pyrenees with an excellent selection of hotels and restaurants and with some of the most beautiful landscape in the range close by. It is exactly the place to be either lazy or active but not intellectual. Spa and sport is what this town is about.

After climbing along the Cauterets valley on the D920 from Pierrefitte –Nestalas and turning into the main square (place de la Gare), the amazing "Wild West" clapboard station (no trains now run) comes into view. But continue on into the town and there is a very different impression of colonnaded buildings that would not be out of place in Paris.

The spa was set up in the 10th century by the monks of St Savin who were funded by Count Raymond of Bigorre. In the 16th century the spa received the royal seal of approval when Margaret of Navarre, sister of Francis I, became a regular client. If you are seriously interested in spas, Cauterets has an interesting mix of sources—four from *schist* and four from granite— considered particularly beneficial for respiratory complaints and for rheumatism. The most famous spa, the César, with its neo-classic entrance, is in the town centre, but two others, the stone-built Les Griffons and the more elegant La Raillére, are near the Lutour waterfall on the road to Pont d'Espagne.

A lovely rendezvous for lunch is the **Pont d'Espagne** by the bridge of the same name, 7 km (4½ miles) from Cauterets. There are also a few inexpensive rooms. Pont d'Espagne itself is

---

The Izard

The izard is the most famous inhabitant of the Pyrenees and the symbol of the national park. Closely related to the chamois of the Alps, it differs only in its smaller size and a slightly different curve to its horns. Although it looks much like a goat, it is in fact a member of the antelope family with an elegance to match.

Your first signs that izards are in the vicinity are often the tracks and the droppings. Since izards have cloven hooves, the tracks are similar to those of goats and sheep but slightly longer, thinner and more angular. The hooves are very elastic and this, coupled with an enormous heart and blood rich in haemoglobin, enables the izards to climb rapidly over rock. The droppings are very small, like those of a rabbit, and are seen on paths in groups.

In France they are known as *isards* or *sarris* and in Bigourdan dialect the word is the same as the English, *izards*. In Spain they are known as *sarrios*, *rebeccos* or *camuzas*. At one time they existed throughout the high Pyrenees but were brought to the edge of extinction by overhunting and only since the creation of national parks and protected areas have they reached a healthy population level. There are an estimated 30,000 in the Pyrenees, equally divided between the French and Spanish sides. Even so, there are many former izard territories where the animals are still not seen.

Izards are gregarious and live in herds of from a score upwards. Before hunting took such a severe toll, herds of 100 animals were not uncommon. A few, particularly the grand old males (life expectation is about twelve years), live alone. The young, born around the end of May, remain with their mothers for a year. At the approach of autumn the scent glands of the males, situated just behind the horns, become enlarged and secrete a musky liquid which each male rubs off on to the bushes which define his territory. The rut runs from October to January, the males fighting to possess and keep a harem of females. During this time the successful males eat and rest little, thus facing the winter in a weak condition. In a severe winter, with the plants thickly covered in snow, the weak die. In a period of a few days, 40 izards were once lost in the Cauterets area.

Normally izards flee at the sight of man but in areas like Pont d'Espagne, where they have become accustomed to people, it is possible to approach quite closely before they move away. The normal pattern of life is for the animals to retire to high ground in the evening, both to enjoy the last of the sun and to find secure places to sleep. In the morning they descend to feed, resting at lunch time in the cover of trees or rocks to chew the food over. There is also a seasonal pattern. The animals are driven down from the ridges in winter and into the woods; they may even approach close to villages. During winter storms the chance of seeing izards is therefore at its greatest, whereas during the height of summer it may be necessary to stalk them on higher ground.

---

a stone built bridge on the traditional footpath to Spain that long-distance hikers still walk. The Lutour waterfall, though, is a greater spectacle and slightly nearer to Cauterets on the same road; there is no good restaurant, but a café perched so excitingly close as almost to feel the spray.

Walking around Cauterets

There are a number of delightful walks, of which the finest is along the **Marcadau Valley**. It begins at the Chalet Clot, a café at the very end of the road (7 km/4½ miles from Cauterets) just beyond Pont d'Espagne. From there the way is well marked, across the Marcadau stream and then along a section of tarmac closed to traffic which suddenly emerges from woods onto a plateau, where the stream, sparkling in sunshine, has widened into lakes. This is a marvellous picnic area, just half-an-hour's walk from the parking. Those with more energy can continue to the Wallon refuge, a highly picturesque route along the river and through trees before the final steep climb. Total time from the parking area is two hours. Meals and refreshments are available at the refuge and there is dormitory accommodation for mountain walkers.

The most popular walk is that from Pont d'Espagne to the **Gaube lake**, the toughest section of which can be accomplished by chairlift. Without the lift the walk takes about 90 minutes but half that with the lift. The Gaube is a famous beauty spot, set in a narrow north-south valley, the trees coming mostly down to the water's edge. It was here in 1832 that William and Sarah Pattison drowned while boating on the lake during their honeymoon, a sad accident that caught imaginations at the time and which has been part of the tourist culture ever since.

Even if you have not time for a long walk, you can still enjoy the **woods** beside the road between Pont d'Espagne and Plateau du Clot. There are often izards here, well used to tourists, which can be photographed without long lenses.

Luz St Sauveur

For motorists, the spa town of **Luz St Sauveur** makes an excellent touring base. It is really two resorts. Luz, the larger part, is on the east bank of the Gavarnie or Pau river, while St Sauveur, the elegant and recently restored spa, is on the west bank.

On the way from Argelès–Gazost it is possible to detour the short distance to Chèze for the studio of potter and sculptor Rémi Trotro. The studio is a landmark because of the giant statue that Trotro has erected outside. The main road can be regained via the village of **Saligos** where there are self-catering studios to rent from mountain guide Jean-Jacques Destrade (Tel. 62-92-82-76).

The main tourist attraction at **Luz** is the **church** where the rare surviving fortifications were the work of the Hospitaliers de Saint Jean de Jérusalem in the 14th century. The Hospitaliers were one of the orders established to protect pilgrims, later changing their name to Knights of Rhodes and then Knights of Malta. The church is at the top of the town, its crenallated outer wall closely hemmed in by the village buildings and its gun slits looking out all over the town and valley.

*R*émi Trotro is one of the leading sculptors working in the Pyrenees, making gigantic statues which frequently engulf his studio at Chèze.

In the lanes around the church there is a market every Monday selling a wide range of goods, an excellent opportunity to buy local cheeses and honey.

Between the church and the river, the Pyrenees National Park has an office (*Maison du Parc*) where there is an exhibition of flora and fauna. It is possible to acompany park guards on walks in the area.

The Tourist Office (Tel. 62-92-81-60) is on the main square where the roads to Lourdes, Barèges and Gavarnie all meet, and there is an office for mountain guides opposite, where all kinds of mountain activities can be organized.

The spa of **St Sauveur** has recently enjoyed a revival, along with the general trend towards health and fitness in France. Napoleon III arrived in 1859 with his wife Eugénie after his victory over Austria at the battle of Solferino. He ordered the construction of the bridge, completed in 1863, which stands 66 metres (215 ft) above the river. He also paid for the building of the Solferino chapel on the south side of Luz, to commemorate his victory. Casualties on both sides had been enormous—22,000 Austrian and 17,000 French plus 25,000 French dead from malaria and typhus.

Gavarnie

From Luz St Sauveur the D921 to Gavarnie climbs steadily south, giving you your first glimpse of the famous cirque and the *brèche* (breach) as soon as you get above the village of Gèdre (11 km/7 miles). In 1837, it was two men from Gèdre, Henri Cazaux and Bernard Guillembet, who were the first to climb Vignemale (3,298 metres/10,720 ft). But they—and the village—have been overshadowed by Henry Russell and Gavarnie, and there is not much to stop for. If you do want to stay in Gèdre, the best hotel is the Brèche de Roland, on the road through.

Just beyond Gèdre, you can take the left turn (N21d) to the less famous CIRQUE OF TROUMOUSE (*see* below), but it is probably best to see Gavarnie first, some 20 minutes on from Gèdre.

Gavarnie is known as the "Chamonix of the Pyrenees" and the setting is undeniably one of the most spectacular in the world. No visit to the central Pyrenees would be complete without reaching the village and making the walk (or ride) to the foot of the mighty cirque, 4 km (2½ miles) away.

The cirque of Gavarnie is a curved vertical wall of rock, scoured by glaciation, and falling some 1,400 metres (4,550 ft) from the 3,000 metre-plus (10,000 ft) peaks at the top. Its main waterfall, the *Grande Cascade,* is one of the longest in the world.

*T*he elegant spa buildings of St Sauveur were just the pick-me-up for Napoleon III and his wife Eugénie.

The village itself seems to be little more than a collection of souvenir kiosks, cafés and hotels along a single road. But it is as redolent of the history of the Pyrenees as it is of the donkeys and horses waiting in the square to give rides to the cirque. The explorer Henry Russell was the heart and soul of this village in the late 19th century and his statue gazes appropriately towards his beloved Vignemale from just beside the bridge. A little further on, the Tourist Office has an exhibition on *Pyrénéisme* and on the fauna of the region. Continue to the little church; in the **cemetery** lie some of the most famous names in the history of *Pyrénéisme*, including Célestin Passet (1845–1917), the greatest of the Gavarnie guides. Without his acrobatic skills and deep knowledge of the mountains many famous ascents would never have been made. Others buried in the cemetery are François Bernat-Salles (1855–1934), another important guide, and Jean Arlaud (1896–1938), a doctor who dedicated himself to mountaineering and who died in a climbing accident near Luchon.

To the Cirque of Gavarnie

Having drunk a coffee in one of the cafés, taken a look at the history and wildlife exhibition in the tourist office, and visited the church, you will be ready to start out for the cirque. On foot it takes about an hour, on horseback about 20 minutes. The tradition of riding to the cirque goes back well over a century and remains an important source of income for the village. The cost is approximately 80F. No hard hats are provided, however, and given the steepness of the trail in

The cirque of Gavarnie attracts hundreds of thousands of tourists every year.

places, and the rocks, there is an element of risk.

The trail follows the Gavarnie stream, soon climbing to the **Botannical Garden** where the tombs of Louis Le Bondidier and Franz Schrader are another reminder of Gavarnie's past. Bondidier (1878–1945) was the founder of the museum at Lourdes, while Schrader (1844–1924) was an explorer and cartographer of the central Pyrenees and also an accomplished painter.

Shortly after the Botannical Garden the track crosses the boundary of the Pyrenees National Park and levels out across the lovely **Prade plateau**, twinkling with streams, where there is an **outdoor theatre** every summer, using the cirque as a stupendous backdrop. There are picnic tables and benches here, if you need a rest. From the end of the plateau, the trail climbs again to a short gorge at the far end of which the old Hôtellerie du Cirque sits just inside the bowl of the cirque. This is as far as the horses—and many walkers—go. In the old days it must have been a marvellous place to stay, to watch the sun go down on the cliff walls or perhaps to listen to the crash of echoing thunder from the safety of a sofa by the blazing fire. Nowadays, sadly, it is only a snack bar.

From the Hôtellerie you can continue, if you wish, to the foot of the **grande cascade** (waterfall) which has a drop of 423 metres (1,375 ft). It will take another half-hour but you can cool off in the spray when you get there and the views all round the towering rock faces are inspiring.

Enthusiastic hikers can return to Gavarnie by a circuitous but well-marked route which climbs up from the side of the Hôtellerie to the Pailla plateau before dropping to Gavarnie once more (allow about three hours by this route).

To the Cirque of Troumouse

An excursion to the cirque at Troumouse, quite different in character to the Gavarnie cirque, makes an enjoyable full or half-day excursion from Gavarnie. After descending to Gèdre, take the N21d which climbs along the Héas valley. After some 7 km (4½ miles) there is a *péage* where a small toll has to be paid in summer. The road then climbs steeply up for another 4 km (2½ miles), right into the cirque itself. Apart from an auberge just before the top, there is no development so that the sense of remoteness remains. This is a lower cirque than Gavarnie's but far wider, stretching for 10 km (6 miles). A walking trail leads right into the centre, at the **Lacs des Aires**.

To the Brèche de Roland

The **Brèche de Roland** is the most popular high-mountain objective for walkers in the Pyrenees on account of its impressive scenery, folklore and history. On a summer afternoon there are walkers of all ages but the route has sufficient difficulty to give a fine sense of achievement. The *brèche* is a way through the cirque of Gavarnie where the top of the wall has collapsed to leave a natural gateway between France and Spain. According to folklore the hole was made by Roland, the legendary commander of Charlemagne's rearguard, as he tried to break his magic sword Durendal to prevent it falling into the hands of the enemy.

Clouds gather in the Pouey Aspé valley, the main approach to the Brèche de Roland.

The easiest way to reach the *brèche* is to drive to the end of the road at the Gavarnie pass—also known as the Port de Boucharo—some 13 km (8 miles) from the village. The road climbs up to give spectacular views of the cliffs at the head of the Ossoue valley, passes the village ski station, and then emerges onto the northern rim of the **Pouey Aspé valley**.

From the parking at the end (right on the frontier), the walk lies along the southern rim of the **Pouey Aspé**, under the pyramid-shaped mountain known as **Taillon** (3,144 metres/10,220 ft). The trail is well marked, climbing gradually as it passes under the north face of Taillon. After an hour, the path intersects with another climbing up from Gavarnie along a steep gulley. (If you want to walk all the way from Gavarnie by this route, the trail begins by the church.) Turn into the gulley and ascend in zig-zags past a glacier to a pass from which there are views of the *brèche* and of the mountain refuge at its foot. The refuge, where refreshments are available, is gained in some two hours from the parking. The final stretch involves the crossing of a short section of glacier, which is at its easiest when it is covered in a little snow. If the ice is exposed, crampons will be useful, but given the short distance they are not essential and most people manage it without.

Wind is considerably accelerated as it passes through the *brèche,* and during a storm it can be a very dangerous place. The view south is over the superb **Ordesa region**, famous for its canyons, while behind there are clear views of **Vignemale** to the north-west, **Piméné** (2,801 metres/9,105 ft), rising on the east side of Gavarnie, and the **Néouvielle massif** to the north-east.

To Russell's Caves

Count Russell's caves, known as **Grottes Bellevue**, are cut into solid rock just below the Ossoue glacier in Vignemale. Russell had them excavated in 1888 so that he could live and entertain on the mountain in summer. The caves are reached from the parking area by the Ossoue *barrage* (dam). Leave Gavarnie on the road to the ski

Co-author Paul Jenner at the Brèche de Roland in winter.

Count Russell

Gavarnie is closely associated with the whole history of Pyrenean exploration and its greatest figures but above all with one particular man, Count Henry Russell (1834–1909) whose statue at the entrance to the village gazes along the Ossoue valley towards Vignemale. Russell was eccentric even by comparison with the many highly individ-ualistic travellers of his time. Vignemale became his obsession. He climbed it 33 times, the last aged 70, took out a 99-year lease on the summit, had caves excavated in which he lived and, one famous August night in 1880, had himself buried on the summit, only his head protruding. God, he reported next morning, when his porters came to dig him out, had been a "palpable presence".

The French have never fully accepted Russell as a countryman, partly because his father was Irish but more pertinently because such eccentricity is rare in French cul-ture. In fact, his mother was French and he was a French citizen. As a young man he travelled all over the world but it was to the Pyrenees he returned to dedicate his life. His first entry in the golden book at the Hôtel des Voyageurs is dated 14 September 1858. He made 16 "first" ascents in the Pyrenees, and his winter ascent of Vignemale in 1869 was the first winter ascent of any major European peak.

In 1882, Russell took his passion for Vignemale to a new extreme when he hired Gavarnie workmen to excavate a cave for him at the head of the Ossoue glacier near the Vignemale summit, adding a second in 1885 and another the following year. But the trio were no sooner celebrated by a great party than the rising glacier (today, on the contrary, it has fallen well below the entrances) made them uninhabitable. Disappointed but undaunted, Russell had new caves excavated below the glacier in 1888, the Grottes Bellevue, which can be visited by most walkers (see the itinerary below). Despite the magnificent view, however, the new position was too earthly for Russell and he finally had a cave excavated just 18 metres (60 ft) below the summit in 1893. He called it "Paradis".

The mountaineering style of a gentleman adventurer like Russell was quite different to the Alpine style of today's climbers. He would go out immaculately dressed, includ-ing collar and tie, normally accompanied by a guide and porters who would carry all his effects. At his caves, his cook would prepare meals which would be served in style on damask tablecloths, with wines and cigars. In fact, catering to the needs of Russell, his associates and guests was for a time a minor summer industry for Gavarnie, with mes-sengers constantly running between the village and his caves each day, carrying letters and supplies. None of this, though, detracts from his achievements. Few today could climb both Monte Perdido (Mont Perdu) and Vignemale, as he did, in under 24 hours. He wrote a book about his exploits, the poetic *Souvenirs d'un Montagnard*.

*O*ne of the three *Grottes Bellevue that Count Henry Russell had excavated below the Ossoue glacier on Vignemale. There was one for himself, one for guests and one for his servants.*

station but turn off to the right almost at once along the Ossoue valley.

This is a beautiful drive but should never be attempted in the spring, when melting snow may sweep rocks down from above. The road first passes under high cliffs, then beech forest and finally pasture where

*V*ignemale was the
*favourite mountain of Count
Henry Russell, who took out
a 99-year lease on the summit,
including the Ossoue glacier,
and spent his summers there
in excavated caves.*

horses are grazed and the whistle of
marmots is frequent. The tarmac
stops after 4 km (2½ miles) but the
track thereafter is in good condition
and it is possible to drive almost to

*T*he view from inside
*Count Henry Russell's cave—in
the distance you can see the
Cirque of Gavarnie.*

the lake (7 km/4½ miles from Gavarnie).

Walk along the east side of the reservoir, continue over the dried-up lake bed and cross the bridge. The path then climbs to the top of a waterfall, continues to a short stretch of permanent ice, which should be crossed with care, passes a second waterfall and finally climbs fairly steeply to the caves (about three hours from the reservoir). Even if you feel unable to get all the way to the caves, the views from even halfway are magnificent. If you do make it, you can sit on Russell's stone bed inside his cave and get a feeling of nights gone by when the fire crackled and Russell and his friends watched the stars twinkle above.

Barèges

Barèges is a summer and winter resort with little to see but plenty for active people to do. Some 7 km east of Luz St Sauveur on the D918, it has a long history connected with exploration of the mountains. It was to Barèges that the young man who was to become the father of *Pyrénéisme* came by chance in 1787 when he was 32. He was Louis François Elisabeth Ramond (1755–1827), known as **Ramond de Carbonnières**.

The story of his arrival is one of those remarkable illustrations of "fate". In 1781 he became advisor to Cardinal Rohan, one of the most powerful men in France. Despite his position, or perhaps because of it, Rohan became the dupe of a confidence trick devised by the Comtesse de La Motte-Valois, in which the cardinal believed himself to be acting as the intermediary in the purchase of a necklace for the Queen, Marie-Antoinette. The 593-stone necklace, however, never went to the Queen but was stolen by the countess, broken up and sold in London. The Cardinal was cleared of any wrongdoing in the theft of the necklace but stripped of all offices as a result of which he arrived the following year in Barèges with Ramond for a "cure" at the spa. Ramond fell in love with the mountains and wrote *Observations faites dans les Pyrénées* (Observations made in the Pyrenees), published in 1789. Narrowly escaping the guillotone in the Revolution, he organized the first ascent of Mont Perdu (3,355 metres/10,905 ft) in 1802, the third highest in the Pyrenees, but then believed to be the highest. He climbed Pic du Midi de Bigorre close to Barèges 35 times and made explorations in many parts of the range, investigating the botany, geology and wildlife.

As for the waters for which the cardinal came, they have more recently been believed excellent for wounds, so that Napoleon made Barèges one of five military *thermes* in a new "welfare" programme for wounded soldiers.

Pic du Midi de Bigorre

The drive up **Pic du Midi de Bigorre** is the classic outing from Barèges. The road is the highest in the Pyrenees, reaching 2,720 metres (8,840 ft), just short of the summit (2,872 metres/ 9,335 ft) where there is an observatory. From Barèges the road climbs slowly eastwards, the hillsides to the north forming an atmospheric and picturesque arrangement of pastures dotted with small farms.

Marmots

The marmot is the most endearing and easily observed of Pyrenean mammals, giving itself away by its own warning whistle long before it would have been spotted. Living in colonies in tunnels, marmots bear a resemblance to prairie dogs but are much larger with thick fur and large tails. They live all over the central Pyrenees at altitudes of 1,500–2,500 metres (5,000–8,000 ft) approximately.

A marmot lookout gives its warning signal when a human approaches to approximately 50 metres (165 ft), disappearing into its hole at approximately 30 metres (100 ft). As soon as a whistle is heard, stand still until the lookout has been located, normally sitting on top of a platform of rock. The tunnel entrance will be nearby, possibly under the rock. Once a marmot has been disturbed and given its warning whistle the colony may remain underground for some time but in areas like the Ossoue valley where human visitors are frequent they are less cautious.

Marmots seldom travel far from their homes, eating only the surrounding plants and drinking dew, so that once an occupied tunnel has been identified observing becomes quite easy.

The most exciting time to watch is April, when they emerge from their hibernation and are at their most playful, wrestling with one another. Although they are vegetarians and look harmless, the wrestling can be in earnest and marmots sometimes fight to the death, especially over territorial disputes. Mating takes place immediately after the end of hibernation and the young emerge for the first time between the end of June and the beginning of July.

Marmots are gone from the valley, and all the Pyrenees, by the end of September, when they disappear into their tunnels to hibernate. During the winter sleep they lose between a third and a half of their body weight and re-awaken, whatever the outside weather, when fat reserves are exhausted.

After the ski station of **Superbarèges**, where the brightly- coloured canopies of *parapentes* are often in the sky, it climbs in steep hairpins into the **Col du Tourmalet** (2,115 metres/6,875 ft), the highest road pass in the French Pyrenees. A small toll is charged for the final section to the summit; to walk is free but on foot it takes three to four hours for the round trip from the toll booth. The views from the summit are immense, from Balaïtous in the west to Andorra in the east.

The **observatory** has functioned year round ever since it opened in 1882. When the road is closed due to snow, the staff ascend by cable car from the ski resort of **La Mongie**, on the eastern side of the pass. There is a **museum** of observatory equipment which can be visited.

Continuing over the Col du Tourmalet, the road descends towards Bagnères de Bigorre.

*T*ourmalet means bad detour and this road snaking down from the Col du Tourmalet, the highest road pass in the French Pyrenees, can be blocked by snow even in early summer, ensuring the area lives up to its name.

Bagnères de Bigorre and the Baronnies

A once-flourishing spa resort now undergoing a long overdue face-lift, Bagnères de Bigorre makes a good base for exploring the Bigorre. The tranquil but easily accessible Baronnies region is nearby and there are plenty of important and fascinating tourist sites within easy reach.

Bagnères, like Pau, had a substantial British community in the mid-19th century—mostly Wellington's men from the Peninsular War. The mountaineer Charles Packe was a frequent visitor who, together with the photographer and inventor Maxwell Lyte, helped set up the **Société Ramond** in Bagnères in 1864. Similar to the French Alpine Club, which it predates, it is now dedicated to research and education. The headquarters are still in Bagnères, in the old town hall, where there are regular meetings.

Bagnères has functioned as a popular spa since Roman times when it was known as *Vicus Aquensis*. In the mid-16th century its waters earned a great reputation for restoring fertility — the birth of the future Henry IV of France was said to have been due to them. Stroll from the main road through the market area and you will come to the *Grandes-Thermes* spa building, huge, classical and very clean looking after a multi-million franc facelift.

Next door are the casino and the **Salies Museum** which has a good selection of pleasing landscape paintings and a sprinkling of modern artists, including *Picabia*, representing **Dada**. The other museum in Bagnères is the **Old Mill** in rue Hount-Blanque, about ten minutes away by foot on the opposite bank of the Adour. It has a satisfying display of Pyrenean furniture, tools, utensils and clothes, for which the bare stonework and original mill fittings provide a marvellous setting.

Best shopping is in the streets around the market between the *thermes* and the tree-lined allées des Coustous, especially rue des Thermes, rue Victor-Hugo and place de Strasbourg, as well as in the square at the bottom of allées des Coustous, place Lafayette. The Tourist Office is in a kiosk at one end of the square; look out also for **L'Isard Blanc**, one of the few bookshops anywhere in the Pyrenees to have a really comprehensive selection on the range.

If you have the opportunity, take in a performance of the **Chanteurs Montagnards**, traditional singers formed in Bagnères in 1832 as France's first "profane" (non-religious) singing group. At the time, hardly anything like them had been heard before and the *chanteurs* travelled Europe-wide on a fabulously successful tour. Though no longer quite so popular, the red-jacketed singers are still in demand and perform frequently in summer.

The Road South

The astonishing **Médous Caves** are some 3 km (2 miles) south of Bagnères on the D935 towards Campan (April to mid-October, 9–11.30 a.m. and 2–5.30 p.m. Be ready to make the turn through the narrow wrought-iron gates of **Château de Médous**, because they are easy to miss. Tours, including a boat ride on the underground **Adour River**, take about half an hour. The stalagmites, stalactites and other concretions are magnificent, most of all the "orchid" wall which experts have rated one of the top ten formations in France. The reason these caves have kept their beauty despite their easy access is that they were only discovered in the private grounds of the chateau in 1948 and therefore escaped the worst of late 19th-century cave vandalism.

There is no entry to the caves until a group of at least ten has assembled, which, out of season, can mean a wait. This is agreeably passed at the Hostellrie d'Asté, just across the main road from the caves in the village of the same name.

If this does not appeal, there are plenty of other restaurants on the way south. You can take the footpath from the end of the Lesponne Valley at the Vieille Auberge de Chiroulet (itself a good rustic eating experience) that leads to **Lac Bleu**. If you go all the way to the lake, you are in for a steep climb rewarded by a magnificent high-mountain ambience at the end of it (5 hours to the lake and back).

Continuing south on the D935, the landscape is glorious — lush green pasture rising up on either side to remote summits. A kilometre (½ mile) beyond the Lesponne turning, the screen inside **St Jean-Baptiste** at **Campan** gleams with the unusual gold baroque decoration which was the work of two local brothers. The church was rebuilt after the 1694 fire which destroyed much of the village, but still incorporating a "Cagot door" through which these mysterious outcasts were supposed to enter (*see* ST JEAN PIED-DE-PORT).

Into the Baronnies

From Bagnères take the D938 towards Capvern, turning right at Haut de la Côte onto the narrow lane to Bulan, Laborde and Esparros. This is a region of rolling, though quite substantial hills, dense forests and often neglected fields, the occasional muffled chug of a tractor the only mechanical sound you are likely to hear. It is a moving and an incredibly beautiful place.

The tiny village of **Esparros** is the "capital" of the region, complete with Tourist Office over the grocery store.

Horseback is one way of seeing the countryside—try **Ranch Les 3 A** (Tel. 62-39-10-82)—but most people will prefer their own feet. There is an easy walk to the waterfall, signposted *La Cascade,* from the centre of the village. Leave your car at the cross beside the road, some 2 km (1 mile) from the village centre, and follow the footpath beside the stream. This is an idyllic walk on a sunny day, leading through meadows and past old stone barns until reaching the mossy and spectacular falls.

An alternative walk starts yet further down the lane. Some 4 km (2½ miles) beyond the cross, the road turns to un-surfaced but easy track. Drive on for

*T*he Baronnies is an area of high rainfall with a vegetation to match.

another 2 km (1 mile), past cattle pens and up to a wide, flat area at the top of the hill where there is a "cross-roads". Park here. The trail heading south is the most delightful (but certainly do not take the trail north, which leads to a mine).

To Escaladieu and Mauvezin

On the northern fringes of the Baronnies the abbey of Escaladieu and the castle of Mauvezin are two of the most enchanting sites of the region. You can reach them directly from Bagnères along the D938 or by taking the D14 north from Esparros.

The **Abbey of Escaladieu** (June to mid-September, 10 a.m.–1 p.m. and 2–6 p.m., in winter, weekends only; April and May, afternoons only) was founded by the Cistercians on its present site at the confluence of the Rivers Luz and Arros in 1142. Having fallen into disrepair, especially after the ravages of the Wars of Religion, the plain but graceful buildings are now been renovated by a group of enthusiasts who are imaginatively turning the abbey into a cultural centre. The corridors hum with earnest voices discussing the latest art exhibition and there are frequent concerts in the abbey church.

Some 5 km (3 miles) east of Escaladieu, perched on top of a hill, the **Castle of Mauvezin** (open daily mid-June to mid-October; the rest of the year 1.30–6 p.m.) was just one of the castles of the flamboyant knight, Gaston Fébus. Born in 1331, he spent much of his boisterous life trying to create a united kingdom of the northern Pyrenees. When he died, in 1391, he had added the regions of Soule and

Bigorre to his inheritance of Béarn and Foix—but it was not until almost 200 years later that the French Pyrenees became united as part of France.

Fébus was a legend in his own lifetime, renowned as a warrior, politician, lover and poet, but his private life was not so successful. He divorced his wife and killed his son and heir in mysterious circumstances, writing, it is said, a prayer book in penance. His other book, *Livre de la Chasse*, is respected as a hunting manual even today.

The ramparts of the castle give magnificent views south over the Pyrenees, while the state rooms are a museum dedicated to Fébus and—because he was a writer as well as warrior—to the *Société Félibré*, a literary organization which keeps alive the *langue d'Oc* (which Fébus would have spoken).

Before leaving the area, also make a point of seeing the Arctic Museum (open daily 2–7 p.m.) at Tournay, a little to the north on the main N17.

The Bigorre is noted for its variety of rock, which includes granite, gneiss, schist, limestone and particularly marble.

The Aure Valley

The Aure Valley, to the east of Bagnères de Bigorre and the Baronnies, cuts through traditional mountain pasture from the major industrial centre of Lannemezan to the Spanish border at the Bielsa Tunnel.

The best way into it from (Bagnères de Bigorre) is over the spectacular **Col d'Aspin**, with its wide views back to Pic du Midi de Bigorre, from where the road redescends to Arreau.

Arreau, old capital of the region some 30 km (19 miles) south of Lannemezan, has retained an authentic medieval ambience. There are half-timbered houses with slate roofs overhanging the narrow streets and a covered, half-timbered market square (the weekly Thursday market attracts shoppers from all over the region). The River Aure, pouring through the centre of town and crossed by several attractive bridges, sets it all off with the melody of rushing water.

There are two minor places to visit, the 13th-century **Chapelle de St Exupère** which has a notable Romanesque doorway, and the **Château des Nestes** where there is a **Pyrenean museum** (open in season 10 a.m.–noon and 2.30–6 p.m.).

From Arreau the D618 climbs south-east to the **Col de Peyresourde**, another pleasant journey through mountains and their villages down to **Bagnères de Luchon**, passing *en route* the holiday resort of the Val Louron. However, to stay in the Aure Valley continue south on the D929, first through the village of **Vielle Aure**, an important walking centre crossed by the famous GR10 footpath. About 12 km (7½ miles) from Arreau, **St Lary Soulan** is one of the leading ski resorts in the Pyrenees. There is also an active programme of summer sports and diversions, from trekking to *parapente*, in which the operator of a small parachute runs downhill until uplifted into flight.

Just a couple of kilometres further south, **Tramezaïgues** is a tiny hamlet built into the cliffs at the meeting of the rivers Rioumajou and Aure, where the remains of an 11th-century watch tower underline its once vitally strategic position. From here you can enjoy the beautiful drive into the **side-valley of the Rioumajou**. There is a superb mix of high-mountain pasture, woods and watercourses and, not to spoil it, the road becomes track for most of the 12 km (7½ miles). In good conditions, the track is passable by car as far as the derelict *Hospice de Rioumajou*, but it may be safer (and certainly more enjoyable) to walk the last part. The hospice was one of many built throughout the range for the shelter of pilgrims en route to the holy places in Spain and is now a well-known landmark for the modern "pilgrims" of the transpyrenean HRP footpath.

To the west of the Aure valley, the popular mountain wilderness of the **Néouvielle Natural Reserve** can be reached from the village of Fabian, a short way south of Tramezaïgues. Take the right-hand turning which climbs the 14 km (9 miles) to the very fringes of the protected area. Seldom is such remote high-mountain country so easily reached, all peaks, forests and lakes. There are two lakeside hotel refuges.

There are well-marked trails throughout the reserve, including the section of the GR10 that runs from Barèges to St Lary. Pic Néouvielle itself (3,091 metres/10,050 ft) can be climbed without resort to rope, but its remote situation makes it a very hard day out. But you do not have to reach the most inaccessible parts of the reserve to have a chance of seeing izards, those lithe members of the antelope family, or to hear the shrill whistles of marmots. Both these creatures have been reintroduced to the reserve, the izard because it had been completely hunted out. Keep an eye on the sky; it is possible to see golden eagles and the even larger lammergeier.

Beyond Fabian, the Aure valley road passes the turn to the custom-built ski station of Piau-Engaly and, after 10 km (6 miles), reaches the **Bielsa Tunnel**, half-way through which is the frontier. This is an easy and direct route into the Spanish Ordesa region.

Tarbes

Almost 19 km (12 miles) north-east of Lourdes and capital of the Bigorre since the 9th century, the long history of Tarbes rests in its museums rather than its buildings, which were razed by the Normans and, later, in the Wars of Religion.

Maréchal Ferdinand Foch, supreme commander of the Western Front in World War I, was born in Tarbes at 2 rue de la Victoire in 1851, a short way east of place de Verdun. The typical flat-fronted and shuttered Bigourdan town house is now a museum of his life, containing photographs, film, sculpture, mementoes, room settings and personal effects from childhood through to the armchair in which he is said to have died in Paris in 1929. Foch was baptised close by in the town's 12th-century **Cathedral de Notre Dame de la Sède**, on place du Général de Gaulle. Built in several different styles, the cathedral is worth seeing for its unusual colour scheme—a mix of ochre sandstone, red bricks and multi-hued cobbles. Finally, there is an equestrian statue of the marshal at the junction of cours Gambetta (which runs south from place de Verdun) and rue Cronstadt.

Remaining with things military, the **Massey Museum** traces the history of the Hussars from 1692—the uniforms, the arms, the men and the horses. The museum is in the Massey Gardens (*Jardin Massey*), off rue Massey, which runs north from place de Verdun. Today, Tarbes remains important militarily. There are two large barracks and the arsenal (ATS) employs a workforce of around 3,000. Other rooms are devoted to the municipal art collection, begun by Achille Jubinal in the mid-19th century and including works by Pontormo, de Keyser, de Clerck, Michelin, Creti, Jongkind, Gerome and Barry. Fresh acquisitions

in the last few years include *Nature Dead* by Ferguson (1632–95), *The Nativity* by de Wittewael (1560–1638) and *Portrait of a Woman* by Van Ceulen (1593–1661). An archaeological and historical section of the museum is under development at the time of writing.

The **Massey Gardens** are an oasis in this bustling town, designed by Placide Massey, whose bust is close to the main entrance. Born in Tarbes in 1777, Massey was landscape gardener to Queen Hortense, step-daughter of Napoleon I and wife of Napoleon III. His projects included Versailles. The exquisite trees, flowers and shrubs include different varieties of magnolia, American sequoias and giant cedars, plus the sassafras, rare in Europe and used by the North American Indians as a medicine. Among the shrubs are the busts of two poets important in the modernist movement, Tarbes-born Théophile Gautier, sculpted by his daughter, and Tarbes-educated Jules Laforgue, who influenced Apollinaire and Eliot but died before he had completed any truly great work of his own. The 15th-century **cloister** taken from the nearby Abbey of Saint Sever de Rustan is a magical place to wander within the gardens. The carved pillars and capitals are intriguing, telling tales of events on the Santiago de Compostela pilgrimages. The **conservatory** contains sculptures by Alicia Penalba (1913–82).

The legendary mount of the Hussars was the Tarbais, still bred today at the *Haras National* (national stud), southeast of place de Verdun, along avenue du Regiment de Bigorre. In the stables here you can also see the black Mérens of the Ariège Pyrenees, thought to be

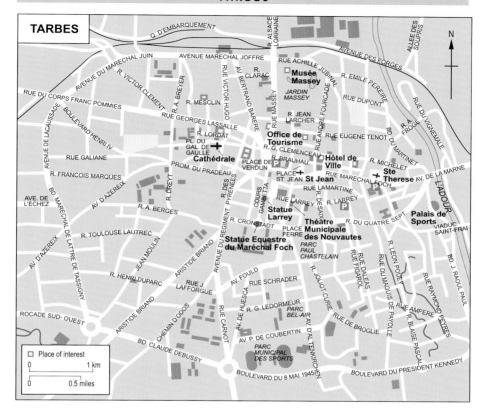

Town plan of Tarbes.

the closest relative of the wild ponies of European prehistory. Various horse shows are held at the *haras*, including the carriage show in May, show-jumping in June and the big sale of stallions in October.

Tarbes is a working town rather than a tourist town with no-nonsense shopping to match. For local produce, go to the daily market in place Brauhauban (take rue Maréchal Foch from the south side of place de Verdun, then first right into avenue Marché Brauhauban, passing the excellent cheese shop **Fromagerie Brauhauban** along the way). Best market days are Tuesdays and Saturdays. The general market is held every Tuesday in place Marcadieu, further along rue Maréchal Foch, a little before the Adour river. Every other week there is a **Grand Marché** which is particularly lively and redolent of all things Bigourdan. Also for local produce try the shops **Le Chai** (53 rue George Lassalle), **Le Fermière Bigourdan** (6 place du Forail) and **Aux Ducs de Gascogne** (21 rue Maréchal Foch). For gifts try **Manuguet** (avenue de la Marne—the continuation of rue Maréchal Foch).

Tarbes is a wonderful town in which to sample Bigourdan specialities.

The Gargas Caves and the Cathars of Mountaillou

Haute-Garonne is a huge *département* stretching diagonally from well to the north of Toulouse as far as the Spanish border. But only a neck of the *département* includes the Pyrenees, beginning at St Gaudens and extending to the frontier peaks near Bagnères de Luchon. The mountains and the Lac d'Oô can be explored from the spa resort of Luchon. The prehistoric Gargas caves are not far from the Romanesque Cathedral of St Bertrand de Comminges.

Bagnères de Luchon

Bagnères de Luchon, normally known simply as **Luchon**, is one of the most popular spas in the Pyrenees. It is the complete Pyrenean resort, with plenty of good (but no great) hotels and restaurants. It makes a comfortable and convivial base for car tours and for exploring the mountains, whether

*H*aute-Garonne is famous for its streams, tumbling down from the frontier peaks to join the mighty Garonne, which rises in Spain and flows into the Atlantic at Bordeaux.

strolling to an idyllic lakeside picnic spot or tackling the highest mountain in the range (Aneto, 3,404 metres/ 11,169 ft, just over the border).

Luchon first became truly fashionable as a spa in the middle of the 18th century when Jacques Barrau and Baron Antoine d'Etigny re-established the old Roman baths, and invited the governor of Gascony, Louis Richelieu, great-nephew of the famous Cardinal de Richelieu.

A Walk around Town
A tour of Luchon's statues serves as an introduction to the geography of the town. Beginning at the station on the north side, where the buses also stop, the first is Allar's **Isis Dévoliée**. Heading into town across the One River

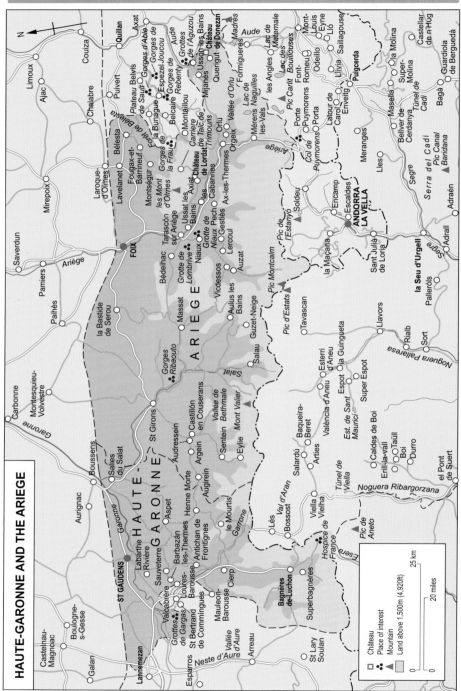

HAUTE-GARONNE AND THE ARIEGE

Château
Place of interest
Mountain
Land above 1,500m (4,920ft)

25 km

20 miles

(from the Celtic *onna* meaning "water") and down avenue Maréchal Foch, the second is Monnard's composed and solid **La Lionne**. You next reach allées d'Etigny, the main boulevard, which is flanked by lime trees and pavement cafés. Half-way along are the Tourist Office and the **museum**. At the far end are the spa buildings (*thermes*), where, in the surrounding parc de Quinconces, are Guyot's **L'Ours**, de Crauk's **Etigny**, and three statues by the local sculptor Jean-Marie Mengue (1855–1939), **La Baigneuse, La Vallée du Lys** and **Caïn et Abel**. From the spa, stroll along allées des Bains towards the Pique River and the **Casino Gardens** where there are three more important works, Christophe's bronze *La Fortune*, Allouard's *Molière Mourant* and Coutheilai's Rodinesque and very lovely *Baiser à la Source*, the male figure lying on a rock, leaning down into the stream to kiss a nymph. Returning to allées d'Etigny via place Richelieu you will come across the final sculpture, Guillaume's *Francois I et sa soeur Marguerite de Valois*.

Luchon has its own ski resort of **Superbagnères**, a custom-built ski-station clustered on a mountain promontory high above, There is hang-gliding and *parapente* in summer and fliers are often seen floating in the sky over the town.

If, as a non-patient, you would like to visit the spa buildings, you must buy tickets at the Vaporium off cours de Quinconces between 7.30 a.m. and 11.30 a.m. Tours are at 2 p.m. Tuesdays, Wednesdays and Thursdays (not Wednesdays in low season).

The **Luchon Museum**, an eccentric and unfailingly compelling collection of this and that to do with the region, is at number 18, allées d'Etigny (summer weekdays only, 9 a.m.–noon and 2–6 p.m.), the same building as the Tourist Office. Old photographs and memorabilia of the town's rich and famous visitors completely cover many of the walls—here are figures as diverse as Henri Gorsse, a writer and local benefactor, Victor Hugo, the Duc d'Orleans, Leopold II of Belgium and a very young Prince Rainier of Monaco.

The **Salle du Pyrénéisme** follows the adventures, triumphs and tragedies of climbing—Pierre Barrau who fell to his death into a crevasse on Maladetta in 1824 and local climber Jean Arlaud who died on Pic Saud in July 1938. There are also exhibits of early climbing equipment—the unwieldy rope, the enormously heavy ice-axes and the so-formal restrictive clothing.

Other rooms display flora and fauna, the finds of pre-history, pictures of old Luchon and a folk museum of tools, implements and furniture.

Because Luchon's main appeal today is as a resort, primarily for summer *curistes* (as visitors to the healing waters are called) or for the increasing numbers of skiers using nearby Superbagnères for winter sports, there are plenty of tourist diversions. The main street, **allées d'Etigny**, is filled with attractive shops, many, as you would expect, concentrating on beauty and health products. Permfumeries, boutiques and

*T*he *Haute-Garonne and Ariège regions.*

139

Above Bagnères de Luchon, the ski resort of Superbagnères offers some idyllic skiing.

health foods are plentiful though there are also regional specialities to be had, such as local cheeses, game, honeys and wines. The best specialist grocers are **Le Cagibi** at 17 allées Etigny and **Gailhou Durdos** at number 71.

Festivals

There are fêtes, festivals and special events through the Spring and Summer. The **fête of St Jean** with bonfires and fireworks is held on 23 June from 10 p.m. in front of the Thermes Chambert building. The impressive flower festival procession is held the last Sunday of August and there is a permanent **festival of folklorique events**, including mountain choirs, dancing and art and craft exhibitions throughout the main holiday period. Each week there are

pelota and **chistera** matches played at the fronton Réserve de la Pique.

As a well-established French summer holiday resort, Luchon has an impressive number of apartments and villas to rent for one week or more. Most offer good quality and value for money, but you are advised to look for one approved and graded under the *Cléconfort* scheme; a list is available at the tourist office. For short-term hire of a television (or even a video recorder), contact Locatel at 69 avenue Maréchal Foch; Tel. 61-79-06-51).

Walking from Luchon

The landscape around Luchon is superb and there are itineraries to suit all hiking abilities. One of the easiest trips is to visit the **Hospice de France**, founded by the Knights of St John in the Middle Ages to shelter pilgrims. You can take the car along the D125 Superbagnères road from Luchon until reaching the Pont de Ravi where you head off south-east along a tiny road which eventually peters out to track. You may prefer to leave the car here and follow the track on foot for about half-an-hour to reach the refuge. From the Hospice de France there are several more demanding walks you can undertake—and you may well be in the company of hardened trekkers as it is from here you can pass through the Port de Benasque to enter Spain and join the transpyrenean footpath the HRP.

From the hospice, the **Port** (pass) **de Benasque** with its magnificent views and its lakes is a tough 3 hour walk. For long-distance hikers it is possible to continue beyond the pass, descending to the *renclusa* or hut (allow a further 3 hours). The renclusa is the normal base from which to ascend **Aneto** (3,404 metres/11,065 ft), the highest mountain in the range (for an account, *see* BENASQUE).

Another favourite is the walk to the ravishing **Lac d'Oô** along the GR10 footpath from Superbagnères (where you can park). A quicker way of reaching the lake is to drive the 7 km (4 miles) along the narrow Vallée d'Oô road to the parking spot at Granges d'Astau. You can buy refreshments here and the lake is just a one hour walk away through inspiring landscape. Keen hikers can continue beyond Lac d'Oô to the high-mountain **Espingo** refuge where it is possible to stay.

*M*any birds, such *as owls, regurgitate food they cannot digest in the form of pellets. These, composed mainly of matted fur, were probably regurgitated by a buzzard. A good tracking book can add immeasurably to the pleasure of walking in the mountains around Luchon—or anywhere in the Pyrenees.*

St Bertrand de Comminges

An easy drive 42 km (25 miles) north of Bagnères de Luchon, the cathedral and tiny village of **St Bertrand de Comminges** is one of the most powerful tourist sites of the region. It has something for virtually every visitor—religious glory, architectural splendour and a fascinating, well-documented history.

Driving from Luchon you can see the magnificent **cathedral** loom up on its hill from some distance away. The well-signposted route leads straight to an enormous parking area. Inside the walls you stroll through the **medieval village** of half-timbered 15th- and 16th-century homes to the imposing cathedral itself, towering over everything.

The site has been occupied since at least Roman times and the vestiges of their *Lugdunum Convenarum* are now being uncovered at the base of the hill. The lower town was sacked by the Vandals in AD 409 and the upper town, to which the inhabitants had then retreated, by the Burgundians in AD 585. After 500 years of desolation it rose again, St Bertrand taking its name from Bertrand de l'Isle, then Bishop of Comminges, who decided to restore the old church in the Romanesque manner (see the **cloister**, **clock tower**, **main doorway** and the **sculpted door arch**). After him there were additions in the Gothic (the nave) and Renaissance styles (the magnificent **woodwork of the choir and the sanctuary**). Unfortunately, during current restoration, there has been some damage to the

The Gargas Caves

Prehistoric hand outlines are known in many European painted caves but **Gargas**, some 8 km (5 miles) from St Bertrand surpasses all of them in the sheer number of its hand images. Over 150 hand outlines adorn the black recesses of the cave system, along with the more familiar engravings and finger tracings of deer, horse, bison and mammoth. There were once superb stalactites and stalagmites but the caves have been known since at least the late 19th-century and many have been cut off as souvenirs. Gargas (you have to join a guided tour—some have English commentaries) is open 2.30–4.30 p.m. and some mornings in high season.

Experts believe the outlines were created around 20,000 BC, which is considerably earlier than the celebrated paintings at Niaux in Ariège, but there is no agreement on how they were made nor on their purpose. Most mystifying of all, many of the hands have whole fingers or parts of fingers missing. Some prehistorians believe they are true outlines, created by spraying pigment from reeds, others that they are merely free drawings. The French prehistorian André Leroi-Gourhan (1911–1986) has postulated some sort of code as used even today by South African Bushmen for silent communication when hunting, in which fingers are folded down. Other more dramatic explanations of the missing fingers include leprosy, frostbite, accident and ritual mutilation.

Tours of the caves are in groups of about 12 people and last about 45 minutes and although there is electric lighting in the caves, the guide also has a hand torch to further enhance outlines which are difficult to ascertain at first. There is some uphill walking involved and quite a steep descent once you have left the cave system. There is a small shop and even smaller museum of cave finds, mostly animal bones and teeth.

magnificent organ, which is rated one of the three "marvels of Gascony".

A couple of kilometres north of St Bertrand, the early Romanesque **church of St Just** is not merely picturesque but all the more fascinating from having been built from stones from the old Roman town of Lugdunum. See if you can spot here and there the Roman inscriptions on the blocks and columns.

St Gaudens

St Gaudens, about 15 km (9 miles) north-east of the Gargas caves, is the main town of the region but there is little reason to visit except to see the **Comminges Museum**, which has a good display of prehistoric finds and an unusual collection of souvenirs of the military men of the Pyrenees—Foch, Joffre and Gallieni. There is a large market each Thursday. Sadly, as yet here is nothing to mark St Gaudens as the home of the pioneering speleologist Norbert Casteret (1897–1987).

Augirein

The most important site in the village of Augirein is the **Museum of Couserans Arts and Traditions** which houses a fascinating collection of exhibits relating to Bethmale Valley folklore and the *Guerre des Demoiselles* (War of the Spinsters). The exhibits come mainly from the private collection of Count Jacques Begoüen who died in 1979, son of the prehistorian Count Henri Begoüen. One of the most famous items is a linen shirt, said to have been worn by one of the *demoiselles*. The museum hours are: 2 p.m.–6.30 p.m. daily from the beginning of July until the middle of September.

The War of the Spinsters

The *Guerre des Demoiselles* (War of the Spinsters) erupted in the hamlet of Autrech, near Augirein, in 1829. The local people rose up against the big landowners who, despite the French Revolution 30 years earlier, still monopolized the forests of the Ariège supplying timber to the iron industry while local people went short.

A colourful folklore is today's most obvious legacy from those turbulent years but at the time the "war" (actually more a series of terrifying and only occasionally violent demonstrations) was a serious protest. By 1818 there were 43 mines in the Ariège and the total was to grow to almost 60 by 1845. As a result, ordinary people were reduced to digging up tree stumps and cutting bushes for firewood, while the real timber went for pit props and furnaces. Worse, the mine owners used their profits to take over all trade in the area, pushing up prices for food and clothing.

The nickname for the troubles comes from the way the rebels dressed up to avoid identification. Each wore a shirt held tightly in at the waist by a red belt, giving the impression of a bust. The aim of these *demoiselles* was to intimidate and to voice discontent rather than to kill. In the 40 years of disturbances, only one person was actually murdered by them. But to heighten terror (and further disguise themselves) the *demoiselles* blacked their faces with soot or wore masks.

The museum exhibits give only an impression of the terror created by the *demoiselles*. For a more vivid experience (and a good night out) enquire about performances by the **Biroussans**.

An Area of Caves and Ruined Castles

A region with a varied history crammed with interesting places to see (*see* map on page 138). The Salat River offers canoeing and gold panning; the many trails provide excellent hiking and riding. Near Tarascon are the caves of Niaux, Vache, Bédeilhac and Lombrives, while visits to Montségur and Montaillou bring alive the history of the Cathars.

There is probably more to see and do in the Ariège than in any other part of the Pyrenees. It is a region with a long, and sometimes terrible, history. And it is curious how often that history comes back to the extensive cave systems of the mountains. The people of the Magdalenian left their strange art behind them in so many caves of the Ariège. The Cathars hid in the same caves to escape persecution. And during World War II the Nazis used them yet again as protected underground factories.

Above ground there are ruined castles, beautiful scenery, marvellous hiking and riding trails, fast-flowing rivers for canoeing, convivial hotels and satisfying restaurants.

Foix

The three unmatching towers of Foix Castle present a dramatic face as you arrive in this capital of the Ariège. Even on closer inspection the town will not disappoint you with its narrow streets and half-timbered buildings. The Ariège is a huge and varied region, and the best time to catch a glimpse of a cross-section of its people is on

The spa town of Aulus-les-Bains, which like so many towns of the Ariège, snuggles at the bottom of a spectacularly steep-sided valley. This is one of the toughest regions of the Pyrenees for hikers.

Wednesday or Friday mornings in Foix, the market days when artisans, farmers and shoppers descend on the St Volusien covered market and the allées de Villote, which is the car parking area on the main avenue Gabriel Fauré.

Like many old towns, streets are narrow and parking is a problem, so on non-market days head straight for avenue Gabriel Fauré; otherwise use the Champ de Mars behind the Post Office (PTT) on the south side of the avenue.

 Wherever you walk in the town the impressive **Château Foix** towers above (open daily). Fortifications are thought to have existed from Roman times but even the oldest parts of the present castle date only from the 11th century. The three towers were built at different times and in different styles while the low connecting building was built in the 19th century.

The **Museum of Ariège** is housed in the 15th-century round tower. Exhibitions cover palaeontology, prehistory, the Gallo-Roman and Barbarian periods, armour and medieval art. There is also a small folk section, illustrating domestic and agricultural life of the Ariège in the Middle Ages.

The first square tower of the **castle** was built in the 11th century, probably by the Count of Carcassonne, Roger the Old. His son, Roger Bernard, was the first to take the title Count of Foix. But Henry of Foix, Navarre and Béarn is more renowned, becoming Henry IV of France in 1607.

The **Church of St Volusien** in place de l'Arget just below the castle is named after the Bishop of Tours who was put to death by the Visigoths in the 6th century. As legend has it, all manner of miracles took place as the body made its final journey on a bier dragged by two oxen—and the final miracle was that the resting spot of the martyr was chosen by the oxen refusing to go any further! Roger Bernard (1071–1121) Count of Foix and great-grandson of the first count, had the church built on the spot. It suffered sorely during the Wars of Religion and was not fully restored until 1965. This count was also responsible for building the second of the castle's square towers.

Just walking in the town centre streets is a varied architectural journey through the centuries. Be sure to visit **place Parmentier** where there are several half-timbered buildings; **rue des Grand-Ducs** with its covered walkway bridges linking houses on either side of the street; **rue de la Préfecture** and the caryatids (pillars depicting classically-clad females); **place de l'Oie** and its medieval bronze fountain in the form of a swan.

Shopping

Some of the shops in the old streets are architectural gems in themselves. The bustling Wednesday and Friday markets are also worth visiting especially if you like some of the local delicacies such as goose and duck liver or cheese. There are also regular general markets (first, third and fifth Monday of each month) when there is a wider range of goods. Worth seeking out are the wine-based aperitif "Hypocras", said to be the drink of Gaston Fébus, (try **Cave de l'Aude** in place Freycinet) and the patisserie at **Mazas** in rue Labistour. For local history or guide books visit the bookshop **Majuscule** in rue Delcassé.

Festivals

Foix has two major events each year—the Medieval Days of Gaston Fébus

---

Food of the Ariège

The Ariège draws much of its gourmet heritage from its traditional agriculture, in some areas still practised without too much recourse to modern high technology. Throughout the region food remains fairly true to its roots but in the mountains you are likely to enjoy your dining in a small auberge, whereas in the town it will be a formal restaurant. The ingredients, however, will be almost the same—*foie gras*, simple chicken or veal dishes, fresh trout or wild mushrooms.

The area, like its neighbouring region the Aude, enjoys a traditional *cassoulet*, a slow-cooking stew of immense richness with the addition of beans. Ariège *cassoulet* chefs insist on local ingredients and a cooking time of not less than seven hours. *Azinat de choux* is another soupy stew but with a basis of green cabbage. Again cooked slowly, this time for about three hours, the *azinat* requires a ham bone, and added pork, sausage and a special stuffing-type mix called *la rouzolle* which is made up with breadcrumbs, eggs, fat and spices into a plump pancake shape and floated in the stew during its last half-hour of cooking. Traditionally the liquid of the dish is eaten first as soup, with grated cheese, and then the remaining solids eaten as the main meal. *Millas* is a form of corn bread served as a side dish with stews and soups. It is made from a basic mixture of corn flour with water, milk and goose fat, stock stirred and cooked until it becomes loaf-like. *La saucisse de foie*, basically a spicy sausage in which liver rather than pork is used, can be found in most charcuteries throughout Ariège. It can be served hot, cold, dry or very dry. It is often cooked with eggs.

A special drink of Ariège is "L'Hypocras", a concoction known to have been made from the Middle Ages. Its basis is sweet wine in which herbs and mountain plants have been marinated. It is available in many restaurants and bars of the region.

---

celebrations in the second week of July and the fête held the first weekend of September.

Medieval Days is an eight-day extravaganza of processions, *son et lumière*, jousting tournaments and medieval-style markets, with costumes, produce, food and entertainment all in medieval style.

The fête, equally traditional, is launched on the Saturday evening at 6 p.m. by three blasts from the giant canon at the castle. This is followed by a torchlit fancy-dress carnival procession. On the Sunday there are free concerts, music, singing and dancing and an all-night open air ball which is repeated the following night with an impressive firework display, claimed to be the largest free event of its kind in France.

Around Foix
By the main D117, St Girons is 50 km (30 mile) west of Foix, an easy day's return trip from Foix which can also take in the underground river of Labouiche, the prehistoric cave of Mas d'Azil and the medieval village of St Lizier.

Labouiche Caves

Leave Foix by the back road via the village of Vernajoul and look out for the **Labouiche** parking after about 6 km (4 miles). This is a fascinating variation on stalactite and stalagmites, because the marvellous limestone formations are not only some 60 metres (195 ft) down, but are seen from a barge floating on the river which carved the chambers out. (Open 22 May to 30 September from

10 a.m.–noon and 2–6 p.m.; open without break in August; for out-of-season times, Tel. 61-65-04-11.)

Beyond Labouiche you can rejoin the main D117 St Girons road. Some 5 km (3 miles) after the substantial village of La Bastide de Serou, take the right turn for Mas d'Azil. The road climbs up to the ruined **castle of Durban**, now being restored by an environmental group, and then drops to the Arize river. Suddenly you are confronted by an enormous cave and the road disappears into it via a service tunnel cut to the side. To drive through is an experience in itself, but if you wish to see the **Mas d'Azil side chambers**, park and enter on foot. There were people living here 15,000 years ago and much of the art they left behind can be seen on the 45-minute

organized tour—decorated pebbles, carved and engraved bone and a fine head of a neighing horse. (July–September daily 10 a.m.–noon and 2–6 p.m.; April–June afternoons only; October–November, Sundays and holidays only).

If you continue to drive through the cave you will be in the village of Mas d'Azil after a kilometre or so. The **Museum of Prehistory** contains more finds from the cave, notably the spear thrower carved in the shape of a deer (open daily mid-June to mid-September 10 a.m.–noon and 2–6 p.m.; April–mid-June Sundays and holidays only).

From Mas d'Azil there is a direct road to St Girons (25 km/15 miles).

St Girons and St Lizier

St Girons is a bustling small town cut in half by the wide swathe of the Salat river. The **Salat** is to the Pyrenees what the Klondike is to Canada. It has gold in it, which accounts for the emphasis on jewellery shops in St Girons. You can even sign on for gold panning courses at the tourist office (Tel. 61-66-14-11). Before you get too excited, the quantities are very small and there is fierce rivalry between the *orpailleurs* (gold-panners), only one or two of whom are full-time professionals.

The medieval **St Lizier** is built on a hill just 5 minutes by car along the

*R*iverbeds in the Ariège can mean gold, trapped under the pebbles by the constant flow of water from seams above. When they dry out they can leave a natural art of a different sort.

D117 from the centre of St Girons. The settlement dates back to Roman times and by the Middle Ages was an important religious centre with two cathedrals. In the 12th century the Count of Comminges rebelled against the power of the church, sacked St Lizier and founded St Girons as an alternative.

The upper cathedral is closed but it is, anyway, the lower **Romanesque cathedral**, consecrated in 1117, that is the most interesting. The **magnificent vaulting** comes from a later date, and the unusual **octagonal tower** from the 13th century. Highlight is the attractive two-storey **cloister**, the lower part Romanesque, the upper storey dating from the 16th century. Every July a classical **music festival** is held in the cathedral.

Organized tours also cover the old cobbled streets overhung by half-timbered buildings, the small **cathedral museum** where religious treasures include a Romanesque silver bust of St Lizier, and the ancient pharmacy within the old civil hospital (10 June to 15 September 10 a.m.–noon and 2.30–6.30 p.m.).

Return to St Girons via the walled village of Montjoie (3 km/2 miles east of St Lizier) most of which was built in the 14th century.

Bear Country

Rather than return directly to Foix, you could make a broad sweep through the mountains of western Ariège. This is magnificent car touring in landscape so remote that bear trainers were still working here in the early years of the 20th century. And there are some convivial rustic restaurants, too. Begin by taking the D618 south-west.

The Bethmale Valley

In the village of **Audressein** just off the main road (12 km/7½ miles from St Girons) L'Auberge has a solid fuel stove, a terrace overlooking the River Lez and superb views of the Pyrenees.

Just beyond Audressein, continue on the D17 for **Castillon en Couserans** (15 km/9 miles from St Girons). The ruined castle above the village was destroyed in the 17th century by Cardinal Richelieu as part of an anti-Protestant campaign to crush regional strongholds throughout the south of France. You can visit the ruins, which include a photogenic three-layer bell-wall.

Beyond Castillon en Couserans, continue along the D1 into the gorgeous Bethmale Valley. Despite its lushness this has been an unprofitable and abandoned place ever since the mechanization of agriculture—holiday homes are only now reviving it. Its eccentric folk culture includes extraordinary pointed clogs, the curved tips extending several centimetres. According to legend, a spurned young man of the valley used his to impale the hearts of his mistress and her new lover.

The road climbs through the valley past farmhouses with large, steep-roofed hay-drying barns, and on up to the **Col de la Core** (1,395 metres/4,533 ft) from where there are views right (south) to **Mont Valier** (2,838 metres/9,223 ft) the highest peak in this area.

At the easternmost end of the Bethmale Valley, **Seix** (62 km/39 miles) from Foix; 18 km/11 miles from St Girons) is a pretty old town on the River Salat, with its photogenic merchants' houses and white rush of the river. Seix is a popular base for canoeing and rafting; if you would like to try, contact the Kayak Club in rue du Maréchal Foch (Tel. 61-96-56-43).

Some 5 km (3 miles) beyond Seix at the tiny village of **Pont de la Taule** is the Auberge Deux Rivières. From here you can really experience the wild Ariège by turning off south. The narrow road plunges into a deep valley among the high border peaks. Keen hikers should park at the **Col de Pause** (1,527 metres/4,962 ft), where tarmac turns to mud, and continue on foot along the track which is an easy but memorable part of the GR10 footpath.

Back at Pont de la Taule, head east on the marvellous D8 through the **Ustou Valley** to the old spa of Aulus les Bains (20 km/12½ miles). The route follows the River Alet past ruined castles and through a succession of tiny hamlets. A little before Aulus, the D68 snakes up south to the ski station of **Guzet Neige**, a chalet-style modern village. Even out of season it is worth the drive for the stupendous view down to Aulus far below in the Garbet valley bottom.

Beyond the Guzet turning, the D8 climbs up to the Col de la Trape and then drops steeply to **Aulus** which is a small but attractive spa.

South of Aulus the rock walls are decorated by the twinkling **Ars Waterfall**, which you can walk to if you wish along a marked path (about 4 hours there and back).

From Aulus the road onwards climbs steeply up to the **Lake of Lers**, a popular weekend water playground, and on through the Lers pass (1,517 metres/4,930 ft). The road descends to **Vicdessos**, the ancient centre of Ariège iron industry from Roman times right up until the early 20th century. The adjoining village of **Auzat** is its more modern counterpart with a large aluminium factory. There are a series of possible excursions from Vicdessos/Auzat—to the ruined Templar **Castle of Sos**, or along the Vicdessos valley to the **Soulcem Dam**, or up to the mountain villages of **Olbier**, **Goulier** and **Sem** (where a huge balancing rock is believed by some to

have been a prehistoric religious site). Continuing east on the D8 for about 6 km (4 miles), a right turn leads to the village of **Siguer**, a favourite hunting spot of Gaston Fébus, and then climbs up in an extraordinary almost never-ending series of loops to Lercoul, clinging like a vine in the sun to the steep south-facing mountain wall.

You regain the Ariège valley about 15 km (10 miles) east of Vicdessos at the town of Tarascon sur Ariège; Foix is some 17 km (11 miles) north and Ax-les-Thermes about 25 km (15 miles) south.

Into the Pays de Sault

Immediately east of Foix lies the mysterious **Pays de Sault**, drenched in a bitter history to which the centuries have imparted their touristic glamour. This was the last significant refuge of the Cathars, the religion brutally cut out of southern France like a sacrificial heart in the 13th century. Its centre was the **castle of Montségur**, now a romantic ruin perched on a high sheer-sided pinnacle of rock. To reach it from Foix, take the D117 from just south of Foix towards Lavelanet and after about 25 km (16 miles) take the small turn south for Montségur.

Montségur

From the large parking area at the foot of the castle mount (and just before the village itself) the footpath climbs steeply up through the Camp des Cremats where the 225 Cathars were burnt alive. In season you will have to pay at the booth in the woods just beyond. The footpath then winds up even more strenuously and it will be 20 minutes before you stand at the entrance. Inside the walls, where most of the internal structure has now collapsed, the most stiking impression is the small size of the fortress that sheltered some 500 people under siege for almost a year. In fact, the *faydits* (dispossessed aristocrats) lived in the donjon, the garrison in the rest of the castle and most of the Cathars in houses which clung to the rock *outside* the walls. There is a sad beauty about the place, reinforced by the climb up the crumbling staircase to the ramparts. From here the inspiring views make such violence seem unthinkable.

You will get at least some of the explanation in the village of Montségur itself, where the **Museum** (same ticket as the ruins; open daily 1 May–30 September 9.30 a.m.–12.30 p.m. and 2–7 p.m.) is largely devoted to the Cathars. There is a fascinating bookshop, **Au Coin des Temps**, which stocks a variety of books on the subject—and on all things religious and occult. Montségur is a delightful place to stay and there are two small hotels, as well as a *gîte d'étape* and several *gîtes de France*.

Two natural attractions lie just to the east of Montségur. One is the awesome **Gorges de la Frau** which connect with Comus (*see* below). The other (about 15 km/9 miles) is the intermittent spring of Fontestorbes, an extraordinary freak of nature, in which now you see the

The balancing rock at Sem is believed by some to have been a prehistoric religious site.

water—now you don't. Because of its passage through a siphon, the river runs for exactly 36 minutes and then stops for 32 minutes. (Due to its pressure, the water is continuous in winter, however.)

The Cathars

For your enjoyment of the Pays de Sault (and, indeed, the whole of the Pyrénées-Orientales) it is essential to know something of the Cathar religion and the terrible years that climaxed with the burning of the leading Cathars at Montségur in 1244.

It was a time at which Languedoc was struggling to maintain some kind of independence from France, Spain and the Roman Catholic church with its hefty tithes and unpopular restrictions. Understandably, then, Languedoc was fertile ground for a new religion which the people could make their own and use as a nationalist badge. And it was for this reason that the Pope and King Philippe Auguste of France combined to bring it down.

The Cathar religion seems to have begun in the Far East. It shared with Zoroastrianism and Manichaeism the belief that the material world was the creation of the "Powers of Darkness". And it shared with Buddhism the belief in reincarnation and eventual attainment of the "Realm of Light". By the late 9th century these ideas had reached the Balkans as Bogomilism and then spread to the Languedoc as Catharism. Followers were also called Albigeois or Albigenses after the Languedoc town of Albi.

The Cathars insisted that they were true Christians, although, to them, Christ was only a messenger from the Realm of Light and not the Son of God. The teachings included pacifism, vegetarianism, anti-materialism and sexual abstinence. In practice, however, only the leaders of the religion (the *parfaits* and *parfaites*) were strict. The ordinary believers (*croyants*) lived much as they liked. Only when death was close did the croyants receive the *consolamentum* or consolation (popularly known as being "hereticated"), after which they would fast (*endura*) until death. Their souls could then enter the Realm of Light.

Pope Innocent III called for a Crusade against the Cathars upon his election in 1198 and with the failure of the missionary Dominic Guzman (later St Dominique) to make any headway in the region, the Crusade began in 1209 with the sacking of Béziers. It was there the archbishop of Narbonne, leader of the Crusade, gave the famous instruction "Kill them all, God will recognize his own". All the 20,000 inhabitants were massacred. The key territories of the eastern Pyrenees then fell in succession, culminating with Muret, in 1213, where King Pedro of Catalonia, fighting on the Cathar side, was killed.

All this conquered territory went to the professional crusader Simon de Montfort, Count of Leicester. De Montfort was one of the ugliest characters in European history whose idea of making Roman Catholic converts was to tear out the eyes of unbelievers. Peace returned temporarily to the Languedoc in 1218 when de Montfort was killed besieging Raymond VI, count of Toulouse.

A new anti-Cathar Crusade set out in 1226, even more ruthless than the first. Raymond VII, son of the now deceased Raymond VI, and Roger-Bernard II of Foix were forced to make a humiliating peace. As the dreaded Inquisition moved in to root out heresy, so Catharism was forced back into the more inaccessible parts of the mountains and, most especially, Montségur whose natural defences and precarious cliff-top position made it almost impregnable. The pacifist Cathars were now without the protection of the regional leaders and their armies, although they were still supported by a small group of professional soldiers. In desperation a group of soldiers from Montségur went to Avignonet, where the Inquisition was set up, and killed all the Inquisition officials and personnel.

The retaliation cannot have been unexpected. Between six and ten thousand Crusaders surrounded the mountain at Montségur in the Spring of 1243 and maintained the siege for ten months until the Cathars finally broke. On 16 March 1244 the 225 Cathars at Montségur were burnt to death.

The fall of Montségur and death of the leading Cathars marked what was virtually the end of the religion. Four escaped the flames, taking with them an unknown "treasure" of the Cathars, claimed by some to be the Holy Grail. What became of that treasure no one knows for sure, but some believe it was recently rediscovered at an old church on the banks of the Aude—only to disappear again.

Those who claimed to have seen the treasure hidden in the church have all since died in mysterious circumstances.

Tarascon and the Caves

Seventeen kilometres (10 miles) south of Foix on the N20, the ancient town of Tarascon sur Ariège is the centre of the richest cave country in Europe.

Before setting off for the caves, though, call in at Tarascon's **Museum of Prehistory and Archaeology** which is on the east bank of the river.

If you want to stay, the best hotel in the town is the two-star **Poste** which also has a good value restaurant.

There are two major annual celebrations in the town which are marked with grand fêtes. The first, on 20 May, recognizes the ascending of the flocks of sheep and herds of cattle, into their mountain summer pastures. The second, on 30 September, welcomes their return for winter.

Niaux and La Vache Caves

The cave of Niaux, 4 km (2 miles) west of Tarascon on the D8, is a site of international importance. The images on its walls, carved or drawn 13,000 years ago, have found their way into the 20th-century consciousness not only through books but also via all kinds of modern decorative art from wall hangings to place mats. Such is the power of Niaux.

For conservation reasons, visits are in small guided parties carrying hand-torches and it is essential to book in advance (*see* below).

Everything about **Niaux** is impressive, beginning with the giant cave mouth, visible from the opposite side of the valley. You then continue through a small tunnel excavated in 1968. Deep inside are the bison and mammoth outlines that have become so famous, and the

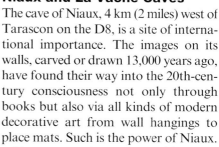

dots and dashes that could have been some early form of writing left by those ancient people in about 10,800 BC (as has been established by modern dating technology).

Before leaving this fascinating and historically significant area, also visit **Grotte de la Vache** (at Alliat, close by Niaux), which has been continuously inhabited for over 10,000 years, and the Niaux village museum where there is an intimate and comprehensive display of Ariège arts, crafts and essentials of life.

Cave Art

When you visit one of the painted caves of the Pyrenees, you are certain to ask, "Why?". What was the purpose of depicting animals in those black recesses? One of the most plausible explanations of cave painting is that it was connected with "hunting magic". This was the view of the famous French scholar Abbé Henri Breuil. In his *Four Hundred Centuries of Cave Art*, he wrote that its main function was: "that the game should be plentiful, that it should increase and that sufficient should be killed".

Others have rejected this theory on the grounds that game in the Upper Palaeolithic was so plentiful as to make magic unnecessary. Furthermore, from the evidence of cave excavation, the animals most often represented in cave art are not those that formed the staple diet. After the discovery of Lascaux during World War II, André Leroi-Gourhan and Annette Laming began to expound a new theory of underground sanctuaries with an organized layout, much as a church has a specific architecture.

A third view holds that cave art is connected with secret initiation ceremonies. This would certainly explain the inaccessibility of the positions within the cave systems and, to some extent, the superimposition of images. This was clearly not decorative art.

Most scholars, with their academic backgrounds, refuse to rely for evidence on the role of art among native peoples today but an understanding of this may be as close as modern man can ever get to understanding the minds of the cave painters 10,000 years ago.

Many of the paintings, for example, bear a strong similarity to those of the Bushmen of the Kalahari Desert. Bushmen in East and South Africa were still making cave paintings in the mid-19th century and in 1874 J.M. Orpen published eight stories that a Bushman named Qing had told to him to explain the paintings in rock shelters—clearly a creation myth and intended to secure the fertility of the species and the success of the chase.

There seems little doubt that native peoples turn to their shamans to appease the spirits and the clearest indication of early shamanic practice in the Pyrenees comes from the cave of Les Trois Frères in Ariège (closed to the public) where a wall engraving seems to show a shaman dressed as a bison plying a hunting bow, surrounded by bison, ibex and horses. The engravings probably date from around 15,000 years ago, each overlaying image added every time a ceremony was held.

One of the latest theories, expounded by Dr Steven Mithen in his book *Thoughtful Foragers: A Study Of Pre-Historic Decision Making*, is that there is no contradiction between the frequency of bison, ibex and reindeer images on the walls and the absence of their remains on the cave floors. If the role of cave art was hunting magic, then the animals depicted would precisely be those that were the most difficult to find and catch.

As a modern witness to cave art you can never put yourself in the position of prehistoric man—but as the lamps flicker in the damp blackness of the caves, your imagination may bring you close to understanding.

Bédeilhac

The artwork in the caves of Bédeilhac, 7 km (4½ miles) west of Tarascon on the D618, differs from that in Niaux in the sheer diversity of art technique employed. Here you can see not only outline paintings and engravings but also half-reliefs in mud and simple "three-dimensional" carvings utilizing the natural shapes of stalactites and stalagmites. There is also the monochrome remnant of what was once almost certainly a bright multi-coloured design.

During World War II, the Nazis used the cave as an aircraft factory.

Lombrives

Lombrives (just south of Tarascon on the N20) is a quite different cave experience. Although it was once inhabited (and, indeed, connects deep in the mountain with the Niaux system), the emphasis here is on the stunning beauty of the natural formations—and on a colourful history which is part legend, part fact. The access train ride is an added excitement, especially for children.

Lombrives is vast—the largest show cave in Europe—and it is no surprise that one of the legends should concern bandits using the network of tunnels as a refuge. Some 250 soldiers are said to have been killed in the caves before the bandits were finally overcome. Another blend of history and legend concerns the Cathars, a group of whom is said to have been walled up alive in the caves by the Inquisition in 1328. As for the formations, like the so-called "mammoth", they are extensive, huge and simply breathtaking.

Ax-les-Thermes

Skin diseases were rife in the Middle Ages—the itch, ringworm, scabies, leprosy, St Anthony's Fire and St Martial's Fire—to which the sulphur baths at Ax-les-Thermes brought relief. But for the Cathars a visit could be cover for a meeting with a *parfait*, as Bertrand de Taix testified to the Inquisition: "I scratched my arms as hard as I could, as if I had scabies; and I lied to people and said, 'I ought to go to the baths at Ax.' "

Ax-les-Thermes remains a popular spa, nowadays specializing predominantly in rheumatic and respiratory problems. Even on a cold day it is not unusual to see scores of people seated around the open-air public footbath, trousers rolled up, feet dangling in. But its 40 sources are also channelled into more luxurious surroundings, like the Hôtel Royal Thermal.

It is best to park in the metered areas in front of the casino (place du Breilh or avenue Delcassé) as the streets within the town itself are narrow.

There is a good, pedestrianized shopping area in the centre of town. For country bread and patisserie, try **Astrié** or **Calvel**, both in rue de l'Horloge. For books, **Beaux Livres** in rue de l'Horloge offers a good selection of guides and histories of the Ariège. For groceries try **Claret**, rue Gaspard-Astrié or **Barata** in place Roussel—local specialities include game, patés and cheeses. For the best choice of wines visit **Cavodoc** in rue Gaspard Astrié or Gianésini at 26 rue Géneral de Gaulle. For souvenirs look at the impressive crystal in the **Hotel Royal Thermal**, **Le Paradis des Enfants** in allées

Ax-les-Thermes is one of the principal spa towns of the Pyrenees, first becoming famous in the Middle Ages when skin diseases were rife.

Couloubret or **La Pastorelle** in avenue du Docteur-Gomma.

There are **street markets** each Tuesday and Saturday morning and also Thursday mornings June to September.

The healing qualities of the waters of Ax-les-Thermes were first recognized in the 13th century, and from the 17th century Ax-les-Thermes started flourishing as a fully-fledged spa. Not surprisingly the town has assembled a wide variety of hotels and guest houses including, more recently, accommodation suitable for winter sports visitors.

Walking near Ax

The tourist offices of Ax are particularly keen to encourage visitors to explore the surrounding Ariège countryside—there are details of fixed itinerary walks of all types available in leaflets. Most of the walks start from the town centre and are scaled according to difficulty. They take between about 20 minutes and a whole day, allowing for picnic and rest stops.

Rated "easy" is the 1 hour 30 minute La Chaumière itinerary which you start from St Vincent's Church following the D613 for a short time until, after a couple of hundred yards, you take a footpath signposted La Chaumière. Good views back to Ax and the Ariège valley. Total time without stops or picnics 1 hour 30 minutes.

For medium-fit walkers, there are gorges, old barns and lakes on an itinerary starting from the bridge in rue du Martinet and exploring the **Lauze Valley** and its gorges. From the starting point, look for the path passing the farm, Entresserres on your right. Climb through a series of bends until reaching the gorge. At the Fournié barns you take a small path to the left up to the village of Ascou. Now follow the path rightwards until reaching the **Goulours Lake**. Return by the same itinerary. Total walking time, 3 hours 30 minutes.

A steep walk up through forest to the village of **Ignaux** is considered suitable only for strong hikers. Start from the town by following the N613 to kilometre marker 1,950. Mid-way through a bend in the road, see a footpath off to the left heading directly into some woods. This leads to the village of Ignaux sited at 1,000 metres (3,250 ft). Return by the same route or by the main road (4–5 hours with stops and picnic).

One of the more popular walking areas close to Ax-les-Thermes is through the **Nature Reserve of Orlu**, 4,250 hectares (10,500 acres) of uninhabited protected countryside giving refuge to izard, marmot, foxes, deer and wild boar. Bird life includes eagles, lammergeiers and capercaillie. The reserve is reached along the D22 which follows the River Oriège through the villages of Orlu and Forges d'Orlu to a parking area. From here the favourite itinerary is to the **lake and refuge d'En Bays**, which is a demanding 8 km (5 mile) walk taking about 4 hours (allowing for rest stops). The route is well signposted and, in summer at least, rewarded with the possibility of a cheap meal, bunk-bed and knowledgeable company at the refuge.

Gorges de la Frau

Ax-les-Thermes is the obvious base for an exploration of the southern Pays de Sault, separated from the area around MONTSEGUR (*see* above) by a barrier of mountains. The only way through this barrier is the magnificent Gorges de la Frau, so narrow that no road has ever been built through it. From Ax leave northwards on the scenic D613 which climbs over the 1,361 metres (4,420 ft) **Col de Marmare** to a fertile plateau. Some 4 km (2 miles) beyond the pass, the village of **Prades** earned a short and scandalous anecdote in the *true book Montaillou*. Pierre Clergue, priest of Montaillou in the 14th century, had brought his lover Béatrice de Planissoles to the church of St Peter in Prades where he had made up a bed. Béatrice was unnerved:

"How can we do such a thing in the church of Saint Peter?" she asked.

"Much harm it will do Saint Peter!" he replied.

Montaillou

From the D613 the tiny village of Montaillou is reached by a narrow lane to the right, just beyond Prades. It has become famous through the book by Professor Emmanuel Le Roy Ladurie, which reconstructed life there in the early 14th century, using records of the Inquisition, now in the Vatican Library. **Montaillou** was the last village in France in which a significant number of families were Cathar. Although the leadership of the religion had been murdered at Montségur in 1244, the Inquisition accused 25 Montaillou villagers of heresy and tried them between 1318 and 1325. The Inquisitor, Jacques Fournier, went on to become Pope of Avignon in 1334 as Benedict XII.

Today only a handful of people live at Montaillou and there is nothing spectacular to see, but given the knowledge of life revealed by the Vatican documents, a visit can be very evocative. The **château**, now in ruins, stands at the top of the village, and the **church** at the bottom.

As you stroll around the village only a little imagination is needed to call back the fields of oats, wheat, turnips and hemp, the women fetching water balanced on their heads, and the men driving their asses and donkeys up from the valley loaded with vital supplies of olive oil, salt and wine.

These stone houses or *ostals* had immense spiritual significance. In the same family for generations—just like the castles and palaces of the aristocracy—each *ostal* brought its own magic or luck, which had to be protected by keeping bits of fingernail or hair from dead ancestors. All socializing went on inside the *ostal* (there was no tavern). Here family gathered around the fire, their only entertainment the meal and their own conversation—illiteracy was high but spinning a yarn was a vital and common skill.

The ordinary people also shared the aristocratic habit of arranged marriages and women were objects used to secure alliances between families in the village. Indeed, the Troubadour poets, who flourished in southern France and northern Spain in the 13th century, sang of a true romantic love that existed only outside marriage. Wife-beating was common and the physical work hard.

The people were literally God-fearing but the church itself was hated for its tithes. Sometimes the church was lax about collection but at other times the demands were rigidly enforced and non-payment could result in a fatal meeting with the Inquisition.

 The **Gorges de la Frau** lie on the opposite side of the D618 from

Montaillou, beyond the village of Comus. There is a **gîte d'étape** in Comus which also doubles as an **adventure centre**, specializing in caving, trekking, horse-trekking and (in season) cross-country skiing: **Centre Ecole de Pleine Nature** (Tel. 68-20-33-69).

From Comus a good track leads to the start of the gorge (3 km/2 miles). Fortunately, the tourism industry has not yet arrived and there are no pavements, handrails or refreshment kiosks, just the magnificent sheer rock walls, towering so high they all but obscure the sky in places. The trickling River Hers which carved the canyon is sometimes steeply below, hidden by woods which positively vibrate with the din of insects and occasionally crack with something larger, such as deer. On the cliffs overhead, choughs spatter their electric cackle.

If you are really efficient you will organize a rota system with your party so that you can make the walk one-way (about 1 hour) and have the car and driver waiting where the road south from Belesta is stopped by the north end of the gorges.

You can also enjoy the spectacle from above by driving (or walking) the forest track that climbs *up* from Comus. After about 3 km (2 miles), turn left at the Col de la Gargante, a crossroads of forest tracks. A little further on you will start to be aware of an enormous drop to your left. This is the **Pas de L'Ours**, a viewing point which is simply breathtaking. Park safely and taking the greatest care, peer over the edge into what seems an almost bottomless abyss.

If you would like to continue on the tracks, you will need a good map,

preferably the *Randonnées Pyrénéenne* 1:50,000 scale Montségur (12)—and a reliable sense of direction.

The Road to Andorra

South of Ax-les-Thermes the N20 climbs along the Ariège valley towards its source high on the encircling frontier peaks of Andorra.

Mérens, about 9 km (6 miles) south of Ax, stands on the GR10 footpath with access to some of the best walking in the region. It is also home of the famous **Mérens horses**. You can combine both by crossing to the left bank of the River Ariège via the attractive old stone bridge beside the main road. The GR10 climbs through woods into the high pasture where you are almost certain to come across the sturdy black horses, believed to be directly descended from the wild horses of prehistory. Some of these belong to an Englishman, Kevin Henshall, who, together with his wife Hélène, has dedicated himself to breeding authentic

M érens horses are believed to be the closest relatives of the wild horses of European prehistory. Nowadays, not so wild, you can see them at Mérens-les-Vals.

Mérens. You can arrange to see the horses by calling at their house in the upper village (Tel. 61-64-03-92).

Some 10 km (6 miles) on from Mérens, the road climb gets really tough at the tiny hamlet of Hospitalet. The long climb over the top is rewarded by exhilarating views and will remain the only eastern gateway into Andorra, the road access for which lies some 8 km (5 miles) above Hospitalet. Alternatively, the new Puymorens tunnel plunges into the mountain at Hospitalet to emerge in the brightly-lit landscape of the Pyrénées-Orientales.

A Centre for Gourmets—
Ruined Castles and Gorges

An out-of-the-way centre, Quillan is ideal for enjoying the Audois cuisine, which offers traditional dishes of note. South of Quillan are spectacular gorges and a landscape dotted with ruined castles. An added bonus is sampling the prize-winning wines of the region.

Quillan

Quillan must rate as one of the least-known touring centres of the Pyrenees, yet it makes an excellent base for some of the most accessible excitments of the range. Sitting squarely on the River Aude, by this stage a river of impressive dimensions, Quillan is the small but vigorous capital of the area known as Pyrénées-Audois.

The rushing torrents which feed into the Aude have scoured out the limestone to create some extensive and fascinating cave systems—some open to the general public, others for dedicated cavers only.

Each July and August Quillan hosts an important arts festival when accommodation is at a premium. Another high spot of the calendar is the arrival of international-class cyclists and special extra traffic police during an important road race each 17 August. Both visitors and local residents pack the pavements and then the restaurants in celebration of the event. Rugby, which was introduced to the town during the two world wars, is also enjoyed with grand passion and, during the winter, local derbies are hotly contested, both on and off the pitch. There are important county markets, a small fruit and vegetable event each Wednesday, swelling to a bumper general market every second Wednesday of the month.

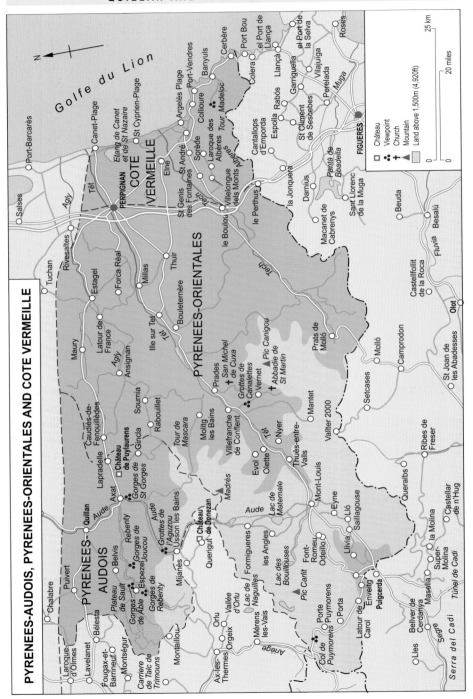

PYRENEES-AUDOIS, PYRENEES-ORIENTALES AND COTE VERMEILLE

Golfe du Lion

COTE VERMEILLE

PYRENEES-ORIENTALES

PYRENEES-AUDOIS

FIGUERES

PERPIGNAN

Port-Barcarès
Port-Barcarès
Salses
Tuchan
Rivesaltes
Estagel
Forca Real
Maury
Latour de France
Ansignan
Ille sur Tet
Bouletemère
Thuir
Millas
Caudiès-de-Fenouillèdes
Lapradelle
Sournia
Rabouillet
Château de Puylaurens
Gincla
Gorges de St Gorges
Quillan
Axat
Aude
Reberty
Gorges de Reberty
Espezel
Joucou
Gorges de Ablé
Belvis
Plateau de Sault
Carriere de Talc de Trimouns
Puivert
Chalabre
Laroque d'Olmes
Lavelanet
Fougax-et-Barrineuf
Montségur
Bélesta
Montaillou
Mijanès
Querigut
Château de Donezan
Madrès
Tour de Mascara
Molitg les Bains
Villefranche de Conflent
Prades
San Michel de Cuxa
Grottes de Canalettes
Vernet
Abbadie de St Martin
Pic Canigou
Evol
Olette
Nyer
Tet
Thuès-entre-Valls
Mont-Louis
Aude
Lac de Matemale
Les Angles
Lac des Bouillouses
Formiguères
Mantet
Prats de Molló
Setcases
Vallter 2000
Eyne
Olló
Saillagouse
Font-Romeu
Odeillo
Llivia
Pic Carlit
Enveitg
Puigcerda
Latour de Carol
Porté
Col de Puymorens
Porta
Puymorens
Mérens les-Vals
Lac de Naguilles
Vallée d'Orlu
Orlu
Orgeix
Ax-les-Thermes
Usson les Bains
Grottes de l'Aguzou
Quérigut
Ille
Ariège
Segre
Serra del Cadi
Túnel de Cadi
Bellver de Cerdanya
Masella
Super-Molina
la Molina
Castellar de n'Hug
Lles
Queralbs
Ribes de Freser
St Joan de les Abadesses
Camprodon
Molló
Castellar
Ribes
Olot
Castellfollit de la Roca
Besalú
Beuda
Fluvia
Sant Llorenç de la Muga
Panta de Boadella
Macanet de Cabrenys
Darnius
la Jonquera
le Perthus
Villelongue dels Monts
Montagnes des Albères
Sant Climent de Sescebes
Espolla
Rabós
Garriguella
Vilajuiga
Peralada
Muga
Roses
el Port de la Selva
el Port de Llança
Llança
Colera
Cantallops d'Emporda
Port Bou
Cerbère
Banyuls
Port-Vendres
Laroque des Albères
Tour Madeloc
Collioure
Sorède
St André
St Genis des Fontaines
le Boulou
Elne
Argelès Plage
St Cyprien-Plage
Canet-Plage
Etang de Canet et de St Nazaire
Tet
Agly
Tech
Tet
Agly
Aude
Ariège

Estagel

Légende / Legend:
- □ Château
- •:• Viewpoint
- ✝ Church
- ▲ Mountain
- Land above 1,500m (4,920ft)

25 km
20 miles

Aude Food and Wine

The Aude region is fast developing a reputation to rival the gourmet sophistication of the Dordogne. An annual culinary prize is given to traditional dishes of distinction. These feature *cassoulet*, created from local produce and, for true authenticity, cooked in local earthenware pottery. Basically beans and meat (pork, goose and/or local sausage), it also reflects the character of the chef in its seasoning, spicing and other vegetable ingredients. The resulting dish is often served straight from the oven in its earthenware pot, boiling hot and crusty. Other local specialities are *fricassées*—another stew-type dish but with the beans served separately. The beans are boiled with garlic and parsley in one pot, while the meat (usually ham or pork) is cooked in another, together with onion, vinegar, wine, gherkins and tomato puree. The rich *civet de sanglier* is made from wild boar, marinaded in wine, oil and garlic and flambéd in brandy. Specialist pâtés are pork liver, chicken liver, game, and giblet. Fish from the Audoise coastline features frequently on inland menus—fresh oysters and mixed fish soup particularly.

Prize-winning AOC wines of the Aude region include: (reds) Terre Natale, a 1985 Fitou; the 1985 Château Etang des Colombes Corbières; 1988 Château de Ventenac Minervois; Château Ste Eulalie Astruc Minervois (1988); Pouzols-Minervois 1988 and the Côtes de La Malepère 1987 from Domaine de Fournery. White wines: Robinson, Blanquette de Limoux; the Blanc de Blanc des Demoiselles and Château Rouguette sur Mer from Jacques Boscary (1988). Rosé: 1988 Corbières from Cucugnan and Château Rivals from Charlotte Capdevila. Prize-winning vin-de-pays are the 1988 Fécos from the Cave Cooperative of Limoux (red), the Domaine Casteras Mièle of Jean and Philippe Mièle (white) and Viven Grandclaus (rosé).

Of interest in the town is the 12th-century **Church of Our Lady** containing a wonderful old organ taken from the former cathedral St Benoit of Alet. The ruins of a medieval fortified castle, its square design unusual for this part of the range, stand on a small hill overlooking the town. Originally built by the Visigoths in the 5th century, it was re-built in 1223 only to be attacked and badly damaged in 1575 by the Huguenots.

If you have any desire to learn or practise river canoeing, this is the place. The fast-running water of the Aude is considered ideal and fully qualified tuition is available at the Canoe-Kayak centre at the Forge Leisure Centre on the southern outskirts of town.

Through the Gorges

There is a whole series of spectacular gorges south of Quillan, carved by the Aude river.

Follow the main D117 towards Axat. First is the smooth- walled **Defilé Pierre-Lys**, cut away on one side to accommodate the road. The first road through the gorge was due to Abbot Felix Armand, a 35-year old priest who, in 1777, decided there had to be a better way of travelling between the villages of St Martin Lys and Quillan than having to

*T*he Pyrénées-Audois, Pyrénées-Orientales and Côtes Vermeille regions.

climb the mountains in between. Fired by his enthusiasm, the road was cut by nothing more than muscle power, picks and spades. The abbot's achievement was recognized even by Napoleon. "It is a pity this man was a priest," he said. "I would have made him into an army general." The tomb of the abbot is in the small cemetery of St Martin Lys.

Some people still take a more difficult route through the gorge—the climbers who swing from the almost sheer walls above the road, and the canoeists who struggle through the foaming waters.

Next come the **Gorges de St Georges**, some 14 km (9 miles) south of Quillan, just past the small town of Axat. Finally, the canyon opens into the long curve of the wider **Gorges de l'Aude**, where the occasional long-deserted home testifies to the gloom of gorge-bottom living. The limestone has been extensively bored out into cave systems and the finest of these, Aguzou, is open to the more adventurous but not to the casual passer-by. Rather, groups of ten are escorted by an experienced caver for the day-long visit. You will need to reserve your place well in advance by phone (Tel. 68-20-45-38), wear sensible water-proof footwear and bring a picnic lunch. The trip costs more than 200F per person which may seem expensive, but the authentic underground experience and the chance to see some exquisite and undamaged concretions and crystals is worth every centime.

The castle at **Usson les Bains**, at the southern end of the Aude gorges, is the place to which the four Cathars who escaped Montségur fled in 1244 (*see* MONTSEGUR above). There is evidence that the four brought with them some kind of "treasure" vital to the Cathars but no scholar has ever discovered what. A few years ago, however, there were rumours that valuable medieval jewellery had been discovered hidden in a church further downstream. What is known for certain is that several people connected with the church have either disappeared or died in mysterious circumstances.

You can visit the ruined castle, above the village on the east wall of the gorge, but because of its poor condition it is dangerous to enter.

Afterwards, you might enjoy a meal at the nearby fish farm, the **Relais de la Pisciculture**.

After Usson you can turn eastwards towards Ax les Thermes and then north following signs for the Col du Pradel from where the road will lead through a succession of minor gorges, **Rebenty**, **Able** and **Joucou** before emerging once more on the main D117 for Quillan, a total of about 90 km (56 miles).

Puilaurens and Puivert

Like Usson, the ruined castles of Puilaurens and Puivert, to the east and west of Quillan, both have important associations with the history of the Cathars.

Puilaurens, some 20 km (12½ miles) from Quillan along the D117, broods high on a ridge above the village of Lapradelle, its outer walls and towers substantially intact. From the parking the castle is a short walk ending in a steepish path which snakes up past the cunning defences which guard the entrance (open at all times). Like other castles of the region, Puilaurens was a refuge for the *faydits* (dispossessed aristocrats) who opposed the extension of "French" power into the Languedoc. It fell to the French in 1255. The ruins on their turret of rock are overgrown now and, although it is possible to get to the donjon and onto the walls in places, great care should be exercised.

The ruins of the **castle of Puivert** lie about 16 km (10 miles) from Quillan along the D117 in the opposite direction from Puilaurens (that is, west). In contrast to the menace of Puilaurens, Puivert stands on a softly contoured hill just above the village and has a more palatial air. In fact, Puivert was the centre of troubadour culture.

Between the 11th and 13th centuries, when marriages were a matter of politics rather than love, the troubadours sang of true love. They were a phenomenon particular to southern France and northern Spain (and northern Italy) and, harmless as they may sound, they were considered dangerous by Paris, for their language was Occitan—the *langue d'Oc* or language of the south of France. As champions of this language they were the natural allies of the Cathars whose growing religious movement was also becoming the "religion of the south". In most respects they were opposites. The Cathars were pacifists but tournaments were a regular feature of celebrations at Puivert. And, in theory, Cathars aspired to abstinence from sex, whereas it was love that the troubadours celebrated. Nevertheless, the troubadours became the messengers of the persecuted Cathars as they moved in secret from one friendly castle to the next.

Standing inside the *donjon* amid the ruins it is not difficult to conjure up the banquets, concerts and tournaments, nor the terrible three days when Puivert fell to the anti-Cathars. The end of both the troubadours and the Cathars was near (*see* MONTSEGUR).

There are *son et lumières* performances at the castle throughout July and August.

Car Tours

Using Quillan as a base there are several undemanding car tours which can be undertaken in a day. It is best, perhaps, to define your specific interest and then follow an itinerary serving that interest. For example, details of a tour of the several marvellous gorges of the region have already been given in the text:

Quillan—Gorges de Pierre-Lys—Gorges de St Georges—Gorges de l'Aude—Gorge du Rebenty—Gorge d'Able—Gorge de Joucou—Quillan (90 km; 56 miles).

Visits to the two main castles of the area, Puilaurens and Puivert, can be pleasantly incorporated into two day-long tours featuring some of the remote countryside, not just of the Aude Pyrenees but also of the neighbouring Fenouillèdes to the east and Ariège to the west.

Quillan—Gorges de Pierre-Lys—Axat—Lapradelle (Puilaurens Castle)—Sournia—Rabouillet—Molitg-les-Bains—Col de Jau—Santa Colombe-sur-Guette—Gorges de St Georges—Axat—Quillan (140 km; 87 miles).

Quillan—Camp-Ferrier (Castle of Puivert)—Belesta—Siphon of Fontestorbes—Belesta—Col de la Croix de Morts—Plateau de Sault—Belvis—Quillan (75 km; 47 miles).

Where the Mountains Meet the Mediterranean

This is an area rich in cultural history and in the Mediterranean climate. Romanesque architectural gems can be seen at Elne, St Martin du Canigou and Serrabone Priory. There is abundant scope for sightseeing, wine tasting, and exploring the mountain regions of Canigou and Carlit (*see* map on page 162).

Perpignan

Perpignan is the most cosmopolitan city in the Pyrenees, and its population of 120,000 is composed of Spanish Catalans, Algerians, Moroccans, Gipsies, French North Africans and immigrants from other parts of France, as well as the city natives. The successive waves of immigration are hardly surprising given Perpignan's position on the flat Roussillon plain close

The Pyrénées-Orientales have a dry climate and are bathed in bright Mediterranean light.

to the Spanish border, its climate, its proximity to both the sea and the mountains and its self-perpetuating vitality. But such an exuberant racial mix has also, sadly, brought its problems and racial violence is on the increase. The more recent immigrants tend to live as communities in the central area, where Arab dress is commonplace; those who arrived earlier have tended to drift out to the modern suburbs and to surrounding villages, some of which are entirely Catalan speaking.

Situated right beside the Narbonne–Barcelona motorway, from which a fast road system leads rapidly to the centre, **Perpignan** is easily reached by car. The old central area is bounded by a pentagonal inner ring

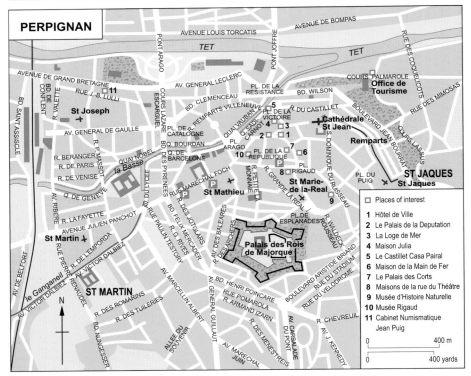

Places of interest

1 Hôtel de Ville
2 Le Palais de la Deputation
3 La Loge de Mer
4 Maison Julia
5 Le Castillet Casa Pairal
6 Maison de la Main de Fer
7 Le Palais des Corts
8 Maisons de la rue du Théâtre
9 Musée d'Histoire Naturelle
10 Musée Rigaud
11 Cabinet Numismatique
  Jean Puig

*T*own plan
of Perpignan.

road with the Têt river to the north and the Palais des Rois de Majorque to the south. Parking on the street is always difficult and it is advisable to use one of the signposted and inexpensive multi-storey car-parks.

The station is outside the central pentagon, about ten minutes walk to the west of it along avenue Général de Gaulle. Long-distance buses stop outside the station but buses into the surrounding area leave from the gare routière, close to the south bank of the

Têt river just off avenue Général Leclerc. The shuttle to Perpignan-Rivesaltes International Airport, just to the north of the city, also leaves from the gare routière.

Sightseeing

Most of the shopping and sites of Perpignan are conveniently reached from place Arago, the square on the canal known as **La Basse,** flanked by lawns and flowerbeds, which cuts through the north-west corner of the city and runs into the Têt. The conservatory-style **Palmarium** café is the main landmark of the square, fringed by palm trees; in World War II it was a meeting place for *passeurs*—the men and women who guided people over the escape routes into Spain.

Just off the square to the east in rue de l'Ange (no. 16) is the recently renovated **Rigaud Museum**. Born in Perpignan in 1659, Hyacinthe Rigaud specialized in portraits and became court painter to Louis XIV. Apart from his works which feature a number of self-portraits, there are also paintings by early Catalan masters and by modern artists, including Maillol and Picasso.

North from place Arago along the east side of the Basse canal is the red-brick gateway-cum-château known as the **Castillet**, built mostly in the 14th century, and which now houses the **Casa Pairal**, the Museum for Roussillon Arts and Crafts. There are eight rooms in the Casa Pairal, exploring life as it used to be lived in rural Roussillon and including a reconstruction of a house in the Haute Aspres, the region of foothills which lie to the west of Perpignan.

Just to the east of place Arago is the famous **place de la Loge**. Given its long history as the focus of city activity, its tiny dimensions come as a surprise, yet the *sardana* is somehow danced here regularly in summer, close up against the tables of the pavement cafés. Visitors are welcome to join the circles of dancers and move to the mournful notes of the cobla band, provided they know the steps.

At the start of the French Revolution, after a five-day hunt for government agents and tax gatherers who were thrown into prison, the local people celebrated with a dinner in place de la Loge and gave thanks in a mass in the cathedral at the far end. When six customs officers arrived in Perpignan two years later to try to enforce duties, one of them was hacked to death with bayonettes and the other five men were severely beaten.

Right by the entrance to the square is the 15th-century **Palais de la Deputation**, followed by the 16th-century **Hôtel de Ville** (town hall) and the 14th-century **Loge de Mer**. Just inside the main gates of the town hall, visible even after closing time, is Maillol's famous statue, **La Méditerranée**, also known as La Pensée; a second Maillol work, **Venus**, stands on the far side of the square. The sculptor was born nearby at Banyuls sur Mer where he also returned to work in later life; both statues are curvaceous nudes in the sensual rather than sexual style for which Maillol is famous. The **Loge de Mer** is now an architecturally unique fast-food restaurant, worth the cost of a bag of chips just for a look. However there are better and more appropriate cafés on the north side of the square. The **cathedral** lies just beyond place de la Loge, along rue St Jean, unimposing with its exterior in brick and pebbles, except for the wrought-iron frame which tops the tower and in which hangs a bell dating from 1418. Work on the church began in 1324 but the plans were altered in 1433 and the finished building, consecrated in 1509, is in Gothic style with a single nave. It became a cathedral almost a century later in 1601. A passage below the organ case leads to the **Chapel of Notre Dame dels Correchs**, part of the original Romanesque church on the site known as St Jean Le Vieux, which was consecrated in 1025.

From place Arago, the **Palais des Rois de Majorque** is best reached by car or taxi; otherwise it's about a

15-minute walk due south. This is the largest site in Perpignan and with a long history. The massive walls are entered by a ramp on the western side in rue des Archers where there is a carpark. The ramp leads up to gardens from which there are marvellous views inland to the Canigou massif. In the centre of the fortifications stands the much earlier, modest palace which was begun in 1276 by King James of Majorca and which has just been restored. Entry is via the cour d'honneur, a warmly welcoming courtyard where the use of pebbles, along with the brick and marble, is sympathetic to the nearby sea.

To the far east of the central area, just inside the ring road, is place Cassanyes, just north of which is the **Church of St Jacques**, the starting point for the Good Friday Procession of the Passion (*Procession de la Sanch*) in which "penitents" dressed in red and black robes with pointed hoods carry the 15th-century wooden Christ.

The best shopping lies around **place Arago**. Immediately on the east side, along rue de l'Ange, there is a Quartier Pieton (pedestrian area) with shops specializing in food, fashion, gifts, jewellery and books. But it is the area between place de la Loge and place Rigaud, where the old warehouses have been converted, that has now become the most chic with all kinds of both elegant and trendy boutiques. Place Rigaud, with a statue of the painter Hyacinthe Rigaud to one side, has a **fruit and vegetable market** every morning. East lies the area into which many North Africans and also gipsies have moved, with only a few, specialist shops but an excellent daily market for general goods in place Cassanyes. On the fringes of this area there are also a number of more exotic restaurants specializing in food from the Far East and North Africa.

As a large, modern city close to a motorway, Perpignan naturally also has its hypermarkets, all built close to the southern ring road. The best of these is **Auchan**, up-market and selling almost every kind of product; the cheapest, with a more confined range, is Leclerc. There are also hypermarkets specializing in products such as sports clothing and in DIY and gardening.

A market stall in place de la Loge, Perpignan—there are markets, too, in place Cassanyes and place Rigaud.

Catalan Food

Long dulled by a frantic rush to satisfy the tourist taste, the cuisine of the
Catalan Pyrenees, especially on the
Mediterranean coast is once again re-
discovering its authentic flavour, a
mixture of the local fish, fruit and vegetables with the spices of southern
Europe. Conversely, in the mountains
where little glamour has been associated with local food and where the introduction of deep-freezes and mi-
crowaves has diverted attention away
from the traditional, there is a growing awareness of the value of regional
cuisine and an understanding that the
visitor seeks quality and integrity in
mountain repasts. The Pyrénées-
Orientales are richly served by nature,
especially the coast with its
Mediterranean fish specialities, such as
anchovies and sardines, oysters and
mussels. The valleys of Roussillon provide a wide variety of fruit and vegetables, including kiwi fruits, peaches,
nectarines, cherries, artichokes and asparagus, while from the mountains
come dairy foods, game and wild
stocks such as mushrooms, berries and
nuts. Now the simple feasts once associated with the village auberges can
be found on international-class restaurant menus. Expect to find cuts of
wild boar, wild pigeon, hare, rabbit
and izard. In season wild vegetable
treats include mushrooms such as
morel, *cep* and the vivid yellow
chanterelle. Wild raspberries, straw-
berries and hazelnuts are also available. Speciality dishes of the region include *cassoulet*, a hearty bean stew
with meat, notably sausage and bacon;
bouillinade, a local mixed fish stew;
esclade, a soup flavoured with garlic,
thyme, oil and eggs; and *cargolade*,
snails barbecued on a fire of vine
branches.

Cultural Tour

Place Arago—rue de l'Ange (Musée
Rigaud at no. 16)—rue de la Clocher
d'Or—place Jean Jaures—place de la
Loge (statue of Venus by Maillol,
Loge de Mer, Hôtel de Ville containing Maillol's La Méditerranée, Palais
de la Deputation)—rue St Jean—place
Gambetta (cathedral)—rue St Jean—
place de la Loge—rue Blanc—place de
Verdun (Le Castillet/Casa Pairal). The
church of St Jacques in the Miranda
Gardens is just to the north of place
Cassanyes and may be best reached by
taxi. The Palais des Rois de Majorque
is also best reached by car or taxi (entrance rue des Archers).

Shopping Tour

Place Arago—rue de l'Ange and the
surrounding streets of the Quartier
Pieton—rue Mailly—place Jean Jaure
—place de la Loge—rue des
Marchands—rue de l'Argenterie—
place Rigaud (morning fruit and vegetable market)—rue Emile Zola—place
Font Neuve—rue Llucia—place Cassanyes (morning market for general
goods). The hypermarkets on the outer
ring road to the south are well signposted, reached by car along avenue
des Baleares; Auchan (pronounced
Ocean) is the best.

The Têt Valley

From Perpignan the RN116 follows
the broad River Têt past fields laden
with vines, peaches, nectarines, apples,
melons and kiwi fruits.

St Feliu d'Amont, 14 km (9 miles)
from Perpignan is worth a stop for its
marvellous **fortified church doors**,

examples of the intricate wrought iron and stud work of the eastern Pyrenees. Next, **Millas** is a once-fortified town with fragments of surviving wall, where a lofty parade of 100-year-old lime trees shelters a natural drinking water fountain, renowned for its theraputic qualities. Buy some of the locally-pressed olive oil and then detour on the D612 to the **Col de la Bataille** where, above the col to the east, the restored hermitage of **Força Réal** gives magnificent views over the plain and into the mountains.

Continuing along the valley brings you to **Ille sur Têt** where there is a daily fruit and vegetable market in the huge square beside the main road (in summer 9 a.m., winter 11 a.m.). This is second in size only to Perpignan. The old town still shelters behind well-preserved walls and ancient gateways, its narrow streets making driving a hair-raising experience. Call in at the **Museum of Sacred Art** in the 16th-century **Hospice of St Jacques**. Then take the road across the Têt for the extraordinary wind-eroded sandstone cliffs, known as **Les Orgues** (organ pipes).

Just beyond Ille lies one of three great Romanesque monuments in the Pyrénées-Orientales. Turn left off the main valley road to the attractive medieval village of **Bouleternère** and continue through the gorge to the hilltop

The exquisite 11th-century priory of Serrabone (or Serrabonne) is one of the three great Romanesque monuments of the Pyrénées-Orientales.

9th-century chapel and a 17th-century church constructed from the ruins of an earlier castle and containing a magnificent retable by the Catalan master sculptor Vincent Sunyer.

Prades

The main town of the valley is Prades, some 50 km (30 miles) from Perpignan. It was here in July 1789 that the French Revolution hit the eastern Pyrenees. Every part of France had its own motives for joining the mass movement. In Roussillon it was the imposition of the hated salt tax known as the *gabelle*, something Louis XIV had promised would never be imposed when he officially annexed the region in 1659. The salt warehouse in Prades was broken open, as was another for tobacco, the local people helped themselves and the tax collectors were thrown out. The first days were heady with the exhilaration of righting perceived wrongs but noble sentiments soon gave way to the personal desire to settle old scores.

Nowadays a faint scent of revolution remains in the air with the summertime influx of hippies, who ignore scornful looks, to make the **Tuesday morning market** a more colourful event. The town's main claim to fame is as home-in-exile of international cellist **Pablo Casals** (1876–1973), a Spanish Republican who fled over the

 Priory of Serrabone. Serrabone is distinguished by an 11th-century construction in local stone, much like mountain homes of the region. But inside, by contrast, a cloister gallery and an even more ornately carved tribune in pink marble, with flower and animal motifs, suggest that something far richer once stood here.

A little further along the main Têt valley, clustering around its hill-top church on the north bank, **Eus** has earned itself the title of one of the prettiest villages in France. Facing **Pic Canigou**, which is the sacred mountain of all Catalan people, the village is flower-filled and shaded by Mediterranean oak trees. Sights include a

Romanesque Architecture

Once you have seen Romanesque architecture you will find it easy to recognize—but it is much harder to define. In the Pyrenees, the style swept in with the Christian Reconquest from the 11th century onwards. As the Moors (who had landed in Spain in AD 711) were forced back, so the Christian church built outposts to consolidate its gains, and these were inevitably in Romanesque style.

Of course, most building was in wood and it is only the few stone buildings that come down to us. The barrel vault, as at Ripoll and St Pere de Rodes, was developed as a replacement for the wooden roofs which were a fire hazard. There were few windows because the full strength of the walls was needed to support the weight. Thus the barrel vault in time gave way to ribbed vaults and windows became more possible. Eventually, windows became the single most obvious feature of Romanesque. The openings were paired in the *ajimez* style, so that there were pillars to either side and a single pillar in the centre, all topped by carved capitals; the openings ended in horseshoe shapes at the top, set off against a rectangular frame (*alfiz*).

As the Pyrenees became "safe" for Christians, so there were pilgrimages into Spain. Along the routes, pilgrimage churches tried to reflect the holy place that was the ultimate goal of the pilgrims. You can see echoes of the cathedral at Santiago de Compostela, for example, at many points. Needed to accommodate huge numbers, these pilgrimage churches were characterized by long naves, extensive galleries and tall towers, which perhaps served as landmarks. Nowhere is this cult of towers more obvious than in the Boí valley where numerous churches compete. Sant Climent de Taüll is the finest in the valley, the windows in its six-storey tower getting bigger as they get higher, so as to compensate for the effects of perspective. The churches of the Boí valley, like those in Andorra and at Serrabone, are in a rustic "dry stone" style but many others are richly ornated, with superb cloisters.

Moorish Spain had some influence on style (the Moors had a higher standard of architecture and culture than the Christians at the time) but France was more significant. In the Catalan Pyrenees, Lombard Romanesque was very powerful, particularly as a result of trade with Italy. Perpignan Cathedral (then in Spain) is an example. Lombard influence is clear in the bell towers which have many storeys with pilaster strip decoration, also known as Lombard bands (that is, a "fake" pilaster or pillar created from raised stonework).

border during the Spanish Civil War. Each summer the music festival that he began is continued in his honour, an unlikely hero of the fight against Fascism, who often played rousing revolutionary songs on his cello to entertain the troops. There is a small **museum to Casals** in the tourist office close to the main square.

The **music festival** takes place in the **monastery of St Michel de Cuxa**, on the outskirts of the town to the south. As you approach, the square tower with its typically Romanesque *ajimez* (paired) windows is dramatically set off against Canigou rising up behind. Founded in the 9th century, remodelled by Abbot Oliver in the 11th century, but abandoned by the late 18th century, St Michel de Cuxa has been extensively renovated, often with new material (some of the original is in the

Cloisters museum in New York). The monastery is open daily (8 a.m.–noon and 3–6 p.m.) but if you are in Prades during July or August, beg, borrow or steal a ticket for the nightly concerts. The **church of St Pierre** in the market square in Prades is also itself worth a visit for a massive screen by Joseph Sunyer.

Accommodation in Prades is limited, although there are two new hotels on the ring road. Alternatively, you could take the road out to the attractive spa of **Molitg les Bains** (7 km/4 miles) where there are several good hotels.

Villefranche de Conflent

Some 6 km (4 miles) beyond Prades, the Têt valley narrows to a gorge, a natural strategic position first exploited in 1092 by William Raymond, Count of Cerdagne and grandson of Wilfred who founded the marvellous Abbey of **St Martin du Canigou** near Vernet. The village was originally called Villa Libéra— today **Villefranche de Conflent**. As you approach along a curve of the valley floor, the steep-sided mountains suddenly crowd in and the mighty fortifications appear, blocking the way. First constructed in the 13th century, the walls were expanded in the 15th century when the unusual vaulted internal wall walkway was created, half destroyed by the French when Villefranche was in Spanish hands, and finally rebuilt by Vauban, King Louis XIV's military engineer, after the Treaty of the Pyrenees (1659) confirmed the town as French.

The main sites of Villefranche are the **ramparts**, the **old cobbled streets** themselves with their arty craft shops and the **Cova Bastéra**, a natural cave enlarged as a gun emplacement. In 1674, anti-French rebels led by Charles de Llar plotted to use a secret tunnel connecting the cave with the town to surprise the garrison. Llar was betrayed by his own daughter, a dramatic twist which Louis Bertrand turned into the novel *L'Infante*.

High on the hill above the town, **Fort Liberia** was added by Vauban to strengthen the defences. It has been by turns a prison (four women accused of an infamous poisoning in the 18th century spent the rest of their lives there) and a World War I POW camp. Access is by a thigh-groaning 999-step underground stairway or by minibus or horse.

The mountains around Villefranche are predominantly limestone and riddled with cave systems. The two most beautiful and awesome, crammed with stalactites, stalagmites and all other kinds of formations are within a short walk of the walls along the road to Vernet. **Grande Canalettes** is the most famous, with well-constructed walkways and extensive lighting. But **Grottes Canalettes**, just beyond, lets you walk amongst the formations and uses hand torches to create a more exciting atmosphere—a joint ticket is available with **Cova Bastéra**.

Le Petit Train Jaune

Villefranche is the start of the picturesque mountain train service, *Le Petit Train Jaune* (Little Yellow Train) which climbs up to Latour de Carol on the high mountain plateau of the Cerdagne. A marvellous day out, you can either ride the train all the way (about 2 hours in each direction), or get off at one of the intermediate stops for sightseeing, hiking or eating. On a hot summer's day, everyone wants the single open carriage—so arrive in plenty of time or you will have to sit in an enclosed carriage. (Note that for certain minor stations, the driver only stops if asked—if you want one of these, sit in the front carriage so that you can tell him.)

Places to consider alighting are **Olette** (for the ruined **Evol Castle**—about an hour's walk from the station); **Nyer** (for the spectacular **Nyer gorge**—about two hours' walk from the station); **Thuès-Les-Bains** (for the **Carança gorge**—about half-an-hour from the station); **Planès** (where there is an unusual small **Cerdagne Church**); and **Odeillo** (for the solar generator). If you stay on the train until at least Planès you will cross the stomach-churning **Gisclard suspension bridge**, 80 metres (260 ft) above the valley floor, one of the first of its kind to be built anywhere in the world.

There are about five *Train Jaune* departures a day; (adequate parking outside the Villefranche station).

Vernet les Bains

Set at the base of Canigou and sliced in half by the River Cady which gathers pace on its northern slopes, Vernet les Bains is an airy flower-decked and somewhat Anglophile spa. Its enthusiasts have included the writer Rudyard Kipling, a regular visitor. There is even a nearby waterfall called the "Cascade des Anglais" about 3 km (2 miles) from the town centre, a pleasant walk along an easy track and through shady woods.

The old part of the town crowds up the hillside to the east of the Cady, topped by the 12th-century church. But the monument everyone comes to see is the gloriously Romantic monastery of St Martin du Canigou, hidden in the mountains above the village of Casteil, some 2 km (1 mile) to the south.

From near the car-park in **Casteil** a wide track climbs in demanding loops for about 30-40 minutes; disabled visitors can organize lifts by jeep by contacting the tourist office at Vernet. Visits are hourly and guided to include the domestic abbey buildings, cloisters and two churches. **St Martin du Canigou** is perched on a rocky outcrop piercing the Canigou forests and surveying a deep ravine. The building seems to fill the small ledge at just over 1,000 metres (3,250 ft), extending in a series of red and grey-roofed rectangles back from the typically Romanesque square church tower.

St Martin du Canigou was founded by Count Wilfred of Cerdagne who, having killed his nephew, sought absolution from the Pope. His penance was to build the Castle of Casteil and in it found a monastic order. The first stone of St Martin was laid in 1001. The abbey was consecrated by his brother Oliver, the Bishop of Elne, in 1009, and here Wilfred lived until he died in 1049. The monks abandoned the abbey in 1783 and by the 19th century the building was suffering pillage and vandalism, the fate of many similarly neglected religious buildings of the Pyrenees. By the beginning of the

The summit of Canigou, the sacred mountain of Catalans, is often sprinkled with snow, but on a fine day the ascent from the Chalet Cortalets is an easy walk.

20th century it was a ruin, restoration starting in 1902.

For the return to Casteil, take the alternative footpath, much narrower, steeper and more dramatic, cutting through the forests and across the waters of the Gorge du Cady.

As a popular spa, Vernet has plenty of accommodation.

To Mantet

From Vernet les Bains another marvellous excursion follows the D6 through to the pretty stone-built village of **Sahorre** overlooked by the rounded Romanesque **Chapel of Torrent**.

Climbing further south into the frontier mountains brings you to **Py**, a cluster of red tile roofs, where there is a **gîte d'étape** and a Haflinger **trekking stable** (for either, Tel 68-05-58-38).

Beyond Py the road narrows and climbs urgently to the remote Col de Mantet (1,761 metres/5,725 ft) before dropping to the village of the same name, sheltering below from the north wind.

This tiny stone-built village today has an international population of around 25—Belgian, Dutch and British as well as French. During World War II on a well-established escape route into Spain, it was a centre of Maquis resistance to the Nazis until the Germans cleared Mantet of its last inhabitants in 1944 and razed the buildings. Many are still ruined today; others have been rebuilt as holiday homes.

If you would like to follow the "escape route" take the marked GR10

The Desman

The desman *(Galemys pyrenaicus)* is one of the most fascinating creatures in the Pyrenees, and found nowhere else in Europe except in the Picos d'Europa in north-western Spain. An aquatic member of the mole family, its most amazing feature is a long trombone-shaped nose which it can use in the manner of an elephant's trunk.

A desman has a body of around 13 cm (5 in), covered in long, thick greyish-brown hair, to which must be added a rat-like tail of similar length. The snout, covered with long hairs near the face, and becoming shiny brown and bulbous at the tip, measures about 2 cm (¾ in).

In the water, the thick fur makes the desman enormously buoyant so that it has to struggle to dive for food. Otherwise, it bobs on the surface like a cork. It eats small fish, crustaceans and aquatic insects, which are captured in the water but eaten on dry land, either on the bank or on a rock. It is then that you have the best chance of seeing one.

If you meet somebody who has seen a desman, find out precisely where, because its range is very small, often as little as 30 metres (100 ft) of river and never more than 200 metres (650 ft).

The great problem for its survival is water pollution. At one time it was reported as low as 30 metres (100 ft) of altitude but nowadays it is never seen below 400 m (1,300 ft), except in parts of the Basque country.

In the traditional mountain village of Mantet, the shepherd still goes out with his flock every day, accompanied by his faithful Pyrenean sheepdogs.

footpath into the Alemany Valley, at least as far as the small stone and wood refuge known as the "**Barraque des Allemands**" (after an earlier German troop shelter, now burnt down). You can reach it in under an hour and the scenery, protected as a Nature Reserve, is glorious. To one side, across the Alemany stream, a dense coniferous forest cloaks the mountains, while on the other the open pasture is sometimes grazed by izards.

Even if you cannot hike far, there are delightful short trails all around, marked with painted symbols—a desman, trout or salamander.

Pony trekking can be arranged at **Ranche Cavale**, the wood-built complex just above the village.

If you are interested in adventure, then stay at **La Girada** (Tel. 68-05-68-69) which specializes in climbing, trekking, caving, canyoning and mountain biking. Experienced guides speak Flemish, French and English.

Canigou

With its fantastic ridges, sparkling streams, forests and saturated Mediterranean light, the Canigou massif is one of the most picturesque mountains in the entire Pyrenees. During World War II it was a *maquis* stronghold, chosen partly, perhaps, because it is a symbol of Catalanism, celebrated in a Catalan hymn; although it isn't the highest mountain in Catalonia it is the most visible and can be seen both from the Côte Vermeille and the northern Costa Brava. From Prades the summit of Canigou (2,785 metres/9,138 ft) rears as a stark pyramid beyond the orchards and coniferous forest. There are two jeep tracks up Canigou, one from Vernet les Bains to the west, but that from Prades is recommended as slightly easier. Non-motorists or those whose vehicles are not suited to track can book a place in a jeep taxi.

The jeep track from Prades is reached by the road signposted "Los Masos" from the roundabout on the main road on the east side of the town. Eventually the tarmac runs out and a solid but often uneven dirt road climbs steadily upwards for 20 km (12½ miles) through superb scenery to the Refuge de Prat Cabrera. Only jeeps can accomplish the next stage to the well-equipped refuge, Chalet Cortalets, where meals and refreshments are available all summer. To walk between the two refuges takes an hour-and-a-half. The Cortalets is a substantial building close to a small lake which is a popular picnic spot. From the Cortalets the ascent of the summit, a walk which never requires use of hands and is well within the reach of most people, takes one-and-a-half to two hours. The summit is just sufficiently sharp to be exhilarating and is marked by a yellow-and-red striped Catalan flag and a *table d'orientation*.

The views are wonderful on a clear day, right down to the coast and far inland to Andorra, but you'll not be alone—this is one of the most popular excursions of the region. However, you can at least make the ascent in relative solitude. as long as you are fit, by taking the steep and slightly exposed route which begins at Mariailles, just above Vernet les Bains.

T he upper Rotja valley, easily reached from Vernet les Bains or Mantet.

To Mont Louis

From Villefranche de Conflent the *Train Jaune* and the busy N116 both climb steeply along the Têt towards the Cerdagne. Though a major artery of the Pyrenees, this is still a picturesque driving route with tiny villages perched back from the traffic on the slopes of such famous peaks as Coronat and Cambre d'Aze.

From Olette it is worth making the 2 km (1 mile) detour north to the village of **Evol** to see its ruined château as well as the 15th-century retable by Maître du Roussillon in the church of St André. The church is in the village centre, the castle just above, on the road that climbs to the Portus pass.

If you like gorge walking you have two possibilities soon after Olette. Immediately beyond the village, a turning left drops to the village of **Nyers** at the mouth of a spectacular canyon, traced by an old track on its east bank. Or you can continue along the main valley, coming first to the tiny spa of **Thuès-les-Bains**, the tell-tale steam rising all around on a cold day, and then to its sister village **Thuès-Entre-Valls**. Here, where the *Train Jaune* passes over a small bridge, is the beginning of the **Carança gorge**, one of the most exciting hikes of the region. The walk begins in the canyon bottom, the cliffs towering overhead, then climbs to vertiginous shelfs, clinging high up on the rock face.

Whether you are actually on the *Train Jaune* or in your own car, you will have the opportunity to see one of the world's first railway suspension bridges just before Mont Louis. It was designed by Albert Gisclard and built between 1905 and 1908, with a main span of 156 metres (510 ft). Gisclard died before it was completed and there is a memorial to him at a vantage point beside the road (but with no adequate parking nearby).

As you approach, Mont Louis is immediately intriguing, its solid brown-grey walls and corner bastions completely hiding the town within. It is a town with statistical claims — the highest fort in France (1,600 metres/5,200 ft), and, rather less glamorously, also the coldest town, thanks to being built in a pass exposed to chilling winds at the crossroads of the valleys of Segre, Aude and Têt.

Mont Louis was the work of Vauban, military engineer to Louis XIV (hence the name). Together they left an enduring military mark throughout the whole of France. Vauban selected the site after seeing the inhabitants of the village of Vilar d'Ovansa, on which it was more or less built. Not only did they live long, he noted, but they had *"dents blanches"* (white teeth) and *"yeux vifs"* (lively eyes). There are none of the high walls of Villefranche, fragile against canon. Instead there is a deep, dry moat behind which the massively thick walls, just high enough to repel infantry, were easily proof against the artillery of the time. "Ville fortifié par Vauban," it was said, "ville imprenable. Ville asiégée par Vauban, ville prise." (A town fortified by Vauban is impregnable; a town besieged by Vauban will be taken.)

The citadel beside the town is still in use by French commandos but you can visit the **town walls**. The statue in the square is of General Dagobert who defeated a minor Spanish invasion at the **Col de la Perche**, 3 km (2 miles) to the west, in 1793. The solar generator is also worth a look but there is a much bigger and more interesting solar development at Odeillo, a little to the east.

The Cerdagne

Leave Mont Louis behind and you find yourself on wide upland plateau noticeably closer to the sun than the plain of Roussillon. All around, the peaks are dwarfed and the August pasture scorched a dull yellow. If you head north from Mont Louis you are on the plateau of the Capcir, but if you go west you are in the Cerdagne (and, further west still, the Spanish Cerdanya). There are three routes across the Cerdagne—along the north-facing slopes via Eyne and Lló, along the south-facing slopes via Font Romeu; or across the middle by the main road.

To Lló

The left turn just after Mont Louis leads through the village of **St Pierre dels Forcats**. From here the little church at Planès is worth the 5-km (3-mile) diversion east for its unusual arrangement of semi-circular half-domed apses, which it was once believed was Moorish in origin. Continuing west from St Pierre, the delightful hike south along the Eyne valley begins at the village of **Eyne**. It is best to park at the start of the dirt track (on the bend just beyond the village going towards Saillagouse). The track itself soon turns to footpath

(marked with red and white stripes) and the scenery is exquisite. If you are reasonably fit you can reach the **Col d'Eyne** on the border (also known as the Col de Núria) in about 4–5 hours. Among birdwatchers this is a famous pass since, from late August to the end of October, it is the second most important bird migration route of the Pyrenees.

Some 5 km (3 miles) after Eyne, the hamlet of **Lló** (pronounced "yo") has one of the few really good restaurants of the region.

After Lló, the main road through the Cerdagne can be regained at Saillagouse.

Font Romeu

Some 10 km (6 miles) west of Mont Louis on the D618, **Font Romeu** is the largest winter sports station of the region and a busy holiday resort in summer, too. The modern **Cité Préolympique**, further up the hill, was the altitude training base for the French team prior to the Mexico Olympics and the French ski team also uses it (snow permitting). But Font Romeu was a place of pilgrimage long before skiing. Over the centuries the faithful have flocked to pay their respects to the wooden statue of the Virgin, kept in resplendence at the **Hermitage**, a sanctuary to the east of the town. According to legend (a common one in the Pyrenees) the Virgin was found by a peasant who saw his bull pawing oddly at the ground. Sweet water then poured from the spot – hence the spring or font of Font Romeu. The sanctuary was built in 1334 but later additions, ever the more splendid, were constructed from the 16th century, culminating with the delectable carved setting for the Virgin by the Catalan artist Joseph Sunyer.

You might witness one of the two main festivals of the Virgin—8 September when she traditionally descends to Odeillo; and Whitsun the following year, when she returns to the sanctuary.

Odeillo

Odeillo, virtually a downhill continuation of Font Romeu, boasts a 10th-century chapel with the oldest portal in Cerdagne, but its more obvious claim to fame is the incongruous giant solar generator which towers above everything in the region. A landmark for miles around, the 40 metre x 54 metre (130 ft x 180 ft) mirrored panel was built in 1968 for experimental purposes—not only generating electricity for local homes but also exploiting the enormous temperatures attained to test materials such as ceramics. Visits are free (daily 9 a.m. to 7 p.m., except holidays). Even more exciting is to catch one of the special *son et lumière* evening entertainments held infrequently during summer, when the mirrors become a giant cinema screen.

several days. You can get right into the heart of the area quite easily by car by taking the road from Super Bolquère signposted to the Barrage (dam) des Bouillouses. This is an exhilarating drive through dense woodlands, full of picnic possibilities, but on a road which is narrow and potholed. There is a large parking area close to the dam wall, on the far side of which the slightly quirky **Hôtel Bones Hores** has rooms with kitchenettes, a good restaurant and cosy bar area with an open fire.

For **Carlit**, it is helpful to have a good map (such as the Randonnées Pyrénéennes 1:50,000 Cerdagne–Capcir). Set out from the dam with a picnic and allow a full day there and back. The most direct route (marked by paint flashes) passes between lakes **Sec** and **Coumasse** and then between lakes **Llong** and **Balleil**. Finally, beyond **Lake Soubirans**, it climbs into a shoulder from which the summit (2,921 metres/9,495 ft) is reached along a ridge.

As with all the high peaks of the Pyrenees, mid-summer afternoons can mean severe thunderstorms and it is advisable to be off the top by late lunch time.

The Carlit Massif

Both the GR10 and HRP footpaths pass close to Font Romeu. In addition the fabulous hiking around **Pic Carlit** lies immediately behind the town. Full of lakes, manageable mountains and high altitude marshlands, this is more than enough to occupy keen walkers or botanists for

The Capcir

The high, naked **plateau of the Capcir** runs north from Mont Louis, relieved by encroaching woods of glistening green and by the blue of its two large reservoirs, **Matemale** at Les Angles and **Puyvalador** at the village of the same name. Apart from the possibility of windsurfing on the reservoir, **Les**

When the wind blows from North Africa, storm clouds can colour the sky yellow, as here descending from Carlit (2,921 metres/9,495 ft). If a thunderstorm should develop, come down immediately.

Angles (30 km/19 miles from Mont Louis) also makes a good walking base. The walks to **Lac des Bouillouses** and to **Lac d'Aude** (the source of the Aude, which plunges through gorges beyond Puyvalador) are especially ravishing. For the less fit, there is a gorgeous drive to the Balcère lake, hidden in dense forest in the mountains to the west of Les Angles. If you would like to stay in the area, there are several hotels.

Formiguères, between Les Angles and Puyvalador, still manages to maintain much of its old village atmosphere. You can find bars and restaurants in the old stone houses of the original hamlet.

Just before Puyvalador you should not miss the **Caves of Fontrabiouse** (a turning to the left). This is an extensive system, of which the small part open to the public is an awesome example, packed with the artistic tricks limestone and water can play.

Bourg Madame, Llivia and the road to Andorra

Bourg Madame is at the westernmost boundary of the Cerdagne and the town is virtually one with its Spanish counterpart Puigcerdà, just across the border. A frantic bustle of border-type shops, cafés and traffic, it was named in 1815 in honour of the Madame-Royale, Marie-Thérèse de Bourbon, wife of Duc d'Angouleme.

From Bourg-Madame, the N20 begins its long climb along the Carol valley towards the **Col de Puymorens** and Andorra. At Ur, you have the option of turning off for **Llivia**, that extraordinary pocket of Spain totally enclosed within French territory. Once in Llivia, signs, language and money are in Spanish, though the total area is only the size of a small town. This oddity was created during negotiations over the 1659 Treaty of the Pyrenees. According to some histories, the French simply forgot to include Llivia when they forced the defeated Spanish to give up 33 villages in Cerdagne. But the significance of Llivia as an old capital of the region makes an oversight unlikely. As you wander around, its history almost oozes out of the ancient stone buildings. There was a pharmacy here as early as 1594, now forming the principal exhibits of the town museum (daily 10 a.m.–2 p.m. and 4–7 p.m.; Sundays, mornings only). In August, the annual classical music festival is held in the 15th-century church, just opposite the museum. Inside, the crucifix is famous for having inspired the French composer Déodac de Séverac to write the strangely titled *Mule Drivers in Front of the Christ of Llivia.* The fortified tower adjacent, known as the **Torre de Bernat** after the seigneur Bernat de So, contains slides of the flowers that in springtime drench the surrounding fields in colour.

Continuing north along the Carol valley brings you to the village of **Enveitg** where, because of the proximity of the Spanish border, the Hôtel Transpyreneen was an important meeting place for escapers and their guides during World War II. In the early days of the war, escapers simply took the Sunday train from Toulouse and then wandered across into Spain through **Latour de Carol**, in a group with local people for whom movement was, initially, little restricted. The line terminates between Enveitg and the village of Latour de Carol, 2 km (1 mile) further north (where you can now switch from French to Spanish railways and, also, to the Train Jaune for the descent to Villefranche de Conflent).

Just across the river from Latour de Carol, it is worth looking for the adjoining hamlet of **Yravals**.

Continuing up the Carol valley, the road climbs past the ruined **towers of Carol**, part of an old castle built to defend the Cerdagne, to Porta. This village of black slate roofs and tight alleyways was once one of the great smuggling villages of the Pyrenees, on account of its easy natural access into Andorra along the Campcardos valley. If the romance of smuggling appeals to you, you can retrace the route (now the GR7 footpath) by following the red and white stripes from the village. The footpath crosses the Carol river, then keeps the Campcardos river to the left. You can reach the Andorran border at **La Porteille Blanche** (2,517 metres/8,180 ft) and get back in one day.

Just above Porta, the village of **Porté Puymorens** is one of the more reliable ski resorts of the Pyrénées-Orientales. From here the road climbs in steep hairpins over the treeless slopes to the desolate **Col de Puymorens** (1,920 metres/6,240 ft), the gateway both to the Ariège and Andorra. By the mid-90s at the latest, there will be a road tunnel option.

Le Perthus and into the Tech Valley

The Tech Valley (also known as the Vallespir) is the southernmost major valley of France, where the familiar east Pyrenean landscape is additionally clothed in cork oak, cherries, bougainvillaea and oranges. This Eden runs west from Le Boulou (about 20 km/13 miles south of Perpignan). Either you go down the motorway or its "shadow" N9, or you cut slowly across country via Thuir and the relatively arid zone known as Les Aspres.

Le Boulou is hardly an auspicious start, a traffic bottleneck famous for its

Wild Mushrooms

All over the Pyrenees, wild mushroom collecting is a great social. During the bright weekends of early autumn, groups of friends, and even entire villages, set out with collecting baskets and picnics in search of the several varieties that are considered worth gathering. There is also one highly prized spring variety, the morel.

Always remember that even wild mushrooms belong to the village in whose woods and pastures they grow and permission should always be sought before setting off. If you are inexperienced, concentrate on species which cannot be confused with others that are poisonous. The best guide is a sample mushroom that a reliable local person has provided. Identification of mushrooms may require careful consideration of spore print colour and gill shape but all those noted below can be verified by a few simple points concerning shape, size, colour and the nature of the spore-bearing surface (gills, folds, pores or spines).

The species most coveted by the French is the cep (*Boletus edulis*). The whitish or yellowish underside of the cap is composed of tiny spongey tubes known as pores. The novice might confuse it with similar edible but less enjoyable species, but these have narrow stems while that of the cep is massive. The cep is excellent fried.

Despite the reputation of the cep, the chanterelle (*Cantharellus cibarius*) is not only visually more attractive but even better to eat. It has the shape of a funnel, the outside fluted so that several held together have the appearance of columns spreading out to a vaulted ceiling, and the whole mushroom is egg-yellow. Once seen chanterelles are never mistaken for anything else. The best way to cook them is to boil them in white wine and lemon juice with parsley and a little chopped onion.

Puffballs are unmistakable and in many parts of the Pyrenees so little regarded that no one collects them. However, when the flesh is firm and white they are delicious fried. There are several varieties, generally with the appearance of a golf ball nestling in the grass. Any that are brown-skinned or not immaculately white inside should be discarded.

Before cooking wild mushrooms, have them verified by someone reliable. In most villages there will be people who have been gathering all their lives and who can be depended upon. Never eat too many at a sitting nor over a period of days—mild reactions are not uncommon, even to species considered edible.

There are many more edible mushrooms than those noted here. The best way to expand knowledge is in the company of informed enthusiasts—but always using a reliable book as a cross-check.

cork and a rather salty mineral water. On the south side of the town (at Bains du Boulou) there is a casino. The nearby St Martin de Fenouillar contains what are considered the finest Romanesque frescoes in Roussillon.

About 8 km (5 miles) further south from Le Boulou, the border town of **Le Perthus** is a bizarre shopper's delight where discounted Spanish prices lure in French shoppers by the coachload. Fresh produce is both inexpensive and of high quality but alcohol and perfume are cheap by French standards only. Le Perthus is half French, half Spanish and either currency is accepted.

However, there is more to Le Perthus than consumer goods. The N9 on the approach to the town is flanked on the heights above by the ruins of twin **Roman forts**, for this was the Via

A basketful of mushrooms collected one morning in the Pyrénées-Orientales—yellow chanterelles, ceps, Lactarius deliciosus *and puffballs.*

Domitia—the old Roman road into Spain. Beside the easternmost fort of Maures (accessed through the village of Les Cluses) the **Church of St Nazaire** contains frescoes almost as good as those in St Martin de Fenouillar.

Once in the main street of Le Perthus itself, a right turn (near the brow of the hill) climbs away from the shops through cork woodland and fragrant Mediterranean scrub to **Fort Bellegarde**. Built in the 16th century, then improved by Louis XIV's military engineer Vauban, this huge and austere hill-top castle is in two parts. The main fortress (daily 10 a.m.–6 p.m. July to September) comprises an oblong of thickly protected buildings around a central courtyard, accessed by a draw-bridge and a steep ramp. Exhibitions inside embrace local prehistory and history, and regional art and sculpture. The smaller and more extensively ruined lower fort to the south can be reached along a rather overgrown path from the car-park at any time.

Slightly beyond the fort and actually in the **Col de Panissars**—the crossing point of the Via Domitia during Roman times and thought to be Hannibal's route in 218 BC—are the partially excavated remains of the Trophy of Pompey. This was a monument erected by the Roman general to celebrate a major victory against Spain. Archaeological work is continuing but it is usually possible to glimpse progress.

To Céret

The little town of Céret, steeped in the folklore of 20th-century French art, lies some 8 km (5 miles) further west along the Tech valley from Le Boulou, but the approach across the Aspres foothills is by far the more attractive.

The Tech valley is the southernmost main valley in France, a riot of colour from huge bougainvillaea to these tiny heartsease.

Thuir is the gateway to this delightful region, 13 km (8 miles) from Perpignan. But do not move on before you have sampled a glass of Byrrh (pronounced "beer") at the cellars near the town centre. The vat containing this delicious aperitif is the largest of its kind in the world (daily in summer, 8.30 a.m.–noon and 2.30–6 p.m.).

From Thuir the quickest way to Céret is via the village of Terrats on the D615, but there is a wonderful loop to be made through **Castelnou**, where the castle above the town has just opened as a **museum**, and past the church of **Fontcouverte**, nestling picturesquely in the hills under the summit of the same name (695 metres/ 2,260 ft).

Céret is passionately Catalan, as you will quickly notice. The musical conversation, overheard at pavement cafés under immense plane trees, is throaty; faces under small black berets are walnut brown and fissured; and the architecture is open to the sun with arches, wrought iron and flower-covered balconies. In August there is a grand festival of the **sardana**, the elegant folk dance that the Catalan people adapted from the Greek two millenia ago. It attracts international dancers and spectators to the circular open-air arena, where concentric circles step with pride, heads held high, backs straight. The sound of the band, or Cobla, is unlike anything else, at once brash but haunting. If you would like to join in one of the street sessions, first memorize the steps very carefully and then choose a group which looks more friendly than perfect—**sardana** here is a serious matter.

Céret's other great quality is its sense of art history, beginning with its selection as a summer home by the Fauves, and now celebrated by its **Modern Art Museum**—just behind the tourist office in rue Joseph Parayre (daily in summer except Tuesdays, 10 a.m.–noon and 2–7 p.m.; in winter, till 5 p.m.).

Catalan sculptor Manolo Hugué was one of the first artists to discover Céret and in 1910 escaped the emotional rigours of Paris to live there. He was soon joined by his friend the composer Déodat de Séverac (to whom he dedicated a sculpture which you can see outside the tourist office in avenue Clemenceau). From 1911 Matisse became a regular, preferring the peace of Céret to the tumult of his nearby summer home at Collioure, which by this time had become popular as an artists' colony. Picasso also preferred Céret to Collioure which he described as *"trop de peintres"*. Georges Braque, Juan Gris and Moise Kisling followed. But there would have been no record and no museum had it not been for the arrival during World War I of the wounded painter Pierre Brune. Collecting donations from his friends among the Céret Fauves and Cubists, including 59 pieces by Picasso and 14 by Matisse, he was finally able to see the museum open in 1950. Today's permanent collection includes these and works by Manolo, Maillol, Gris, Chagall and Dalí. Many, like the sketches for the Céret War memorial by Maillol and Dalís annotated photograph are minor works, but others like the two Cubist works by Gris—Torero of 1913 and the more famous Arlequin of 1923—are more substantial and well worth the journey. Normally, there are also temporary exhibitions, usually devoted to contemporary work by artists connected with the region.

Céret has no fewer than three bridges over the Tech. According to the lore of the town, the oldest—built in the 14th century—is cursed and therefore used only by the unsuperstitious. The devil is said to have helped build this bridge in return for the soul of the first to cross it. The locals tricked the devil by letting a black cat be the first. The debt was therefore repaid, but it is said the devil may still be planning revenge.

The town enjoys a very sunny climate and takes great pride in its early **cherry harvest** (usually around the end of April) amounting to about 4,000 tons of fruit. It is marvellous to visit when the cherry blossom turns the outskirts of the town into a mass of fragrant flowers.

Amélie les Bains

Eight kilometres (5 miles) west along the D115 from Céret, Amélie les Bains is one of the most popular spa towns of the Pyrenees, bursting with life and set beside the river amid mimosas and orange trees. The sun shines here 300 hundred days a year, which certainly makes you *feel* good. More attractive still than the centre of Amélie itself is the linked medieval town of **Palalda**, on the opposite north bank of the river.

Even if you are not in need of a cure, the two spa buildings of Amélie are well worth visiting (there is a third for military use). The **Thermes du Mondony** is the more elegant with its graceful arches and balconies, while the **Romains** is more modern and functional. They share the same thermal source (as well as the strong odour of hydrogen sulphur) and specialize in treating respiratory and rheumatic complaints.

One of the more compelling sights of the area is the **Mondony Gorge**, which empties into the Tech near the town centre. A stroll in the gorge, along a well-constructed walkway, takes just half-an-hour. The riverside walk along the north side of the Tech is also worthwhile for the ancient engraved stones displayed on a small green in avenue de la Petite Provence. Discovered in the 1940s following a severe flood and dating back to 800 BC, they are believed to form part of a prehistoric cromlech.

Arles sur Tech

Arles sur Tech, 4 km (2½ miles) west of Amélie, is an architectural treat on account of an **old quarter** centred on the **10th-century abbey**, of which the highlight is the **cloister**. As you enter the abbey, notice the 11th-century sculpted arch moulding and the typically Catalan lintel, engraved with a cross. The church is built as three naves surrounded by side chapels with several ornate screens and a magnificent 18th-century **organ**. The 14th-century white **marble sarcophagus** of St Tombe is said to "miraculously weep" litres of liquid each year. The much-photographed 13th-century cloister is quite ravishing in white marble quarried from nearby Céret.

Some 3 km (2 miles) from Arles sur Tech, the **Gorges de la Fou** are breathtaking even by the standard of Pyrenean canyons because they are so narrow. The walls tower above, often blocked by giant boulders which have been arrested in their fall, and even light often fails to penetrate. The full length of the walkway takes about an hour-and-a-half, there and back.

Prats de Mollo

Hidden away in the furthest recesses of the Vallespir, 19 km (12 miles) from Arles sur Tech, the medieval walled village of **Prats de Mollo** was outside any laws but its own right up to the early 19th century. When France tried to impose its salt tax (*gabelle*) in Roussillon at the end of the 17th century, the inhabitants of Prats de Mollo were among its fiercest opponents in what became known as the "revolt of the Angelets". After murdering Louis XIV's tax collectors, the villagers held off two French batallions and were only forced to submit after a surprise attack by Maréchal de Noailles, whose forces climbed up to Py and around, the western flanks of Canigou to take the village from the rear. France then built Fort Lagarde overlooking the village, not merely to patrol the frontier but to keep the villagers under control.

After the Revolution of 1789, there was another revolt against the *"sangsues du peuple"* (people's leeches), particularly because ordinary people paid taxes, while the aristocracy and clergy had been exempt.

In World War II, the numerous smuggling trails into Spain radiating out from Prats de Mollo became the escape routes from Nazism. A rendezvous for guides and escapers was the Hôtel Touristes, now one of the nicest hotels in the village.

All this history conjures a romance which the appearance of Prats de Mollo does not disappoint. Just outside the walls there is a huge square where boules is regularly played by leather-faced locals in black berets. Inside the walls, parts of which date back to the 14th century, there is pleasant strolling and shopping along streets which are mainly pedestrianized.

Beyond Prats de Mollo the valley road continues to the tiny spa of **La Preste** (8 km/5 miles), from where there is good walking among the frontier peaks, while the main road climbs to the border at **Coll d'Ares**, a bleak spot where short-toed eagles are sometimes to be seen.

Into the Fenouillèdes

The Fenouillèdes is a region of low and often bizarrely eroded mountains, its summits strewn with the crumbled remnants of medieval castles, for this was once the heavily defended border between "Spanish" Catalonia and "French" Corbières. To reach the Fenouillèdes from Perpignan (a daytrip—or more if you prefer) cross the River Têt, following signs north for the airport, and then continue on the D117. Nowadays this often barren-seeming region is, in fact, a major wine-producer so that castle-hopping can be punctuated by wine-tasting.

Notre Dame de Pène

About 15 km (9 miles) from Perpignan, the extraordinary 17th-century **hermitage of Notre Dame de Pène** is perched on a high ridge overlooking the road just beyond the village of Cases de Péne. The walk up is not difficult and is strongly recommended, beginning at the parking area from which a rocky footpath curves around and up to give marvellous views over the Agly Valley and back to the coast. The white hermitage with its single bell arch is all the more striking for its grand 60-step staircase leading up from the naked rock and more suited to a city opera house.

Estagel

Estagel, 8½ km (5 miles) further west along the D117, was the birthplace of François Arago (1786–1853), an illustrious astronomer and philosopher who was born in the village and whose statue now stands in the square beside the main road. Behind it, the **Commerce** snack bar, a pretty place with lots of greenery and a pleasant conservatory, makes a good place to break the journey. For more substantial eating try **La Petite Auberge**, instantly recognizable from its frescos of unclad ladies, where the road sweeps around to the left. If views are more important than food, there is a wonderfully sited café in the old **hermitage of Força Real**—drive south 7 km (4 miles) to the **Col de la Bataille** and then turn left, following the road for another 4 km (2½ miles) to its end where the restored hermitage stands on top of the hill.

Tautavel and Europe's Oldest Man

Ten kilometres (6 miles) north of Estagel (less than an hour's drive from Perpignan), the village of **Tautavel** shot to international fame in 1971 when fragments of a skull almost half a million years old were discovered in a cave nearby. "Tautavel Man" (*Homus erectus*) seems to have looked much like us, yet these remains are as old as any human remains found anywhere in Europe. There is a **museum** in the village dedicated to him and other archaeological finds from the continuing excavation, supplemented by murals, charts and constructions. You can also visit the cave itself.

Quéribus

The **castle of Quéribus** is one of the most impressive ruins in this frontier zone, so rich in ancient forts. It is reached by taking the right-hand turn at Maury, 9 km (5 miles) west of Estagel.

Though ruined, Quéribus remains a marvellous example of 10th-century engineering, cunningly perched on a tiny pinnacle of rock. From a distance it is difficult to spot, so well does it blend into its limestone landscape, and the climb up from the car-park is dauntingly steep (entrance 10F March to October; the rest of year free). The highest part of the castle is the best preserved, especially the strategic donjon with its ribbed vault. The east face is pitted by projectiles, emphasizing the value of the "secret" passage for use in times of siege. In the 13th century some of the few Cathars who had escaped the Inquisition and the fall of Montségur (*see* above) took refuge at Quéribus before finally disappearing from the pages of history into Spain.

Back on the D117, St Paul de Fenouillet (15 km/9 miles west of Estagel) is capital of the region and a well-placed though unexciting base for touring the Fenouillèdes.

The **Gorges of Galamus** start about 10 km (6 miles) north of St Paul. Cut deep, narrow and dark by the River Agly, the gorge shelters the **hermitage of St Antoine de Galamus**. The hermitage used to be tended by a hermit, but now operates as a small *gîte d'étape* where you can stay if you have a sleeping bag. The chapel of St Antoine is a place of pilgrimage each Easter and

Pentecost and as it cannot be seen from the narrow and busy road above it is worth parking and following the marked path down to the river.

To Sournia

There is another but much shorter gorge south of St Paul which cuts through the massive limestone "wall" of the Fenouillèdes. Known (like several others in the Pyrenees) as the Gorges de la Fou, it gives access to the heartland of the Fenouillèdes, with its fabulously remote touring along a maze of narrow country roads connecting traditional villages. One of the best of these is Ansignan, just 9 km (5½ miles) south of St Paul, a pretty village with giant plane trees and a picturesque arched aqueduct which dates back hundreds of years and possibly to Roman times.

Alternatively, it is possible to get into the central Fenouillèdes by turning south at the village of **Caudiès de Fenouillèdes**, 11 km (7 miles) on from St Paul, a popular local summer holiday resort with fishing, horse-riding, canoeing and caving. By this route it is possible to see the 15th-century **Hermitage of Notre Dame de Laval** which is on the heights above Caudiés, and a centre of pilgrimage each 15 August. South of the hermitage, the village of **Fenouillet** was founded by Charles the Bald for strategic reasons but the castle today is severely ruined.

Sournia, about 25 km (15 miles) from either St Paul or Caudiés is a **wine-making centre** (Côtes du Roussillon) and site of two early **Romanesque churches** which also carry vestiges of Visigothic styling. The road westwards connects with the château

The Pyrénées-Orientales enjoy magical sunsets.

of Puylaurens in the départément of the Aude (*see* above) via the tiny village of Rabouillet on the edge of the magnificent **Boucheville forest**.

Returning to Perpignan, take the Agly valley via **Caramany**, a fortified village dominated by a photogenic church bell-tower; **Planézes**, with a 12th-century chapel and ancient iron mines; and **La Tour de France**, which, before the Franco-Spanish Treaty of the Pyrenees in 1659, was considered the "last" village in France. Alternatively, you can drop into the Têt valley via the *caves* of **Montalba le Château** or via the ruined 12th-century priory at Marcevol.

ARISTIDE MAILLOL
1861   1944

Colour and Light on the Edge of Catalonia

The southernmost tip of France, the Vermillion Coast (*see* map on page 162), was the centre for Matisse and artists of the Fauvist movement at Collioure. To the south are the contrasting towns of Port Vendres, still an active fishing port, and the chic resort of Banyuls.

Collioure

The painter Matisse wrote that he had only to open the shutters of his room to see all the colours of the Mediterranean, a scene he painted with richly coloured exuberance in *The Open Window* (1905). At Collioure the strong colours used for emotional effect almost existed in reality—the geraniums on the balcony, the shutters, the boats in the harbour. In 1911, he painted the

The famous Thinker (La Pensée) marks the grave of its sculptor Maillol who lived on the Côte Vermeille at Banyuls sur Mer.

view from another Collioure window, looking inland over the rooftops to the vineyards. Matisse and Derain painted the mountains, the church tower, olive trees, the graceful *barques catalanes* and the vermillion of the cliffs from which the coast derived its nickname— Côte Vermeille. Collioure was almost Spain, at once exotic and sufficiently far from St Tropez for Matisse to feel free to develop new ideas. It was here the colour-clash school of Fauvism was first nurtured.

Today's Collioure is no less colourful. On a hot summer afternoon the wind-surfing sails, the beach umbrellas and the general hotch-potch of holidaying humanity conspire to outdo the natural colour Matisse admired so much. If you don't mind

195

crowds, Collioure remains an attractive place to visit. Nothing can detract from the intimacy of the main harbour and its small beach, guarded by the bulky buildings of the **Château-Royal** on one side, now an art gallery and museum, and by the **Church of St Vincent** on the other.

The heavily fortified church was built in the 17th century to withstand the ravages of enemy and sea. Inside, in contrast to the light and colour of the Côte Vermeille, it is dark, dank and pungent, and lit only when the timed light-switch illuminates the gleaming altar and glumly religious paintings. The tragedies that have been mourned here with the sighing of the sea are almost palpable. The adjoining domed bell-tower dates from the 13th century and has also been the harbour lighthouse—today's lighthouse is on the edge of the tiny Island of St Vincent, linked by causeway to the mainland.

In the harbour, the restored fleet of ancient Catalan fishing *barques,* brightly painted in primary colours and lateen-rigged, is a reminder of the rugged past. Around 1900, Collioure fishermen operated about 120 barques and the village was the centre of the Roussillon anchovy and sardine fishing industry. The traditional way of life only went into decline from the end of the 19th century, and the last barque was constructed in Collioure in 1914. By 1928, all the barques had been motorized. During World War II fishing was forbidden and in 1947 only 22 of the traditional boats were in use. Their last working appearance was in 1967. Many of these marvellous wooden craft were destroyed, but a number have been restored by enthusiasts who form the Lateen-Rig Association, based in the village. Fishing itself is of small importance in Collioure today, though locally caught sardine and anchovy are still available.

The **Château-Royale**, was built in the 12th century by the Templars, dominating the village with its huge blank walls and fortress gates. After Spain ceded Collioure to France by the Treaty of the Pyrenees (1659), the castle was strengthened by Vauban. Inside, it is now the inspiring setting for art and sculpture and for other exhibitions of the life and culture of the region.

There are several good hotels and restaurants in Collioure, of which the best, and most expensive, are close to the harbour.

Walking from Collioure

Collioure lies at the very edge of the Alberès mountains (the easternmost chain of the Pyrenees), an area of arid scrub, with here and there a *mas* (farm) growing olives and vines. There are miles of easy walks, often with spectacular views back down to the coast, of which one of the best is to the **Madeloc tower**. The tower is visible from Collioure on the hills to the west, distinguished by its radio mast. Distant as it looks, it can be reached in under 4 hours (and about 3 hours for the return). Begin by following signs for the **hermitage Notre Dame de Consolation**, set amid sweet chestnuts. If you have already had enough, stop here for your picnic, otherwise the marked route carries on climbing to the tower with its spectacular views. If you prefer, you can make a complete circular tour by descending on the GR10/HRP foot-path to Banyuls sur Mer and return to Collioure by bus.

Cycle Tour

Argelès—St André—Palau del Vidre—Elne—St Cyprien-Plage—Canet Plage—Perpignan—Canohès—Pon-teilla—Trouillas—Passa Llauro—Torderès—Banyuls dels Aspres—St Genis des Fontaines—Laroque des Al-berès—Sorède—Argelès (57 km/35 miles).

Argelès sur Mer

If you would like a change from the tiny coves around Collioure, the im-mense sandy beaches of the **Côte Radieuse** begin only a little to the north at **Argelès sur Mer** (20 km/12 miles from Perpignan).

The town is divided into three. Argelès village, which has the shops and permanent residents, is slightly in-land. Argelès Plage is the seaside part with a casino and two main beaches (Front de Mer and Plage Nord) and is almost deserted in winter. Le Racou is a smaller, more intimate part of the de-velopment retaining some of the flavour of the Côte Vermeille. A fourth sector, Port Argelès, is under con-struction and will primarily function as a yacht marina.

When you have had enough of the beach, take a look at the **Catalan Mu-seum** (rue de l'Egalité; open June–September 9 a.m.–noon and 3.30–6 p.m.; closed Sundays) which gives something of the flavour of Catalan culture and history. One of the most interesting periods locally was the set-ting up of refugee camps for the thou-sands of Spaniards who fled the Civil War in 1939, their misery only em-phasized by the beauty beyond the wire.

There are hotels and restaurants in all quarters (*see* HOTELS and RESTAU-RANTS), but if there are high-season problems, ask at the Tourist Office.

Elne

Seven kilometres (4½ miles) inland from Argelès, on the main road from Perpignan, **Elne** was the ancient cap-ital of Roussillon during Roman times when it was known as Helena. After the construction of the cathe-dral of St Eulalie in the 11th century, Elne became seat of the Roussillon bishopric until the growing commer-cial importance of Perpignan stole it away in 1600. The huge fortified cathedral, with its Romanesque and Gothic influences, reflects that long period of power. The **cloister** is the most beautiful part. Particularly note the **carved capitals**. Climbing a stair-case within the cloister, you will come to a terrace with marvellous views over the Albères mountains. There is a small **museum** in the St Laurent chapel with local archaeological finds on view.

South to the Border

From Collioure, a corniche twists, climbs and descends like a roller-coaster all the way to the border with Spain, an invigorating drive with superb views.

Port Vendres

Port Vendres, which is just 4 km (2½ miles) south of Collioure, is the least touristic of the seaside towns on the Côte Vermeille. It is still an active trading and fishing port and this gives it an unusual attraction. It was a particularly important port in Roman times, when it was known as Portus Venerus. In the 18th century Roussillon wines were the main cargo. Then from the early 19th century it was the port of embarcation for the French military in Algeria. Today, some of the biggest fishing boats on the coast operate from Port Vendres and the early-morning fish market on the quay is substantial.

The war memorial on the quay is a rather uncharacteristic work by the great sculptor Maillol, born near Banyuls sur Mer.

There are a number of hotels, mostly in the budget category. Most restaurants in Port Vendres concentrate on fish (see HOTELS AND RESTAURANTS).

Banyuls sur Mer

Banyuls sur Mer, 6 km (4 miles) from Port Vendres, is the most chic resort on the Côte Vermeille, with top-class hotels and restaurants, a popular yacht marina and a pleasant beach. It is famous for three things—its wine, its artistic heritage and its important marine life.

The bustling town was the birth place of world-renowned sculptor Aristide Maillol (1861–1944). He was born at 6 rue du Puig del Mas, now a shoe shop and identified by a plaque. At the age of 20 he moved to Paris, working as a painter and tapestry designer, and it was not until he was nearly 40, his eyesight too weak for tapestry, that he turned to sculpture. By 1910 he was internationally famous

for his monumental female nudes, breaking with the emotion of Rodin and developing instead the more serene classical traditions.

There are several Maillol sculptures to be seen in Banyuls (and others in Port Vendres, Céret and Perpignan). These are in the garden of the town hall; on **Ile Grosse**, a small island connected to the mainland by a causeway, where there is the artist's controversial half-relief war memorial; and at his home, 4 km (2½ miles) inland, where his most famous work *The Thinker* (in French, La Pensée) has been set above his tomb.

Maillol's home, set among vineyards, has recently been converted into a museum of his life. It makes a pleasant walk from the town. Starting at the sea front, follow avenue Général de Gaulle, pass under the railway bridge, and where the road curves sharply right take the left turn beside the river. After about 90 minutes, take the bridge across the river and follow the road for another half-hour. The same itinerary can be followed by car but this is to miss the scent of resin and vines and the ambience which attracted the artist back home.

Banyuls is at the northernmost tip of the underwater reserve of Cerbère-Banyuls, the first protected zone of its type in the entire Mediterranean. But

*M*ountain oaks are a feature of the landscape—look out also for cork oaks, whose thick bark provides the stopper for your wine bottle.

even if you neither dive nor snorkel, you can still get an idea of the kaleidoscopic marine life of the region by visiting the Arago Laboratory on the south side of the marina. In its aquarium (daily in summer, 9 a.m.–noon and 2–10 p.m.) there are more than 40 tanks of fish and invertebrates—colourful, bizarre, beautiful and sometimes simply unbelievable. There is also a display of local birds.

There is plentiful accommodation in the town and a choice of restaurants (*see* HOTELS AND RESTAURANTS).

Banyuls is a well-known label especially renowned for its sweet dessert wine. The most enjoyable way of sampling it is to take a **wine tour**, which can be booked at the Tourist Office by the harbour. Most famous are the ancient underground cellars of **Mas Reig** and the historic **Templiers**.

Walking from Banyuls

The famous transpyrenean footpaths GR10 and HRP begin and end in Banyuls so that among the lightly clad sunbathers it is not unusual to see the occasional red-faced hiker carrying a heavy backpack.

You can reproduce something of the excitement by following these classic footpaths yourself, if only for a short way. Begin by following avenue Puig del Mas away from the seafront until red and white stripes indicate a concrete path to the right. The path leads across a road and under the railway line, from where the GR10/HRP begins a steepish climb

The Passeurs

The men and women who acted as guides across the Pyrenees during the Spanish Civil War and World War II were known as *passeurs*. They were by no means all professional smugglers and very few were shepherds or mountain guides; instead they tended to be waiters and hoteliers, mayors and clergy and even members of the police and frontier guards.

The first clandestine crossings of the Spanish Civil War were from France to Spain as members of the International Brigade made their way over the closed frontier to join the Republican forces. Liverpool docker, Frank Deegan, was one who took the train to Perpignan and then hiked for 16 hours over the mountains, mostly at night, eventually arriving at the castle at *Figueres* to join "hundreds of men from almost every country in the world".

As the Nationalists advanced through Aragón, so the defeated Republicans began making their way north over the Pyrenees. Many still hoped to regroup but in the end strategic retreat turned to flight and thousands began arriving at French border posts with Catalonia.

During World War II it is estimated that some 35,000 people escaped over the Pyrenees, both from Occupied and Vichy France, into a technically neutral Spain, either intending to pass on to Britain or to another safer country. The first wave came with the capitulation of France in 1940 and General de Gaulle's radio appeal for Frenchmen to join the "Free French" army. Another rush came in 1942 when German troops moved into the Vichy zone in response to Allied landings in North Africa. Half of the French fugitives joined the Free French forces and 9,000 of them were later killed in action.

Many of the guides were Spanish Republicans who had become fugitives living along the frontier, wanted both by the Spanish authorities and by the Nazis. In the early days of the war a crossing was relatively easy and the penalty for failure not severe. Escapers often simply took a train or strolled across the frontier at one of the border villages like Latour de Carol. For a Frenchman who was caught there could be a month in prison and a 200F fine. All that changed with the German occupation of the Vichy zone. The French frontier guards, numbering no more than 800 men including reserves, were joined by some 1,200 Germans and Austrians, usually picked for mountaineering skills honed in Bavaria and the Alps. In addition, the Nazis employed intelligence agents along the frontier. About 15 people were shot dead trying to escape but between 2,500 and 5,000 escapers were caught and 1,000 of them were subsequently executed or died in concentration camps. As many as 30 may have died in accidents in the mountains. As for the *passeurs*, half of them were eventually caught, of whom a dozen were shot; 150 died in concentration camps.

up towards the **Madeloc tower**. Somewhat before the tower, the GR10/HRP begins a level traverse towards the **Col de Baillaury**, deep in the heart of the Albères. Here you can either continue, turn back, or climb away from the GR10/HRP on another footpath which zig-zags up to the Madeloc tower (3 hours from Banyuls).

The historic and isolated **Col de Banyuls**, right on the frontier, is another worthwhile hiking goal. Begin as for Maillol's tomb (*see* above), but rather than cross the river, continue ahead following signs for the col (pass). The road eventually turns to track, climbing steadily through olive groves and vineyards and finally reaching the Col de Banyuls after about 3 hours. This pass, with its lovely views into a deserted corner of Spain, was the site of an historical battle. In 1793, a small force of French from Banyuls held a Spanish attack at bay, helped by their women who risked their lives carrying ammunition and supplies. The defence of the col is commemorated in a giant painting in the Hôtel de Ville (town hall) in Banyuls.

Cerbère

Ten kilometres (6 miles) south of Banyuls sur Mer, France comes to an end at Cerbère, named after the mythological three-headed dog (in English, Cerberus) who guarded the entrance to the Underworld. Yet beyond Cerbère lies not Hell but the Costa Brava, equal in beauty to the Côte Vermeille. The frontier post is on the hill beyond the village (15 June–30 Sept 24–hours a day; 7 a.m.- midnight rest of the year).

Cerbère is also the terminus of the French rail services. Either here (or across the frontier at Port Bou) you will have to change trains. The giant railway arches are a feature of the town and some have been converted into shops and boutiques.

The beach is small but there are attractive coves nearby and the 30 minute walk to Cap Cerbère, beginning by the church, is recommended for its views along the coast.

Car Tours

A fabulous range of touring in the Côte Vermeille area includes inland vineyards, acre after acre of stone terracing with tiny huts and sheds used to store equipment and even, occasionally during harvest-time to accommodate pickers. The coastal corniche offers fabulous seaward views but, alas in summer, is very busy and often choked. Early morning or evening is the best time to avoid crowds though it is always advisable to allow extra time for this route.

Collioure—Argelès sur Mer—St André—Soréde—St Génis des Fontaines—Laroque des Albères—Le Boulou—Céret—La Jonquera—Figueres—Lança—Portbou—Cerbère—Banyuls—Port-Vendres—Collioure (136 km/ 84 miles; passports required).

Collioure—Argelès Plage—St Cyprien Plage—Etang de Canet and St Nazaire—Canet Plage—Perpignan—Elne—Argelès—Collioure (72 km/ 45 miles).

The Megastore in the Mountains

No longer a mountain fortress, Andorra attracts tourists and visitors from France and Spain in their thousands to take advantage of the huge range of duty-free goods on offer in Andorra la Vella. Keen walkers can escape the hectic valley to find a bit of paradise.

Ringed by high mountains, Andorra's first road access was not constructed until 1913. The second came in 1931. Even in the 1950s Andorra remained a sort of Shangri-La, cut off from the rest of Europe in its mountain fastness, just as it had been for hundreds of years.

Today Andorra is still the outsider and a Shangri-La of another sort. Surrounded by France and Spain it is a non-EU country in the midst of the EU Without the burden of armed forces, its taxation and duty-free policies have turned it into a kind of mountain megastore, its shop windows gleaming with consumer treats.

From the crammed valley roads the first impressions of this tiny country (just 462 km²/178 miles²) can be deceiving. But if you follow some of the side roads described, climbing high above the valley floor, you can still discover in the mountains the traditional Andorra of yesteryear.

The unusual round tower of the delicate Romanesque church at St Coloma near Andorra la Vella—the principality boasts many more like this.

Andorra la Vella

Andorra la Vella, capital of Andorra, lies in the eastern Valira valley, some 11 km (7 miles) from the Spanish

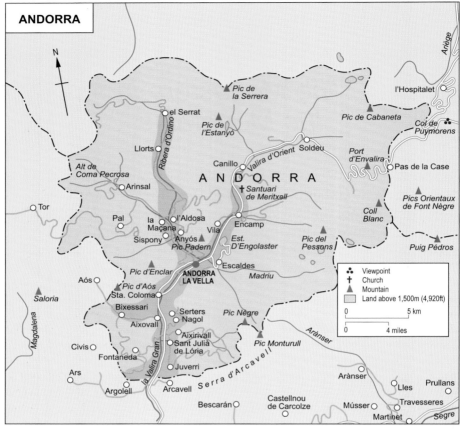

ANDORRA

Pic de la Serrera
l'Hospitalet
el Serrat
Pic de Cabaneta
Col de Puymorens
Pic de l'Estanyó
Llorts
Port d'Envalira
Pas de la Case
Canillo
Soldeu
Valira d'Orient
Ribera d'Ordino
Alt de Coma Pecrosa
ANDORRA
Arinsal
Santuari de Meritxell
Pics Orientaux de Font Nègre
Tor
Pal
la Maçana
l'Aldosa
Coll Blanc
Vila
Encamp
Sispony
Anyós
Pic Padern
Est. D'Engolaster
Pic del Pessons
Puig Pédros
Pic d'Enclar
ANDORRA LA VELLA
Escaldes
Madriu
Aós
Pic d'Aós
Sta. Coloma
Bixessari
Serters
Nagol
Pic Nègre
Aixovall
Aixirivall
Civis
Sant Julià de Lória
Pic Monturull
Fontaneda
Juverri
Ars
Argolell
Arcavell
Serra d'Arcavell
Aránser
Lles
Prullans
Saloria
Magdalena
la Valira Gran
Bescarán
Castellnou de Carcolze
Músser
Travesseres
Ariège
Martinet
Segre

	Viewpoint
†	Church
▲	Mountain
	Land above 1,500m (4,920ft)

0   5 km
0   4 miles

*T*he Principality of Andorra.

border and about 30 km (19 miles) from the French border. If shopping is the aim then Andorra la Vella is the town above all others in Andorra in terms of the sheer variety of goods. Here you can buy anything from a new car to a roll of film, at prices which undercut the French by anything up to 30 per cent and the Spanish by up to 20 per cent. But be warned, prices may not be so keen by the standard of, say, British or US shops (*see* SHOPPING below).

The old part of Andorra la Vella, known as the **Barri Antic**, is the most interesting to stroll around. Camouflaged by modern high-rise development, it stands on a high shelf above the Gran Valira river, straddling the main through road. The parish church of **St Esteve** has been somewhat spoiled over years of renovation and enlargement but the **Casa de la Vall** (government building) at the very heart of the old quarter has been sensitively preserved. Unprepossessing as it looks, this has been the seat of government since 1580. The coat of arms, over the door, was added in 1761. The interior is richly panelled in wood and stone and the inner chamber, for use by the "Very Illustrious Council General of the Principality", can be seen on a free guided tour. Almost wholly in wood from the bare floor and carved panelling to the seating upholstered in purple, there is a sense of history that is almost palpable. Casa de la Vall has a strong sense of history yet is uncharacteristically simple—but, then, the whole history of Andorra displays a certain naïvety.

History

The early history of Andorra is shrouded in mystery. Some have conjectured that the ancient Andorrans were the Pyrenean tribe of the Andosines who, according to the Greek historian Polybe, fought against Hannibal. This seems unlikely, however, since Hannibal almost certainly crossed the Pyrenees at le Perthus, far to the east. Later, Andorra was probably under Visigoth rule. According to legend, the son of Charlemagne, Louis le Débonnaire, liberated Andorra from the Moors but there is no hard evidence that the Moors even reached Andorra, let alone ruled it.

In fact, the first written reference to Andorra is not before AD 839, in the Acta de Consagració which is in the archives at La Seu d'Urgell. From this it is clear that the villages of Andorra la Vella, San Juliá (then called Laurédia), Santa Coloma, La Massana, Ordino, Encamp and Canillo already existed.

In this historical mystery it is rather easier to unravel the way Andorra became a principality co-ruled by Spain and France. A document dated 1133 provides the first clue, showing that Andorra was ruled by the counts of Urgell. The French interest arose by the simple process of marriage. Ermensende de Castellbó married Roger Bernard II, Count of Foix, bringing with her the extensive Castellbó possessions in modern Andorra. There was considerable friction between Urgell and Foix as a result but by 1278 all was resolved by the act of Pariatge, sharing control between the bishops of Urgell and the counts of Foix. On the Spanish side, that is how things remain today. But on the French side, the coronation of Henry II of Foix as King of France in 1589 effectively brought half control of Andorra under the French state.

There was one attempt to end the "French connection" in 1793 when the French revolutionary government refused to accept the Andorran tribute or *quista* because it was a remnant of the hated feudalism. The Andorrans, however, preferred the old relationship and Napoleon restored the *quista* in 1806.

Today Andorra is still theoretically ruled by its Spanish and French "co-Princes" but, in reality, power has been devolved to the 28-member Council General, comprised of four representatives for each of the seven parishes. Government was entirely in the hands of the richest families until the vote was extended to all heads of families in 1866 (*see* ORDINO below). The vote was only extended to all men in 1933 and to women in 1970.

Shopping

Prices may look good in Andorra and the frenzied activity of other shoppers

205

is encouraging, but if you are contemplating spending big money make sure you first know what the price is back home. Although there are tourists in Andorra from all over the world, shops primarily set their prices to undercut Spain—not London, Hong Kong or New York.

Furthermore, prices are not the whole story. Andorra made a new agreement with the EU in 1991 but is not a full member, and any purchases you make may be subject to duties and taxes at the border. Check before you buy! There is a good deal of petty smuggling but Customs checks are becoming more and more rigorous. To get into Spain you have to pass through a factory-sized Customs shed with a high chance of being stopped and searched. For France, the border check is less careful but there are spot checks along the way. Many a holiday smuggler has breathed a sigh of relief after the French border, only to be pulled up on the approach to Ax-les-Thermes!

Remember, too, that Andorra is not subject to the same consumer protection regulations that exist in many other countries. Competition is fierce and free enterprise is king. The digital watch you have your eye on, for example, may be a factory clearance manufactured five years ago and its internal battery half used up. Film could be out of date. Foodstuffs may not be fresh. And that famous brand name might be a pirate imitation. Check carefully and (in the case of durables) make sure that you get the packaging and guarantee.

Having said all that, there are some tremendous bargains to be had in Andorra. Compare prices in several shops (in both French and Spanish currency) and then try to negotiate. It is possible to buy at below the stated price, especially if you are buying more than one item.

Specialists shops tend to group together, car accessories, electrical, sports, etc. though in the main one-way system in Andorra la Vella you will find just about anything you seek —with the high rates these are the most glamorous of the shops, the glass and brass gleaming. Here as elsewhere you may find the prices are not displayed and you will have to go into the shop and enter negotiations. Smaller, side-street shops may be more accommodating with discounts. There is a trend for large superstores, a number of different outlets including a giant food and drink section

Andorra is a shopper's paradise. Punt de Trobada is just one of several huge new American-style shopping malls.

under one roof. In the south of the principality, a brand-new store called **Trobada** just outside **St Julia de Lloria** has eveything—including covered car parking and several cafés and restaurants. Just a couple of hundred yards further on is another complex, **Jumbo**.

Just outside St Julia are a number of large petrol stations—these take francs or pesetas, but definitely no credit cards. Prices are very good, significantly lower than in France and a shade cheaper than Spain.

If you are looking for car accessories the ugly stretch of built-up road between St Julia de Lloria and Andorra la Vella should furnish your needs, though parking is difficult.

In Andorra la Vella casual parking is almost impossible so head for one of the multi-storey or pay-and-display town centre parking areas. Also remember never to leave purchases on show in a parked car—this is a thieves' as well as a shopper's paradise. If you like department stores, head for the **Pyrenees Center** on the main shopping street of Andorra la Vella. Individual shops nearby include Suissa watches, Benetton fashion woollens, Pentax cameras and Technics hi-fi.

If you want to stay in Andorra there is a choice of relatively inexpensive hotels (*see* HOTELS AND RESTAURANTS).

Along the Valira d'Orient to Pas de la Casa

From Andorra la Vella the valley of the Valira d'Orient climbs steadily eastwards until just beyond Soldeu, where the road snakes up in steep hairpins to the highest road pass in the Pyrenees, the Port d'Envalira (2,408 meters/7,900 ft). From there the road drops just as steeply again to the Andorran frontier town of Pas de la Casa.

Escaldes, Engolasters and the Madriu Valley

Escaldes is virtually an extension of Andorra la Vella, famous for the hot spring that splashes down on the right-hand side of the main road (and which froths and steams in the glass pyramids to the right). Strongly sulphurous, these waters are said to be good for rheumatism, blood circulation, respiratory problems, and the laundry—you can tell people from Escaldes because their clothes are immaculate! And at a maximum temperature of 61°C (14°F), the waters are even used for heating some of the hotels. While in **Escaldes** you may like to try a change of pace and visit the **exhibition of sculptures** by local artist Josep Viladomat i Massanes. The 140 works are highly regarded figures from religious characters through society men and women to simple nudes. Find the exhibition in the Edifici Salita Parc, avenida Parc de la Mola in Escaldes (5 p.m.–9 p.m. and also 11 a.m.–2 p.m. Sundays and holidays).

Just beyond the steaming pyramids, a right turn climbs up the steep valley side to a top road high above the valley floor. By turning left on to the top road you can reach the beautiful 12th-century Romanesque church of **St Miquel d'Engolasters** (4 km/2½ miles from Escaldes). The tower is unusual for the narrowness of its three groups of *ajimez* (paired) windows, which get longer towards the steep slate roof.

207

Continue driving past the church and you will come to the picturesque **Engolasters** lake, fringed by mountain pines, aromatic in the sun. To stretch your legs, follow the track that goes off south-west from the final bend before the lake. Those really keen on hiking can keep on it over the **Coll Jovell** into the **Madriu valley**, one of the most entrancing in all Andorra.

The direct way into the Madriu is the GR7 footpath which climbs up from Escaldes and crosses the top road near the Engolasters turning. From there the initial climb is steep, but once at the hamlet of Entremesaigues the path levels out somewhat. This is a little bit of paradise, the hectic world of the valley floor so far below as to seem another planet.

Beyond Escaldes the CG2 road climbs on via Encamp and the little church of **St Roma de les Bons** to Canillo. The dense urban landscape is left behind and the ever-present but distant peaks become more insistent. Immediately before Canillo, a turning right leads to the new **sanctuary of Meritxell**, where thousands of Andorrans gather every 8th September, the National Day. It was in 1972 that fire ruined the original Romanesque church and destroyed the wooden image of the Virgin of Meritxell, since 1873 the patroness of the Principality. Beside it, the unusual new sanctuary designed by the famous architect Ricard Bofill was inaugurated in 1976 and a replica Virgin, with huge mournful eyes, installed in the gleaming white and black interior. The burned-out ruins have been preserved, a rare opportunity to compare ancient and modern treatments of the same theme.

Canillo to Soldeu

Canillo is an attractive town which has responded to tourism without losing too much of its Andorran charm. Its most important development is the **Ice Palace** (Palau de Gel), containing not only the largest ice rink in southern Europe, but also a swimming pool, squash court and small cinema. The church has the highest tower in Andorra (30 metres/100 ft). But it is across the river at the village of Prats that the atmosphere is at its most authentic, some of the lanes still cobbled and flanked by old stone houses.

Beyond Canillo this traditional flavour of Andorra strengthens. Architecturally, it is at its most glorious in the **church of St Joan** (John) **de Caselles**, on the right of the road after about 1 km (half-a-mile). Stone built in the 12th century, it has the usual Romanesque tower, somehow so sympathetic to the mountains, and its porch—where horses would have been tied up in the old days—is a particularly attractive feature. The inside is even more impressive for the restored fragments of a polychrome stucco Christ and a fresco of the Calvary which date from the building of the church. The magnificent screen, from around 1525, is the work of the "Master of Canillo".

Ransol, just above the road to the left some 5 km (3 miles) after Canillo, is another gem of old Andorra, a picturesque clutter of stone walls, wood beams and slate roofs. The valley behind, climbing north to the frontier, is a delight for hikers and car tourers alike with a tabled picnic spot at the far end.

A second opportunity to explore one of the high northern valleys by car

208

comes just before Soldeu, a ski development some 2 km (1 mile) after Ransol. Where the road sweeps round the tight bend just before the resort, watch out for the left-hand turn into the **Incles valley**. This is a more open valley than the Ransol, dotted with well-restored stone houses. It is a favourite with hikers because it gives a not too difficult access to the GR10 and HRP long-distance footpaths. From the head of the valley, where there is a campsite, you can choose routes of varying degrees of difficulty, but all of them through some of the remotest scenery of the range. No bears have been sighted within Andorra itself for several years but there remains the faint possibility that one or two may survive on the French side of the border.

Over Port d'Envalira to Pas de la Casa

A little after Soldeu, where the CG2 begins its final well-engineered climb to the Envalira pass, a right turn leads to the small ski resort of **Grau Roig**, towards the head of the **Envalira valley**, above which ski lifts swarm down the slope from the ridge. You can park here and take the footpath through the woods to the **Pessons lakes**, a whole series of sparkling blue pools on a summers day against the raw nudity of the rock. The athletic can alternatively climb east on the GR7 to the frontier at the **Porteille Blanche** (2,517 metres/ 8,258 ft), thus linking with the old smuggling trail up from Porta (*see* ARIEGE above).

Back on the CG2 the views become more and more overwhelming as the road climbs. Sometimes in the early morning or on an overcast day, it is possible to emerge from cloud into

brilliant sunshine, the white mass swirling below like an ocean. Once over the crest the road drops steeply to Pas de la Casa, just inside the Andorran border. Hugely popular with the French at weekends, Pas de la Casa is positively bursting with bargain hunters and the effervescent atmosphere of a frontier town continually in festival mood. The stock is less extensive than in Andorra la Vella but many French shoppers feel no need to go further. Watches, cameras, electronic goods and sports clothing are the main buys, together with foodstuffs —especially butter.

Along the Valira del Nord to Arcalis

The northern Valira valley is undoubtedly the most picturesque part of Andorra's main valley bottom. From Andorra la Vella to La Massana (5 km/3 miles) the road remains quite built up, but it is still worth pausing to see the Romanesque **bridge of St Antoni** in the Grella gorge.

At **La Massana** you have the opportunity to detour westwards on the minor road that climbs to the ski villages of **Arinsal** (4 km/2½ miles) and **Pal** (5 km/3 miles), nestling in a soft curve of the mountain high above the valley floor, the houses huddled together beneath the Romanesque church tower. Driving on, the road climbs towards the frontier, turning to track at the airy **Botella pass**, which at 2,069 metres (6,788 ft) makes a wonderful viewpoint over the bare uplands. A few native Andorrans with jeeps continue along the track which connects with Alins and the Cardos valley in Spain. Doubtless, this route is sometimes also used by smugglers. Smuggling was a common and colourful part of the history of Andorra for centuries. The local name for a man who carried goods over the mountains was *paquetaire*. Unlike most World War II escapers, their knowledge of the mountains was so exact that they could march at night when the chance of interception was minimal. But it was not these men who grew rich; rather it was the entrepreneurs and many an Andorran family fortune has been founded on contraband tobacco.

Back on the main CG3 road, the landscape beyond La Massana opens out to tobacco fields and green pasture capped by forests of mountain pine and bare rock peaks. **Ordino** (2 km/ 1 mile from La Massana) is the most attractive of the major Andorran holiday resorts. Here construction has been limited to traditional houses and low-rise apartments and hotels, all sympathetic to the stone and timber tradition.

Be sure to visit the ancestral home of the d'Areny de Plandolit family (**Casa d'Areny de Plandolit**). It is a fascinating house for two reasons. Firstly, the family is closely linked with Andorran history, most notably Guillem, baron of Senaller, who introduced the reform of 1866, giving the vote to all Andorran heads of family (*Caps de Casa*). Secondly, it is a wonderful example of traditional Andorran architecture and furnishing (though an atypical aristocratic family).

After Ordino, all of urban Andorra is left behind and the road is fringed by tobacco fields dotted with houses, whose open lofts are hung with the drying leaves. Andorran agricultural conditions are hardly favourable for tobacco but it is a question of fiscal conditions rather than climate. The two tobacco companies based in

Andorra (Reynolds and Philip Morris) can import Virginia tobacco tax-free but only so long as they buy an equivalent quantity of Andorran tobacco. Hence Andorran tobacco is grown and sold but almost none of it is good enough to be used.

The road passes through a series of delightful villages—**La Cortinada**, **Arans** and **Llorts**. Finally, some 16 km (10 miles) from Andorra la Vella, you reach the well-spaced buildings of the hamlet of **El Serrat**, gleaming against the velvet green grass on a gentle rise at the head of the valley. If you want to explore seriously, then this attractive little village has to be your base.

 Beyond El Serrat, the road changes direction and climbs the side valley of the Tristaina to the west, to the **Tristaina lakes** and the ski resort of **Arcalis**. All situated at over 2,200 metres (7,218 ft), the lakes are set amongst truly savage high-mountain landscape. A circular itinerary takes in the three largest lakes (**Primer**, **Mig** and **Amunt**) and can be completed in about 4 hours of fast walking. If you are staying in El Serrat, you will be better to make a day of it and carry a picnic. The HRP footpath also crosses this neck of Andorra.

In the opposite direction, the HRP follows the track that rises eastwards from the road 5 km (3 miles) above El Serrat. You can drive on the track as far as the **Borda de Sorteny** refuge, the best mountain refuge in all of Andorra with about 30 places.

Daytime moon on the road to Arcalis, one of the most picturesque parts of Andorra.

South along the Gran Valira

The **church of St Coloma** at Santa Coloma (virtually the southern extension of Andorra la Vella) is one of the most unusual Romanesque buildings in the Pyrenees. In complete contrast to traditional Romanesque architecture, its 12th-century tower is round. Moreover, some experts believe the apse dates from the 10th century, making the church possibly the oldest building in Andorra. It stands just to the west of the main road.

Continuing south on the CG1 watch out for the Romanesque **bridge of La Margineda** on the left-hand side of the road. Almost immediately afterwards, a turning right climbs along the Os valley to the village of **Beixissarri**, sympathetically renovated by well-to-do Andorrans. The road then divides. A left turn climbs in exciting tight bends to the old church at **Canolic** and a splendid restaurant. Ahead, the road crosses the frontier to the gorgeous village of **Os de Civis**, which although Spanish can only be reached from Andorra.

Back on the CG2, your last chance for shopping before leaving Andorra comes at **St Juliá de Lória**. From the centre of St Juliá, two roads climb up eastwards. One leads to Nagol, where the little **St Cerni** hermitage contains the oldest Romanesque fresco in Andorra, believed to date from 1055. The other climbs to Aubinya and the even tinier **St Roma** chapel, endearingly set on a shoulder among the pine scrub. From the south end of St Juliá, a road climbs west to the village of Fontaneda where there is a ruined castle and an 11th-century church.

Seaside Capital of the Spanish Basque Region

The city resort of San Sebastián is an interesting and ideal base for seeking out the delightful villages of the coast or touring inland. There are plenty of excellent restaurants in which to sample the seafood specialities of Guipúzcoa.

In Guipúzcoa, the Pyrenees roll down to the sea, in contrast both with the flat coastal plain of the French Basque country and the dramatic cliffs of the Mediterranean end of the range. Here gently rounded hills dotted with sheep and whitewashed and red-roofed farms curve down into mightly Atlantic surf. Only a few sharper peaks stand out, notably the triple summits of Peñas de Haya, visible behind San Sebastián and Fuenterrabía.

In Guipúzcoa the Pyrenees roll down to the sea, providing beautiful walking country immediately behind the coast.

For holidaymakers there is a tremendous diversity. San Sebastián is a sophisticated city resort, its famous La Concha beach recalling Rio de Janeiro. But this coastline also hides exquisite seaside villages like Pasajes. Inland there is delightful touring. And when it comes to eating, Guipúzcoa has a great culinary tradition, as underlined by San Sebastián's 30 dining clubs.

San Sebastián

The city of **San Sebastián** is an immensely attractive base for a beach holiday and for touring the region. Despite its up-to-date business image, the busy docks, modern shops, neon lighting and apartment block suburbs, it is

213

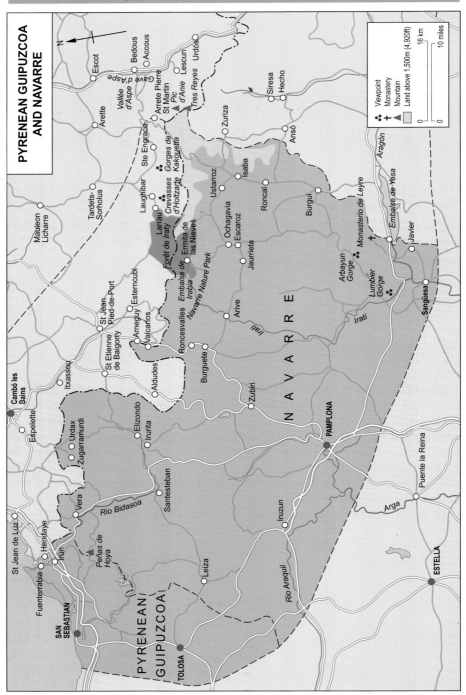

PYRENEAN GUIPUZCOA AND NAVARRE

Key
- Viewpoint
- Monastery
- Mountain
- Land above 1,500m (4,920ft)

16 km
10 miles

Escot
Bedous
Accous
Urdos
Arette
Lescun
Arrete Pierre
St Martin
Pic d'Anie
Tres Reyes
Siresa
Hecho
Ste Engrace
Gorges de Kakouetta
Zuriza
Ansó
Vallée d'Aspe
Gave d'Aspe
Mauleon
Licharre
Tardets-Sorholus
Laughibar
Crevasses d'Holtzarte
Ustarroz
Isaba
Roncal
Burgui
Aragón
Arbayun Gorge
Lumbier Gorge
Monasterio de Leyre
Embalse de Yesa
Javier
Larrau
Forêt de Iraty
Ermita de las Nieves
Ochagavia
Escaroz
Jaurrieta
Sanguesa
St Jean Pied-de-Port
Esterncubi
Arneguy
Valcarlos
Embalse de Irabia
Navarre Nature Park
Roncesvalles
Arive
Irati
Irati
St Etienne de Baigorry
Itxassou
Aldudes
Burguete
Zubiri
Cambó les Bains
Espelette
Elizondo
Irurita
Urdax
Zugarramurdi
PAMPLONA
Puente la Reina
St Jean de Luz
Hendaye
Vera
Rio Bidasoa
Santesteban
Inzun
Arga
Fuenterrabia
Irun
Peñas de Hoya
ESTELLA
SAN SEBASTIAN
Leiza
Rio Araquil
PYRENEAN GUIPUZCOA
TOLOSA
NAVARRE

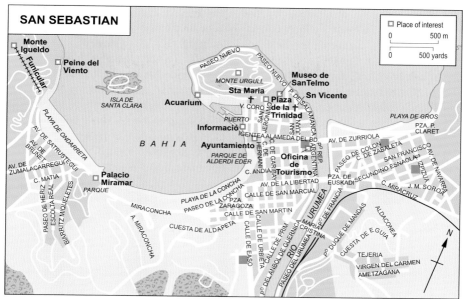

SAN SEBASTIAN

☐ Place of interest

0 | 500 m
0 | 500 yards

Monte Igueldo
Funicular
Peine del Viento
ISLA DE SANTA CLARA
PASEO NUEVO
MONTE URGULL
Sta Maria
Acuarium
V. CORO
PUERTO
Informació
Museo de SanTelmo
Sn Vicente
Plaza de la Trinidad
IGENTEA
ALAMEDA DEL BDO
AV. DE ZURRIOLA
PLAYA DE GROS
PZA. P. CLARET
B A H I A
Ayuntamiento
PARQUE DE ALDERDI EDER
Oficina de Tourismo
PZA. DE EUSKADI
PASEO DE COLON
C. DE ZABALETA
SAN FRANCISCO
AV. DE NAVARRA
J. M. SOROA
PLAYA DE ONDARRETA
AV. DE SATRUSTEGUI
AV. DE BRUNET
AV. DE ZUMALACARREGUI
C. MATIA
PASEO DE HERIZ
ESCOLTA REAL
BIARRITZ MIQUELETES
Palacio Miramar
PARQUE
MIRACONCHA
A. MIRACONCHA
PLAYA DE LA CONCHA
PASEO DE LA CONCHA
PZA. ZARAGOZA
CUESTA DE ALDAPETA
C. ANDIA
AV. DE LA LIBERTAD
CALLE DE SAN MARCIAL
CALLE DE SAN MARTIN
CALLE DE EASO
CALLE DE URBIETA
CALLE DE SAN MARTIN
C. DE PRIM
C. DE GARIBAY
RIO URUMEA
P DE FRANCIA
AV. MARIA CRISTINA
PASEO DEL URUMEA
P DUQUE DE MANDAS
CUESTA DE EGUIA
ALDACONEA
SECUNDINO ESNAOLA
C. MIRACRUZ
EIZIZUA
TEJERIA
VIRGEN DEL CARMEN
AMETZAGANA
N

*T*own plan of San Sebastián.

as much a resort of gentility, with elegant turn-of-the-century villas and classical seaside frontages.

San Sebastián was orginally a fishing village, predominantly catching cod and whales, from which it expanded into an important trading port handling the oil and wine of northern Spain for markets in France, England and the Low Countries. The port still flourishes. The commercial part of the town starts south of the street known as the Boulevard which runs east–west to Puente la Zurriola, the city's most seaward bridge. It was from here that the old city walls were demolished in 1863 to make way for expansion.

*T*he Guipüzcoa and the Navarre regions.

The civic architecture here is grand and the main bridges heavily decorated. St Catalina bridge over the Urumea river, second down from the ocean, is particularly ornate. It is overlooked by the magnificent de-luxe hotel **Maria Cristina**, one of the finest in the Pyrenees (*see* below). The shopping in San Sebastián is stylish as befits its status as one of Spain's most elegant holiday resorts. High fashion, especially in leather wear, predominates in the wide central streets like **calle de St Martin, avenida de la Libertad** and their smaller cross streets. Parking is predictably difficult in the city centre and is therefore restricted to 90 minutes. You must buy a parking ticket in a tobacconist.

Beaches

San Sebastián's best beach, **La Concha**, which is moon-shaped and sheltered by hilly promontories on both sides, is right in front of the city centre.

Breakers are also dampened by the tiny island of St Clara, which can be visited by ferry. Some of the best hotels are around this beach, together with fashionable restaurants, bars and clubs. San Sebastián's glory as a summer beach resort was at its height from the 1880s when it became a favourite haunt and then official summer residence for Queen Maria-Cristina and the Spanish royal family who had the Palace Miramar built overlooking the Concha Bay. The presence of the royal family, their royal friends and court of Madrid gave San Sebastián enduring appeal and although royalty is no longer the major attraction, many of Madrid's old families still retain property in the resort. Its accessibility from France and reverence of gastronomy also makes it appealing to the French.

The westward extension of the crescent-shaped Concha beach is known as the **Ondarreta**. It begins beyond the rocky outcrop backed by the **Miramar Palace**. The palace was designed, in part, by British architect Selden Wornum and its gardens are open to the public. At the far end of the Ondarreta, there is a park from which a funicular climbs to the top of **Monte Igueldo**, where there is a hotel and a small zoo. Also make a point of seeing the water's edge modern sculpture, *Peine del Viente* (Comb of the Wind) by a local artist. A third beach, Playa de Gros is not recommended as it is close to the mouth of the River Urumea and subject to pollution.

The Old Quarter

The **Old Quarter** of San Sebastián with its narrow streets and tall cramped houses is packed onto the lower slopes of Monte Urgull, topped by the giant statue of Christ. Although the buildings with their wooden shutters and balconies, the cobbles and the lay-out of the quarter give it an authentic medieval appearance, it was in fact almost entirely rebuilt after 1813. The Anglo-Portuguese alliance celebrated victory over France by razing the city which had been occupied by Napoleon's troops for almost five years. And it was not the first such

tragedy for, vulnerable in its position close to the Franco-Spanish border, San Sebastián has been destroyed many times.

For lovers of seafood, the Old Quarter is also the centre of the shellfish industry, sold everywhere from inexpensive kiosks to fashionable restaurants soon after landing at the old port from which the streets of the Old Quarter rise. Search particularly the area around the **Plaza de la Constitutión** for bars serving seafood speciality *pinchos*, as Basque-style *tapas* are called. You pay about 100 ptas a portion. The plaza is one of the most architecturally attractive sites in the city. The balconied tall houses which surround it were once used as grandstand seats for bullfights. Nowadays it is still a social centre, catering for large crowds who come to dance on high-days and holidays.

Also in the old quarter near the foot of **Monte Urgull** are two interesting churches, the baroque-style **St Maria** and the less ornate **St Vincent**, parts of which date from the 11th century. Between the two is the **St Telmo Museum**, a mixture of art gallery and folk museum with exhibits ranging from folk dress to ancient Basque grave stones (displayed in stunningly attractive cloisters with intricate vaulting). There is also a small selection of Spanish painting, including works of **Zuloaga, El**

Whitewashed farmhouses reflect the sun on the rolling clifftops on the south side of San Sebastián.

Greco and the more recent frescoes of **José Sert**. The museum is housed in a 16th-century monastery, parts of which operate as a conference centre. Behind the museum, several footpaths rise to the peak of the hill, a steep climb through parkland to the statue of Christ and the **Military Museum** housed in the small castle of **St Cruz de la Mota** built by Sancho the Strong. There is a sad little cemetery on Monte Urgull where a number of British soldiers are buried along with their Spanish comrades, victims of a botched-up British intervention in the Carlists' wars of the 1830s. Less challenging is the stroll or drive around the Paseo Nuevo, a corniche on the seaward side of the base of Monte Urgull which ends at the **Maritime Museum** housed with an interesting aquarium in the **Palacio del Mar**. Directly across La Concha Bay you can see Monte Urgull's "twin" peak, **Monte Igueldo** which protects the beach at the westernmost end of the bay.

San Juan Pasajes and San Pedro

The most photogenic area of town is **Pasajes** —a community split in two by the River Oyarzun with San Juan Pasajes on the right bank and San Pedro on the left. San Juan is the less spoiled of the two though it is difficult to find by road. It is far easier to take the tiny ferry-boat from San Pedro, a journey which will give you the best views of these attractively painted waterside homes built around a Basque-style church and moodily reflected in the waters of the tiny fishing harbour.

The idyllic harbour of Pasajes, on the north side of San Sebastián, has long attracted artists and writers like Victor Hugo.

To find **San Pedro**, simply follow signs for Pasajes from the centre of San Sebastián. You will have to cross the Urumea river by the ornate **Sta Catalina bridge** and drive some 2 km (1 mile) east. First you will pass **Pasajes Ancho**, the busy commercial docks, active with the loading and unloading of containers for the Madrid–Irun railway which runs behind the docks. There are also large fishing fleets and their necessary accoutrements—huge warehouses, crates, crushed ice, lorries and fishermen's cafés, bars and restaurants. Finally, you come to a collection of colourful old fishermen's cottages, once inhabited not by Basques but by fishermen from Galicia, in the north-west of Spain. It is from here, right by a modern war memorial, that you catch the ferry past the little fishing boats for the ten-minute journey to San Juan Pasajes. San Juan is tiny and picturesque with what are now converted bijou residences with lots of flowering plants and colourful shutters. The views back to the harbour through ancient stone arches are memorable. Look out for the house numbered 59 in San Juan's main street; this was the temporary home of writer Victor Hugo when, on 4 September 1843 he heard the tragic news that his daughter Léopoldine had drowned.

(To find Pasajes San Juan by road follow signs from San Sebastián to Lezo; at Lezo take the Fuenterrabia road, almost immediately turning left along the river to San Juan.)

Festivals
San Sebastián has several major celebrations thoughout the year—periods when the city can be visited or avoided depending on your temperament. In February there is a grand carnival, lasting several days. In July the city hosts a major international jazz festival. The week of 15 August is **Semana Grande** with carnival parades, fireworks and street dancing. The second fortnight of August is dedicated to a **music festival**. Finally, on the first two Sundays in September are the annual **Trainera**

218

rowing races, which arouse great passions.

It is obviously advisable to book in advance for festival periods and there are plenty of hotels to choose from (*see* HOTELS AND RESTAURANTS.)

There is no shortage of eating places in San Sebastián and its surrounding area and there are also a disproportionate number of highly recommended restaurants when compared with other cities of the Pyrenees.

Trips from San Sebastián

West along the delightful Basque coast, the tiny port of Guetaria (30 km/19 miles) was the birthplace of Sebastian Elcano (also known as Del Cano), the Basque captain who completed Magellan's attempted circumnavigation of the globe after Magellan himself was killed in the Philippines. Elcano's ship, the *Victoria*, was the only one of the five which started out in 1518, crawling back to Spain in 1522. The ship and its crew were much lauded on their return and hailed as the first circumnavigators. Others insist that Magellan had made an earlier journey from the Philippines to Europe and therefore qualified as the first circumnavigator, and others still bestow the honour on his slave, Enrique de Malacca.

While in **Guetaria** you may like to visit the highly recommended restaurant **Elkano**, named after the captain and specializing in fresh fish such as sole,

Spanish Basque Cuisine

The Basques eat three times more fish than other Spaniards and four times more than the average French person—which is why you will find plenty of good fish eating in San Sebastián, capital of this section of Spanish Basque country. The locals are well aware of their preoccupation with eating. The 30-plus *Sociedades Recreativas* or eating clubs are over-subscribed; prospective members join a waiting list to rub elbows with other local foodies.

Nouvelle Cuisine, or delicate portions, have little to do with Basque cooking. This is a weatherbeaten but immensely fertile land where produce grows fat and the wine is strong. Guipúzcoa specialities include *besugo* (sea bream) or *merluza* (hake, often served in a green sauce created from asparagus, clams and parsley), *shangurro*, *centollo* or *tsangurro* (all names for spider crab), *chipirones en su tinta* (squid in its own ink), *sardinas asadas* (grilled sardines), *angulas* (baby eels) and dishes based around *bacalao* (salt cod).

General Basque specialities also are much in evidence on the Atlantic coast. These include *txistorra* (spicy sausage), *marmitako* (fish and vegetable, especially pepper, stew) and *toro* (mixed fish stew). Spanish Basques have a favourite locally produced wine to accompany their fish dishes. Called *chacoli*, it is a pleasantly acidic white, produced in the area around the village of Guetaria, a coastal settlement 30 km (19 miles) west of San Sebastián.

turbot, sea bream and squid grilled over an oak fire. Expect to pay 5,000 ptas–7,000 ptas à la carte.

Just before Guetaria is **Zarauz**, once an important centre of the bacalao or salt-cod industry from where, after it was treated, it would be sent in large amounts all over Spain and Portugal.

There are two main routes into Navarre and the high mountains from San Sebastián. The smaller, prettier road initially follows the line of the **River Urumea** and passes through **Hernani**, a pleasant 10 km (6 miles) drive. There is not a great deal to stop for at Hernani, though its initial, unattractive face is misleading as, at the centre, there are a number of well-maintained Basque town houses complete with coats of arms and wrought-iron balconies. A faster, dual carriageway road leads south from San Sebastián 20 km (13 miles) to Tolosa.

Tolosa

Primarily an industrial town, ringed by high-rise flats, Tolosa has one of the least glamorized and intriguing medieval centres of the region. There has not been much money spent on conservation here so the glasswork panels of the old market are broken, the narrow streets are dimly lit by old-fashioned lanterns and black-clad widows and old men look from the upper windows of buildings you would think were derelict. Small wood and metal workshops still use the lower floors, as do dusty grocery shops and bars. Hanging over everything is the smell of strong Spanish tobacco. There are some better homes, once lived in by the successful traders of the region, though most of the town's better off, such as the owners of the giant papermills which create so much of the local employment, now have large whitewashed houses on the green hills surrounding the town. The parish church, which is in the centre of a maze of narrow streets, is impressively huge and heavily baroque. It is just beginning to undergo renovation.

Monte Jaizkibel, Fuenterrabía, Irún and the French border

You can travel the 20 km (12½ miles) to the French border at Irún in minutes on the motorway from San Sebastián. Far more attractive, however, is the almost secret back road over the coastal mountains to Irún via **Fuentarrabía**, a walled and well-preserved medieval town.

To find this back road from San Sebastián, follow signs for Lezo. **Lezo** is a pretty stone-built village, some of the wood-balconied houses bearing the family coat-of-arms. The surprisingly large village church, **Basilica del Santo Christo**, houses a statue of Christ, which, according to legend, helps local young women find happiness, sufficient wealth and a good husband.

From Lezo the road climbs steeply through pine forest and bracken, almost immediately giving views down to the Spanish Basque coast, which at this point is quite uninhabited, wild and windblown and used only by a few farmers and the army for military manoeuvres. There are a number of tracks which allow for marvellously bracing walks and from near the summit of **Mount Jaizkibel** (543 metres/1,781 ft) the views are most dramatic, especially at sunset.

After Mount Jaizkibel, the road drops to the hamlet **Guadalupe**, where the small chapel is the destination of an annual pilgrimage from Fuenterrabía during its summer *fiesta*. From here you start encountering the outlying buildings of Fuenterrabía, more French than Spanish at this stage, and see ahead the Bidasoa river which marks the border, and the beaches of the French Pays Basque.

Fuenterrabía

As you reach the valley floor, the massive 15th-century defensive walls of the old part of **Fuenterrabía** loom up. As a frontier town it has certainly seen a great deal of war action, and survived several attacks from the French. The 8 September pilgrimage to the shrine of **Our Lady of Guadalupe** is in gratitude for deliverance from one of these—a two-month battle in 1638 when it was attacked 20 times; when the lead ammunition ran out, the local women bought out their precious metal valuables and the muskets fired gold and silver.

You can drive through the old town but it is very narrow and it is better to go on foot. The main gateway is again dedicated to Our Lady of Guadalupe and carries the town coat of arms above the arch. Once through the arch you are in calle Mayor, a steep, cobbled street lined with medieval houses with their ground floors converted to shops—souvenirs, books, chemists and *objets d'art*—whilst washing and geraniums garland their upper wrought-iron balconies. There is an attractive small hotel in the street, the **Txoko Goxoa**. At the top of the street is the 11th-century Gothic church of **Santa Maria**, famous for having hosted the 1660 proxy wedding of Louis XIV of France and the Spanish Infanta Maria Teresa. A few days later the couple attended the official ceremony in St Jean de Luz across the River Bidasoa. Right at the top of calle Mayor is the large and light plaza de Armas, its far end open to wide views over the port of Fuenterrabía and the ocean. On your right, looking to sea, is Charles V Castle, part of

221

A sleeping dog lies in Fuenterrabía. This marvellously preserved town is noted for its traditional architecture.

which was also known as the Palace of Joan the Madwoman after the Spanish queen who married the unfortunately short-lived Phillip of Burgundy. She was grief-stricken by his death and refused to bury her beloved, instead keeping his corpse constantly by her side. The building is a huge, square, slate-grey fortress, now an unusual Parador hotel.

Irún

It is difficult to escape memories of the Spanish Civil War anywhere in Guipúzcoa, since devolution if not separatism is still such a live issue. The fall of Irún to the Fascists and the sealing of the Basque–French border, through which the Republicans had hoped for aid, was one of the turning points of the war. But, in fact, little aid was forthcoming, for Léon Blum, head of the French Popular Front government, refused to intervene in the hope that Italy and Germany would keep out of the war, too. Unfortunately for the Republicans, Germany and Italy did not.

Irún is today a typical frontier town with lots of shops dedicated primarily to the constant search by the French for cheap spirits and butter. But it sells a lot of other things besides, including olive oil, fruit and vegetables, perfume and souvenirs. The **church**, Our Lady of Juncal, is ornately decorated and the **Town Hall** is 16th century.

Just behind Irún, the **Peñas de Haya mountains** with their three distinct peaks (also known as the Three Crowns) make a wonderful viewpoint for a last (or first) panorama of the region. Best access is from the southern side of Irún, close to the Matadero General Frigorifico e Montero, a huge green factory building about 2 km (1 mile) from the motorway (A8).

Follow the small road signposted Barrio Meaka which climbs rapidly away from the urban sprawl of the valley into these heavily wooded mountains. The road hits its highest point after 8 km (5 miles) at the **Picoketa Pass** (490 metres/1,605 ft) and shortly afterwards there is a parking area (identified by a giant electicity pylon) which is where walkers should leave their cars. A poorly marked path climbs south and links the peaks **Muganix** (786 metres/2,580 ft) which you can reach in about half-an-hour; **Irumugarrieta** (806 metres/2,645 ft) another 15–30 minutes on and then **Txurrumurru** (826 metres/2,710 ft) to be reached after a total of about one hour.

Inland from San Sebastián

The north-western corner of Navarre, which pushes up to within a few kilometres of the coast, is a region of low, often densely-forested mountains and sparse habitation.

Even on the main N240 route between Pamplona and San Sebastián the remote nature of the landscape is apparent, only occasionally tamed by a sprinkling of grazing sheep like hailstones on a summer's day. But a far more exciting way of passing between San Sebastián and Pamplona is the road over the mountains via Goizueta, which follows the narrow gorge of the Urumea river amid dense black forest.

Between Pamplona and Irún (95km/ 60 miles) the most direct route is the N121 which follows the Bidasoa river for much of its length. About half way it gives access to the Baztan valley, the largest parish in Navarre. The valley of the Baztan is intensely rural and among its emerald green fields the ancient Basque "tower houses" are still to be seen. There is a marvellous example at Arráyoz at the entrance to the valley, the brick lower storey topped by a wooden upper storey and a short central defensive tower.

Some 12 km into the Baztan is **Elizondo,** the tiny but graceful capital of the parish. Just beyond Elizondo, a side road climbs eastwards to the French border at the southern end of the spectacular Iparla ridge, from there descending to St Etienne de Baïgorry. Meanwhile the main Baztan valley road continues northwards to meet the French frontier at **Dancharia**. From there, a minor road cuts back the short distance south-westwards to **Zugarramurdi**. The caves here were said to be the haunt of witches. Every August a festival known as *zikiro-jate* is held in the main cave, where a whole sheep is roasted. There are also caves, with stalactites and stalagmites, at Urdax, just off the main road a short distance back from Dancharia.

A rugged way of returning to Pamplona from the Baztan is to take the minor road from Irurita, just south of Elizondo, which climbs over the **Oyalegui pass** into the Arga valley (19 km/12 miles). A short section is unsurfaced but easily negotiated by family saloons. Once on the main Arga valley road, Pamplona lies 35 km (22 miles) south, while the French border is 12 km (7½ miles) north. From the frontier the road drops into the French Aldudes valley, leading to the villages of Aldudes and St Etienne de Baïgorry.

A Remote Area of Rolling Basque Mountains

Around Pamplona, renowned capital of Navarre (*see* map on page 214), the historic and natural sites to consider are Sangüesa, city of sculpture; Javier, birthplace of St Francis; and the Navarre Nature Park, refuge of the brown bear. Note that the Navarrese eat hugely and well.

For travellers, Pyrenean Navarre provides the perfect mix of ingredients. It has a long and often mysterious history to which its surviving ancient monasteries, churches and castles can only provide a few romantic clues. It has a landscape so remote that it provides the only real refuge of the Pyrenean brown bear; the huge silhouettes of lammergeiers and griffon and black vultures are always visible in the sky. The culture is refreshingly different

Pyrenean Navarre provides the perfect tapestry of ingredients for travellers— history, a refreshingly different culture and beautiful landscape, like the embalse de Yesa.

(although only partly Basque). And the exploration is always congenially punctuated by a veritable feast of a meal and a comfortable bed, whether in an expensive city hotel or the most remote mountain village.

Pamplona

Pamplona, the capital of Navarre, is world famous for its **San Fermin fiesta** (6–14 July). But it remains a fascinating town the rest of the year when it is also less expensive and far more comfortable.

It was the American writer Ernest Hemingway who really put Pamplona on the traveller's map in his novel *Fiesta* (equally known as *The Sun Also*

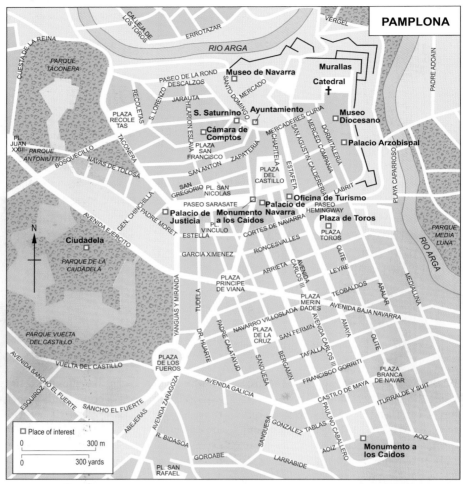

*T*own plan
of Pamplona.

Rises). A regular visitor for San Fermin, he was drawn not only by the bull-fighting but also the party spirit.

The bullring is on the west side of the town. The famous bust of Hemingway is in the street named after him—Paseo Hemingway. But bullfighting, it should be remembered, is illegal in many countries, including most of Europe and the USA, and you may think the fiesta best avoided.

When planning your day, note that siesta is strictly observed. Many government offices work right through the morning until 2 p.m. and then close for the day. However shops open again between 4 and 7 p.m. and the city returns to life with the cool of late afternoon.

History

Pamplona has been by turns Roman, Basque, Frankish, Moorish and

Spanish. It first became Frankish in the 6th century and was taken by the Moors in 738, but only for 12 years. In 778, the Frankish emperor Charlemagne, who had crossed the Pyrenees into Spain to re-establish Frankish influence in the wake of the Moorish retreat, almost inexplicably sacked Pamplona. It is possible that Charlemagne suspected the nominally Christian city of Moorish sympathies, but the plunder may equally have been a "reward" for his soldiers.

During the Middle Ages, by which time Pamplona was capital of the Kingdom of Navarre, there was a 300-year struggle against the mightier

The bust of the American writer Ernest Hemingway is outside the bullring in Pamplona, which he made famous in his novel Fiesta.

neighbouring kingdoms of Castile and Aragón. Pamplona also endured considerable internal as well as external strife and the town was literally partitioned into three distinct neighbourhoods, separated by walls. These internal walls were not demolished until 1423, following the successful peacemaking of Charles III (the Noble) but the fortifications around the city were strengthened (and substantial sections still remain). They could not keep out Castile, however, and King Ferdinand of Castile took the city in 1512. Within nine years Castilian troops were defending Pamplona against Jean d'Albret, King of Navarre, at the head of French troops. It was during this siege in 1521 that one of the defenders, Iñigo de Loyola, was severely wounded in both legs. His slow and painful recovery became a religious experience which led to his founding the Society of Jesus (known to outsiders as the Jesuits).

In the First Carlist War (1833–39), Pamplona and Navarre supported the ultra-right-wing pretender Don Carlos against the more liberal Isabella II—and lost. Navarre was forced to renounce its status as a separate kingdom, but it did not give up its *Fueros*, a type of Bill of Rights setting out the freedoms and responsibilities of the people, which are still in force today.

In the Spanish Civil War, Pamplona and Navarre similarly adopted the Fascist position and broke with the other Basque provinces. Because of this reliable Spanish nationalism, Navarre was able to establish the first of Spain's post-Franco autonomous parliaments in 1978.

Sights

The most social square in the city is the central **Plaza del Castillo**, from which all Pamplona's sights are within easy walking distance. Shaded by plane trees, furnished with comfortable benches and surrounded by cafés like the fashionable **Iruna**, locals and tourists mingle here to relax, watch the world go by and, on summer afternoons, listen to musicians.

The main boulevard leading into the square from the south is Avenida Carlos III and the rather austere building on its west side by the square is the **Regional Parliament** (Diputación Foral). Inside, however, the throne room of the former kings of Navarre is in complete contrast, hung with tapestries and fine paintings (including a Goya portrait of Ferdinand VII), crystal chandeliers and huge mirrors. In this complex of buildings is also the **Navarre Archives** (Archivo de Navarra) where an ancient copy of the regional laws of Navarre (Fueros) can be viewed. The lofty **Monument to the Fueros** opposite, erected in 1894, is an extravagant column, layered like a wedding cake topped with a large, bronze figure of liberty.

The evidence of Pamplona's past and present tensions is everywhere as you stroll around, from the modern graffiti for ETA-Militar, the Basque nationalist terrorist organization, to the ancient heavily fortified churches. The most formidable of these is **San Nicolás**, half-way along Paseo de Sarasate which exits from the south-western corner of the square. San Nicolás dates from the early 13th- century, in a style reflecting the slow changes from Romanesque to Gothic tastes. Above the northern door is a parapet with eight machicolations—fortifications through which missiles could be dropped or fired. **Paseo de Sarasate**, a busy boulevard with a central tree-lined promenade, was named after the violinist Pablo Sarasate.

A native of the city, Sarasate was born at 19 Calle San Nicolás and there is a museum dedicated to him in the Town Hall, a few minutes stroll to the north of Plaza de Castillo. This is a marvellous baroque extravagance of sculpted twirls, wrought-iron balconies and flamboyant statues, beautifully cleaned and renovated in 1990. Inside, the **Sarasate Museum** has a collection of the violinist's music, instruments and other memorabilia.

Just around the corner from the Town Hall, the church of **San Saturnino** was important on the pilgrim route (as witness the scallop shell symbol). It was rebuilt in 1276 and later fortified with two defence towers.

Notice the scallop shell, symbol of pilgrims to Santiago de Compostela, on this carving on the church of San Saturnino.

Cathedral

The huge primarily Gothic **Pamplona Cathedral** is a few streets to the east of the Town Hall. A mixture of different architectural styles, it is an impressive building distinguished by its two pepper-mill towers. Hanging in one of these is the second largest bell in Spain made in 1584 and weighing 12,000 kilograms (12 tons). Originally there was a Roman acropolis on the site. Next, a Romanesque cathedral was consecrated in the early 12th century. The present building was begun in the late 14th century, much of the Romanesque having collapsed. Inside, look out for the marble **mausoleum** of Carlos III and his wife Eleanor in the nave, and in the main chapel the ornate choir stalls, carved in English oak by a French sculptor in the 16th century. The **cloisters** are memorable and certainly amongst the finest examples of Gothic styling in Spain. The intricate carving of the arches and decoration of the doorways is particularly impressive. There is a good **Dioscesan Museum**, notable as much for its impressive setting within the vaulted **Old Cathedral Refectory** as for its exhibits. These include 13th- and 14th-century sculptures, and Gothic and Renaissance paintings as well as sacred works.

City Walls

From the cathedral it is only a short stroll northwards to the old city walls at the **Zumalacarregui gate**. If you follow the walls westwards you will come in a few minutes to the **Navarre Museum**, established in the remains of the 16th-century civil hospital building. Note the doorway as you go in, sculpted with mythical beasts and, ominously for a hospital, a skull. On the ground floor there is a comprehensive regional collection of early art, including prehistoric, Roman, Arabic and Mozarabic (work of Christian artists under Moorish occupation and influence). On the first floor are some marvellous murals, particularly the delicate 14th-century works taken from the cathedral, and Romanesque and Gothic architectural exhibits. Among the 18th- and 19th-century paintings is Goya's *Marqués de San Adrián* (1804). Another gem is the *Abd-al-Malik* carved ivory box, made at the very beginning of the 11th century, and decorated in unbelievably intricate half- relief birds, fish, beasts and human

Navarrese Food

The Navarrese tend to eat hugely and well, especially of locally caught dishes, such as Pyrenean trout (traditionally served with ham), salmon from the Bidasoa river, game and of course, beef, pork and lamb in pepper sauce. Local preference is for a wide range of stew-type, one-dish meals, like *calderete* made from vegetables and meat, or the more spicy *migas* whose ingredients include breadcrumbs, garlic and either herb sausage or the hard thin and peppery *chistorra* sausage of Pamplona. The excellent vegetable stews known as *menestres* are based on kidney beans and artichokes but (vegetarians take note) invariably also contain some form of animal flavouring, from a ham bone to goose fat.

Local cheeses include *Roncal*, a raw sheep's milk cheese which is tangy and firm, *cuajada* (curd) and *requesón* (cottage cheese).

For the sweet course there are white coffee caramels, pastries (*coronillas* and *mantecadas*), and *arroz con leche* (rice pudding).

Festivals are associated with particular dishes. At fiesta time the traditional dish is *relleno* which is a black pudding made with rich eggs. At Christmas the speciality is *sopa cana*, an unusual mixture of milk, bread, cinnamon and turkey fat. And in September and October you will see *pimiento del pico* (meaning "red peppers with a beak") which grow throughout Navarre. They are often grilled outside and sold warm, especially in the villages. Wild mushrooms are another autumn delicacy, gathered by hand from the nearby mountains.

figures. It is an important example of the integrated Roman, Greek and Arabic design known as Umayyad after Abd Al-Rahman, last of the Umayyad family which ruled the Muslim world after the death of Muhammad. His conquest of southern Spain in AD 756 brought new styles which endured for three centuries.

Parks

The city is bounded by parks. On the west of the central area, the traditional star formation of the citadel and surrounding walls contains gardens planned by King Philip II of Castile (who was also Philip IV of Navarre).

Spanish sausages come spicy. Be sure to try them barbecued in the traditional way with the fiery red peppers of the region.

The deer are a great attraction. In summer from 8 a.m. to 9.30 p.m. you can walk along the grass-topped walls, or picnic on the lawns. **Parque La Taconera** is a continuation to the north. The **Parque de la Media Luna**, with its canals, archways and fountains, is on the opposite side of town by the Arga river.

There is a good choice of hotels in all categories. Note that during the San Fermin fiesta hotel prices may double.

Shopping

Pamplona's traditional product is the leather wine bottle. Two specialist shops are **Boteria G. Perez Daroca** in Calle Comedias, 7 or **Boteria Eustaquio Echarri**, Travesia Mendaur, 5.

The town is also noted for its ceramics and ornamental glass.

All of the main shopping streets are close to the Plaza de Castillo; they are Avenida de Carlos III, Chapitela, Garcia Castañón, Avenida de San Ignacio and Zapateria.

To Roncesvalles

North of Pamplona, the rolling Basque mountains, drenched in pine, larch and beech, have recently been protected by "Nature Park" status. But to take the road into the mountains (C135) is also to follow the path of history. This was the route of the Roman legions and of the thousands of pilgrims who came through France and over the Pyrenees on their way to Santiago de Compostela in Galicia, the most important Christian shrine of the Middle Ages outside of the Holy Land. But most of all it was the route of the emperor Charlemagne after his sacking of Pamplona and scene of the famous revenge attack that destroyed his rearguard.

Some 21 km (13 miles) north of Pamplona on the C135, **Zubiri** was probably the seat of the monastery of St Zacharias, visited around AD 848 by the Cordoban priest Eulogius. According to the *Life of Eulogius* written after his death in 859, he discovered there lost manuscripts of Augustine's *City of God*, Virgil's *Aeneid* and Juvenal's *Satires*.

Beyond Zubiri the main C135 forks right and begins its meandering ascent to the village of **Burguete**, made famous by Hemingway in his novel *Fiesta*. As you come over the little pass before the village you glimpse the tantalizing metalled roof of Roncesvalles in the distance ahead. Before going on it is worth exploring the village, especially the Hotel Loizu, a marvellously atmospheric inn that can hardly have changed since Hemingway's day.

The **Royal Collegiate Church** of Roncesvalles, a few minutes drive beyond Burguete is a huge complex in locally rare Gothic style and capped by a striking zinc roof. It is surrounded in legends of Charlemagne as mysterious as the frequent mists which hang in the encroaching forest. In fact, none of it goes back to Charlemagne, and the oldest building, the **Sancti Spiritus chapel**—which is said to have been built where Roland, legendary commander of Charlemagne's rearguard, knelt to pray—actually dates from the 12th century, some 400 years after Roland was killed.

The 13th-century **church** was built by Sancho the Strong, one of the victors over the Moors at the key battle of Las Navas de Tolosa in 1212. Sancho's mausoleum is in the chapter house. His statue, said to be life size is 2¼ metres (over 7 ft). On the wall, the chain is a memento of his victory over the Moors, and there are other Sancho (and "Roland") memorabilia in the **museum**.

Charlemagne's troops would have followed the established trail over the mountains, which is nowadays the marked GR65 footpath, winding up through the beech woods from the back of the Collegiata to the Ibañeta

The woods above Roncesvalles are often gloomy, as if mourning the tragic events that took place here in the 8th century.

Pass. You can do the walk in less than half-an-hour. Alternatively you can drive up to the pass, where two memorials to Roland confirm this as the generally accepted view of the battle site. From the pass the road descends along the Valcarlos valley and to St Jean Pied de Port in France. The original pilgrim route, however, turned east on a line now followed by a narrow tarmac lane. After some 4 km (2½ miles) the GR65 leaves the tarmac behind and heads into France via the **Lepoeder pass**, the

ruins of the **Elizacharre chapel** and the Bentarte pass. It is in the **Bentarte pass**, close to the modern border, that another group of scholars locates the battle. If you would like to see the site, it is a 2-hour walk from the tarmac lane.

To Sangüesa and Javier

Forty kilometres (25 miles) east of Pamplona there is a combination of important natural and historical sites that can be seen during a memorable day out, or as part of a car tour.

You can begin by visiting the gorges of Lumbier and Arbayun by taking the Lumbier turn off the N240 after some 35 km (22 miles). The gorges are not merely spectacular in themselves but support the greatest concentration of griffon vultures anywhere in the Pyrenees. At the **Foz** (gorge) **de Lumbier**, these huge birds can be seen from below, winding up into the sky as they scan the ground for carrion. A footpath goes right through the gorge bottom (reached via Lumbier village). At the **Foz de Arbayun**, the viewing platform is close by the road on the edge of the cliff (14 km/9 miles from the N240) where there is literally a vulture's eye view. Sometimes a vulture will be below, sometimes flying close by the platform, its white head distinct against the brown body and wings.

Sangüesa
Back on the N240, continue for 6 km (4 miles) and then turn south for the very atmospheric old town of Sangüesa. Despite outskirts which are disappointingly industrial, Sangüesa

might be nicknamed "city of sculpture" for once you cross the bridge you are in a very different ambience. Immediately to the left is the 12th-century **church of St Maria**, the glory of which is the intricately carved multilobed doorway. Two of the sculptors are known. One was the **Master of San Juan de la Peña**, whose large-eyed statues were something of a trademark (*see* JACA and ARAGON), and the other was Leodegarius—look out for his signature to the left of the door, carved into the book the statue of Mary is holding. The tympanum (above the door) depicts God sorting saints from sinners. The spandrels and covings are all vigorously carved and the miniature arches above, which date from earlier, depict God surrounded by the disciples and angels.

There are other worthwhile carvings in Rúa de los Sebastianes (previously Rúa Mayor), in which St Maria stands. Look closely at the imposing houses, especially the eaves and the woodwork under the first floor windows. Incidentally, Enrique de Labrit, son of King John and Queen Catherine of Navarre, was born at number 56. A right turn brings you to the **Vallesantoro Palace**, with, if not the finest, certainly the most powerful of all the carvings, its giant eaves decorated with fantastic and often grotesque beasts.

The Foz de Arbayun, a magnificent limestone gorge between Jaca and Pamplona, the well-known haunt of griffon vultures. There is a viewing platform close to the edge of the cliff.

The former Viana palace, on the north side of the church, is now the **town hall**.

Javier

The **castle of Javier**, some 7 km (4 miles) east of Sangüesa, was the birthplace of St Francis Xavier (1506–1552), an early disciple of Iñigo de Loyola, founder of the Society of Jesus (known as the Jesuits—*see* PAMPLONA). Most of the castle dates from the 16th century but it may have been begun as early as the 10th century and in 1236 was given to the de Sada family—Francis's maternal side. In becoming a

The fairy-tale castle of Javier, birthplace of St Francis Xavier (1506–1552), an early disciple of the Jesuits.

Jesuit, Francis would have had to renounce all worldly wealth—including the castle that stands on a hill overlooking the beautiful Aragon valley and the Pyrenees beyond. The figure of Christ seen in the chapel is said to have sweated blood during the last years of Francis's life, which were spent as a missionary in Japan. He died on his way to China. In season, there are daily guided tours and weekend performances of *son et lumière*.

From Javier take the road which descends to the Aragon valley at Yesa. The valley bottom has been flooded to create a huge lake, popular with windsurfers in summer. A side road climbs up from Yesa to the **Leyre monastery**, built on a shelf under the vertical cliffs of Sierra de Leyre and looking out over the valley. Vultures are often to

be seen along the cliffs—probably from the nearby Foz de Lumbier. Leyre is as immaculately restored as Javier even though surviving fragments are even older, possibly 9th century. By the 11th century—from which most of the monastery dates—this was the spiritual centre of all Navarre, with dominion even over San Sebastián on the coast. Within a century, however, Leyre was losing ground to both San Juan de la Peña (*see* ARAGON) and Pamplona and in the 19th century was utterly abandoned. The restoration, from 1954 onwards, is the work of a Benedictine community.

Highlight of the visit is the massively constructed 11th-century **crypt**, the vaulting and capitals bizarrely supported on narrow and irregular stumps.

*C*arvings above the south door of St Maria la Real at Sangüesa, the work of the Master of San Juan de la Peña and Leodegarius.

The Navarre Nature Park

Almost all of Pyrenean Navarre east of Roncesvalles is now protected by nature park status (*El Parque Natural Pirenaico en Navarra*), including the immense Irati beech forest and the *karst* zone around the mountain of Tres Reyes. Another substantial area of Pyrenean foothills has been designated as a "peripheral zone". Brown bears live within this protected area as well as izards, desmans, lammergeiers and griffon and black vultures.

The park is all a marvellous area for car touring and hiking. It is possible to make a circuit around Pamplona in a single day, but the itinerary described would be better broken up by at least one night in one of the mountain villages such as Isaba.

A Tour of the Park

From Pamplona follow the road to Burguete (*see* above), but just before the village turn right along a minor road which picks its way eastwards amongst beech-covered hillsides to the picturesque village of **Arive**. A side trip from here is north to the Irabia lake, a popular beauty spot along the GR11 footpath. Otherwise continue driving through the lush woods via the delightful Basque villages of **Abaurrea**, **Jaurrieta** and—in the Salazar valley—**Escaroz** and **Ochagavia** (about 32 km/20 miles from Burguete). Ochagavia is a marvellous village of cobbles and white-painted houses, their windows framed by huge stones and overhung by intricate wooden balconies. If you would like to stay, the tiny Laspalas is recommended.

Ochagavia is immediately south of the impressive Sierra de Abodi and the massive Irati forest which extends into France. Two small but charming chapels deserve further exploration.

The nearest is **Our Lady of Musquilda**, built at just over 1,000 metres (about 3,250 ft) to the north of Ochagavia on the road towards Isaba. The chapel dates from the 12th century, sited where the Virgin appeared to a shepherd boy; her festival is 8 September, celebrated by a procession and dancing in traditional dress. The other chapel, the **Ermita de las Nieves**, is considerably more remote, some 20 km (12½ miles) north of Ochagavia on a dead-end road over the Abodi mountains. The little white-painted chapel is set amid spectacular scenery at the foot of magnificent beech forest, home to a growing population of red and roe deer. Look out, too, for the Laminak, the Basque equivalent of pixies, said to live in the forest.

This is wonderful walking country, of course, and you should not miss the stroll to the **Irabia lake** to the west, which can be done in under an hour from the Ermita de las Nieves along the GR11 footpath. If you fancy something longer, the hike from Ochagavia eastwards on the GR11 to Isaba is strongly recommended. It can be done in a day. By road, the distance is some 25 km (15 miles), covered in a broad curve through often dense forest. About half way, a road climbs off north over the mountains and into France via the Larrau pass; this is certainly one of the most atmospheric ways of connecting with the French Basque country, especially when the bare tops are shrouded in mist.

Isaba, in the Roncal valley, is the unchallenged tourist capital of the region, its cheerful orangey-red tiled roofs set off by the deep green of the surrounding woods and pastures.

The heart of the park lies to the north-east of Isaba, the sector that was the first to receive protection (as the *Parque Natural Pirenaico Larra-Belagoa*). To begin with, the road climbs only gradually from Isaba, following the Belagoa river, framed by fields and forest of beech and silver fir. Then the mountains rise dramatically and ahead to the east stands the mass of **Tres Reyes**, its naked pinky-grey summit rising from the kaleidoscopic green of pasture, light deciduous woodland and the dark green bands of mountain pine. The road now doubles back and climbs in steep hairpins to a high shelf from which the summit peaks make their final effort. There is a mountain refuge which is always open, just to the right of the road.

Continuing towards the border, the scenery becomes more and more fantastic with stunted pines pushing through weirdly contorted grey limestone. This is the beginning of the *karst* which can be seen more plainly around **Arette la Pierre St Martin** on the French side of the border and by hiking on foot towards Tres Reyes, the highest summit on the Spanish side. If you are doing any long-distance walking, be sure to carry plenty of water with you for there are no streams at altitude. This may seem paradoxical in a region of high rainfall. The explanation is that the rain immediately percolates down through the limestone, eroding tunnels and caves as it goes.

One of these caves is the famous **Sima de San Martin** (known in France as the *Gouffre Pierre St Martin*), a grilled-over entrance to which is just beside the road on the Spanish side of the frontier. When discovered in 1950, San Martin was the deepest known cave in the world. Coincidentally, men first reached the bottom in 1953, the same year that men reached the summit of Everest—but with the tragic loss of one of the speleologists, Marcel Loubens.

Close by, also make a point of seeing the frontier stone that is the very "stone of San Martin". Here every 13 July people from both sides of the border gather for the 600 years old ceremony of the *Tributo de las Tres Vacas* (tribute of the three cows). The respresentatives of the Roncal valley in particular are always colourfully and traditionally dressed, placing their hands on the stone together with their French counterparts to chant "*Pax avant*" (peace before all).

The choices now are to continue into the French Basque Region (see above), to take the road from just north of Isaba into the Anso valley in Aragon (see below) or to descend the Roncal valley. In the last century, the river itself was a common way of making the journey—the lumberjacks would lash logs together into rafts to deliver them downstream to the mills. About 7 km (4½ miles) south of Isaba, **Roncal** is the actual capital of the Roncal valley. You should make a point of seeing the elaborately sculpted **mausoleum** of the famous tenor Julian Gayarre (1844–89). There is one dependable hotel in Roncal, the simple **López Sanz**. A further 11 km (7 miles) south, **Burgui** is another marvellous old village, built by a weir on the river crossed by a lovely old stone bridge draped in creepers. From Burgui the road continues south along the Esca river to the Yesa reservoir.

Exploring the Secret Landscape of the Ordesa

The Ordesa National Park has some of the remotest and most exciting landscapes in the world. The canyons of Ordesa and Anisclo are set in wild and spectacular terrain which can be explored on foot and, in places, by jeep. For the athletic, the sport of canyoning will add to the thrills of the area. Around Benasque, the ascent of Aneto, the highest summit in the range, requires stamina but not climbing skills.

Aragón encompasses all of the most dramatic scenery of the Spanish Pyrenees, including the highest peak (Aneto 3,404 metres/11,168 ft) and especially the Ordesa National Park, that region of high peaks and deep steep-sided canyons which links with the French Pyrenees National Park at the cirque of Gavarnie. Pyrenean Aragón includes no significant town bases except Jaca, well to the west. For a more intimate exploration of mountain Aragón you

The Ordesa National Park is one of the best-kept secrets of Europe, its scenery ranging from dramatic summits and deep canyons to this enticing beech forest.

should also plan to stay in villages like Torla (for the Ordesa) and like Benasque (for the Maladeta massif).

Jaca

Not since the days of the huge pilgrimages to Santiago de Compostela has Jaca been a major tourist town and this is its great attraction. From the Somport Pass at the head of the Aragón valley, the pilgrims of the Middle Ages would descend the 32 km (20 miles) to Jaca and there rest and reprovision after the rigours of the mountains. Today, Jaca seeks a new kind of pilgrim—the 1998 Winter Olympics. Meanwhile, the shops, the cafés and the people in the streets have an invigorating authenticity.

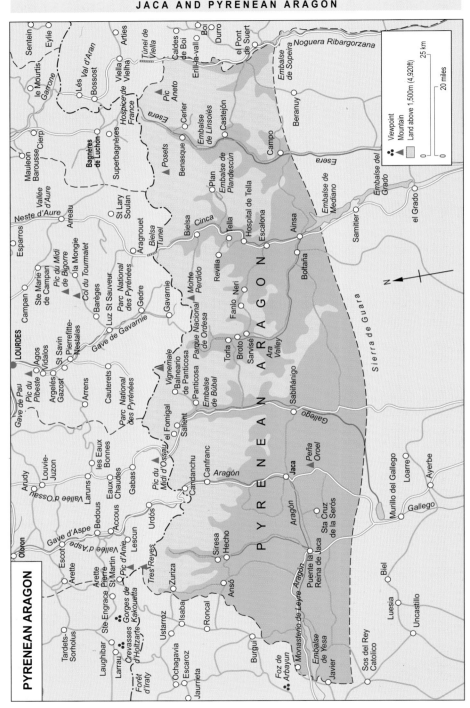

PYRENEAN ARAGON

JACA AND PYRENEAN ARAGON

Viewpoint
Mountain
Land above 1,500m (4,920ft)

25 km
20 miles

Sentein
Eylie
le Mourtis
Garrone
Lès
Val d'Aran
Bossost
Arties
Viella
Tunel de
Viella
Boí
Caldes
de Boí
Erill-la-vallo
Durro
el Pont
de Suert
Embalse
de Sopeira
Noguera Ribargorzana
Beranuy

Mauleón
Barousse
Cierp
Hospice de
France
Pic
Aneto
Cerler
Castejón
Embalse
de Linsoiés
Esera

Bagnères
de Luchon
Superbagnères
Posets
Benasque
Plan
Embalse de
Plandescún
Campo
Esera

Esparros
Vallée
d'Aure
Arreau
St Lary
Soulan
Aragnouet
Bielsa
Tunel
Bielsa
Cinca
Tella
Hospital de Tella
Escalona
Ainsa
Samitier
Embalse del
Grado
el Grado

Neste d'Aure
Campan
Ste Marie
de Campan
Pic du Midi
de Bigorre
la Mongie
Col du Tourmalet
Barèges
Luz St Sauveur
Gedre
Gavarnie
Monte
Perdido
Revilla
Fanlo
Neri
Boltaña
Embalse de
Mediano
Esera

LOURDES
Pic du
Pibeste
Agos
Vidalos
St Savin
Pierrefitte-
Nestalas
Parc National
des Pyrénées
Gave de Gavarnie
Parque Nacional
de Ordesa
Torla
Broto
Sarvisé
Ara
Valley
Sierra de Guara

Gave de Pau
Argelès
Gazost
Arrens
Cauterets
Parc National
des Pyrénées
Vignemale
Balneario
de Panticosa
Panticosa
Embalse
de Búbal
Sabiñánigo
Gallego

Arudy
Louvie-
Juzon
les Eaux
Bonnes
Eaux
Chaudes
Gabas
Pic du
Midi d'Ossau
el Formigal
Sallent
Candanchu
Canfranc
Aragón
Jaca
Peña
Oroel
Murillo del Gallego
Loarre
Ayerbe
Gallego

Oloron
Escot
Pierre
St Martin
Accous
Bedous
Urdós
Pic d'Anie
Tres Reyes
Siresa
Hecho
Aragón
Puente la
Reina de Jaca
Sta Cruz
de la Serós
Biel
Luesia
Uncastillo

Arette
Ste Engrace
Gorges de
Kakouetta
Zuriza
Ansó
Monasterio de Leyre
Javier

Tardets-
Sorholus
Laughibar
Larrau
Forêt
d'Iraty
Crevasses
d'Holtzarte
Ustarroz
Isaba
Roncal
Burgui
Embalse
de Yesa
Sos del Rey
Catolico

Ochagavia
Escaroz
Jaurrieta
Foz de
Arbayun

Vallée d'Ossau
Gave d'Aspe
Vallée d'Aspe
Lescun

PYRENEAN ARAGON

A   R   A   G   O   N

P   Y   R   E   N   E   A   N

The Pyrenean *Aragón region.*

Aragonese Food

Aragonese starters include *ensalada Aragonesa* which is a simple mixture of lettuce, tomato, onion, black olives, raw green pepper and perhaps ham or hard-boiled egg. *Sopa roya* is a rich soup of vegetables with *chorizo* (sausage). Almonds are used in many dishes, especially *guirlache*, a rich sweet made with sugar and eggs. In the south of the region, specialities include ham (*serrano*), local olive oil, and *salmorrejo*, a name which covers quite a few egg dishes. *Tortilla al salmorrejo*, for example, is potatoes and rice covered with a garlic sauce, while *huevos al salmorrejo* is eggs poached in white wine with chorizo or ham and sometimes asparagus. At some places you can still find the traditional *al entiero* style of cooking when a small animal, usually rabbit, is cooked whole (first gutted, though not skinned) by being buried in a hole, covered with a fire and cooked slowly.

The Cathedral

The most important building in Jaca is the **cathedral**, for it was the first significant Romanesque building in all of Spain—that is, built in the style of the Christian Reconquest over the Moors, who occupied Jaca in AD 716. It dates from the early 9th century (although most of what you see was added in the early 11th century) and its very presence was both a celebration and a triumphal war cry. Driven out in 760, the Moors were prevented from retaking Jaca in 795 by a determined force of inhabitants which included many of the city's women—an annual fiesta, held on the first Friday of May, celebrates the occasion with some good natured female skirmishes. Not surprisingly, the cathedral's architecture was echoed in other churches built along the route westwards to Santiago de Compostela.

Corn on the cob, drying in the sun near Jaca.

The bell-tower, most of the outside walls and doorways with carved decorations are the remaining vestiges of Romanesque ancestry. Slightly overwhelming this is the later Gothic and Renaissance construction. There are several **side chapels** with good wrought-iron work, frescos and reliefs and in one, the shrine of St Orosia, patroness of the cathedral. Her fiesta and procession is held 25–30 June.

In the beautifully vaulted rooms of the **Diocesan Museum**, accessed through the 12th-century **cloisters**, are paintings and frescos taken from churches from all over the region.

There are still pilgrims walking to Santiago today and they still cross the Rio Aragón into the town by the same bridge as their predecessors, the stone-arched **Puente San Miguel** leading to the **Camino el Puente San Miguel.**

Main Part of Town

From the cathedral, **Calle Major**, one of the main shopping streets of the city, is a short stroll to the south. Here, the exterior of the 16th-century **Ayuntamiento** (town hall) is a fine example of the Plateresque style, a term derived from the very detailed filigree carving of the Renaissance, similar to that employed by silversmiths. Inside, **El Libro del Cadena**, the 13th-century book which details Jaca's ancient Fueros or "Bill of Rights" is a source of great pride. Just across Calle Major in Calle de Ramón y Cajal, the **Torre** (tower) **de Reloj**, notable for its Gothic window arches, was built on the site of a former Royal Palace.

A little further along Calle Mayor are the 12th-century **Benedictine Monastery** in Romanesque style, and the **church of San Salvador y San Ginés**. Inside the church is the tomb of Doña Sancho, whose father Ramiro I founded Aragón. The tomb was transferred from the nearby Monastery of Santa Cruz de la Serós which Doña Sancho founded in the 11th century.

The **ciudadela** (citadel), a short stroll to the west of the cathedral, is the only fortification of its type to have survived complete in Spain. The huge dry moat-ringed pentagon was started by Philip II, whose first wife was Mary Tudor of England. But it was completed by Philip III, to a design by Vauban, the celebrated military engineer to king Louis XIV of France. It is still in military use.

Sculpture

Jaca has committed itself as a showcase of sculpture and sponsors an important annual competition. As you stroll around the city there are several interesting pieces to see, both traditional and innovative. **Jacetania** is a modern sculpture in iron. This huge figure with windswept hair and gaunt features symbolizes the union of all men of the region. It is the work of the sculptor Angel Orensanz and towers over the traffic in Avenida Regimiento Galicia, just south of the Paseo General Franco. Nearby, actually in the Paseo, is an unusual monument dedicated to the art of promenading. It is the work of Miguel Cabré. Mariano Andrés Villegas was one of the competition prizewinners and his work, **Presa**, is in place Calvo Sotelo, just across the main road from the Paseo.

West of Jaca

Athough Jaca itself stands on a flat plain, the ever-present vultures in the sky over the town announce that marvellous wild country is waiting close by to be explored.

Immediately to the south of Jaca and clearly visible from the town, the cloud-draped **Peña Oroel** (1,769 metres/5,804 ft) beckons with the insistence of an enchantress. You can walk up in about 3 hours, via the chapel of **La Virgen de la Cueva** where medieval aristocrats are said to have sworn a pact to drive the Moors out.

From the mountain, drive on via the village of Bernues and the HU230 the short distance to the **monastery of San Juan de la Peña**. Of all the religious buildings in the Pyrenees, the lowest (and oldest) of the two monasteries is one of the most engaging because of its unusual situation right against the cliff. The 12th-century **cloister** is particularly beautiful and although it has had to be extensively restored, the **capitals** by the "Master of San Juan de la Peña" (*see* also SANGUESA) are original. The founding of the monastery goes back even further, to at least AD 858. There are, in fact, two churches, the earlier lower church subsequently becoming the crypt for the later fortified Romanesque stucture. It was here in 1071 that the first Roman Mass was held in Spain.

The upper monastery, dating from the 17th century, is closed to the public.

Descend to the main Aragón valley road (C134) via the Romanesque church of **Santa Cruz de la Seros**. At Puente la Reina (9 km/5½ miles to the west after regaining the valley) cross the bridge and head north along the Aragón Subordan river to Hecho. The relatively flat agricultural land gradually gives way to steep valley sides and dense forest.

Hecho (24 km/15 miles from Puente la Reina) is an extraordinary place. This very traditional village was both the birthplace of Alfonso I and the 9th-century seat of Aznar Galindez, one of the founders of Aragón, yet in complete contrast, huge modern art sculptures erupt from the surrounding fields. The idea of a mountain-inspired open-air art exhibition was that of sculptor Pedro Tramullas who, from the mid-70s, was joined by other like-minded artists. The majority of villagers, however, turned against the sculptures and the summer art sessions have now been brought to an end.

Hecho makes an attractive and convenient place to stay. Particularly note the strange round chimneys and the white-framed windows. Beyond Hecho, on the far side of the gorge, look up to the right for the 9th-century monastery and 11th-century church of **San Pedro at Siresa**. As you continue to drive north the full beauty of the valley becomes apparent, the fields and woods of the valley bottom dwarfed by immense cliffs. Some 10 km (6 miles) further on you enter the quiet of the dense **Oza woods** where there is a substantial refuge and campsite. The tarmac ends soon afterwards, but walkers have the choice of numerous tracks and paths. The GR11 cuts right across, following the course of the Aragón Subordan to the east and connecting with Zuriza in the Ansó valley to the west.

A classic walk is the ascent of **Castillo de Acher** (2,390 metres/7,841 ft), a peak to the east of the Oza refuge which—as the name suggests—looks like a huge castle. It can be done in a day.

Whereas the Hecho valley is fairly open, the **Ansó valley** immediately to the west is both narrower and with a greater sense of remoteness. You begin to notice the difference almost as soon as you take the connecting road which begins just south of Hecho. The road climbs among glorious woodland then descends through tunnels and a narrow defile. The village of Ansó (12 km/7½ miles from Hecho) has been meticulously restored but not so much that you cannot sense the history in its ancient cobbles and the generations of Basque peasants who have sat inscrutably on the ornate wooden balconies, half hidden by their broad black berets. There are several simple hotels to cope with the visitors attracted to this ambience, although the only tourist site is the 15th-century church of San Pedro which has now become an ethnological museum. Try the **Fonda Estanés** (Tel. 974-37-01-46).

North of Ansó the road follows the Veral river though forest and amongst pastures where it is still possible to see a shepherd dressed in the traditional way. After some 9 km (5½ miles) the valley narrows to a vertically-sided gorge. Look up and you may see a huge black vulture in the sky above, distinguished from the far more common griffon vultures by the dark head and solitary habits.

Through the gorge you emerge into a broad open flat area, a gleaming green in contrast to the bare rock left behind. Here are the few buildings of the hamlet of **Zuriza**, including a refuge, a restaurant and a campsite. The hamlet is a popular walking base for the Navarre Nature Park, and especially for the karst scenery around Tres Reyes to the north-east. Beyond Zuriza the road climbs westwards to a ridge and drops the other side into Navarre.

To the Ordesa National Park

The western part of the Ordesa National Park, which includes the fabulous Ordesa canyon itself, lies 60 km (40 miles) from Jaca by road, via Biescas. But it is also possible to reach the eastern side of the park directly via the desolate and little-populated Serrablo valley to the north of the Sierra de Guara, a journey of about 80 km (50 miles). The two can be combined to make a circuit, but if you are continuing eastwards after the Ordesa you will have to choose between them.

Whichever way you decide you will have to drive first to the industrial town of **Sabiñánigo**, about 18 km (11 miles) east of Jaca on the C134, where there is an interesting **museum** of traditional Aragónese arts. Known as the *Museo de Artes Populares de Serrablo*—Serrablo is the ancient name for the area around Sabiñánigo—it is situated on the south side of town, on the way out towards Huesca (11 a.m.–1 p.m. and 4.30–7 p.m. daily, except Sunday afternoons and Mondays).

A second museum devoted to drawings, the **Museo de Dibujo**, is situated in the 14th-century castle at Larres, about 6 km (4 miles) north-west of Sabiñánigo.

The Serrablo Valley Route

By heading south at Sabiñánigo and then turning east towards Boltaña after about 12 km (8 miles), you can follow the desolate **Serrablo valley** directly to Boltaña, near the south-eastern tip of the Ordesa National Park. A few hamlets, mostly concealed from the road, punctuate the route, and here and there small fields have been excavated in the sparse, rocky soil. Otherwise, this is a wilderness of rock and stunted vegetation and all the more exciting because, to the south, rivers have cut deeply into the limestone to excavate some of the most amazing canyons in the Pyrenees. It is here (and in the Ordesa itself) that small groups of devotees come each summer to practise the sport of canyoning. The most frequently-visited canyons by this route are the Guatizalema and Pillera, both accessible by taking the track to Nocito from the village of Villobas, some 9 km (5½ miles) along the Serrablo valley. Most of the others are more easily reached from the south of the Sierra de Guara.

The **Guatizalema** and **Pillera** are canyons for walking rather than swimming and you can explore them along footpaths from the village. You need a full day for the Guatizalema but the Pilliera can be fully explored in 2–3 hours. From Nocito it is also possible to hike up the "look-out" mountain of **Tozal de Guara** (2,077 metres/6,815 ft), south-east of the village and taking a full day there are back.

Back on the road, and having reached Boltaña, you have the choice of returning westwards on the C138 along the Ara valley to the Ordesa Canyon (34 km/21 miles), or of continuing eastwards via Ainsa to the south-eastern region of the Ordesa National park (24 km/15 miles).

The Biescas Route—and Panticosa

From Sabiñánigo, the C136 follows the broad Gallego river north to the little town of Biescas (14 km/9 miles). For the Ordesa National Park you now turn right on the C140 to Torla (24 km/15 miles). The road all the time keeps south of the beautiful and mysterious Tendeñera range, first climbing to and then descending from the Cotefablo tunnel (1,423 metres/4,669 ft).

Alternatively, continuing along the Gallego takes you towards France (via the Portalet pass) and to the hiking and ski resorts of Panticosa and El Formigal.

Panticosa is some 18 km (11 miles) north of Biescas, at the north end of the **Bubal reservoir**. The creation of the reservoir in the 1950s flooded villages, the remains of which can be seen projecting sadly as you drive along. Panticosa itself is a modern but quite sympathetic resort in largely chalet style. There is an older and much higher resort, however, at the far end of the Escalar gorge, known as **Balneario de Panticosa**. This is a recommended excursion, some 7 km (4½ miles) on from Panticosa, through a narrow defile sprayed by waterfalls and inhabited by marmots, the giant "prairie dogs" of the Pyrenees.

This old spa, which claims the Emperor Tiberius as an early client, is one of the highest occupied villages of the Pyrenees. It makes an excellent base for hiking trips, especially as it is on the GR11 footpath. Two recommended ascents are **Pico de Baldairan** (2,702 metres/8,865 ft) and the "three-thousander" **Pico de Argualas** (3,046 metres/9,993 ft).

The Upper Aragón Valley

The Aragón valley leads north from Jaca and over the Pyrenees into the French Aspe valley. The way through the mountains is the **Somport pass**, a major road which is kept open all year (continuously in summer; 8 a.m.–10 p.m. in winter). The ski resorts of Candanchu and Astun stand on the bare uplands of the Spanish side but across the frontier, the Pyrenees National Park has so far prevented development.

This has always been an important route over the mountains. After the fall of Granada, some 1,400 Moors paid for permission to go to France, in order to escape the persecution and enforced conversion to Christianity. When they reached Canfranc, 9 km (5½ miles) before the frontier, they were stopped and many subsequently died in the long trek back.

Today Canfranc poses an obstacle of another sort since it is now the end of the train line from Jaca. It used to be possible to continue into France but the tunnel has been closed and rail passengers must continue by bus.

Torla and the Ordesa National Park

The Ordesa National Park is one of the best-kept secrets in Europe, so spectacular that it must rate with the Grand Canyon and the Victoria Falls as one of the great natural wonders of the world. The walls of the **Ordesa Canyon** itself are almost 1,000 metres (3,250 ft) high, dwarfing forests of ancient beech, silver fir and mountain pine far below. You can enjoy the canyon even from your car, but your enjoyment will be immeasurably increased if you put on a pair of hiking shoes.

Near the entrance to this mighty canyon at the Mondarruego cliffs (2,615 metres/8,500 ft), slate roofs shining in the sun, stands the beautiful, traditional village of **Torla**. Predominantly stone built, its centre is a maze of narrow streets still frequently blocked by herds of cattle making their way to and from their fields and the weekly market. But it is a comfortable village, many of the old houses having been skilfully converted into hotels and restaurants (*see* HOTELS AND RESTAURANTS.)

Into the Park

The 2,066 hectare (5,105 acre) Ordesa National Park was created as early as 1918. In 1982 it was expanded to 15,608 hectares (38,567 acres) (plus a "buffer zone" of 19,679 hectares/ 48,627 acres) and officially known as the *Parque Nacional de Ordesa y Monte Perdido*. It embraces three main canyons (the Ordesa, Añisclo and Escuain), the northern tip of the Pineta valley and the massif of Monte Perdido (3,355 metres/10,905 ft), the highest limestone peak in Europe.

The National Parks

The Ordesa

The most spectacular national park in the range is the Ordesa (known in Spanish as the *Parque Nacional de Ordesa y Monte Perdido*). The great walls of the Ordesa Canyon itself rise more than 1,000 metres (3,300 ft) above the Arazas river but climb from a lush vegetation of beech, mountain pine, Scots pine and silver fir. Moreover, the entrance to this park is accessible to motorists and a wide and easy trail for walkers runs through to the end.

The 2,100 hectares (5,200 acres) of the Ordesa Canyon were first protected in 1918 and the park was subsequently extended to 15,608 hectares (38,500 acres) to include all the summits between the canyon and the French frontier, the narrower but equally dramatic Añisclo Canyon, the Gargantas (gorge) de Escuain and part of the Pineta valley. Its highest point is Monte Perdido (3,355 metres/1,100 ft; Mont Perdu to the French), the highest limestone mountain in Europe. The park also includes the Casteret ice-cave, the highest cave in the world known to contain permanent ice.

The Ordesa is home to the only ibex surviving in the Pyrenees. Quite large numbers of ibex live in other parts of Spain but this sub-species (*Capra pyrenaica pyrenaica*) has existed on the edge of extinction for decades and, still numbering only 30, may yet prove beyond saving.

The Egyptian vulture is a summer visitor all along the Pyrenees—you may also see griffon and black vultures and the rare lammergeier (bearded vulture).

Only fit walkers can gain access to the heart of the park from the Pineta side—the mountains will prove too steep for many.

A total of 32 other mammal species live in the park. These include the izard, roe deer, wild boar, fox, wild cat, genet, otter and desman. Among the birds, the lammergeier or bearded vulture is the largest, easily told from the golden eagle by its diamond-shaped tail and, closer up, by its pinky-gold chest. There are also griffon vultures and summer-visiting Egyptian vultures.

Among the reptiles, the Pyrenean brook salamander is common in the Escuain sector and there are several species of viper.

Pyrenees National Park

Since the Ordesa adjoins the Pyrenees National Park (*Parc National des Pyrénées*) it is quite easy to devise an itinerary to visit both. It was created in 1967 and stretches along the frontier as a 100-km (60-mile) long ribbon, from near Pic d'Anie in the west to the cirque of Troumouse in the east, and totals 45,700 hectares (113,000 acres). The highest peak is Vignemale (3,298 metres/11,000 ft). The Néouvielle Nature Reserve (*Reserve Naturelle de Néouvielle*) extends the protected area north at the eastern end.

The best bases for visiting the park are (from west to east) Gabas, Cauterets, Gavarnie and the modern development of Piau Engaly. Of these Gavarnie is the best choice if you would like to hike in both the PNP and the Ordesa National Park, staying in refuges. The most famous "gateway" between the two parks is the Brèche de Roland, a breach in the wall of the celebrated Gavarnie cirque. The brèche is a strenuous hike but nevertheless probably the most popular in the entire range. An easier route connecting Gavarnie and Torla lies through the Col de Boucharo. For confirmed mountaineers there is the Brèche de Tuquerouye, which connects the two

The drumming of woodpeckers is frequently heard in the lower mountains of the Pyrenees National Park. This dead tree has been excavated by a woodpecker in search of ants. Varieties include the green woodpecker, the great spotted and the lesser spotted.

parks on the north side of Monte Perdido. Existing wildlife is comparable to that of the Ordesa. However, some poaching of izards takes place. Nevertheless, numbers inside the park's protection have risen from 1,200 in 1967 to some 4,000 today. Of the large birds, there are some 30 golden eagles in and around the park and 22 lammergeiers. For griffon vultures, the best area is the Ossau valley.

The park has not been able to help two creatures in particular, the brown bear and the capercaillie, both of which live mainly outside its protection. Both face extinction.

The best way of getting to know the park is to take a guided walk with one of the park guards.

The Aigües Tortes

The third national park of the Pyrenees is the Aigües Tortes, the only national park in Catalonia (*Parc Nacional d'Aigüestortes i Estany de Sant Maurici* in Catalan). Covering 10,230 hectares (25,300 acres) in the north-west corner of Catalonia, close to the wild Maladeta massif, it differs from the more central parks in its granite and slate relief, producing sharp summits and boulder-littered screes above impermeable bowls which give the park its 200 lakes. The name of the park means "twisted waters" and its lakes, sparkling streams and upland marshes are its most memorable feature, often lined with silver fir and Scots pine. Unfortunately a number of hydro-electric projects were sanctioned before the park was set up in 1955. This exploitation is contrary to the internationally recognized rules governing national parks and is a visual blot in what would otherwise be one of the most beautiful areas of the world. The Aigües Tortes also differs from the other two Pyrenean national parks in its extensive jeep tracks, served by jeep taxis from both Espot and Boí. Whilst this makes it possible to penetrate to some relatively remote spots without effort or mountaineering skill, it also reduces the tranquillity of the park.

The highest summits are Pala Alta de Serrader (2,983 metres/9,639 ft) in the western part of the park and Peguera (2,982 metres/9,636 ft) in the eastern part. But the most famous mountain is Els Encantats (2,747 metres/9,012 ft), meaning "enchanted". According to legend, the twin summits of Els Encantats, divided by an *enforcadura* (gully), are two shepherds turned to stone one Sunday morning for refusing to descend from the mountain at the sound of the Espot church bells.

The wildlife of the park includes izards, wild boars, pine martens, stoats, the desman and a variety of large birds of prey including the golden eagle, buzzard, honey buzzard and red kite. There are also black woodpeckers, the largest of the European woodpeckers, wallcreepers and capercaillie.

The Navarre Nature Park

The Navarre Nature Park, established in May 1990, is the only protected area of the Pyrenees where a significant number of brown bears still survive. The chances of actually seeing a bear, however, are remote. More visible wildlife includes lammergeiers, griffon vultures and black vultures.

The Navarre Nature Park stretches south from the French frontier from Valcarlos in the west as far as the Mesa de los Tres Reyes in the east and includes the villages of Roncesvalles, Ochagavia, Isaba and Roncal. There is also a peripheral zone to the south of the park, stretching from Burguete to Burgui. The character of the Navarre Nature Park is quite different from most of the Pyrenees. In the east the valleys have an almost Alpine character with extensive coniferous forests, contrasting dramatically with naked limestone or karst summits eroded into fantastic shapes. In the west the lower, gently rounded peaks support deciduous tree cover, notably the Irati Forest, once one of the greatest woodlands in Europe.

Just across the frontier and outside the park lie the four famous French gorges of the Basque country, Kakouetta, Ehujarré, Holzarté and Olhadybia, which should be included in any visit to the park itself. The most comfortable base for exploring the Navarre Nature Park is Isaba.

Garrotxa Volcanic Park

The Garrotxa Volcanic Park (*Parc Natural de la Zona Volcanica de la Garrotxa* in Catalan) extends over a wide area behind the Costa

Brava, taking in some 30 extinct volcanoes. Most of them lie within an area bounded by Olot and the villages of Santa Pau and Castellfollit de la Roca. The last eruption was 11,500 years ago and all the cones are now disguised in a lush vegetation. One of the most famous is Santa Margarida, a short walk to the west of the medieval village of Santa Pau, where a small chapel has been built inside the ancient cone. Between Santa Margarida and Olot lies a once great beech wood, the Fageda d'en Jorda. The Garrotxa is celebrated for its strange light which gives to the landscape the quality of an Impressionist painting.

The Park's mammals are highly elusive, including wild boar, beech marten, wildcats and genets. But there is a chance of seeing goshawks, peregrine falcons and short-toed eagles. The principal vegetation is the oak in a variety of both deciduous and evergreen forms, including several hybrids.

The Cadí-Moixeró

The Cadí-Moixeró Natural Park (*Parc Natural del Cadí-Moixeró* in Catalan) is an outstanding area of 41,342 hectares (102,156 acres) lying to the south of Andorra and the Cerdanya. Its highest peak is **Puig de la Canal Baridana** (2,647 metres/9,000ft) but its most celebrated is **Pedraforca** (2,497 metres/8,190 ft), memorable for its twin summits separated by a deep gully or *enforcadura*. Less distinct gullies, known locally as *canals*, can be seen all along the Serra de Cadí, whose north face facing on the side of the Cerdanya is famous for its near vertical drop. Other distinctive features of the park are the curious red gulches of the Gosol area, and the half-abandoned stone villages, such as Josa de Cadí, Cornellana, Fornols and Adraén, often perched on low defensive hills. It is possible to drive across areas of the park on dirt track and that from **Gosol** to **La Seu d'Urgell** is highly recommended.

The animal life of the park includes izards and red and roe deer. Bird life includes the black woodpecker, the symbol of the park, capercaillies, partridges and golden eagles. Amphibeans include the Pyrenean brook salamander. Plant life includes a rare species endemic to the eastern Pyrenees, the rather ugly Xatardia, and the much more pretty violet-flowered Ramonda, a member of the Gloxinia family named after Ramond (1755–1827), an early explorer of the range.

Recommended places to stay are **Castellar de N'Hug** for the eastern sector of the park, and **Gosol** and **Tuixent** for the western part.

On the French side of the Pyrenees there are a number of *Réserves* which give some degree of protection and where hunting is controlled. These include **Orlu**, near Ax les Thermes, **Carlit** near Font Romeu and **Mantet** near Villefranche de Conflent. The Pyrenees is, however, still underprotected, especially the French side, given that the PNP includes no brown bear habitat.

The nest of the pine processionary caterpillar looks like a snowball in summer. But the caterpillars emerge at night to wreak havoc in the forests, feeding on huge quantities of pine needles.

The Ordesa Canyon rivals America's Grand Canyon in its breathtaking views. The canyon walls are up to 1,000 metres (3,250 ft) high.

The presence of so much limestone, in which small sea shells can be found, accounts for the marvellous cliffs and canyons, eroded by water and ice to create the vertiginous ledges or fajas which are a memorable feature of so many hikes in the park. Other spectacular geological features include cirques such as Soaso and Pineta, hanging valleys such as Balcon de Pineta and U-valleys such as the Ordesa itself.

The climate of the park is virtually always at its driest and most invigorating in the early autumn. On the heights of Puyarruego, in the south of the park, it rains (or snows) for about 80 days a year and at the border almost 110 days, much of it in spring or during violent summer thunderstorms—

at least 25 a season. Winds can also be violent—the north wind is *Le Cierzo* (dry) while the south wind is *Le Bochorno* (bringing rain and cloud). In winter, access can be cut off to all except skiers and ski-mountaineers—in fact, at altitudes of 1,900 metres (6,235 ft) and over, there are almost 200 days of ice a year.

Almost a fifth of the total area of the park is wooded. Right at the base of the valleys and canyons are oaks, limes, alders, hazels and silver birch interspersed with ferns, myrtle and rhododendron bushes. Beeches and fir trees follow, up to about 1,600 metres (5,250 ft). Scots pine, Pyrenean oak and masses of box inhabit the slopes and ridges with minimum sun, while a few Aspens flourish in shady parts where the humidity is high. The upper forest level is generally around 2,000 metres (6,500 ft) but the mountain pine (*Pinus montana*, sub-species *Uncinata*) manages to survive, gnarled and windblown, up to about 2,400 metres (7,800 ft).

There are 1,500 plant species in the park, of which the rare cylindric rock

The Ibex

The Ordesa National Park is the only place in the world it is possible to see the variety of ibex that has been categorized as *Capra pyrenaica pyrenaica*. Known in Spain as the *bucardo* (and by the French as the *bouqetin*), the ibex of the Pyrenees is a handsome mountain goat with thick corrugated back-curved horns. In the 14th century the Count of Foix reported seeing herds of hundreds but today the 30 that live in the Ordesa are sadly the sole survivors in the range.

Before protection, the ibex was easily hunted, being reluctant to give ground, and maintaining only a distance of 200–300 metres between itself and the hunter. Nevertheless, the horns are highly coveted and the animals were decimated by British hunters in the late 19th century, particularly Sir Henry Halford and the irresponsible Sir Victor Brooke who, together with friends between 1878 and 1887, more or less exterminated the species.

Why the now-protected animals of the Ordesa are not reproducing successfully remains something of a mystery; probably the genetic pool is too small. The Pyrenees certainly cannot be repopulated with animals from the Alps, which are slightly larger and which have different markings and a different shape to the horns. Ibex live in large numbers elsewhere in Spain, however, and many naturalists believe some should be relocated in the Pyrenees. But ever since the early 20th century, a distinction has been drawn between the variety in the Pyrenees and the varieties that now thrive elsewhere in Spain, and interbreeding has always been blocked. Possibly the old classifications will be swept aside and all the Spanish varieties of *Capra pyrenaica* considered as one.

France would also like to see ibex on its side of the Pyrenees, and although Spain had previously refused to cooperate, a programme of reintroduction in the Pyrenees National Park and elsewhere now looks imminent.

From a distance the ibex is distinguished from the izard by its sturdier appearance and the absence of facial stripes. Except for animals under three years of age, the horns are longer than those of the izard. Closer up, it is possible to judge the age of an ibex by the length and shape of the horns and by its markings. Each year the ibex adds a further segment to its horns so that an animal with four segments is four years old. By the age of eight the tip of the back-curved horn is becoming parallel with the ground. In the male, the darker areas of red-brown or grey-brown coat become more extensive with age. They are almost non-existent at one year, but by the age of ten years envelope the legs, shoulders, spine, belly and the front of the face. The females are cinnamon-coloured.

The rut takes place from the beginning of November to early January but the clash of heads to establish hierarchy goes on long before. The females give birth in May and June.

For a chance of observing ibex in the Ordesa you will need good high-powered binoculars to locate the herd and, preferably, also a telescope with a magnification of 20 times or better for a "close-up" view. They favour the inaccessible south-facing ledges like those of Mondarruego behind Torla.

jasmine (*Androsace cylindrica*) is only found on Monte Perdido and at Gavarnie just across the border. Amongst the endemic species are the long-leaved butterwort (*Pinguicula longifolia*), a delicate mauve flower with yellow throat and long, curved spur which likes wet rock up to 1,600 metres (5,250 ft) and flowers in July. Another is the Spanish speedwell

(*Veronica aragónensis*), a low, blue small-flowered trailing plant found only in the central Pyrenees; it likes limestone rocky areas where it flowers June–July. Ramonda (*Ramonda pyrenaica* or *myconi*), a plant very special to the Pyrenees, was named after one of the first explorers of the region, Ramond Carbonnières. A deep-violet five-petalled flower with cabbage-crinkled leaves, it flowers July–August. Among high-altitude plants, mossy saxifrage (*Saxifraga broides*) grows up to 4,000 metres (13,125 ft), its single pale yellow flowers projecting from a mat of small succulent leaves. The local variety, the Pyrenean saxifrage (*Saxifraga longifolia*) is identified by its long stem emerging from a single round succulent base and capped by small white flowers.

There are 32 species of mammals making their home in the Ordesa, most notably the ibex and the more visible izard (*isard* in French, *rebecco, sario* or *camuza* in Spanish) a small mountain antelope (*see* CAUTERETS for a detailed description). Altogether on the Spanish side of the Pyrenees there are about 15,000 izard and although they are normally extremely timid, there is a good chance of sighting a group in the Ordesa, where the herds are used to the thousands of walkers. Harder to spot are the wild boar (*sanglier* in French, *jabali* in Spanish), though you might be lucky enough to bump into one on a woodland trail in the late evening.

Among reptiles, watch out for the mountain lizard (*Lacerta monticola*) which is highly adapted and lives amongst the rocks at more than 2,000 metres (6,560 ft) altitude.

Birds include the rare bearded vulture, or lammergeier (*Gypaetus barbatus*), three pairs of which nest within the park. These glorious birds are recognized by their golden fronts and distinctive diamond-shaped tails. They eat bones, the largest of which they drop from the air to break on the rocks below. They nest and lay one or two eggs in January, usually high on an almost totally inaccessible cliff face. The more common griffon vultures are also to be seen high above, working together to spot carrion. Griffon vultures have white necks and heads, contrasting with brown wings and bodies.

Lammergeiers, griffon vultures and eagles cannot be guaranteed to accompany your high mountain walks, but there is one inhabitant of the high mountains almost always present, especially in limestone terrain. It is the Alpine chough. It resembles a jackdaw but is easily distinguished by its yellow bill and orange legs. Even before you see it, you will hear its easily identifiable, weird, trilling calls which have an almost supernatural quality. Also in the Pyrenees is the close relative known simply as the "chough"; it is the same size as the Alpine chough but with a long red decurved bill.

Alpine choughs nest in colonies, often of 100—200 birds, laying their eggs on twig and grass-lined ledges in caves and potholes. A legend has grown up in the Pyrenees that if you find the nesting place of choughs then you may find the entrance to a major cave system. But in fact choughs only seem to nest in shallow potholes, perhaps up to 50 metres (164 ft) deep. Barring accident, the birds normally pair for life, although one male will occasionally be accompanied by two females. The female lays four or five eggs, occasionally six. Once the young are able to leave the nest, the family makes excursions a short distance from the cave mouth. It is mainly the work of the male to feed them, flying backwards and forwards to regurgitate insects, while the slightly smaller female keeps watch for predators.

The experiments of the late Konrad Lorenz have shown that the Corvidae family, to which Alpine choughs belong, are the most intelligent of all birds. At least 15 different combinations of whistles and postures have been identified as chough language, many of which can be seen if you are fortunate enough to be able to watch the young being fed. Once they can look after themselves, the young birds leave their parents to live together in adolescent groups. These can be identified by the lack of the characteristic colouring—until maturity the beaks are grey and the legs dark. Eventually only a few birds hatched during the summer seem to remain with the colony. The remainder fly off to form new colonies and grey-beaked Alpine choughs are often seen in mixed flocks of birds migrating south in the autumn.

The spiral of up to 200 birds from the same colony, circling upwards in rising air currents as they feed on flying insects, remains one of the great bird spectacles of the range.

Amongst butterflies, the rare Argus, (*Aricia morronensis ordesiae*) is a sub-species only found in the Ordesa.

Park Regulations
*No camping outside the authorized sites (around the Goriz Refuge at the foot of Monte Perdido; near Lago Helado, close to the Brecha de Tucarroya; and around the San Vicenda refuge).
*No fires.
*No dogs.
*Nothing to be picked or collected.

The Ordesa Canyon

From Torla the short drive north to the Ordesa is one of indescribable beauty, with great swathes of rock

The Canyons

The mighty canyon of the Ordesa can be enjoyed even through the windscreen of a car and those like the Anisclo have carefully engineered walking tracks. But there are at least a score of other "secret" canyons which can only be visited by the intrepid, equipped for the new sport of canyoning. This means following the course of a river through a gorge, sometimes splashing along knee-deep, sometimes shooting waterfalls carved glass-smooth over thousands of years. If you would like to experience this exhilarating sport, it is best to sign on with a professional guide who can supply all the necessary hardware. Only go as a party of friends if you already have some climbing expertise, equipment and a guide book. The canyons naturally vary in degree of difficulty, from those requiring no equipment at all to those calling for wetsuits, ropes, abseiling skills and even inflatable boats.

If you are at all athletic, try it at least once. The combination of scenery and excitement is something you will never forget.

defying anything to climb them. Yet humans can join the fluttering wall-creepers on these cliff faces without any climbing skills whatsoever, thanks to the natural ledges, well-engineered footpaths and, occasionally, to simple hand rails *(clavijas)* to overcome the difficult sections. If you have a fear of heights, check which routes are "exposed" and which are not, before you set out.

Where the road comes to an end some 9 km (5½ miles) beyond Torla, there is a large car-park together with toilets, resturant and a park office with uniformed park monitors on hand to answer questions and give advice.

The easiest and most popular route lies along the right (north) bank of the Arazas river to the **Circo de Soaso**. It is a wide and well-marked route at first, among giant oaks and beeches, and with no chance of getting lost. After an hour of easy strolling a look-out has been built above a spectacular series of waterfalls. The track then climbs more steeply through the woods to the open pastures of the upper valley at the far end of which the famous **Cola de Caballo** (horse's tail) waterfall splashes down to the left hand of the cirque. Monte Perdido rises up behind. A round trip to the waterfall, a popular picnic spot, takes about 7 hours.

Rather than picnic, you can actually buy a meal (and stay overnight) at the **Goriz refuge**, just beyond the top of the cirque—but this is not recommended in high season. There are two ways up the cirque. You can either

M̄onte Perdido (3,355 metres/10,905 ft) is the highest limestone peak in Europe and the third highest summit in the Pyrenees. It was first conquered by Ramond de Carbonnières in 1802.

follow the path which zig-zags up to the right, or you can scramble directly up with the help of the *clavijas*. Quite likely you will see izards as you make your way. Once up, the refuge is to the north (allow 1 hour 30 minutes from the foot of the cirque).

Hikes from Torla

Another easy walk in the Torla area lies along the upper Ara valley, which is not inside the park but no less wild. From Torla head north towards the Ordesa, but after some 5 km (3 miles) turn left onto the track through the narrow Navarros gorge. This is also the route of the GR11 footpath but an ordinary car can continue without problem as far as the ruined hamlet of Bujaruelo (6 km/4 miles from the road), where a bar and refuge operates in summer. Park here and either stroll along the valley or climb up to the frontier pass of **Bujaruelo** (2,257 metres/7,405 ft), according to your inclination.

Confirmed hikers might like to try some of the alternative signposted routes around the Ordesa canyon. For example, the return from the Soaso cirque can be made along the left bank of the river, by the **Faja de Pelay route**, a high but broad ledge on the canyon face. A slightly more demanding faja is the **las Flores**, which is reached via the Salarons cirque to the north of the parking area. But enthusiasts will not consider you have done the Ordesa until you have tackled the **Cotatuero cirque**, also to the north of the parking area, and which has to be climbed with the aid of *clavijas*.

Long-distance walkers who have reached the Goriz refuge (*see* above)

might consider continuing to the Sarradets refuge in the cirque of Gavarnie in France, a four-day round trip. Only the most experienced and properly equipped should consider the ascent of Monte Perdido from the Goriz. It is not a climb but it is an all-day expedition which requires perfect weather and knowledge of snow and ice technique.

The Añisclo Canyon

The Añisclo is second of the great canyons of the Monte Perdido region but totally different in character from the Ordesa. From Torla it is about 25 km (15 miles) through superb wild scenery (for those without cars, jeep tours can be booked in the village). Head south 7 km (4½ miles) to Sarvisé and there take the tiny side road east to **Fanlo**, a ruined and almost deserted village where the national park has recently opened an information office. Beyond Fanlo the road follows the Asa river along the Valle de Vió and past Nerin, the only one of nine more abandoned or semi-abandoned villages to have a café. Finally the road drops in steep zig-zags towards the dramatic mouth of the gorge. The start of the walk is so spectacular that few can resist crossing the bridge from the parking and following the high ledge along the cliff to the little chapel of **San Urbano**, fashioned out of a natural

Viewed from the steep head of the Añisclo Canyon, the Larri Valley is a clear example of a glacier-formed hanging valley.

cave high above the frothing greeny confluence of the Ara and Añisclo rivers.

Beyond the chapel, the path drops to the bottom of the canyon, crosses the river by a bridge and then continues along the right bank. The ever-present noise of rushing water, the waterfalls, the high cliffs and the spray-soaked vegetation combine to make every step an unforgettable experience. You can walk for just a few minutes but by continuing for 2 hours or so you can reach an attractive picnic spot known as **La Ripareta**, where the canyon walls open out and griffon vultures are often to be seen in the sky above. If you are really fit, the **Fon Blanca** waterfall makes a suitably spectacular goal, some 2 hours beyond La Ripareta.

From the Añisclo canyon, you can retrace your route to Torla or make a circuit by continuing east through the **Las Cambras gorge**, one of the narrowest and most exciting road gorges in the Pyrenees. After some 12 km (7½ miles) turn south for 9 km (5½ miles) on the main road to Ainsa, and then west along the Ara valley back to Torla—a marvellous route past weird rock formations and mysterious abandoned villages.

From Ainsa to the Pineta Valley

The little town of **Ainsa**, in the Cinca valley at the north end of the Mediano lake, is an excellent rest stop in the Ordesa region. In the **Casco Antiguo** (old town), high on the hill and surrounded by fortifications, there are several good restaurants and bars in the arcaded Plaza Mayor. The best of these is the **Bodegas del Sobrarbe**, created from two marvellous old houses just through the arch at the east end of the square and dating from the

11th and 12th centuries. Sobrarbe is, in fact, the name of the old kingdom founded by Garcia Jiménez following the expulsion of the Moors and Ainsa was its capital in the 11th century. The food matches the earthy ambience; specialities include mountain soup, trout, and lamb cooked in a wood oven. Expect to pay from 2,500 ptas–5,000 ptas whether for menus or à la carte.

Actually in the square, the **Mallacan** (by the ancient wooden wine press) is a mid-price alternative while for inexpensive eating go to the **Albas** where the menu is around 1,000 ptas and *bocadillos* (rolls) are available for 250 ptas.

To the north of Ainsa lie the Añisclo Canyon (already described above) and the less well-known **Tella valley**, carved by the Yaga river and ending at the **Escuain gorge**. There are minor roads and tracks along both sides of the valley but the north side is recommended. From Ainsa follow the C138 for 15 km (10 miles) to Hospital de Tella and there take the side road which climbs westwards to the meticulously renovated village of Cortalaviña and then to Tella where there is a **dolmen** and the 11th-century **hermitage of Juanipablo**. Between Cortalaviña and Tella a track to the left heads deeper

*I*ntricate tiles create traditional street names in the old centre of Ainsa. Here in the Plaza Mayor are a number of excellent restaurants.

into the canyon as far as the ruined village of **Revilla**, built facing the sun below an orangey-coloured cliff. You can park here and continue on foot the short distance to the *mirador* (viewing point) over the canyon. This is a popular river with experienced canyoners.

The final valley of the Ordesa region is the **Pineta**, which begins some 18 km/11 miles north of Hospital de Tella. This is a spectacular open valley, burning in the hot summer sun, the Cinca river gurgling lazily over bleached rocks, and with formidable mountains rising steeply on the western side.

The obvious village base for the Pineta is **Bielsa** at the southern end (and some 11 km/7 miles from the Bielsa tunnel to France). But atmospheric as Bielsa is with its old square and stone-built houses, the **Parador Nacional de Monte Perdido hotel** at the far (north) end of the Pineta (13 km/8 miles from Bielsa) has to be preferred both for sheer comfort and the spectacle of its setting.

The road between the two ends of the valley makes a memorable drive, but any walking will be even more indelibly imprinted on the mind. Behind the Parador there is a charming hike into the hanging Larri valley, and there are several easy tracks on the east side of the valley, but almost anything else is ferociously demanding. The two classic hikes of the valley are, firstly, the ascent of the cirque to the mercifully flat ground of the **Balcón de Pineta**, and secondly, up the west side of the valley by the GR11 footpath to the **Collado de Añisclo**. Both look impossible from the valley floor but it is

amazing what a well-engineered path can do. For the Balcón, follow the path from the Parador to the foot of the cliffs and then up the tight switch-back for an unrelenting and often frightening three hours. The GR11 can be picked up some 3 km (2 miles) back down the road from the Parador, where a signpost indicates the way over the wide river bed. Once across, follow the cairns to the base of the cliff from where the path climbs steeply through the woods towards the cirque and finally in a more exposed series of steep zig-zags. The views are literally breathtaking from well before the top (5 hours if you go all the way). It is not recommended going beyond the Collado (pass) de Añisclo because the route ahead is narrow and dangerously exposed.

To Benasque

Benasque is the perfect base in the up-per Esera valley, which lies between the two highest massifs of the Pyrenees.

From Ainsa the Esera valley lies 30 km (19 miles) east along the C140, a delightful route under the mass of Peña Montañesa. Once in the Esera, Benasque lies a further 30 km (19 miles) to the north, beyond the

The lower reaches of the idyllic Pineta Valley where straight-sided cliffs give way to softer lakes and forests.

in the 17th century by the summer homes of the Aragónese aristocracy and most recent development and refurbishment has been sympathetic. The modern ski development of **Cerler** stands above the village to the east (9 km/5½ miles).

The Benasque Pass
Benasque is an historic and exhilarating area for the mountain walker. The highest mountain in the range, **Aneto** (3,404 metres/11,168 ft) is immediately to the east, and the second highest, **Posets** (3,375 metres/11,073 ft) is immediately to the west. Moreover, looking northwards, the Benasque valley is cut off from France by a

Linsoles reservoir and the little village of Eriste. This is grand country, indeed, on a scale which is Alpine rather than Pyrenean.

Benasque is equipped with good hotels and is chic by Pyrenean standards without having lost its traditional ambience. The peasant houses were joined

The route up from the Pineta Valley to the Añisclo pass is incredibly steep and as there can be snow on the upper slopes even in summer, great care should be taken.

sharp line of high peaks so that the village is in a deep cul-de-sac. One of the most exciting walks in the area is to the **Benasque** (or Venasque) **pass** (2,448 metres/8,031 ft), for hundreds of years the crossing point of the frontier on foot between Benasque and Luchon in France. This is not a difficult walk but it does involve an ascent of some 550 metres–700 metres (1,800 ft–2,300 ft) according to route, which is strenuous for those not used to it. The recommended way, with the least vertical ascent, is from the parking area at the end of the road, approximately 17 km (11 miles) north of Benasque. About 3 hours should be allowed for the ascent and almost as much for the descent. From the parking area a path climbs northwards, gradually at first and then in steep zig-zags, after which it traverses the slope climbing north-westwards into the pass. The views from here are hugely impressive, with Aneto and its surrounding glaciers due south and the Posets massif to the southwest. When the going becomes difficult reflect that this was for hundreds of years one of the normal ways of crossing the Pyrenees.

Forau de Aiguallut

An easier walk, but with an equally spectacular climax, is the excursion to the **Forau de Aiguallut**, the pit into which the waters from Aneto and the surrounding peaks disappear. The waters remain underground for 4 km (2½ miles) before re-emerging in the valley of the Artiga de Lin to the east, a side valley of the Aran valley, at a point known as the Güells de Joeu. The starting point, as for the Benasque pass, is the parking area at the end of

the road. From here, the track climbs slowly eastwards, reaching the hole in under an hour. The Aiguallut plain beyond makes an excellent picnic spot.

Ascending Aneto

The ascent of Aneto is made by thousands of people every summer and is a walk rather than a climb. Every fit and experienced mountain walker staying in Benasque should consider it, but it has to be stressed that it is a long way. The ascent involves a distance of some 10 km (6 miles) there and back and a total vertical ascent of approximately 1,500 metres (5,000 ft). Walkers who are comfortable with those figures should experience no great problem. There are, however, two hazards on the route which walkers should be prepared for. The first is the crossing of the **Aneto glacier** which for safety requires the use of a rope and, for ease, the use of crampons and an ice axe (all of which can be hired in Benasque). The second difficulty is the short, sharp ridge of rocks known as the bridge of Mohammed (in the Muslim religion, the bridge between Hell and Heaven), which has a frightening sense of exposure to those not used to heights. The best advice to the inexperienced is to book with the *Guias de Montaña* (Mountain guides) at the tourist office.

Most dedicated walkers stay in the **Renclusa refuge** but the ascent is quite possible from Benasque provided a start is made by about 6 a.m.—it is essential to be off the summit by early afternoon when thunderstorms are apt to strike. The way up is from the same parking area as for the other walks described, some 17 km (11 miles) north of

Benasque. From there, a clear path climbs southwards to the Renclusa refuge, reached in well under an hour. It then continues southwards, climbing quite steeply into a pass known as the **Portillon Superior** (2,850 metres/9,350 ft), which looks out over the Aneto glacier and its famous summit which is at the far end. The **glacier** should be joined approximately 1 km (½ mile) beyond the Portillon. The route across the ice is normally clearly defined by the footprints of those who have gone before and leads eventually to the Coronas pass where a small sapphire-blue lake sometimes forms in the ice. From the pass, the way lies up out of the sea of ice across the bare rock to the south-east and finally over the short but precarious ridge of broken rock that leads to the summit. Eight hours should be sufficient for the ascent, allowing for stops, and fit and experienced walkers do it considerably faster.

The descent from Aneto can be by the same route or, more usually, descending from the Coronas pass north-eastwards to the Forau de Aiguallut described above.

Ascending Posets

Posets (3,376 m/11,076 ft), although lower than Aneto, is no easier to get up. But even if you are not planning an ascent, the approach walk along the Estós valley is recommended. The track begins some 3½ km (2 miles) north of Benasque, just over the bridge, curving away westwards beside the stream. Eventually track gives way to path and forest to upland pasture. You can easily reach the Estós refuge in time for lunch if you set out around 8 a.m. and be back in Benasque for dinner. The

A family welcome awaits you at the Viados refuge if you choose it as a base for an ascent of nearby Posets (3,376 metres/11,076 ft).

ascent of Posets is another day there and back from the refuge and, since it involves a glacier crossing, is for experienced and well-equipped walkers only.

Into Catalonia

To continue eastwards into Catalonia, pick up the C144 14 km (9 miles) south of Benasque. It climbs through lush sheep country via the Fabas and Espina passes to the Noguera Ribagorçana, the first main valley of Catalonia (32 km/20 miles). Viella lies some 34 km (21 miles) north while the Boí valley begins some 5 km (3 miles) to the south.

A Variety of Natural and Historic Highlights

From typically Spanish Girona you can discover Pyrenean Catalonia: Besalú, one of the best-preserved medieval villages in Spain, the Aigües Tortes National Park, famed for butterflies, the volcanic zone of the Garrotxa, the wild-west region of the Cadí-Moixeró National Park, and what was, until recently, the most remote part of Spain, the delightful Aran Valley.

The Catalan Pyrenees stretch half-way across the range from the still rugged beauty of the Costa Brava to the flashing streams of the Aigües Tortes National Park. In between lie two lesser known but equally inspiring landscapes, the volcanic Garrotxa and the "wild-west" Cadí. But the works of man are nevertheless more important here than in any other part of the Spanish Pyrenees, from the cityscape of Girona to the preserved medieval village of Besalú. In terms of architecture there are not only literally hundreds of Romanesque monuments but also Modernist ones. And this is the only region of the Pyrenees to have inspired a genuine art movement.

Girona

With its international airport, and rail and coach connections, Girona is an important gateway to the southern flank of the Pyrenees. It is an immensely Spanish city, but also reflecting the many different cultures (Roman, Visigoth, Muslim and Frank) that have left their mark over the centuries. More recently (late 18th century) the Modernists arrived and left

The 12th-century Benedictine monastery of Santa Maria at Gerri de la Sal is ruined but still beautiful.

CATALONIA

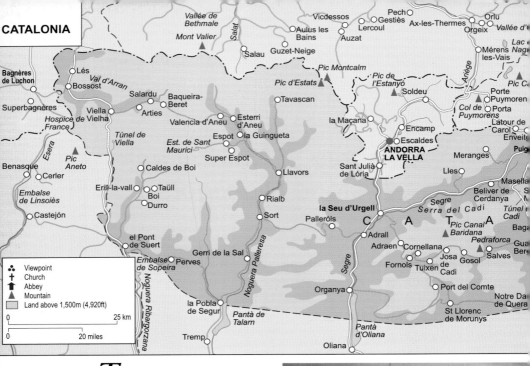

The following place names appear on the map:

Vallée de Bethmale, Mont Valier, Salat, Salau, Guzet-Neige, Aulus les Bains, Auzat, Vicdessos, Gestiès, Lercoul, Pech, Ax-les-Thermes, Orgeix, Orlu, Vallée d', Lac, Mérens Nag les-Vais, Ariège, Pic C

Bagnères de Luchon, Lés, Bossost, Val d'Arran, Salardu, Baqueira-Beret, Tavascan, Pic Montcalm, Pic d'Estats, Pic de l'Estanyó, Soldeu, Porte Puymoren, Porta, Puymorens

Superbagnères, Viella, Arties, Valencia d'Aneu, Esterri d'Aneu, la Maçana, Encamp, Col de Puymorens, Latour de Carol, Enveitg

Hospice de Vielha France, Túnel de Viella, Est. de Sant Maurici, Espot, la Guingueta, Escaldes, ANDORRA LA VELLA, Meranges, Puig

Esera, Pic Aneto, Caldes de Boi, Super Espot, Sant Julià de Lória, Lles

Benasque, Cerler, Erill-la-vall, Boi, Taüll, Durro, Llavors, Serra del Cadi, Masella, Beliver de Cerdanya, S

Embalse de Linsoiès, Rialb, Segre, Túnel Cadi, Bag

Castejón, Sort, Palleróls, la Seu d'Urgell, C A A T A, Pic Canal, Pedraforca, Baridana, Gua

el Pont de Suert, Adrall, Adraen, Cornellana, Josa de Cadi, Gosol, Salves, Ber

Embalse de Sopeira, Perves, Gerri de la Sal, Noguera Pallaresa, Fornols, Tuixen, Notre Da de Quera

Noguera Ribagorzana, la Pobla de Segur, Organya, Port del Comte

Tremp, Pantà de Talarn, Pantà d'Oliana, St Llorenc de Morunys

Oliana

Key (legend):
- Viewpoint
- † Church
- Abbey
- ▲ Mountain
- Land above 1,500m (4,920ft)

0 — 25 km
0 — 20 miles

*T*he Catalonia region.

*T*he subtle colours of Girona's waterfront reflected in the River Onyar.

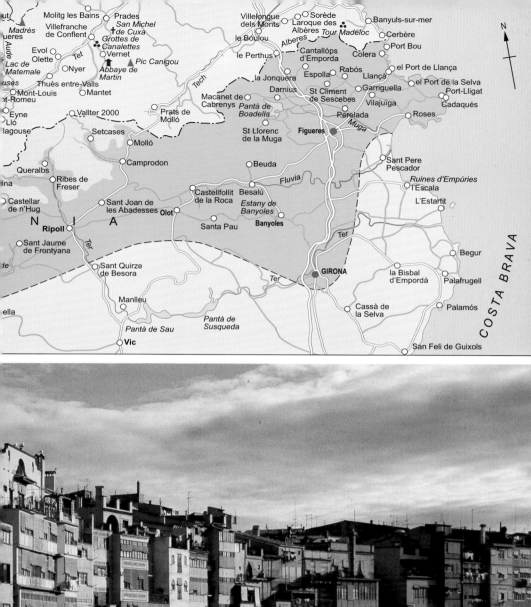

some idiosyncratic architecture, such as the Farinera Teixidor flourmill. The city is small enough to get to know in a couple of days and can be used as a touring base for northern Catalonia.

Normally, the easiest place to leave your car is the parking under the railway line on the south bank of the Onyar river. From there stroll along the river bank, through plaça de la Independencia and cross the river by the footbridge to **rambla de la Llibertat**.

The riverside houses here are extraordinary and well worth a photographic stop. In differing shades of ochre, umber, flakey-blue and pastel-browns these thin tall buildings are reflected in the muddied waters of the river where giant fish hang around under the bridges in the hope of receiving some titbits.

Once across the bridge you are immediately in a good shopping, strolling and café area and close to the most historic part of town.

Catalan Food and Wine

Spanish Catalonia has a huge reputation for food, both from the sea and from the mountains. Portions tend to be generous, lean cuisine non-existent and the contemporary demand for presentation is largely satisfied by the reds of tomato and pimiento.

The Costa Brava is naturally famous for its fish dishes such as the stews *suquet de peix* and *sarsuela* (which is often very rich, and seasoned with anis and herbs). But the preference is for plain, grilled or barbecued fish. *Rape* (monkfish) and locally caught sardines and anchovies (often served as a starter with toasted bread and olive oil) are favourites. *Bacallá*, made from dried salt cod, was traditionally the meal of the poor but has become a classless delight—there are several versions, some very garlicky but none too salty. *Arroz negro* is rice flavoured and coloured with squid ink. Away from the coast, locally caught river trout is frequently on menus and is usually fairly reasonably priced—thanks to local amateur fishermen. Honey often figures in trout recipes, sometimes lusciously spread on the fish before it is wrapped in foil and cooked in an open fire.

The mountain influence is felt strongly in meat dishes. There are tasty and filling stews such as *escudella*, usually made with a veal or ham stock and a combination of meats and sausages. *Estofat* is a stew of meat with vegetables, most often beans. Truly bold gourmets will want to try *manos de cerdo estofadas* (stewed pig's trotters) or *el estilo del Ampurdán* (rabbit with snails).

Desserts are dedicated to custard-type fillings—try *crema Catalá*, an enormous deep-fried doughnut stuffed with custard. Mountain Catalonia is particularly rich in fresh fruit and nuts, especially almonds and walnuts, and these are often served after dessert as coffee-nibbles. A special coffee is *el cremat* which is made with burnt rum.

As far as snacks are concerned you will find that Catalonia does not have the same quality of bar snacks (tapas) as southern Spain. The choice is normally restricted to *bocadillos* (sandwiches), *butifarra* (Catalan sausage) and the Catalonia-wide traditional snack of *pan amb tomáquet*, a hearty portion of fresh bread rubbed with garlic, moistened with olive oil and flavoured with tomato.

For local wines, try those from Empordá, often under the label El Ampurdán. These are produced in the fertile vineyards behind the Costa Brava such as Perelada (sparkling), Espolla (rosé) and Campmany (red).

Around the Cathedral

The **cathedral** is the obvious place to begin, a short stroll along the narrow, cobbled carrer de la Força, from where the broad staircase leads. Of giant proportions, and a technically brilliant example of how to design for maximum visibility, the cathedral boasts the widest **Gothic nave** in the world. Within this vast and vaulted interior are the **tombs** of Cardinal Berenguer, intricately carved in the 15th century, and of Bernardo de Pavo, a work of meticulous detail probably done by Lorenzo Mercadante, also in the 15th century. The **high altar screeen** is one of the finest examples of Gothic silver-gilt in Spain, the work of three men over a period of almost 30 years.

Also, make a point of seeing the largely Romanesque **cloister** of twinned columns, where the capitals are particularly elaborate and well crafted.

Among the important religious art in the **Capitular Museum** (entered via the cathedral), are the **Creation Tapestry**, dating from the beginning of the 12th century, and a copy of Beatus's *Commentary on the Apocalypse*, made in 974.

On the east side of the cathedral, in the renovated former Bishop's Palace, the hugely enjoyable **Art Museum** is spread over five floors and moves on chronologically as you climb up, from Romanesque to contemporary. Illuminated manuscripts, such as the 11th-century Beda Homily, are among the earliest artworks. Notable religious art includes the work of Bernat Martorell (died 1452) for the church of Pubol in Baix Empordá.

A number of works are important not only artistically but also for their comment on Girona's history. These include Ramon Martí i Alsina's (1826–94) *Siege of Girona*, the *Walls of Girona* by Modest Urgell (1839–1919) and *Girona* by the sculptor Miquel Blay (1866–1936).

Of the Olot School (*see* OLOT), there is a good selection, evocatively capturing the strange light of the Garrotxa region to the north-west of Girona. Impressive 20th-century contributions include the ceramic *Duet* of Claudi Casanovas (1985) and *Robot* by Maese (also 1985). The museum is particularly visitor friendly with lifts, toilets, good air conditioning and plenty of comfortable chairs.

Arab Baths and an Archaeological Walk

From the art museum, descend the cathedral steps and turn right through the Sobreportas Gate to the **Arab Baths**. These are the best you will see in Spain outside the Moorish stronghold of Granada, yet they date from the 13th century, long after the Moors were forced out of Girona. The **cooling room** is the most elegant and evocative with its octagonal skylight supported on columns.

Stone steps lead up from near the baths to the "Archaeological Walk" around the old walls, while strolling westwards over the often dry River Galligans brings you to the Romanesque **church of St Pedro**, now the Provincial **Archaeological Museum**. This is a marvellous setting for the exhibits which include Roman finds from the Ampurias site on the Costa Brava, impressive amphoras recovered by underwater archaeologists and collections of ancient ceramics, jewellery and tools.

Back over the Galligans, the landmark church of **St Feliu** is just to the south of the Arab Baths, its easily recognized steeple having been damaged by lightning in 1581. From here retrace your steps through the Sobreportas gate to the **City Museum**, just to the right. From there continue along the carrer de la Força and into the Call or Jewish Quarter.

Carrer de la Força itself is the centre of the most interesting part of town and there is always some sort of live music in one of the bars or restaurants.

Into the Garrotxa

The Garrotxa is a region of extinct volcanoes to the north-west of Girona

---

The Jewish Quarter

When Muslim armies first appeared from North Africa in 710, the Jews welcomed them as their saviours from the Visigoths. And indeed, as a minority themselves, the Moors did not persecute either Christains or Jews. Jews were active in military and in public life and though the Girona ghetto was not compulsory they tended to live together and in an area that was constructed with an eye to defence. In fact Jews could travel freely and many reached the heights of politics and scholarship. Spanish Jewry had their own courts and could pass the death sentence for a crime to which Christian or Moslem law did not apply.

All this, however, ended with new waves of Moorish invaders. The Almoravides, who came in 1090, imposed a narrower regime. They were followed in 1145 by the Almohades, who were even more fanatical and demanded immediate conversion of both Christians and Jews. In Catalonia, the Call became the place Jews were confined between dusk and dawn. The Cabala was a Jewish movement which had originated in Languedoc, and its great master in Catalonia was Isaac el Cec (the Blind; 1165–1235) of Girona, author of various mystical works. There were probably no more than 100 synagogues in Catalonia and only a third could provide formal teaching, as they should. There were three in Girona; others in Pyrenean Catalonia were at Vilajuïga, Besalú and La Seu d'Urgell.

From the 14th century, the Jewish situation deteriorated even further. In a movement known as the Pastoureaux, French shepherds attacked Jewish communities as a prelude to an intended Crusade to the Holy Land, and this soon spread to Spain. Other waves of anti-Semitism came with the cleric Fernando Martinez, from Seville, and the Dominican friar Vincente Ferrer and finally with the uniting of the thrones of Castile and Aragón under the Catholics Ferdinand and Isabella in 1479. Their purge against non-Catholics led to the setting up of a Spanish Inquisition and Jews either converted, fled the country or were killed. Today there are still no more than a few thousand Jewish people in Catalonia.

The Girona Jewish Quarter or Call is typically dark, with narrow streets and faceless houses. One of the best ways of understanding what life in the Call was like is to visit the Isaac el Cec Museum, right in the heart of the district, up a long flight of steps from the carrer de la Força—a fascinating reconstruction of life behind the closed doors.

dotted with ancient villages and towns —a marvellous area for enjoying the real Catalonia.

Just 20 km (13 miles) north-west of Girona along a the C150, **Banyoles** is the first of these towns. Its industrial outskirts conceal a historic heart, centred on a square of porticoed arches and shady trees, where a bustling market is held every Wednesday. To find the square—the plaça Major—follow signs from the main road marked "*centro antic*". The shops on the square include a mouth-watering bakery with both bread and traditional pastries, and there are also cafés, bars and an ice-cream parlour.

The **Archaeological Museum** is just to the east of the square, established in the well-restored shell of a 14th-century palace. Exhibits include the bones of animals long since extinct locally (including elephant and lion), prehistoric tools and the replica of a pre-neanderthal (200,000–90,000 BC) human jawbone found in the nearby Serinya caves (organized visits in summer).

The **Darder Natural History Museum**, just to the north of the main square, is based on the life's collection of a local botanist, and is highly recommended.

Banyoles is built on the eastern bank of a huge natural lake, scene of the 1992 Barcelona Olympics rowing events. On a pleasant Sunday its pleasure boats and picnic sites are always full and the lake has also become a centre for underwater orienteering. The drive round the lake, which takes in the tiny village of Porqueres and its 12th-century church of St Maria, is 8 km (5 miles) long.

Besalú

Continuing on the increasingly scenic C150 for 14 km (9 miles), you reach Besalú, one of the best-preserved medieval villages in the region. Your first glimpse of the village is of its beautifully restored fortified bridge, **Pont Vell**, built in the 12th century and painstakingly restored in the mid-1960s. To park, continue along the main road until the left turn into the centre where there is a car-park. From here you can walk though the narrow, cobbled streets to the bridge.

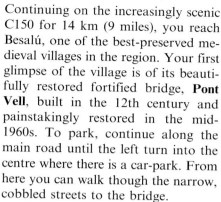

From the 9th century when the Counts of Girona also adopted the title Counts of Besalú, until the 12th century when the county of the Garrotxa and its capital Besalú passed to the Counts of Barcelona, the village was a major strategic and religious base. Almost every building in the central part is of historic importance. As you walk from the parking into the centre, the first significant building you see is the 12th-century church of **San Pere**, all that remains of the architecture of the Benedictine community which came to Besalú in the 10th century. The huge square on which the church stands, the **Prat de San Pere**, was once the municipal cemetery. Although very plain on the outside save for the 17th-century balustraded **bell-tower** and for **sculptures** of two bizarre lions, one with a snake and the other with a monkey, the **interior** is an important example of Romanesque decoration.

If the door of the church (or any of the buildings you wish to visit) is locked, enquire at the Tourist Office.

On the opposite side of the square, wedged between a café and a tabac, is

Whereas Romanesque churches are common in the Pyrenees, it is much harder to see Romanesque homes. A good example is the Casa Cornellà in Besalú.

the dark entrance of **Casa Cornellà**, a rare Romanesque example of a private house, the rooms opening onto a secluded inner courtyard and an upper columned balcony. The rooms beside the entrance contain a small **museum of farm and household implements**. This was the elegant home of the Cornellà family until the 15th century.

From the Prat de San Pere continue to the porticoed plaça Major, where there is an enjoyable market on Tuesdays and *sardana* dancing on summer evenings. Here you will also find the tourist office.

Strolling on towards the bridge, the *mikwah* (Jewish ritual bath house) is down an alleyway to the right by the banks of the river. After the Jews were hounded from Besalú by Christian persecution the mikwah became a dye works and was eventually lost until modern excavation. There are indications of the existence of an ancient synagogue nearby, though this has not yet been found.

Looking down from the bridge to the waters of the Fluvia, an intriguing little balcony on the walls catches the eye. This belongs to the Pont Vell one of the most romantically situated restaurants in all of the Pyrenees.

Castellfollit de la Roca and Olot

About 14 km (9 miles) west of Besalú on the C150 an extraordinary cliff of sheer tree-clad basalt rises up from the side of the River Fluvia. Clinging to the top is the tiny village of **Castellfollit de la Roca**, its church perched right over the leading edge and looking as if it is about to be elbowed into the abyss. The formation is caused by different layers of lava from subsequent volcanic eruptions solidfying and being eroded into spectacular columns. It is particularly eye-catching at night when floodlit from below.

A further 7 km (4½ miles) brings you to **Olot**, the largest town of the Garrotxa and the only one in the entire Pyrenees to have spawned an art movement—the Olot School. It grew precisely from the characteristic diffuse light of the Garrotxa and the way **Joaquim Vayreda** (1843–94) in particular translated that onto canvas. Nowadays, **Ramon Casas** is the best-known name of the Olot School, partly because he was a friend of Picasso. But it was **Joaquim** who founded it, together with **Josep Berga i Boix** (1837–1914). Joaquim's brother Maria, who first found fame as a writer, was another key figure. Their paintings and many other marvellous works, including the sensitive scuptures of **Josep Clara** and **Miquel Blay** can be seen in the **Garrotxa Comarcal Museum** housed in the newly converted ancient hospice, just a short stroll from the tourist office on the main road through the town. There is still a highly regarded Fine Art College in the town.

Olot's other main museum is the **Casal dels Volcans**, a car-ride south of the town on the main Santa Coloma and Vic road. This is housed in the flamboyant **Palladian Palace** surrounded by the botanical gardens of **Parc Nou**. Worth visiting for the well-tended gardens alone the museum is a bonus, crammed with scientific and geographical information about the volcanic region. Sadly, however, there are no English-language translations.

Once you have seen these two, take a stroll around the **old centre** of the town with its elegant villas, fountains, statues, and park squares. Most interesting of all is the area around passeig d'en Blay, a huge town-centre square on which stand the delightfully ornate **Municipal Theatre** and the extraordinary **Casa de Solá Morales**, the best example of Modernist architecture outside Barcelona. The Modernist movement had much in common with Art Nouveau, an influence which is easily seen in the extravagance of the wrought-iron balconies, the figureheads and the classically styled plaster decoration.

Also in the square are the sculpture **La Lectura**, by Blay, and a bust of **Joan-Pere Fontanella** by Olot sculptor Celesti Devesa.

Visiting the Volcanic Zone

The Garrotxa is one of the most surprising areas of the Pyrenees. Not far inland from the crowded resorts of the Costa Brava it is nevertheless little known and little visited, yet it is one of the most important volcanic zones in Europe. There are more than 30 cones, but all festooned with the dense greenery that the rich soil of weathered ash eventually produces. It is 11,500 years since the last eruption.

All of the volcanic zone to the south-east of Olot has been protected by Natural Park status since 1985, within which there are also more rigorously conserved nature reserves. However the business of cinder quarrying (a building material) leaves ugly scars in places past which hikers must walk. Conservationist groups are fighting it but the problem remains and the best way to avoid it is to stay on the south side of the C524.

A wonderful traditional mas *(farmhouse) of the Garrotxa, a region of extinct volcanoes and luminous; an easy drive from Girona.*

From Olot, follow signs for the beech forest called Fageda d'en Jorda and for the superb medieval village of Santa Pau, turning off the main through road near the tourist office along avenida Maria Vayreda. If you do not have a car there is a taxi rank beside the tourist office, but buses are too infrequent to be of much use.

After about 6 km (4 miles) look out for a parking space on the left side of the road. You can cross and follow marked footpaths through the **Fageda d'en Jorda**, the ancient trees especially magnificent in their autumn reds and golds. Keen hikers can then continue on foot to the medieval village of **Santa Pau** (about 3 hours); otherwise, drive on by car.

Santa Pau is a tiny and historic village 9 km (6 miles) east of Olot in the heart of the Garrotxa. In the style of the Middle Ages, the outermost houses of the village are built so close together as to form a continuous defensive wall and the lanes within are so narrow that it is best to park outside. At the heart of the village is the well-preserved 13th-century porticoed plaça Major, on which stands the pretty Romanesque church of **Santa Maria** (and the tourist office).

The carved doorway of the Monastery of Santa Maria at Ripoll depicts religious scenes as told through the dreams of Saint John and the visions of Christ.

Between the Fageda d'en Jorda and Santa Pau lies the most famous crater of the region, the **Santa Margarida**. It is actually accessible from the main road but anyone reasonably fit who has not walked from the Fageda should certainly walk to the volcano from Santa Pau— a mere 40 minutes or so. The route is well marked through glorious countryside of alternating sheep pasture and oak forest. Finally, there is a short ascent to the rim of the crater, well concealed by dense vegetation, and in the bottom of which lies neither ash nor larva but a pretty little chapel set on a broad swathe of grass, probably dotted with sheep.

There are well-signposted footpaths, giving approximate walking times to other volcanoes or monuments (**San Miquel Sacot** or **San Llucia**, for example) and further exploration is recommended. Thousands of years have weathered volcanic ash into fertile soil and around the traditional old farmhouses with their huge balconies and drying areas, agriculture seems to go on much as it did a century ago.

Ripoll and Central Pyrenean Catalonia

From Olot, Ripoll lies 31 km (20 miles) west along the C150 via the Coll de Caubet. It is a magical drive through mountainsides lushly draped in pine and cork oak and with marvellous views of a seemingly endless succession of peaks and ridges. At the **Coll de Caubet**, with its tantalizing vista, the main road drops to the Vallfogona river, while a a minor road heads off directly to St Joan de les Abadesses (*see* below) which you can also visit from Ripoll.

The great jewel of **Ripoll** is the **monastery of Santa Maria**, in the old part of town, to the right of the main through road. This Benedictine abbey-church was architecturally one of the most important in the Romanesque style in all of Spain, the equivalent in Catalonia to the church of Santiago de Compostela in Galicia. However, having fallen into ruin, mainly thanks to a couple of earthquakes in the 15th century and a fire in 1835, it had to be

rebuilt in the late 19th century and, although the work was done using drawings of the original, what remains today is only an approximate reproduction. The style comes from Old St Peter's in Rome, a cruciform layout with double aisles and seven apses. Some of the early building survives however, particularly the west doorway, surrounded by a profusion of marvellous 12th-century sculpture, and part of the two-storeyed cloister, which dates from around 1125.

The **carved doorway** depicts religious scenes as told through the dreams of St John and the visions of Christ. You can obtain a full key to the scenes from the tourist office. The **barrel vault**, an early architectural solution to the problem of supporting a heavy stone roof, was erected over the tomb of the monastery's founder, Count Wilfred the Hairy by Abbot Oliva in the 11th century. It became the favoured resting place of the family, though the only tomb remaining is that of Ramon Berenguer III.

Wilfred, count of Barcelona, Besalú and Cerdanya, patriach of one of Catalonia's leading medieval families, created a Benedictine community in Ripoll in the 9th century. His descendents continued to enlarge it and in the early 11th century, Abbot Oliva committed himself to creating an internationally reputed seat of learning at the monastery, establishing one of the world's most important libraries.

A small **folk museum** in the neighbouring church of St Pedro is the only other real sight of the town. This has predictable exhibits though, including some unusual old foundry equipment. There is a good Saturday market.

North from Ripoll

From Ripoll it is just 10 km (6 miles) north-east to **St Joan de les Abadesses**, a small mountain town with which it has strong ties. An abbey was founded here in the 9th century by Wilfred the Hairy (who also founded the monastery at Ripoll) for his daughter Emma who became the first Abbess. However the town was not destined to become as important as Ripoll and by the 12th century it operated simply as a parish church. Apart from the pleasing architecture of the **abbey**, the town has retained some authentic medieval charm and it is pleasant to stroll around perhaps shopping. Around the abbey are some arcaded shops where you can buy good quality souvenirs such as home-made candles and locally produced fabrics. Each Sunday there is a market under the arcades.

Heading further north on the C151, you come to **Camprodon** (14 km/9 miles), a lovely old mountain town at the confluence of the rivers Ter and Ritort and overlooked from high on the hill above by the Romanesque **Monastery of San Pere** with its photogenic square bell-tower. The beautifully curved stone bridge, the **Pont Nou**, dates from the 16th century. In the winter Camprodon welcomes a growing number of skiers using the nearby resort of Vallter 2000 and there has been a rash of sports shops to meet this demand. Other specialists goods here are sausages, hams, cheeses, furs and leatherwear. There is a general market every Sunday.

Every August the town holds the **Festival de Música Isaac Albéniz** (1860–1909) in honour of the composer who was born here.

Tiny villages cling to the slopes of the upper Ter Valley near Camprodon. Streets are often too narrow for tourist cars.

The Ter flows down to Camprodon from its source near the ski resort of Vallter 2000 (20 km/12½ miles), a route which makes a hugely enjoyable drive. Where the open valley steepens, about half way, stands the pretty village of **Setcases**, rescued from decay by renovation for summer homes and ski lodges. This is an excellent walking base.

Beyond Setcases the road climbs in steep hairpins to the ski lifts and runs of **Vallter 2000**. In the summer this is also a good place to start high-level walking. You can pick up the HRP footpath and head either east towards Canigou in France or west towards Núria, or you can connect with the thrilling Freser gorge. The ascent of **Pic de la Dona** (2,702 metres/8,865 ft) right on the border is a popular itinerary within the range of any moderately fit walker.

Back at Camprodon, the main C151 climbs north along the remote Ritort Valley to the tiny village of Molló with its Romanesque church.

From Molló the road climbs on to the border with France at the Coll d'Ares (18 km/11 miles from Camprodon). The border is open 7 a.m.–midnight from June to September and also at weekends; the rest of the year the border is open 8 a.m.–8 p.m. The attractive walled town of Prats de Mollo is 14 km (9 miles) beyond the frontier.

Ripoll to Ribes, Queralbs and Núria

Ribes de Freser, 14 km (9 miles) north of Ripoll along the Freser valley, is a busy market town, best known for its eponymous brand of mineral water. It is also the terminus for a breathtaking rail journey into the high mountains by the little **Cremallera rack railway** (the last of its type in Catalonia). From Ribes the mountain train climbs first to the gorgeous mountain village of **Queralbs**, popular with artists in summer for its narrow cobbled streets and lovely views. Queralbs is also accessible by road, but no car

can follow as the train cranks its way on up from Queralbs and through the gorge to the extraordinary sanctuary of **Núria**. The sanctuary was founded in the 11th century after the discovery of a sacred statue on the spot. It has been used as a place of pilgrimage ever since and you can follow a unique outdoor **Twelve Stations of the Cross route**, marked with huge religious sculptures. Outdoor masses are often held in this spectacular natural setting.

It is very exciting to hike back to Queralbs through the gorge along the route of the railway. A longer and

---

Salamanders

With their brilliant black and yellow (occasionally orangey-red) markings, the fire salamanders are among the most spectacular inhabitants of the Pyrenees. As nocturnal creatures, they emerge from their daytime hiding places under tree stumps, rocks and carpets of moss to appear on forest paths, especially after rain. Black and yellow is a warning colour combination (as with wasps) and fire salamanders do indeed secrete a poison which makes them inedible to predators. You should therefore wash your hands after handling them although they are not particularly toxic to humans. Protected by this, their movements are extremely slow in contrast to those of lizards which they otherwise resemble.

Females return to the streams to give birth to tadpoles, otherwise the entire adult life is spent on land. They eat slugs, worms and other invertebrates. The best way to see fire salamanders is to set off at dusk with a torch along the Freser gorge (or any similar damp, green location in the Pyrenees).

The other salamander of the range is the slightly smaller (up to 15 cm) Pyrenean brook salamander which occurs only here and, in closely related forms, on Sardinia and Corsica. Although they lack the tropical spectacle of the fire salamanders, they are an important species and are rightly protected. Emerging from hibernation under rocks in early spring, Pyrenean brook salamanders—in contrast to the fire salamanders—spend their active lives in water, feeding on insect larvae. Mating takes place throughout the summer and the adults return to land to hibernate when the water temperature falls below 6 °C (43 °F). With their pale brown coloration, the perfect camouflage against the stream beds, Pyrenean brook salamanders are therefore very difficult to see. The tadpoles take 40–50 days to emerge from the eggs, which the female hides beneath stones, and when winter comes they bury themselves in sand, to resume development the following year. The young are darker than the adults with a yellowish strip along the spine.

Two other salamander-like Pyrenean inhabitants are the stream-living marbled newt, which is recognized by its green colour, and the tiny palmate newt which is terrestrial and nocturnal.

even more spectacular itinerary, which will make a full day out, lies through the truly magical Freser gorge. The walk is not technically difficult but it is long and you should aim to leave Núria by mid-morning to be back at Queralbs before dark. The Editorial Alpina 1:25,000 Puigmal/Núria map is recommended.

To pick up the well-trodden path, cross the railway line at Núria and follow the track beyond the cable-car station to a large outdoor stone altar with a huge suspended crucifix. From here you drop slightly south-east across pasture to join a narrow but well-defined dirt path which continues into the **Freser gorge** and then works its way eastwards along the rock walls. Finally the path drops to the river and works its way back to Queralbs along the opposite bank.

An alternative hike lies north from Núria to the beautiful **Carança lakes** which lie just across the border in France.

To Puigcerdá

From Ripoll you have the choice of three westbound routes. The southernmost (to Berga) runs across marvellous rolling foothills. The middle route (to Guardiola de Bergueda) runs along the southern edge of the Cadí-Moixeró Park. But first, the northern route, the main N152, which connects directly with the Segre valley and Puigcerdá.

After reaching Ribes de Freser, north of Ripoll, the N152 becomes a marvellous corniche above the Rigart river, winding around buttresses and in and out of gulleys as if to give every possible viewpoint on the luscious Serra Mongrony to the south. The **Toses pass** is the high point, some 25 km (15 miles) from Ribes. There is a restaurant here. For botanists the pass is especially exciting. Terrain and climate conspire to give life to a number of rare plants, including the Rhaetian poppy, Pyrenean pheasant's eye, decumbent treacle-mustard and the Parnassus-leaved buttercup.

Once over the pass, the ski resorts of **La Molina** and **Masella** are seen on the hillsides to the south. In the summer there are organized sporting activities.

The upper Freser Valley is a wonderful place to see fire salamanders which, with their brilliant black and yellow markings, are amongst the most spectacular inhabitants of the Pyrenees.

Puigcerdá

More attractive than its sister border town of Bourg Madame, **Puigcerdá**, makes a convivial stop for refreshment and shopping. It is some 45 km (28 miles) from Ribes and 38 km (24 miles) east of La Seu d'Urgell. Head for the main square, the huge plaça de Santa Maria where there is plenty of parking and an assortment of bars and restaurants. Try **Bar Kennedy** for *tapas* and sandwiches or the next door **El Galer** restaurant, or for a snack one of the kiosks where *churrios* (long, sausage-shaped deep-fried doughnuts) are always available. On Sundays a lively market is held in the square.

The main sights of the town are the 42 metres (160 ft) **bell-tower** in the square, all that the Civil War has left of the church of Santa Maria, and the church of **San Domines** in passeig 10 Abril, just off the main square. Inside are some fragments of an important medieval mural by Guillem Manresa who was born in Puigcerdá. You will find it in an alcove on your left as you face the altar, opposite a modern stain-glass window. The main section shows the martyrdom of St Dominic.

Puigcerdá's shopping is surprisingly good with a number of high-quality fashion outlets to choose from. Best street is **calle Mayor** which is pedestrianized and leads into the older part of town with its few remaining medieval arcades. Any right hand turn here will lead to the **plaça Cerdanya Balcon** which is a natural viewpoint out over the Cerdanya plateau. A seemingly endless stone staircase leads down to the lower end of town by the RENFE station which you can see below. Amongst the old-looking buildings near the top of the stairs are the restored **town hall** and **tourist office**. Shops to look out for are **Carol** for leather goods; **Margal** for fine shoes; **Caçu** for high fashion and **Bartoch** for more leather fashion.

From Puigcerdá to La Seu d'Urgell

From Puigcerdá the main C1313 cuts through the Segre valley to La Seu d'Urgell. But first there are several glorious diversions along the way. Begin with the village of **Meranges**, 8 km (5 miles) west of Puigcerdá on the main road and then a further 10 km (6 miles) north on a minor road. A summer art community, it is also a good base for day walks. In fact, it was also popular with smugglers who would use it as an emergency bolt-hole should they encounter a frontier patrol on the heights of Andorra to the north.

Next, some 18 km (11 miles) west of Puigcerdá, the balconied houses and cobbled streets of **Bellver de Cerdanya** stand engagingly on an isolated hill. Just to the south of the village, the importance of the 12th century Romanesque church of **Santa Maria de Tallo** is underlined by its local nickname, "cathedral of Cerdanya". Make a point of seeing the **wooden Virgin** inside, a carving that is 800 years old.

Lles, another 9 km (6 miles) west, is a true mountain village, at the top of a steep climb. The drive is worth it for the views alone. In winter this is a cross-country ski resort and in summer the same trails make delightful walking. There are several small hotels and restaurants in Lles but, if you feel like something special, descend to the main

The dramatic north face of the Serra del Cadí as seen from the village of Gers near La Seu d'Urgell.

valley again and the Michelin rosette-holding **Restaurant Boix** in Martinet, run by the family of the same name. The menu is divided into regional and *haute cuisine*.

La Seu d'Urgell

The town of **La Seu d'Urgell** stands on a broad agricultural plain overlooked by the imposing and magnificently striated cliff faces of the Cadí mountains. Seu means seat and the town's name is derived from its importance as the episcopal seat of the region of Urgell. First its counts and then its bishops jointly ruled nearby Andorra together with the counts of Foix, from the Middle Ages onwards.

The main sight of the town is its 12th-century cathedral, consecrated in 839, rebuilt in 1175, embellished in the baroque style and finally restored in the Romanesque manner. The lovely 13th-century cloister gives access to the **Diocesan Museum** containing the 10th-century illuminated manuscript of Beatus' *Commentary on the Apocolypse*. This commentary on the Revelation of St John, originally written by the Asturian monk, Beatus of Liébana before AD 785, contains dream-like illustrations (or "illuminations") influenced by oriental imagery and by the visionary qualities of the apocalypse. The Beatus manuscripts are characterized by Mozarabic style—two dimensional, with strong colours, especially yellows and reds, unrelated to true colours, and with the convention that interiors are revealed through walls.

The recently renovated **Parador de la Seu d'Urgell** is a marvellous place to stay, right beside the cathedral.

La Pobla de Lillet and into the Cadí

As an alternative, quieter route west from Ripoll, take the GE402 to Guardiola de Berguea via La Pobla de Lillet. From the village of Campdevanol 4 km (2½ miles) north of Ripoll, the GE402 climbs first to Gombren, just after which there is an optional diversion to the **Mogrony Sanctuary** along a well-made track. The sanctuary is not open to the public but the 5-km (3-mile) route is so spectacular that it should not be missed. The sanctuary has been built high up on a shelf at the base of enormous cliffs, from where the surrounding peaks seem to roll on forever. It is possible to continue on track right into the **Mogrony nature reserve**, where there is a refuge, picnic spot—and memorable hiking.

At **La Pobla de Lillet** there are two Romanesque churches worth looking at as well as an unlikely example of Modernist architecture. The churches are the ruined **St Maria** and (to the south of the main road on the east side of town) the more interesting **St Miquel** which is circular and contains a rare 12th-century *Christ in Majesty*. The Modernist building is in fact a cement factory, no longer in use, which was designed by Rafael Guastavino in 1901. Less famous than his contemporary Gaudi, he was considerably more practical and the inventor of the so-called "brick vault", now widely adopted. The factory lies 3 km (2 miles) north of La Pobla de Lillet on the side road north to **Castellar de N'Hug,** where its "cascade" appearance reflects the waterfalls of the nearby river Llobregat. The **Llobregat** is the sacred river of Catalonia because it runs into the sea at Barcelona. The source (**Fonts del Llobregat**) lies a short way south towards Castellar and, having seen it, you might as well continue into Castellar itself in a most magnificent setting in the Serra de Mogrony and on the edge of the Cadí-Moixeró park.

From Castellar you have the choice of continuing north the 15 km (9 miles) to the Coll de Toses (*see* above), or of retracing your steps to La Pobla de Lillet.

Cadí-Moixeró Natural Park

West of La Pobla de Lillet, on the GE402, you soon enter the **Cadí-Moixeró Natural Park**, a huge protected area of little inhabitation. After 9 km (6 miles) you will reach the main north–south C1411 at Guardiola de Bergueda. Here you can choose to head north through the Cadí Tunnel and on the fast way to Puigcerdá or La Seu d'Urgell. Or you can head west to plunge still deeper into the Cadí wilderness on an itinerary which ultimately involves some long sections of good but unsurfaced track. To continue in the Cadí, turn south at Guardiola for just 2 km (1 mile) then take the minor road to the right for Massanes and Gosol. The road at first follows a narrow shelf spectacularly above the Saldes river but then, as Massanes approaches, a new and even more arresting vista takes over as the curious forked mountain of **Pedraforca** (2,497 metres/ 8,192 ft) takes shape behind Massanes.

Motorists can drive right to the base of the peak by continuing to the village of Saldes and, just beyond, taking the

A full artist's palette of colours emerges over the autumn period as different trees stagger their seasonal changes.

route signposted "Mirador (viewpoint) de Gresolet". A steep road, unsurfaced for a section, climbs to a viewing platform from which the **panorama** is one of the finest in all of the Pyrenees. A ten-minute climb on foot through the woods from the lookout will bring you to the **Lluis Estasen refuge** where meals and refreshments are available in summer.

Hikers can continue along the track from the lookout which heads northwest through beech forest until, after about an hour, it reaches the pass and crossroads of tracks known as **El Collell**. From this pass it is possible to descend to **Gosol** on the far side of Pedraforca. From Gosol you may then return to your car by taxi (Tel. 973-37-00-65). If you plan to do this walk, or any other in the area, you should obtain the *Editorial Alpina* 1:25,000 map "Serra del Cadí and Pedraforca".

Petrol stations are few and far between in this area, but if you are desperate, ask at the general store in **Saldes** and it may be possible to buy a couple of cans in a "psst, come round the back" style transaction.

Continuing along the valley road from Saldes the lush scenery changes unexpectedly to an Arizona-type landscape of bizarre pink soil and deeply eroded gulleys. **Gosol**, 10 km (6 miles) west of Saldes is the village to which Pablo Picasso came to paint in 1906 at the age of 25, attracted by its remote location, its people and its memorable scenery. His stay is commemorated by a small plaque on plaça Major, the tiny central square with its three trees, fountain and benches. The ruins above Gosol, reached in a few minutes walk, are of an earlier abandoned village.

If you want to continue onwards from Gosol you will have to be prepared to drive on track—but it is well maintained and passable to ordinary family saloons. The track first heads towards the Serra del Cadí, a long line of peaks of which the highest is

*B*elow the distinctive peaks of the Serra del Cadí lies a lonely landscape of scrub, red rock and tiny stone villages such as Fornols.

Baridana (2,648 metres/8,688 ft). Unfailingly impressive in any light, the Cadí peaks are very special when snow-capped. Once over the little Josa pass, the track drops to the very foot of these impressive peaks and then turns west to the hamlet of **Josa del Cadi**, perched on a hill with its old church at the very top. Take your camera as you will fall in love with the narrow streets, roughly painted houses, the cobbles and the gated farmyards.

Tuixent, some 8 km (5 miles) on from Josa and 6 km (10 miles) from Gosol, is a more substantial village where the Tourist Office for the region is located.

At Tuixent you have the choice of continuing on track north to La Seu d'Urgell or of rejoining tarmac and driving south to St Llorenç de Morunys over the Port pass 1,636 metres/5,367 ft. La Seu d'Urgell is 38 km (24 miles) through some of the most remote and spectacular scenery of Catalonia, a lonely landscape of scrub, vivid red rock (called *puzzolana*) and tiny stone villages such as Fornols or Adraen.

Ripoll to Berga

The most southerly itinerary from Ripoll towards the Cadí lies along the C149, an attractive, undulating road, at every bend giving new views of the ravishing peaks and valleys of the gleaming Pyrenean foothills. After 24 km (15 miles) there is a possible detour from the village of Borreda to see the best Romanesque church of the region, the 11th-century **St Jaume de Frontanya**. Some 10 km (6 miles) north of Borreda on a side road this parish church, looking like some frightened castle with its massive blank walls, is actually in the shape of a Latin cross. It is distinguished by its 12-sided "lantern" of which there is only one other comparable example in all Catalonia—at Ripoll.

Back on the C149, another enchanting 21 km (13 miles) bring you to the ankle of the boot-shaped **Baells reservoir** which you cross for the historic town of **Berga**. It is here at the beginning of June every year that Catalonia holds what is probably its greatest celebration, the **Festa de Patum**. Lasting three days around Corpus Christi, it is a spectacular event involving dancing, singing, colourful processions of giant figures, fireworks and much eating and drinking. The general theme is good versus bad and the highlight always comes on the Saturday night with a dragon breathing fire and fireworks amongst the revellers.

During the **Festa** there is very little room left in the town but at other times there are few visitors. The old town is partially pedestrianized and makes for good strolling. There is also a small local **museum** next door to the tourist office in Carrer des Angels, unfortunately only open on Sundays (tourist office Monday–Saturday 9 a.m.–3 p.m. and Sunday 9 a.m.–noon; museum Sundays 11 a.m.–noon).

The Monastery of Queralt and St Llorenç de Morunys

The drive from Berga to St Llorenç de Morunys (32 km/20 miles) and onwards into the Segre valley near Organya is one of the most spectacular routes along the Pyrenees. For much of its length, the road traces the final cliffs of the range with impressive views south; at other points, the succession of ridges and summits is hauntingly beautiful, especially at sunset. But before setting off, first see the **monastery of Our Lady of Queralt** on the mountainside behind Berga, an easy drive from the town, recommended for its attractive gardens and breathtaking views over the plain of Lower Bergueda.

St Llorenç is an ancient town of narrow cobbled streets contained behind a remarkably well-preserved medieval wall. The **church** dates back to the 11th century and is extravagantly decorated inside.

In the mountains to the north of St Llorenç, the small ski resort of **Port del Comte** also makes an attractive summer walking base. Beyond, the road climbs on to the Port pass and then drops to Tuixent.

From La Seu d'Urgell into Western Catalonia

West of La Seu d'Urgell and the Segre valley, the marvellous Aigües Tortes National Park is one of the natural highlights of Catalonia. From La Seu d'Urgell, take the C1313 Lleida road, turning right towards Sort, just after the village of Adrall. For those interested in Catalan history, however, there is first a worthwhile diversion another 16 km (10 miles) south on the C1313 to Organyá. Motorists coming from the St Llorenç de Morunys direction will pass through Organyá without diverting.

In a little round building in the square in **Organyá** (beside the tourist office) is kept what could be the earliest example of written Catalan. In the 12th century somebody took a Latin sermon and made annotations in the Catalan language. These **Homilies of Organyá**, were uncovered in a local religious institution at the beginning of the 20th century and have fascinated scholars ever since.

Having climbed from the Segre valley to the Cantó pass, the road westwards descends to the mighty Noguera Pallaresa river—one of the most powerful in the Pyrenees—at the village of **Sort**. Various signs immediately underline the importance of the river for modern tourism—canoeing and rafting are the great attractions. The more atmospheric old part of town lies up the steep streets behind the main road. Here are cobbles, tall, thin washing-hung houses, small shops and some cheap hotels and restaurants.

A brooding sunset throwing into haunting relief the succession of ridges and summits leading to St Llorenç de Morunys.

A Circular Tour from Sort

The Aigües Tortes National Park lies north-west of Sort. No roads run through the park so that to see both sides by car it is necessary to make a circle around it. The following itinerary visits the east side first, circles anti-clockwise to the west side via the Aran valley, and finally returns to Sort via La Pobla de Segur.

From Sort head north on the C147 along the wide Noguera Pallaresa through Rialb (4 km/2½ miles) to Llavorsí (12 km/7½ miles), a picturesque village at the convergence with the **Cardos** river. For energetic hikers the Cardos and its side valley of the **Vallferrera** are highly rewarding, both rivers having their sources in the high peaks of the frontier.

Some 13 km (8 miles) along the Noguera Pallaresa from Llavorsí, just at the bottom tip of the Torrassa Reservoir, the road for the Aigües Tortes National Park is signposted left. After 7 km (4½ miles) this side road climbs to Espot, a lively village now surviving almost exclusively as a gateway to the park, which lies 3 km (2 miles) beyond.

Espot is in two parts, the more touristic on the south bank of the San Maurici river and the agricultural part on the north side, where you will also find the 9th-century parish church of **Santa Llogaia**. The two parts are connected by the inverted horseshoe of the **Capella bridge**.

The Aigües Tortes National Park

In an area of sharp granite peaks, characterized by a profusion of sparkling lakes and streams, the Aigües Tortes is the only national park in Catalonia. With its easy road access and network of jeep tracks its beauty is accessible to the picnicker and casual stroller but the landscape also contains tough summits and remote unmarked traverses suitable for the mountaineer and dedicated hiker.

Butterflies are the most visible wildlife in summer, flicking brilliantly across the meadows and upland marshes. The diversity of terrain attracts many species and a short stroll should reveal anything up to a dozen.

Next come the large birds of prey, the golden eagles, often seen spiralling upwards, singly or in pairs, and the slightly larger griffon vultures, normally in a flock. Individuals too high for their markings to be distinct can sometimes be identified by silhouette—the tail and head of the golden eagle are quite prominent in flight whereas the massive wings of the griffon vulture dwarf the tail and particularly the head almost into invisibility. The black woodpecker, the largest of the European woodpeckers, is the symbol of the park but fiendishly difficult to spot. In flight it resembles a crow but with a much longer, pointed tail, more rounded wings and a flash of red on the head.

On the rock faces wallcreepers climb with the adhesive qualities of spiders as they search for insects; little larger than sparrows, they have downcurved bills and grey bodies but the wings are a marvellous red spotted with white.

The capercaillie is now extinct in the French Alps but occurs both in the French and Spanish Pyrenees, especially the Aigües Tortes. The male is considerably larger than the female, approximating to a turkey with a

Butterflies

The intoxicating colours of a Pyrenean meadow are not due solely to the flowers but also to the kaleidoscope of butterflies that flicker in the sun. If you have just a little knowledge of these amazing creatures your rambles will be all the more exciting.

Fragile and simple as they seem, butterflies are capable of covering vast distances and of astounding aerobatic feats to escape birds. They are so sensitive that they can differentiate flower species through their feet and a male can detect a female several kilometres away by her release of an attractant scent or pheromone. Even the immobile pupa is capable of surprises, assuming the colour of surrounding vegetation and, in many cases, producing squeaking noises which somehow deter predators. A few butterflies and moths are pests, particularly the pine processionary moth whose caterpillar is responsible for the white "snowballs" seen on pines in many parts of the range. These are in fact nests from which the blue-black caterpillars emerge in procession at night to devour the pine needles.

The Aran Valley and Aigües Tortes National Park are famous for their butterflies but, in fact, most parts of the range have significant populations. These are some of the varieties you may see:

The chequered skipper (*Carterocephalus palaemon*) is a handsome dark brown and pale ochre, with a wingspan measuring up to 29 mm (1.15 in). The eggs are laid on ground ivy, plantain and various grasses.

The Apollo (*Parnassius apollo*) is a huge and striking butterfly. Its forewings are grey with black spots and have an incredible span of up to 85 mm (3.3 in); the hindwings are black edged with orange spots. It flies during July and August at up to 2,000 metres (6,500 ft) altitude. The incandescent clouded Apollo (*Parnassius mnemosyne republicanus*) is an endemic sub-species which is white or creamy with black veins and a wingspan of up to 75 mm (3 in). The caterpillar is black with rows of red spots. The adult can be seen at the same time and altitude as the Apollo, often feeding on members of the poppy family.

The great banded grayling, also known as the greater wood nymph (*Brintesia circe*) has a prominent off-white band across the back of the fore and hindwings. Towards the fore wingtip there is a round black spot in the white which identifies it. The wingspan is up to 72 mm (2.85 in). The adult flies in early summer.

The clouded yellow (*Colias crocea*) is an amazingly powerful flier and long-distance migrant. An acid yellow, it is identified by a black spot on the forewing and an orange spot on the hindwing. The wingspan is up to 58 mm (2.2 in). In summer it survives up to 2,000 metres (6,500 ft) altitiude but it cannot survive the winters and probably migrates. There are several other notable yellow species in the Pyrenees. Berger's clouded yellow (*Colias australis*) is also present, similarly sized, but its colour less clean. The Brimstone (*Gonepteryx rhamni*) is yet another yellow species, but paler—the colour of butter, from which some experts believe all butterflies got their name. The Cleopatra (*Gonepteryx cleopatra*) is similar to the brimstone, except that the male has an orange-red forewing and the female an orange streak. It flies in late spring and early summer up to 2,500 metres (8,200 ft).

Extinct in much of northern Europe, the Mazarine blue (*Cyaniris semiargus*) still lives in the Pyrenees. A lovely dark blue, the wings are edged white and black. Its wingspan is up to 34 mm (1.3 in). The marsh fritillary (*Eurodryas aurinia*) is a small but magnificently coloured butterfly in brown, orange and yellow, like an early church fresco. It flies in May and June, over marshy ground.

fan-shaped tail, blackish plumage and a red flash over the eye. The females, though, are quite different, with mottled brown plumage. Capercaillies are most usually seen when accidentally flushed from cover in the woods, or during the spring courtship display around dawn.

All the mammals are difficult to see, with the exception of the squirrel. The izards (Pyrenean chamois) live on the uplands in summer and are only likely to be seen by motorists when winter weather drives them down into the valleys. The Aigües Tortes is also home to wild boar, pine martens, stoats and the curious desman, an animal that has the appearance of a long-nosed mole but that swims in the streams where it feeds on aquatic insects.

Covering more than 24,000 hectares (60,000 acres), the park has a shape somewhat reminiscent of Australia. Sadly, when it was established in the 1950s, hydro-electric power development was also allowed to take place. Technically, the dams and pipework are in contravention of national park status and they certainly do detract from the sense of wilderness. But it is still an area of astounding beauty. The two main entry points for motorists are the village of Espot in the east and the Boí valley (see below) in the west— also famous for its Romanesque churches.

Inside the Eastern Park

The park information office is at the far end of Espot village, near the bridge. Beyond the village, a good tarmac road continues for 7 km (4 miles), going inside the park boundary as far as the parking area at the St Maurici

lake. When the lake is full and reflecting the famous Encantats mountains on the south side, this is a very beautiful spot indeed. The surrounding meadows abound with butterflies. A short walk south of the lake, and signposted from the dam wall, refreshments are available at the **Ernest Mallafré** refuge; for serious hikers, there are also 36 places available here in dormitories.

The **Encantats** (2,747 metres/9,012 ft) are the distinctive twin peaks of a single cloven summit of naked granite beyond the refuge. According to legend, the twin peaks are two shepherds turned to stone—from which derives the name, meaning "enchanted".

Ordinary cars cannot go further than the St Maurici lake but it is possible to take a jeep taxi from the rank outside the Hotel Saurat in Espot, either for a tour throughout the eastern park along its jeep tracks, or to visit one of the more remote picnic spots. The jeep taxis follow two tracks. One climbs north from the St Maurici lake for a distance of about 4 km (2½ miles) to the Amitges lake, where refreshments are available at the refuge on the south side. This is a harsh and treeless high-mountain landscape of weather-shattered rock but the views are impressive. To the south you can see the Encantats with, to the right of its divided summit, **Monastero** (2,878 metres/9,442 ft) and, to the right of that, Peguera (2,892 metres/9,488 ft), the highest mountain in the eastern park.

The second jeep track begins approximately half way between Espot and the St Maurici lake and climbs southwards 8 km (5 miles) to the **Tort de Peguera** lake and the huge **Negre**

lake, both popular picnic spots where the terrain is a little softer than at the Amitges lake. Walkers can follow either of the jeep tracks; an alternative, away from tracks and hydro-electric development, is the **Monastero valley** which runs south from the St Maurici lake, an area of outstanding and almost untarnished beauty.

It is possible to walk right across the park from the St Maurici lake, spending the night in the Boí valley before returning next day. Hotels in Espot can arrange for a jeep taxi to cover the final section from the refuge at Lake Llong to whatever overnight accomodation has been booked. The walk is 15 km (9 miles) and takes approximately 6 hours.

Super Espot, an ugly block of apartments calling itself a ski resort is at the end of a 2 km (1 mile) road well signposted from just outside the village. At only 1,500 metres (5,000 ft) it does not enjoy a good snow record but the views are worth the trip.

A storm descends suddenly on Pic de Peguera. The Aigües Tortes National Park is an area of high rainfall, hence the name which means "twisted waters".

Aran Valley

If you follow the C147 past the Espot turn you will be driving into what, until fairly recently, was considered one of the most remote parts of Spain. The Vall d'Aran was often completely cut off in the winter and the area even had its own language, Aranese. Today you can still find yourself in pretty uninhabited country if you come off the beaten track—especially if you hike south towards the Aigües Tortes National Park which, save for a couple of tracks, has virtually no sign of human habitation. Not so the main routes, however, now marked and marred by electricity pylons of which you will see plenty as you climb up towards the Bonaigua Pass.

Descending on the far side to the River Garona (the famous River Garonne of France), the first village is the modern ski resort of **Baqueira-Beret**. A more traditionally attractive place to stay is **Salardú**, 5 km (3 miles) further on. Salardú is a good base for exploring the several small villages of the immediate Aran Valley, several of which have very well-preserved Romanesque churches. Salardú also has a marvellous church of its own, the 13th-century St Andreu. The others are at **Unya**, a short walk higher up the hill, **Bagergue**—2 km (1 mile) beyond Unya—and at Tredos, on the opposite side of the river.

Arties, 4 km (2 miles) further west has an interesting **church** built on the site of a 12th-century castle originally belonging to the Knights Templar. Another plus point of Arties is that it has a Parador.

Viella

Capital of the Aran valley, **Viella** is 6 km (4 miles) past Arties, standing at the junction with the N230, the final north–south artery of Catalonia. It is a fair-sized shopping centre and increasingly a holiday town catering for the ever-growing numbers of winter sports enthusiasts using the slopes of Baqueira-Beret or Le Tuca just up the road. This means there is a constant building programme of chalet-style apartments, fast-food restaurants and a rash of expensive skiing shops.

A major sight in the town is the church of St Mique in the central plaza, set back from the road and instantly recognizable by a massive studded door. It is pleasant to park and walk through this square and into the old town climbing a hill at the back. The little River Nere runs down to meet the larger Garona and in summer its banks will be crowded with butterflies. You can also visit the small but fascinating **Ethnological Museum** in a well-restored medieval building, which gives some insight into the history and life of the Aranese people.

From Viella, head south through the 5-km (3-mile) Viella Tunnel (which now keeps this once-remote area of the Pyrenees accessible throughout the whole year) and down the fast N230 for 40 km (25 miles) to the entrance to the Boí valley, just before El Pont de Suert.

The Boí Valley

This is the gateway to the western side of Aigües Tortes National Park, traced by a long, winding and bumpy road beside the Noguera de Tort river. This route presents a feast of Romanesque monuments—perhaps nowhere else in the entire Pyrenees has such a fine collection within so small an area. First church is the 12th-century **Santa Maria** at **Coll**, 8 km (5 miles) into the valley and only a short steep diversion off the main road. At **Barruera**, **San Feliu** is next, clearly visible from the road and a beautiful photographic composition when taken with the wide river behind. The church at **Durro**, a couple of kilometres east from this village, boasts the largest bell-tower in the valley. The church of **Santa Eulália** at **Erill la Vall** on the west bank of the river comes next—it has a six-storey tower.

Just beyond Erill, the road divides. One part heads on along the main valley bottom. The other swings up the eastern slope of the valley to Boí village itself. Some 16 km (10 miles) from the valley mouth, Boí is one of the high-spots of any Pyrenean tour. Picturesque, despite its popularity with tourists, it still manages to operate as a traditional farming community against a backdrop of superlative mountain views. Its church of **St Joan** was formerly much greater, but is now reduced to a single apse and a square three-storey tower of perfectly balanced solid stone squares. The **mural** inside, showing the stoning of St Stephen, is a reproduction, the original of which is in the Museu d'Art de Catalunya (MAC) in Barcelona. The church is right in the centre of the village in the little main square surrounded by huge boulders, a number of hotels and not unattractive apartment complexes. Walk through

One of the many fine Romanesque murals in the Boí valley—this one is in the church of Santa Maria in Taüll.

the stone arch and you are in the most ancient part. There are inexpensive, clean and attractive rooms here at the recently converted **Casa Marco**.

From Boí the road climbs 3 km (1 mile) to Taüll with its two **Romanesque churches** and **medieval village centre**, now being renovated to meet the needs of the ski station which is being developed above the village. **Santa Maria** is the church in the higher part of the village, containing a reproduction mural showing the Virgin and Child—the original is now in Barcelona. Surrounded by fields on the outskirts, **San Climent de Taüll** is easier to see and appreciate as the perfect example of Romanesque architecture that it is. Like Santa Eulália in Erill la Vall, it has a six-storey

The village of Perves is set in bleak landscape along the road connecting El Pont de Suert and La Pobla de Segur.

The distant Collegats gorge framed by the belltower of the church at Montcortes.

bell-tower, the windows increasing in size as they go up to counter the effects of perspective. The murals were transferred to Barcelona in 1907 but the reproductions capture the ambience accurately; they are strongly and brilliantly coloured, showing Christ in Majesty and scenes from the New Testament and the Apocalypse.

Returning to the main valley road below Boí village, the most luxurious hotel in the entire Boí valley is at the spa of **Caldas de Boí**, some 5 km (3 miles) north of Erill. This is the **El Manantial** standing in a park with its own indoor and outdoor swimming pools and tennis courts. It is possible to continue along the valley beyond Caldas de Boí as far as the huge dam wall at lake Cavallers. Hikers can take the path along the eastern shore that climbs up to the **Ventosa i Calvell**

refuge in a beautiful region surrounded by lakes. From the dam, the walk takes a full day, allowing for stops.

Between Boí and Caldas de Boí lies the access to the western sector of the Aigües Tortes National Park, along a track which climbs up to the right. Ordinary cars cannot cope with this route but it is possible to go by jeep taxi, bookable at your hotel (or Tel. 973-69-60-37 or 973-69-60-34). The standard excursion is to **lake Llebeta** on the boundary of the park, immediately south off **Pala Alta de Serrader** (2,983 metres/9,787 ft), highest mountain in the park, and then on to **lake Llong**. Dedicated walkers may like to stay in the refuge on the lake, which has 50 places in dormitories. Attractive itineraries in this part of the park include the hike to the **Dellui lake** to the south of lake Llong.

To the Collegats Gorge and Gerri de la Sal

Returning to El Pont de Suert at the entrance to the Boí valley, motorists should head east on the C144 to complete the circuit of the Aigües Tortes region. Alternatively, if you are touring westwards, take the N230 north for 5 km (3 miles) and then the C144 west towards the Benasque valley (*see* above).

Eastwards, the C144 climbs through bleak and treeless scenery to the Perves pass, redescending along the Bellera valley to Senterada. Here there is the chance to explore some little-known scenery on the southern fringe of the Aigües Tortes by turning off into the narrow Vall Fosca to Capdella, otherwise continue to La Pobla de Segur (42 km/26 miles) where the Noguera Pallaresa valley is regained.

On the first Sunday in July each year **raft races** are held on the river at La Pobla to commemorate the way logs used to be floated down from the mountains to the town's sawmillls.

Some 8 km (5 miles) north of La Pobla the spectacular **Collegats gorges** begin, a superb "wild-west" of high cliffs, bluffs and gulleys.

Beyond the gorge the road emerges at the village of **Gerri de la Sal**. Sal is Catalan for "salt" and the abandoned salt pans are on the far side of the village beside the river. The other sight of Gerri is the magical but crumbling monastery on the far side of the river.

*T*he Paseo leads to the magnificent Arbolo monastery at Gerri de la Sal.

Gerri has a marvellous old core, reached by walking through an archway and down towards the river. Across the bridge the **monastery of Santa Maria** was once glorious, but most of its gilded interior decoration was destroyed during the Civil War. Nevertheless, so romantic is the setting that many people from the area come here to get married.

From Gerri, it is 13 km (8 miles) north to Sort.

*T*he former salt-producing village of Gerri de la Sal scrambling up the hillside above the mighty Noguera Pallaresa river.

Coastal Catalonia for the Independent Traveller

Cosmopolitan Roses is the main resort on a delightful section of coast (*see* map on pages 266–267), far less busy than the main beaches of the Costa Brava. El Port de la Selva is a lovely working fishing village. Inland is the town of Figueres, centre of the Empordá wine-growing region.

The easternmost point of the Pyrenees is Cape Creus on the northern Costa Brava, where the mountains meet the Mediterranean. From the wide sandy beach at Roses it is possible to look back and see the line of summits, often snowcapped in early season. Look for a pyramidal peak, slightly lopsided, but quite distinct from its surrounding mountains. This is **Canigou**, the sacred mountain of all Catalan people and a great beauty spot. But the mountains

*P*rehistoric people favoured the Costa Brava just as much as people do today, leaving their ancient standing stones like this one at Vilartoli.

are not just the backdrop to the coast, for here on the eastern side of the range they stretch right down to, into and under the sea, unlike the western Pyrenees which fade away before the coastal plain. Driving between Roses and Port Bou on the coastal frontier with France you are still very much in the mountains, twisting around cliffs and folds, but here with wonderful views out over blue sparkling sea.

Costa Brava means "Rugged Coast" (a title invented by the Catalan poet Fernando Agulló in 1908), and although the southern part was one of the early discoveries of mass tourism, the resorts of the Pyrenean Costa Brava are small and visited mainly by independent tourists. This is the territory of holiday villas and apartments,

owned mainly by the French, British and Germans. Spring and autumn are particularly wonderful when the tiny coves, fascinating countryside and aromatic mountains can be enjoyed in tranquillity.

Roses

Roses is the largest holiday resort on this section of the coast, a cosmopolitan sort of place with 4 km (2 miles) of wide, safe, sandy beach. Because it faces south at the edge of the Cadaqués peninsula it has wonderful sunsets, best enjoyed, cocktail in hand, as the waters of the broad Bay of Roses turn a delicious pink.

As an important port **Roses** goes back a long way, its name derived from Rhode, a colony founded on the site by the ancient Greeks. However, there were inhabitants even before the Greeks as witnessed by the existence of **La Creu d'en Cobertella**, a magnificent dolmen (a megalith of prehistory)

Cap Norfeu lies just to the north of Roses. You can explore this wild stretch of the Costa Brava on foot from Roses, eventually reaching Cadaqués.

some 5,000 years old, in the hills just behind the resort. To see it, turn left from the seafront road into avinguda de la Cuana (just before the harbour). Next, turn right into carretera Montjoi i Joncols. Follow this beyond the last buildings of Roses until a sharp right bend where there is a small parking spot from which a footpath leads through resinous shrubs to the dolmen. After about ten minutes on foot the huge blocks of stone appear in a shady grove of trees, highly scented in the heat and full of grasshoppers.

If you return to your car and carry on along the potholed road you will discover several lovely bays, including cala Montjoi and cala Joncüls, both far less busy than the main beaches of the Costa Brava. At **Cala Montjoi** there is a Michelin rosette restaurant **El Bulli**, with breathtaking views and atmosphere of rustic sophistication. For accommodation and eating out *see* HOTELS AND RESTAURANTS. Roses is not a great shopping centre, mostly holidaywear and souvenirs, but if you are self-catering you can buy good fish at the evening fish market down at the port and fruit and vegetables at the daily covered market.

Coastal Catalan Food

Finding somewhere to eat in Roses is no problem—finding somewhere quiet may be. As in most Spanish holiday resorts dinner hours are late, the rush not really starting until 10 p.m., so your favourite restaurant may have room earlier rather than later. There is a wide range of prices, from hamburger and chips to international cuisine. In coastal Catalonia fish is understandably top priority and it is almost always possible to find paella although it is not a speciality of this area—squid is, either battered or in a variety of sauces. Sardines and anchovy, both caught by local fishermen, are also widely featured on menus; anchovies are served on great hunks of bread or toast, often as a piquant first course. Sardines are favoured fresh and grilled often on outdoor barbecues. Costa Brava specialities include *suquet*, a rich mixed fish dish stewed in a court-bouillon stock, *langoustines* (giant prawns) and mussels served in a number of different sauces, such as garlic and chilli. It is advisable to choose a good specialist fish restaurant if you are going to treat yourself to a fishy meal as standards vary a great deal, especially in the mixed dishes

such as paella. Non-fish lovers can try snails, again served in all manner of different sauces and quite an everyday dish, especially after heavy rain when you can see families collecting the tiny molluscs by the roadside. A more exotic version is *al estilo del Ampurdán* which is snails served with rabbit. There is plenty of grilled meat (no longer just the thin, tough bifstec) and, thanks to the mountains closeby, game will often be available in season. *Faves estofades* is stew with white beans and *carn d'olla* is a thick meat stew. *Manos de cerdo estofadas* is stewed pig's trotters. *Butifarra* is a highly spiced Catalan blood sausage. *Samfaina* is a side dish of peppers and tomatoes; *escalivada*, is almost the same though with the addition of aubergines. *Aminada* is Catalan for salad. *Aminada Catalá* is with garlic sausage and even *aminada verda* (green salad) is invariably an imaginative creation including mild onion, sweet pepper, olives and tomatoes.

As in the inland regions of Catalonia, the local wine is supplied by the El Ampurdán wineries. Try the sparkling whites from Perelada, the whites, rosés and reds from Espolla (Torres is a particularly well-thought-of label) and reds from Campmany.

Aiguamolls de l'Empordá

The bird and wildlife sanctuary of **Aiguamolls de l'Empordá** just inland from Roses on the marshy plains between the rivers Muga and Fluvia makes a beautiful evening excursion after a day on the beach. For the visitor centre, take the busy C260 from Roses towards Figueres. At the ancient town of Castelló d'Empuries

The wetlands of Alt Empordá are only a fraction of their former size, but still form a magnificent wilderness to the south of the range.

white storks, because there is a breeding programme for them—as there is for fallow deer. Of entirely wild birds, in an hour or two at the various hides and lagoons you should see (according to time of year) kingfishers, bee-eaters, marsh and hen harrier, stone curlews, black-thoated divers, maybe the odd Kentish plover and hundreds of ducks. The rare glossy ibis is an occasional visitor. All this is punctuated by the croaking of frogs—and the whine of mosquitoes (so take the repellent).

(9 km/6 miles), the major port of the region before the Muga silted up, turn left towards Saint Pere Pescador. After about 4 km (2 miles) the **visitor centre** is reached along a track to the left. You can hire binoculars here and see an exhibition of the birds you might be able to observe. You will certainly see

North from Roses to the border

Roses is on the southern side of a wondrously unspoiled rocky headland, the rounded and multi-bayed Cadaqués Peninsula. Almost opposite Roses on the north side is the much

smaller El Puerto de la Selva and in the middle of the eastern side, looking directly out to open sea, is the arty resort of Cadaqués itself.

Cadaqués

Energetic walkers can make their way directly around the coast from Roses to Cadaqués, following a track so badly eroded that even a four-wheel drive jeep would have difficulty. Ordinary motorists have to take the road over the mountains, descending to Cadaqués in scenic hairpins through vineyards and aromatic scrub.

This was the coastline that the great Surrealist artist Salvador Dalí fell in love with and no wonder. He bought and converted some fishermen's cottages in the hamlet of Port Lligat, adjoining Cadaqués. The town itself is an immensely likeable place, full of hilly, narrow streets, creeper-clad walls, cafés and—because of the Dalí legacy—art galleries. The traditional fishermen's waterfront homes have also been joined by two Modernist buildings which, somehow, are not out of place. Leave your car in the parking area at the approach to the village and just wander. Steep alleys cut between protruding rocks lead up to the white-painted 17th-century church which has always doubled as a lighthouse. Inside

There is a breeding programme for fallow deer in the Aiguamolls de l'Empordá, where they are easy to see. You will also spot white storks and a variety of ducks, divers and wading birds.

These heads identify the wall of Dalí's house at Port Lligat, empty since his death in 1989. There are plans to open it as a museum.

is a remarkably ornate gilded altarpiece which has only survived since the decline of pirate attacks which were the ruin of an earlier church on the site.

The **Municipal Art Museum** is close to the church, its walls crammed with an invigorating display of local artists and local themes. But Dalí is not to be found here. Only some of his drawings are to be seen in Cadaqués, at the **Perrot-Moore Museum**, just behind the seafront. It is the private collection of a former secretary of Salvador Dalí. Under the influence of the eccentric artist, the museum is an extravagent imaginative romp, downstairs centred around a gold and velvet theatre displaying prints from Dalí (and a number of other famous artists) all with Don Quixote as the central theme. Upstairs, the centre of attraction is a huge old automobile, now filled with models of Dalí, his wife Gala, Picasso and some other artistic friends.

To see Dalí's house, you need to drive to the next bay by taking the small road signposted to **Port Lligat** on the outskirts of Cadaqués. This takes you, through the expanding suburbs, down to the tiny bay and bohemian resort where Salvador Dalí and his wife Gala made there longtime home. Since Dalí's death in 1989, Casa Dalí has been empty and is now locked up and flaking. It is easily identified by a number of Daliesque touches—the giant heads and eggs on the walls. It is the central part of a charming beachside hamlet, all white wash, bougainvillaea and stray cats. Brightly coloured fishing boats cram on to the small beach and yachts rock gently in the protected bay.

North of Port Lligat the peninsula is quite wild and makes for wonderful hiking with the opportunity to drop down into idyllic little bays to swim. Club Mediteranée has a holiday complex close to the tip of the headland at Cape Creus.

El Port de la Selva, San Pere de Rhodes, Llança and Port Bou

To head north from Cadaqués along the northern Costa Brava you will first have to drive back inland 5 km (3 miles) until a junction of main roads from where you go north west for 8 km (5 miles) to **El Port de la Selva**, a lovely old fishing village, still working commercially and thus only touched and not ruined by tourism and full of good eating possibilities. It has a wonderfully atmospheric restaurant, specializing in fish and Catalan dishes, cheap and very cheerful with red-checked table cloths.

Piracy was once rife along this coast and a number of the small ports, such as Selva de Mar and

Llança 8 km (5 miles) north were built back from the sea, merely fronted by their ports.

El Port de la Selva is a paradise for small boat owners. With its small marina, yacht club and chandler's stores it has all the facilities but none of the crowds found in the more southerly ports. There are miles of uninhabited coastline and plenty of small coves in which to drop anchor or land.

Just above El Port de la Selva are the ruined Benedictine **monastery of San Pere de Rhodes** and the **castle of San Salvador**, both looking down from

The ruined castle of Saint Salvador stands on the summit of Mount Vedera, just above El Port de la Selva. The visit here, and to the monastery of Saint Pere de Rhodes just below, is highly recommended.

Mount Vedera. They are reached in an easy 6 km (4 mile) drive along a newly metalled track ending in a huge carpark with marvellous views back down along the coast. The **monastery** is a magnificent monument both in architectural and historical terms. As you follow the steeply climbing road you will see the dark walls loom overhead, the crenellations and the symmetrical window arches of the typically Romanesque church tower standing out against the sky. It was a huge structure, now largely ruined but in the slow process of restoration (open daily 10 a.m.–2 p.m. and 4 p.m.–dusk). The **11th-century church** is moving in its raw state, dark, damp and in advanced collapse and there are still vestiges of Romanesque decoration such as carved capitals and elegant if decrepit cloisters.

If you want to visit the severely **ruined castle** of San Salvador you must follow a steep footpath climbing above San Pere for about 20 minutes. It is worth the effort for its views both to the coast

you have just left and behind to the Bay of Roses and the Empordá plain.

Close to the car-park is a third ruin, the **church of St Elena,** a pretty though somewhat despoiled pre-Romanesque building.

If you do not want to return the way you came, you can continue over Mount Vedera dropping down on a good road through a landscape of cork and olive to the village of Vilajuïga

(9 km/6 miles) on the Empordá plain. En route you will pass a series of **five dolmens** (prehistoric megaliths), the first of which is marked left of the road as you descend. Watch out for small wooden signs and scraps of red cloth as you come to a long sharp bend about 3½ km (2 miles) from the car park. From the first dolmen the others are relatively easy to find, again marked with scraps of red cloth. By searching out the whole series, you actually walk virtually down to the plain where you could be met by your driver just over a kilometre (under one mile) from the village of Vilajuïga. If you choose to drive the 9 km (5½ miles) to Vilajuïga you will be well-placed to explore the wine-growing region of Alt Empordá or take the fast road back to the coast.

Vilajuïga itself is worth visiting for its **ancient synagogue** preserved in the outer hall of the plain old building on the main square which now functions as a Christian church. Ask in the souvenir/bookshop for a key if the church is locked. Also close to the village is the hill-top ruin of the Visigothic **castle of Quermanço.** The Visigoths, who invaded Spain in the 5th-century AD, were not enduring builders and this is a rare opportunity. You

The dolmen de la Cabana Arqueta stands close to the road near the village of Espolla. It dates from around 2,500 BC.

can stay in Vilajuïga at the hotel/restaurant **Xavi**.

From Vilajuïga you can take the C252 9 km (6 miles) north-east to Llança; if you have not made the San Pere de Rhodes/Vilajuïga diversion you simply continue north on the coast road. Llança was built in two parts as protection against piracy—a port and an inland residential area. The village is popular with the home market; it has good beaches, simple accommodation and a range of restaurants, several of them making the most of the busy fishing industry.

The dolmen del Barranc, just to the north of Espolla, is the only one in the region to bear an inscription. This dates from between 3,200–2,700 BC.

Activity centres around the fishing port where there are several inexpensive restaurants and—in the inland part—the plaça Major. Here there are more traditional café-bars where locals and visitors sit outside and watch the nightly procession of local youths on their noisy motorbikes. The square has two landmarks, a picturesque part-Romanesque belltower—all that survives of an early church—and the newer edifice, a huge rather plain 18th-century church with imposing stone steps.

Some 7 km (4 miles) north of Llança, **Colera** is an even smaller seaside resort, again popular mostly with Spanish holidaymakers. From Colera the Costa Brava is at its most dramatic and there are no more expanses of sand until **Port Bou**, 8 very winding kilometres (5 miles) further north. But even here the beach is quite tiny and the resort's main function is as an international rail terminus. The frontier is just 2 km (1 mile) further on, at the top of the next ridge. There is a petrol station just before (fill up—it is much cheaper than in France!). The customs are open 24 hours a day between 15 June and 30 September but otherwise close at midnight.

Inland from the Costa Brava

Figueres

Figueres is a major inland centre, just 18 km (11 miles) west of Roses and by-passed by the fast N11 trunk road and A7 (E15) motorway. It is an important public transport hub with buses and trains linking with international lines, but its main claim to fame is as birthplace of the famous Surrealist artist Salvador Dalí (1904–89) and home to his extraordinary **theatre museum.** You cannot miss the museum; its white dome, huge eggs and other eccentric exterior decorations are as intriguing as the interior. You can use the same entrance ticket for the nearby **Empordá Museum** where exhibits include Greek and Roman local finds, and paintings by artists with local connections, including Picasso, Miró, and of course, Dalí. There is also a **toy museum** and, in the main square, La Rambla, a statue of **Narcis Monturial** (1819–85) the town's famous son, inventor of the submarine. His early underwater vessel, the wooden *Ictineo* which had a crew of six, was launched into and under the water in Barcelona harbour in 1861.

North of Figueres

North of Figueres the plain of Alt Empordá begins to tilt up into the Albères mountains, the easternmost chain of the Pyrenees where strongly-scented Mediterranean scrub has here and there been tamed into vineyards and plantations of cork oak.

For the main wine-growing region, leave Figueres on the C252 towards Llança and after 7 km (4 miles) turn north-west on the minor road to the village and castle of **Perelada** which has given its name to a popular slightly sparkling white wine. The 14th-century castle has been renovated into a casino and entertainment complex which attracts big-name interntional stars.

From Perelada continue north to Espolla, through the now drained wetlands. **Espolla** is a traditional village not only at the heart of the Empordá wine-growing region but also of prehistoric settlement in the region. Close by are a number of dolmens and monoliths. Most of the main sites are accessed off rough tracks and although marked by scraps of red cloth are difficult to find. One of the easiest is the **Dolmen de la Cabana Arqueta**, just about 1 km (½ mile) south-west of the village on the St Climent road. At the first sweeping bend take a small track to the right going through vines. After a few minutes' walk the track divides and the dolmen is found close by, along the left-hand fork, the mighty slabs standing in a grove of trees surrounded by fields.

The region of **Alt Empordá** west of the main Costa Brava motorway is, if anything, even more remote. Here the vast Boadella reservoir, when full, dwarfs the lake at Banyoles and, ever since the draining of the marshland, its fringes have become an important refuge for birdlife. From Figueres take the minor road west to **St Llorenç de Muga** on the south side of the Boadella Reservoir. From the village a track leads north through marshland where huge herons strut and fly. Again, an ordinary saloon can only go so far but a jeep can reach the surfaced road on the north side of the reservoir. Ordinary motorists will have to return east from St Llorenç for 5 km (3 miles) and then turn north to Boadella (where there is a mighty view along the reservoir from the dam wall) and then to Darnius and **Maçanet de Cabrenys**, where there is a huge prehistoric menhir.

Activities for All Ages

Interesting ways to fill your days, and keep you occupied from dawn until dusk. Leave the car behind and take off for a ramble or a hike, hire a cycle or a horse, or take a mountain train. The Pyrenees are not just about skiing—you can find diving, surfing and windsurfing on beautiful beaches, not to mention golf. Whether your idea of a happy day entails an afternoon stroll or a wild raft ride down a river, here are some ideas to set you off.

Sport and Recreation

Coastlines included, the Pyrenees is an exceptional playground for outdoor enthusiasts. In general you will find that the French side of the range offers the greatest variety of activities and is the better organized, while the Spanish Pyrenees are for the slightly more adventurous.

Hiking and Rambling
Above all, the Pyrenees is known for its thousands of kilometres of walking

There are far fewer ski resorts in the Pyrenees than in the Alps, leaving the region a savage paradise for ski tourers.

trails. The most famous and most tough is the **Haute Randonnée Pyrénéenne** in 45 stages, which stays close to the crestline, mostly in France but occasionally straying into Spain. While the HRP is a recognized itinerary it is not a marked and engineered path and there are long sections where navigation is by map and compass. In the high passes, particularly early in the season, crampons and ice axes are essential. However, there are stretches of the HRP that are well within the capability of most fit walkers and no one need be put off those by the HRP's reputation as the mountaineers' route.

The two standard lower-level traverses are the **Grande Randonnée 10** in France, and the new **Gran Recorrido 11** in Spain.

*H*ikers should remember that in the high mountains, snow can last until summer. At the Sarradets refuge above Gavarnie the only way in and out is through an upstairs window.

The GR10 is generally well trodden and well marked and, as far as possible, is designed to allow overnights in refuges, gîtes d'étape and occasionally village hotels rather than in the open. Only completed at the end of the 1980s (although many sections were long-used local footpaths), the GR11 is generally clearly marked but a few sections still need attention. It is less

known and therefore more tranquil than the GR10. It also visits some of the most powerful Pyrenean scenery, such as the Ordesa Canyon, which both the HRP and the GR10 miss. You may be best, therefore, to plan an itinerary drawing on the best of all three.

The final recognized traverse is the French **Chemin de Piémont** which skirts the entire range by its northern foothills. It can be completed at any time of year.

If you are a history-lover, the partial traverse from Foix to the Mediterranean along the **Sentier Cathare** is particularly recommended. It includes the famous ruined castles of Montségur, Peyrepertuse and Quéribus. Designed to be accomplished in eleven stages, overnighting in gîtes d'étape, it can be walked at any time of year. In addition there are several north–south traverses, the most famous beingthe **Chemin de Santiago de Compostelle** (the **GR65**) which crosses the Pyrenees between St Jean Pied-de-Port and Pamplona via the Ibañeta Pass and Roncesvalles. This is a historic segment, a route that has been trodden by Roman legions, by Napoleon's troops and by pilgrims for hundreds of years. Two other major north–south routes are the **GR36** (known as the GR4 in Spain) which connects Albi in the Languedoc with Montserrat near Barcelona, via the Canigou massif and the Cerdagne; and the **GR7**, which runs from the Montagne Noire, north of Carcassonne, to Barcelona, via Andorra.

If you do not have the time for a traverse but would like to have the satisfaction of completing a recognized itinerary, there are more than a score of local circuits on the French side of the range, taking from three to seven days (or more for the less fit). Most tourist offices can also supply itineraries, taking from an hour or so up to a day.

Walking Skills and Equipment

Walkers in the Pyrenees often opt for unnecessarily tough boots. Ordinary flat shoes and trainers are quite adequate for walks on prepared paths and rubber-soled canvas boots are popular in the Pyrénées-Orientales, where the ground is normally dry. Traditional walking boots become necessary when tackling routes not on prepared paths, especially long-distance walks. In a few parts of the Pyrenees like the Baronnies, where rainfall is high and drainage poor, rubber boots are recommended.

There can be a wide range of temperatures in the Pyrenees in summer, between morning and midday, and between valleys and summits—on average, temperature falls by 1°C for every 100–200 metres of ascent (1°F for every 150–300 ft). The range is also plagued by frequent summer thunderstorms, especially in August. These characteristics require the all-day or long-distance walker to be equipped with suitable clothing. Shorts and T-shirt are ideal for ascents in hot weather, with a sun-hat and dark glasses. As the temperature falls, so you can pull on a jumper and trousers. For storms, a lightweight plastic raincoat, cape or purpose-designed waterproofs should be carried. All of this, together with the picnic, should be in a backpack.

The greatest problem for inexperienced walkers lies in estimating the degree of difficulty and the time necessary to complete a particular route. The system of hours used on signposts and most guidebooks is based on fit walkers, lightly loaded and makes no allowance for stops. Less practised walkers carrying camera equipment, picnic, extra clothing—and even more so those carrying climbing equipment, tent and sleeping bag—will certainly move more slowly. At least ten minutes per hour should be added for rests and, during the course of a day, there will have to be longer stops for picnics and, perhaps to take photographs. Therefore, a walk described as taking "3hrs" will more likely take five hours and a sign that reads "6hrs" should be interpreted as indicating a gruelling all-day itinerary.

If you are unused to walking, you will probably find 10 km (6 miles) as much as you can manage at first and 20 km (12 miles) would take on the character of an endurance test. The amount of ascent is also crucial. A hike involving up to 500 metres (1,600 ft) of ascent should be within most people's capabilities, 750 metres (2,500 ft) can be considered demanding and anything over 1,000 metres (3,300 ft) is really for the young or athletic.

Water can be one of the heaviest items in a backpack. Fortunately, most Pyrenean high-mountain torrents are safe to drink, *provided there are no villages or habitations upstream.* Generally, you will have to be above 1,500 metres (5,000 ft) to avoid sources of pollution —the only way to be sure is to consult a map.

Climbing

Climbing has now become very chic, demanding the latest fashion in climbing tights, boots and equipment, plus a rockface close to an appreciative audience. There is no need to head off into the roof of the Pyrenees since all of the high peaks (Aneto, Posets, Monte Perdido, Vignemale) can be reached by experienced mountain walkers. Some of the toughest climbing routes are right by the roadside, such as the Vénus route at Urdos in the Aspe valley, which has been free-climbed despite its 6b rating. The cliff of Sarrancolin in the Aure valley is also well known to climbers and that at Troubat to the south of Montréjeau has become the most famous of all in the French Pyrenees as the site of many international competitions. In Spain, the Mallos de Riglos between Jaca and Huesca provide some of the most exciting routes for this new kind of gymnastics. For "old style" climbing, classics include the north face of Vignemale and the Ordesa Canyon.

If you would like to learn to climb, schools exist throughout the French and Spanish Pyrenees. The cost of six two-hour lessons, enough to get you started, is around 760F/14,400 ptas. There are artificial climbing walls at Seix, Tarbes, Font Romeu, Luz St Sauveur and Pau.

Horse-riding

Horse-riding is becoming increasingly popular, especially in the foothills of the French side. The Mérens is the famous black pony of the Ariège-Pyrenees, believed closely related to the wild horses of prehistory. In terms of its strength, it should be considered a horse rather than a pony. Its sure-footedness makes it ideal for the mountains. Mérens les Vals, a pretty hillside village close to Ax-les-Thermes is home of the authentic Mérens breed and one of its most passionate defenders is Englishman Kevin Henshall, who runs a stud and can advise on suitable trekking (Tel. 61-64-03-92). Another mountain breed, from the Alps is the highly attractive golden-

Schools for climbing exist throughout the Pyrenees. Take proper tuition and you can learn in safety.

Well-marked horse trails cover the Pyrenees. The favoured mount is the local Mérens, pony-sized but with the strength of a horse and the sure-footedness of an izard.

maned Haflinger, employed by a few stables, notably at Py in the Pyrénées-Orientales (Tel. 68-05-58-38).

A word of warning: because of the seasonality of Pyrenean riding, the animals run semi-wild in the winter and are often tended by inexperienced casual labour in summer. Check the calibre of a horse-trekking company before booking a holiday. Treks of several days are possible and a complete traverse of the Pyrenees has been described in French in André Berrotte's *Grande Traversée des Pyrénées*.

Cycling

The sport of mountain-biking has become hugely popular in the French Pyrenees and there are hire shops in most towns and resorts (around 90F a day). Mountain bikes are stronger and consequently slightly heavier than touring bikes, with broad, deeply treaded tyres, robust frames, powerful brakes and a wide-range of gears—usually 18 or 21. In theory, mountain-bikers can go just about anywhere. In practice, few riders are strong enough and tough enough to contemplate anything more demanding than a well-graded track and plenty of holidaymakers simply stick to the roads. If you do not intend to go off road, consider hiring a touring bike instead, generally cheaper

than a mountain bike and better suited to road use. One of the most important things is to check the lowest gear ratio (calculated by dividing the number of cogs on the *smallest* front chainwheel by the number of cogs on the *largest* rear sprocket and multiplying by the circumference of the road wheels). Typically, mountain bikes for hire have a lowest ratio of around 24 —that is, each complete rotation of the pedals moves the bicycle 60 cm (24 inches). Although adequate for the toughest mountain roads, you should seek out a bottom ratio of under 20 for steep off-road work.

Check the bicycle out thoroughly before leaving the vicinity of the shop by riding it around, going through all the gears and testing the brakes. Mountain bikes for hire get a lot of rough use and are not always as well maintained as they should be.

Canyoning

Canyoning is one of the new sports of the Pyrenees, which involves following

313

watercourses through the deeply fissured limestone terrain of regions such as the Monte Perdido massif. Some of the routes require no more skill or pluck than is necessary for an artificial waterchute at the seaside. Others, however, demand considerable stamina, wetsuits and helmets for protection, and knowledge of specialist disciplines such as abseiling. The best advice is to go with an experienced guide; your hotel or local tourist office will be able to advise. Apart from the Monte Perdido region, there is excellent canyoning to be had around the Canigou massif in the Pyrénées-Orientales.

Rafting, Canoeing and Hydrospeed

A ride on the Noguera Pallaresa on an inflatable raft is an unforgettable experience. You will be saturated and you could even be pitched into the river. As a precaution you will be required to wear a helmet and buoyancy aid. The steersman sits in the middle controlling a long pair of oars but the passengers—up to a dozen—have to work too, using lightweight paddles. The best time on the Noguera Pallaresa is from April to the end of June.

Spring is equally the best time for canoeing in the Pyrenees, when the melt fills the streams. Because of their smaller size, canoes are less restricted than rafts and there are suitable rivers throughout the range. The most important in France are the Aspe, Mauléon, Lourdios, Oloron, Pau, Ossau, Aldudes, Adour, Arros, Aure, Louron, Salat, Garbet, Ariège, Têt and Tech. In Spain the best rivers include the Bidasoa, Irati, Esca, Noguera Pallaresa, Segre, Llobregat and Ter.

The newest way of tackling the Pyrenean torrents is hydrospeed. You need a wet suit, buoyancy jacket, helmet, protective pads, fins and a special float, holding on to which you flash along the torrent virtually at the mercy of the foam and rocks. Only a few schools have as yet been established. One of the main ones is Ecolorado at Lourdes (Tel. 62-96-46-28) where hydrospeed (and also rafting and canoeing) is possible from Easter until October.

Caving

In the extensive limestone regions of the Pyrenees there are literally hundreds of known caves for the enthusiast to visit. The most important areas are around Arette la Pierre St Martin (where the Gouffre de la Pierre St Martin is one of the deepest in the world) and the Ariège. The easiest way to enjoy the formations is to visit a show cave like **Grandes Canalettes** near Villefranche de Conflent. Many show caves have also been shelters for prehistoric people, like Niaux in Ariège.

If you want to pursue caving more actively you can make contact with guides, instructors and clubs through the tourist office. With a modicum of experience and equipment there is no danger in entering most horizontal caves in the Pyrenees. The minimum equipment for short visits consists of a helmet, water resistant head torch, overalls and wellington boots. Longer expeditions will call for spare bulbs and batteries (or a special-purpose rechargeable caving battery pack and lamp), emergency candle, marker arrows and compass, water and food

(all stored in a waterproof container like a metal ammunition tin obtainable from army surplus outlets). Vertical cave systems should never be entered without proper equipment and training in the specialist skills for using it properly.

Skiing

Without any argument, the Pyrenees are second best only to the Alps in terms of the quality of snow. Climatic factors make the French side of the range more dependable than the Spanish, and the central area more dependable than the areas nearer the coast. From west to east, the leading resorts are Cauterets, Luz-Ardiden, Gavarnie, Barèges, La Mongie, Piau-Engaly, St-Lary-Soulan, Peyragudes, Superbagnères and Ax Bonascre in France; Candanchu, Baqueira-Beret, Cerler, La Molina and Núria in Spain; Arcalis, Pal, Arinsal, Soldeu and Pas de la Casa in Andorra.

The sun-drenched Pyrenean ski resorts cannot always guarantee snow, but the ski tourer can be sure of finding it—and solitude, too.

In the Pyrenees it is as important to consider the altitude of the ski station as it is the height of the top lift. If there is insufficient snow at the ski station level then the resort may not be able to function, even though the top runs have adequate snow cover. For this reason, **Pas de la Casa** has proven the most reliable of Pyrenean resorts since the ski station stands at 2,100 metres (6,890 ft). In general, look for top lifts at around 2,500 metres (8,000 ft) and ski stations at around 1,800 metres (6,000 ft) or more.

For cross-country skiing the leading resorts are Iraty, Cauterets, Gavarnie,

Saint-Lary-Soulan, Superbagnères, Plateau de Sault, Plateau de Beille and the Capcir in France; and Tuixent in the Cadí in Spain. Prepared cross-country ski trails, however, are generally at low altitude and suffer from the same unreliability as downhill pistes.

If you can ski off piste, whether on cross-country or mountaineering skis, you will be less vulnerable to the vagaries of snowfall. Cross-country skis are longer, thinner and lighter than downhill. To ease climbing, the sole is normally covered with "fish-scales" so that the ski can slide forwards but not backwards. Purists, however, prefer the traditional smooth-soled skis where adhesion is obtained using waxes. The cross-country binding secures only the toe of the boot so that in the event of a fall there is little danger of a broken leg. Mountaineering skis, on the other hand, are similar to downhill skis, except that they are lighter in weight. Adhesion for climbing is achieved using stick-on "skins". The bindings allow the heels to be lifted on ascents but to be fastened down for descents. Downhill boots can be worn but purpose-made ski-mountaineering boots, allowing more flex, will be more comfortable.

If you have the necessary skills and fitness, the Pyrenees can provide outstanding ski touring and with less danger than in the Alps. Recommended resorts include Gavarnie and Barèges for ski mountaineering while the Cerdagne, Capcir and Cadí are excellent for cross-country. If you prefer to practise ski-mountaineering on a more Nordic-style terrain, you will greatly enjoy the uplands between Canigou and Núria.

Diving

At the Mediterranean end, the Pyrenees extend under the sea to create an underwater paradise for divers. Most dramatic are the two immense underwater canyons or "rechs", the one to the north known as Le Rech Lacaze Duthiers (after the founder of the Arago Laboratory at Banyuls) and that to the south Le Rech Du Cap Creus. The canyons are around 22 km (14 miles) in length, up to 9 km (5½ miles) across and as much as 1,000 metres (3,300 ft) deep, but here and there the "summits" come sufficiently close to the surface for diving.

From just south of Banyuls to just north of Cerbère, lies the Réserve de Cerbère/Banyuls sur Mer covering an area of 650 hectares (1,600 acres), the first marine reserve created in French waters. Within the reserve fishing is controlled; in the central area of 65 hectares (160 acres), around cap Rédéris, all fishing, gathering of shellfish and diving is banned. The result is a well-balanced ecosystem with plenty of plant and animal life.

There are diving schools and places to fill bottles all along the coast. For British divers the English-speaking Unisub at l'Estartit operates according to British Sub-Aqua Club rules as well as offering tuition in accordance with the US Professional Association of Diving Instructors (PADI): Unisub Internacional, Ctra Torroella de Montgri, s/n., 17258 l'Estartit, Girona (Tel. 972-75-87-68).

Surfing and Windsurfing

The best surfing in Europe is on the Atlantic beaches of the Pyrenees, especially at **Biarritz** where tuition and board hire are available. Windsurfing is possible all along both the Atlantic and Mediterranean coasts and at a few locations inland, including the **Embalse de Yesa** to the east of Pamplona, the **Barrage of Vinça** near Perpignan and the **Lac de Matemale** near Font-Romeu.

Parapente, Hang-gliding and Gliding

Parapente is one of the new sports, known also as paragliding, which has caught on rapidly in the Pyrenees. It is similar to hang-gliding, except that instead of a semi-rigid structure, parapente utilizes a parachute-type wing which can be folded away into a backpack. Lift is obtained by running down a slope and the resulting flight can last anything from a few seconds, in the case of a novice, to 20 minutes or more in the hands of an expert able to utilize rising air currents.

In the early days of the sport the accident rate was high but a proven and reliable teaching method has now been established. On no account should a beginner attempt self-teaching. In the French Pyrenees, the main centres are Bedous, Barèges, St Lary and Mont Louis and in Spain Pamplona, Benasque and Núria. New schools are opening all the time. In winter parapente is possible on skis and there is the additional advantage that winds are generally lighter and more consistent. Ensure that any school you intend to sign up with is using parapentes not more than a year old. Technical advance has been so

*P*arapente, or paragliding, is one of the latest crazes to hit the Pyrenees. What finer way to descend a mountain peak!

rapid that you will be at a disadvantage with older designs; moreover, parapentes are not safe for more than around 300 flights. The school should also be equipped with two-way radios for ground to air tuition. The cost of a week's course is around 1,900F; double that for the two weeks necessary to attain a standard at which you can safely go off on your own.

Hang-gliding is now well known. Resorts which have schools include Foix, Bagnères de Luchon, Argelés-Gazost, Loudenvielle, Viella and Benasque. Gliding is available at Foix, Bagnères de Luchon and Val Louron.

Golf

The first golf course in Continental Europe was opened at Pau in 1856 but that was to satisfy the large contingent of British residents. Only recently has there been an explosion of interest in golf in France, taking the number of courses from around 130 in 1980 to 300 in 1990. Half as many again are expected to be added in the next ten years. The main courses of the French Pyrenees are Golf de Biarritz, La Nivelle, Chantaco and Chiberta (all on the Atlantic coast), Pau, Luchon, Lannemezan, Labastide de-Sérou, Font-Romeu and, on the Mediterranean coast, St Cyprien. Despite the popularity of Andalusia with British golfers, there are few Spanish courses close to the Pyrenees. The main ones are San Sebastián on the Atlantic coast, and Pals, just behind the Costa Brava.

Pyrenean courses generally have room for visitors. Expect to pay between 115F/2,760 ptas and 190F/3,600 ptas a round outside the high summer season.

Activities for Children

Walking and Exploring

In families where walking is not a regular activity, itineraries cannot be too ambitious. Infants can be carried either in slings which hold them against the chest or in backpack-style seats, available in outdoor equipment shops. Once children outgrow that stage long walks become impossible for a few years. By the age of ten, however, children should be capable of walking several miles in a day and carrying the same proportional load as adults—about a fifth of body weight. A 30 kg (60 lb) child should therefore be able to carry 6 kg (12 lb), the equivalent to food and water for a day, extra clothing, a book and perhaps some sort of game to play at a picnic spot.

Children do not respond to hiking in the same way as adults and a daytrip will become much more compelling with a little invention. It is best to have a definite place to walk to, such as a waterfall or the summit of a mountain. Tales of smuggling and wartime escape can fire the imagination. Or the family can split into two with the advance party laying a trail of cairns or arrows made of twigs. The following group should clear these away as it goes.

Older children should be allowed to plan the route and do any necessary map reading and compass work.

Most children respond to the idea of seeing wild animals but the day out can be disappointing if nothing is found. Read the sections of this book dealing with wildlife and try to go where wild animals are virtually guaranteed. Izards, marmots and the large birds of prey are the easiest. A pair of lightweight binoculars will add enormously to the enjoyment. Buying a book of animal tracks and signs is also a good idea. A marmot's tunnel is not as rewarding as an actual marmot but it is some sort of reward for a day's exploration.

Mountain Trains

The miniature and mountain trains of the Pyrenees are very exciting to children and these can be worked into a walking itinerary—perhaps taking the train one way and walking back. The most famous train of the Pyrenees is the **Petit Train Jaune** which runs from Villefranche de Conflent in the Têt Valley to Latour-de-Carol. Children will want to ride in the central open carriage, so make sure you arrive in good time to take up your position on the platform.

At the western end of the range the **Petit Train d'Artouste** is even more exciting for children. The day begins with an eight-minute cablecar ride from the Fabrèges lake to the station. The train, composed of four open carriages, then heads south to the Artouste lake, situated at 2,000 metres (6,500ft), a picturesque journey that takes just under an hour. There is only 1 hour 26 minutes before the train leaves again, just long enough to stroll along the lakeside and have a picnic. If you wish to spend all day, you have to buy the special *randonnée* ticket, departing on the 8.30 a.m. train and returning on the 7.18 p.m. Older children will be able to manage the walk back which takes four to five hours.

On the Spanish side of the range, the *cremallera* is a rack railway which climbs from Ribes de Freser to Núria where there is a small lake and a sanctuary that was founded in the 11th century. There is no road up. The return journey can also be by *cremallera* or on foot.

Caves

Caves are fascinating to most children and at **Lombrives** in Ariège it is possible to combine a train ride with a cave visit. Lombrives is the largest show cave in Europe and contains some magnificent formations, of which the most famous is the "Mammoth". There are also legends of bandits. Situated just to the south of Tarascon sur Ariège, the entrance is gained by a short miniature train ride and the whole guided visit takes about 90 minutes. Lombrives is open daily throughout the summer from 10 a.m. until 7 p.m. (June and September until 5.30 p.m.).

The other subterranean experiences of the Ariège are the prehistoric caves of **Niaux**, **La Vache**, **Bédeilhac** and **Mas d'Azil,** plus **Labouiche** which involves a mile-long underground boat ride. In the western Pyrenees there are show caves at **Isturitz** near Cambo and at **Sare**, and in the eastern Pyrenees at **Fontrabiouse**, near Mont-Louis, and at **Villefranche de Conflent** (Canalettes and Grandes Canalettes). For adventurous youngsters the **Grotte L'Aguzou** in the upper Aude Valley is strongly recommended. The visit is expensive but the guided party spends an entire day underground in one of the most beautiful cave systems in the Pyrenees, using head torches for illumination.

Language Guide

Only if you are an accomplished linguist could you possibly deal with the four main languages of the Pyrenees—French, Basque, Spanish (Castilian) and Catalan. To complicate things further, the people of the Aran valley claim Aranese as a separate tongue and there are also numerous patois. However, you can manage perfectly well with French in the French Pyrenees, Castilian in the Spanish Pyrenees, and either in Andorra (where the official language is Catalan). If you have the time for a crash course in a single language, French is the obvious choice since there are more Spaniards speaking French than there are French speaking Spanish.

If you speak only English there is no need to worry as it is widely understood in major tourist areas. But a knowledge of French or Spanish will certainly ease the way in more remote regions, and generally add enormously to the enjoyment of the holiday and to an understanding of the people. If you are driving and have a cassette player in your car, a taped language course is strongly recommended. At the very least, buy French and Spanish phrase books and learn some key words and sentences. If there are problems over pronunciation, find the phrase you want in English and point to, rather than speak, the translation.

Below are some "master" words and phrases which may prove useful in the absence of all other assistance. The Spanish is given first, followed by the French.

General

Do you speak English?	**Habla usted inglés?** **Parlez-vous anglais?**
Does anyone here speak English?	**Hay alguien aqui que hable inglés?** **Quelq'un sait-il parler anglais?**
I don't speak much Spanish/ French.	**No hablo mucho español.** **Je ne parle pas beaucoup français.**
Please could you speak more slowly?	**Puede usted hablar más despacio, por favor?** **Vous pouvez parler plus lentement, s'il vous plaît?**
I understand.	**Comprendo.** **Je comprends.**
I do not understand.	**No comprendo.** **Je ne comprends pas.**
Yes	**Si** **Oui**
No	**No** **Non**
Please	**Por favor** **S'il vous plaît**
Thank you	**Gracias** **Merci**
Thank you very much	**Muchas gracias** **Merci beaucoup**
Don't mention it.	**De nada.** **De rien.**
Can you help me?	**Puede usted ayudarme?** **Pouvez-vous m'aider?**
Can you direct me to...?	**Puede usted indicarme la dirección a...?** **Pouvez-vous m'indiquer la direction de...?**
Good morning	**Buenos dias** **Bonjour**
Good afternoon	**Buenas tardes** **Bonjour**

Good evening	**Buenas tardes**
	Bonsoir
Good night	**Buenas noches**
	Bonne nuit
Goodbye	**Adiós**
	Au revoir
How are you?	**Cómo está usted?**
	Comment allez-vous?
Very well. And you?	**Muy bien. Y usted?**
	Très bien. Et vous?
Sorry!	**Lo siento!**
	Pardon!
Where?	**Dónde?**
	Où?
How?	**Cómo?**
	Comment?
When?	**Cuándo?**
	Quand?
What?	**Qué?**
	Quoi?
Why?	**Por qué?**
	Pourquoi?
Who?	**Quién?**
	Qui?
Where is...?	**Dónde está...?**
	Où se trouve...?
I'm looking for...	**Estoy buscando...**
	Je cherche...
How do I get to..?	**Cómo podria ir a..?**
	Comment puis-je aller à..?
Where are the toilets?	**Dónde están los servicios?**
	Où se trouve les toilettes?
I'm lost.	**Me he perdido.**
	Je me suis perdu.
I'd like...	**Quisiera...**
	Je voudrais...
We'd like...	**Quisiéramos...**
	Nous voudrions...
How much does it cost?	**Cuánto cuesta?**
	Ça coûte combien?

Is that correct?	**Es correcto?**
	C'est juste?
Where do you come from?	**De dónde es usted?**
	De quel pays êtes-vous?
I come from...	**Soy de...**
	Je suis...
See you later.	**Hasta luego.**
	A plus tard.

Food and Eating

Assorted appetizers	***Entremeses variados***
	Hors d'oeuvres
Anchovies	**Anchoas**
	Anchois
Asparagus	**Espárragos**
	Asperges
Avocado	**Aguacate**
	Avocat
Cheese	**Queso**
	Fromage
Clams	**Almejas**
	Clam
Crayfish	**Cigalas**
	Langouste
Eggs	**Huevos**
	Oeufs
Fritters	**Buñuelitos**
	Beignets
Ham	**Jamón**
	Jambon
Kebab (meat)	**Pinochos**
	Brochette
Kebab (various)	**Palitos**
Meatballs	**Albóndigas**
	Boulettes de viande
Melon	**Melón**
	Melon
Mussels	**Mejillones**
	Moules
Olives	**Aceitunas**
	Olives

Oysters	Ostras Huîtres		*Scallops*	Veneras Coquille St Jacques
Sardines	Sardinas Sardines		*Sole*	Lenguado Sole
Sausage	Chorizo Saucisson		*Steak*	Filete Bifteck
Shrimps	Gambas Crevettes		*Sucking pig*	Cochinillo asado Cochon de lait
Squid	Calamares Calamars		*Swordfish*	Pez espada Espada
Tart	Tartaletas Tarte		*Tuna*	Bonito Thon
			Turkey	Pavo Dindon

Main Dishes

			Veal	Carne de ternera Veau
Beef	Carne de buey Boeuf			
Chicken	Pollo Poulet			

Chops	Chuletas Côtelette

Vegetables — Duras Legumes

Cod	Bacalao Morue		*Artichoke*	Alcachofas Artichaut
Duck	Pato Canard		*Asparagus*	Esparragos Asperge
Lamb	Carne de cordero Agneau		*Aubergines*	Berenjena Aubergine
Liver	Higado Foie		*Beans (broad)*	Habas Féve
Mackerel	Caballa Maquereau		*Beans (green)*	Judias Verdes Haricots verts
Mince	Carne picada Bifteck haché		*Beetroot*	Remolacha Betterave
Mutton	Carnero Mouton		*Cabbage*	Repollo Chou
Octopus	Pulpo Poulpe		*Carrots*	Zanahorias Carottes
Pork	Carne de cerdo Porc		*Cauliflower*	Coliflor Chou-fleur
Salmon	Salmón Saumon		*Courgettes*	Calabacín Courgettes
Sausages	Salchichas Saucisses		*Mushrooms*	Champiñones Champignons

Peppers	Pimiento Poivrons		Caramel	Crema Catalana Crème caramel
Peas	Guisantes Pois		Cheesecake	Pastel de Queso Flan au fromage blanc
Spinach	Espinacas Epinards		Ice cream:	Helado: Glace:
Sweetcorn	Maiz Maïs		Chocolate	Chocolate Chocolat
Tomatoes	Tomates Tomates		Strawberry	Fresa Fraise

Fruit / **Fruta / Fruit**

Apple	Manzana Pomme		Lemon	Limón Citron
Apricot	Albaricoques Abricot		Vanilla	Vainilla Vanille
Banana	Plátano Banane		Rice pudding	Arroz con leche Riz au lait
Cherries	Cerezas Cerises		Waffles	Tortitas
Figs	Higos Figues			

Other Useful Phrases and Words

Grapes	Uvas Raisins
Lemon	Limón Citron
Melon	Melón Melon
Orange	Naranja Orange
Peach	Melocotón Pêche
Pineapple	Piña Ananas
Plums	Ciruelas Prunes
Watermelon	Sandia Pastèque
Pyrenean desserts	postres desserts
Apple tart	Tarta de manzana Tarte aux pommes

The bill, please.	La cuenta, por favor. L'addition, s'il vous plaît.
Is everything included?	Está todo incluido? Tout est compris?
Do you accept credit cards?	Acepta tarjetas de crédito? Acceptez-vous les cartes de credit?
Suntan cream	una crema solar une crème solaire
Sweater	un suéter un pullover
Sweatshirt	un suéter de tela de punto un sweat-shirt
Torch	una lintertna une torche
Trousers	unos pantalones un pantalon
T-shirt	una camiseta un T-shirt
Umbrella	un paraguas un parapluie

The Right Place at the Right Price

Hotels

Whichever town you visit in the Pyrenees there will be a good range of hotels from which to choose, with several dozen in each of the larger towns and cities. Hotels in France are classified from one- to four-star and in Spain from one- to five-star on the basis of their facilities, but below an indication of price per room is given. The hotels in the region normally charge per room which gives good value for couples. In the more expensive hotels most rooms will come with an adjoining bathroom.

The hotels listed below have been classified with regard to price as follows:

in France
▌   up to 400F;
▌▌   300–600F;
▌▌▌   over 600F:

in Spain
▌   up to 7,500ptas
▌▌   5,500–10,000ptas
▌▌▌   over 9,000ptas

This is the cost per night for a room. Breakfast is usually charged as an extra. These price ranges should only be viewed as rough guides as most hotels have rooms of various prices, hence the overlap in the bands above.

Ainsa
Mesón de L'Ainsa ▌
Avenida Sobrarbe 12
Tel: 50-00-28
40 rooms.

Sánchez ▌
avenida Sobrarbe 10
Tel: 50-00-14
39 rooms. Central. Swimming pool.

Amélie les Bains
Hôtel Gorges ▌
Place Arago
Tel: 68-39-29-02
Restaurant.

Grand Hotel de la Reine Amélie ▌▌
Tel: 68-39-04-38
Restaurant Le Provence.

Palmarium ▌
avenue Vallespir
Tel: 68-39-19-38

Andorra la Vella
Andorra Palace ▌▌▌
rue de la Roda
Tel: 21-0-72
One of the best hotels in the capital with prices on a par with Novotel.

Hôtel Celler d'En Toni ▌
4 Verge del Pilar
Tel: 21-2-52
Situated on the south side of the river. One of the best restaurants in Andorra la Vella.

Novotel ▌▌▌
Prat de la Creu
Tel: 61-1-16
Overlooks the Valira River. Established in 1990.

Mercure ▌▌▌
58 avenue Meritxell
Tel: 20-7-73
Well established French chain.

La Rosa ▌
Antic carrer Major 16
Tel: 21-8-10
Close to the Casa de la Val. Cheap but pleasant hotel.

Anglet
Château de Brindos ▌▌▌
Tel: 59-23-17-68
Three and a half kms (2 miles) to the south side of town by the eponymous lake. Restaurant.

Argelès sur Mer
Hôtel du Lido ▌▌
50 boulevard de la Mer
Tel: 68-81-10-32
73 rooms. Restaurant. Luxurious.

Hôtel les Mouettes ▌▌
route de Collioure
Tel: 68-81-21-69
Away from the beach, towards Collioure.

Hôtel Soubirana ▌
58 route Nationale
Tel: 68-81-01-44
18 rooms. Restaurant.

Argelès-Gazost
Hôtel Miramont ▌
rue Pasteur
Tel: 62-97-01-26
29 rooms. Restaurant.

Printania ▌
avenue Pyrénées
Tel: 62-97-06-57

Aulus

Beauséjour
Tel: 61-96-00-06
Pleasant restaurant.

Terrasse
Tel: 61-96-00-98

Ax-les-Thermes

Hotel de la Paix
place du Breilh
Tel: 61-64-22-61
36 rooms. Restaurant. In the shopping area.

Royal Thermal
Esplanade du Couloubret
Tel: 61-64-22-51
63 rooms. Overlooks casino. Modern.

Bagnères de Bigorre

Hôtel du Commerce
4 place André-Fourcade
Tel: 62-95-07-33
23 rooms. Restaurant.

Hôtel Trianon
place des Thermes
Tel: 62-95-09-34
30 rooms. Restaurant. Pool.

Hôtel la Residence
Parc Thermal du Salut
Tel: 62-95-03-97
40 rooms. Restaurant.

Bagnères de Luchon

Hôtel des Bains
75 allées d'Etigny
Tel: 61-79-00-58
Large hotel with 52 rooms, opposite the spa. Restaurant.

Concorde
allées d'Etigny
Tel: 61-79-00-69
22 rooms. Restaurant. Popular meeting place.

Inter Hôtel Corneille
5 avenue Alexandre-Dumas
Tel: 61-79-36-22
58 rooms. Restaurant. Set in its own park.

Banyuls sur Mer

Hôtel Canal
9 rue Dugommier
Tel: 68-88-06-75
30 rooms. Restaurant.

Hôtel Le Catalan
route de Cerbère
Tel: 68-88-02-80
36 rooms. Restaurant. Modernized.

Les Elmes
plage des Elmes
Tel: 68-88-03-12

Barèges

Hôtel Central
rue Principale
Tel: 62-92-68-05
20 rooms. Restaurant.

Hôtel Richelieu
rue Ramond
Tel: 62-92-68-11
36 rooms. Restaurant.

Bayonne

Le Grand Hôtel
rue Thiers
Tel: 59-59-14-61
Conveniently situated in the old city.

Mercure
avenue Jean Rostand
Tel: 59-63-30-90
Outside the old walls to the south. Modernized.

Biarritz

Comfort Inn
19 avenue Reine Victoria
Tel: 59-22-04-80
40 rooms.

Hôtel Eurotel
avenue Perspective
Tel: 59-24-32-33
Overlooking the start of Plage de la Côte des Basques.

Hotel Miramar
avenue de l'Imperatrice
Tel: 59-41-30-00
Restaurant has a Michelin rosette. 109 rooms.

Hôtel du Palais
avenue de l'Imperatrice
Tel: 59-41-64-00
Built by Napoleon III. 133 rooms. Looks out over the Grande Plage. Michelin rosette restaurant.

Bielsa

Hotel Bielsa
carretera de Ainsa
Tel: 974-50-10-08
60 rooms.

Bielsa-2
carraterra Francia-Bielsa
Tel: 50-01-08
39 rooms.

Parador Nacional de Monte Perdido
Tel: 974-50-10-11
North end of Pineta Valley. Spectacular setting 13 km (8 miles) from Bielsa. One of the best hotels in the Pyrenees. Good restaurant.

Le Boulou

Le Relais des Chartreuses
Les Chartreuses du Boulou
Tel: 68-83-15-88
Traditional château with only ten rooms. Restaurant.

Cadaqués

Marina
carrer La Riera Sant Vicent
Tel: 972-25-81-99

Playa Sol
platya Pianch 3
Tel: 972-25-81-00
On the water's edge.

Caldas de Boí

El Manantial
Tel: 973-69-62-10
One and a half kilometres (1 mile) north-west of Taüll. Most luxurious hotel in the Boi valley.

Cauterets

Hôtel Club Aladin
avenue Général Leclerc
Tel: 62-92-60-00
70 rooms. Restaurant.

Hôtel de Bordeaux
23, rue Richelieu
Tel: 62-92-52-50
26 rooms. Restaurant.

Céret

Hôtel les Arcades
1 place Picasso
Tel: 68-87-12-30.
26 rooms. No restaurant.

Hôtel la Terrasse au Soleil
route de Fontfrède
Tel: 68-87-01-94
26 rooms. Terrace restaurant; the best in Céret.

Hotel Vidal ▮
4 place du 4 Septembre
Tel: 68-87-00-85
11 rooms. No restaurant. Centrally situated.

Collioure
Hôtel le Bon Port ▮▮
route de Port-Vendres
Tel: 68-82-06-08
22 rooms. Restaurant.

Hôtel la Frégate ▮▮
24 boulevard Camille Pelletan
Quayside
Tel: 68-82-06-05
24 rooms. Good fish restaurant.

Hôtel le Méditerranée ▮▮
avenue Aristide Maillol
Tel: 68-82-08-60
23 rooms. No restaurant.

Escaldes
Roc Blanc ▮▮▮
Placa Co-Princeps
Tel: 21-4-86
A fine hotel which also operates a spa.

Figueres
Bon Retorn ▮
Old French Road
Tel: 972-50-46-23

President ▮▮
ronda Firal 33
Tel: 972-50-17-00

Ronda ▮
ronda Barcelona 104
Tel: 972-50-39-11

Foix
Hôtel la Barbacane ▮▮
avenue de Lérida
Tel: 61-65-50-44
21 rooms. Restaurant.

Hôtel Lons ▮
6 place G.-Duthil
Tel: 61-65-52-44
35 rooms. Restaurant.

Hôtel Pyrène ▮
2km along N20
Tel: 61-65-48-66
20 rooms. No restaurant.

Fuenterrabía
Parador, El Emperador ▮▮▮
plaza de Armas
Tel: 943-64-21-40
One of the most exotic properties in the state-run chain. Recently reopened. No restaurant.

Gavarnie
Vignemale ▮▮
Tel: 62-92-40-00
45 rooms. Refurbished in 1988. Best restaurant in Gavarnie.

Girona
Costabella ▮▮
avenida de Franca 61
Tel: 972-20-25-24
47 rooms.

Hotel Sol Girona ▮▮▮
carrer Barcelona
Tel: 972-40-05-00
114 rooms.

Ultonia ▮▮
Gran via de Jaume
Tel: 972-20-38-50
45 rooms. No restaurant.

Isaba
Isaba ▮▮
Tel: 948-89-30-00
Excellent modern hotel.

Lola ▮
Tel: 948-89-30-12
Recommended budget hotel.

Jaca
Hostal Aboira ▮
calle Valle de Anso 3
Tel: 974-36-35-28
30 rooms. No restaurant.

Condé Aznar ▮
paseo de la Constitucion 3
Tel: 974-36-10-50
23 rooms. Highly recommended restaurant.

Gran Hotel ▮▮
paseo de la Constitucion 1
Tel: 974-36-09-00
165 rooms. Swimming pool.

Jurançon
Castel du Pont d'Oly ▮▮
2 avenue Bansky
Tel: 59-06-13-40
Quiet terrace restaurant.

Lló
Hôtel Auberge Atalaya ▮▮
Tel: 68-04-70-04
13 rooms. One of the really good restaurants of the region.

Lourdes
Hôtel Campanile ▮
route Tarbes
Tel: 62-94-07-07
49 rooms. Restaurant.

Hôtel Gallia et Londres ▮▮
26 avenue Peyramale
Tel: 62-94-35-44
90 rooms. Restaurant.

Hôtel Jeanne-d'Arc ▮▮
1 rue Alsace-Lorraine
Tel: 62-94-35-42
156 rooms. Restaurant.

La Molina
Adsera ▮▮
Tel: 972-89-20-01
Renowned restaurant El Tirol.

Els Isards ▮▮
avenida Supermolina
Tel: 972-89-21-01

Molitg les Bains
Château de Riell ▮▮▮
Tel: 68-05-04-40
18 double rooms and 3 suites. Restaurant with Michelin rosette.

Núria
Hotel Vall de Núria ▮
Tel: 972-73-03-26
65 rooms. Comfortable hotel in converted sanctuary.

Pamplona
Maisonnave ▮▮▮
calle Nueva 20
Tel: 948-22-26-00

La Perla ▮
plaça del Castillo
Tel: 948-22-77-04

Tres Reyes ▮▮▮
Parque La Taconera
Tel: 948-22-66-00
168 rooms. Swimming pool. Air conditioned.

Pau

Continental
2 rue Maréchal Foch
Tel: 59-27-69-31
Largest hotel in Pau with one of the best restaurants.

Bayonne
rue d'Etigny
Tel: 59-27-01-06

Paris
80 rue Emile Garet
Tel: 59-82-58-00

Perpignan

Hôtel de la Loge
place de la Loge
Tel: 68-34-41-02
22 rooms. No restaurant. Central area.

Hôtel Park
18 boulevard Jean Bourrat
Tel: 68-35-14-14
67 rooms. Finest in central Perpignan. Best restaurant in the city. Michelin rosette.

Hôtel le Berry
6 avenue Général de Gaulle
Tel: 68-34-59-02
Near station.

El Port de la Selva

Hostal Comercio
Fish Market
Tel: 972-38-70-14
Fish restaurant and Catalan dishes.

Porto Cristo
carrer Major 59
Tel: 972-38-70-62
Set back from beach.

Port Vendres

Hôtel St Elme
2 Quai Pierre Forgas
Tel: 68-82-01-07
28 rooms.

Hôtel les Tamarins
Plage des Tamarins
Tel: 67-82-01-24
37 rooms. Restaurant.

Puigcerdá

Chalet de Golf
Devesa de Golf
Tel: 972-88-09-62
16 rooms. Three kilometres (2 miles) south-west of the town.

Del Lago
avenida Dr Piguillem
Tel: 972-88-10-00
16 rooms.

Tixaire
carrer Escuelas Pías 5
Tel: 972-88-01-26
44 rooms.

Quillan

Hôtel la Chaumière
258 boulevard Charles de Gaulle
Tel: 68-20-17-90
16 rooms. Recommended restaurant.

Hôtel la Pierre-Lys
avenue Carcassonne
Tel: 68-20-08-65
16 rooms. Restaurant.

Hôtel Terminus
45 boulevard Charles de Gaulle
Tel: 68-20-05-72
20 rooms. Restaurant.

Ripoll

Hotel Monasterio
plaça Gran 4
Tel: 972-70-01-50

Payet
Plaça Nova 2
Tel: 972-70-02-50

Solana del Ter
Barcelona road
Tel: 972-70-10-62
One and a half kilometres (1 mile) south of the town.

Roses

El Parque
avenida Rhodes 2
Tel: 972-25-60-24
13 rooms. Restaurant.

La Terraza
passeig Maritim
tel: 972-25-61-54
112 rooms. Restaurant.

St Etienne de Baïgorry

Hôtel Arcé
Centre Ville
Tel: 59-37-40-14
Local produce and regional specialities. Terrace and gardens on the river.

St Gaudens

Hôtel Beaurivage
Pont de Valentine
Tel: 61-89-06-47
14 rooms. Restaurant.

Hôtel du Commerce
avenue Boulogne
Tel: 61-89-44-77
54 rooms. Restaurant.

Esplanade
7 place de Mas Saint-Pierre
Tel: 61-89-15-90
12 rooms. No restaurant.

St Girons

Hôtel Eychenne
avenue Laffont
Tel: 61-66-20-55
48 rooms. Restaurant with Michelin rosette.

Hôtel le Vallier
20 avenue d'Aulot
Tel: 61-66-22-25
10 rooms. No restaurant.

St Jean Pied-de-Port

Central
pl. Général de Gaulle
Tel: 59-37-00-22
Restaurant highly recommended.

Continental
3 avenue Renaud
Tel: 59-37-00-25

Pyrénées
pl. Général de Gaulle
Tel: 59-37-01-01
Situated opposite the old walls. One of the best hotels and restaurants in the Pyrenees. Two Michelin rosettes.

San Sebastián

Avenida
Igueldo district
Tel: 943-21-20-22

Buenavista
Igueldo district
Tel: 943-21-06-00

Maria Christina
paseo Republica Argentina
Tel: 943-42-49-00
Own gardens. 139 rooms. Luxury-class hotel. One of the finest in the Pyrenees.

Hotel Parma II
calle Général Jáuregui
Tel: 943-42-88-93

La Seu d'Urgell
Hotel Andria I
passeig Joan Brudieu
Tel: 973-35-03-00

Duc d'Urgell I
carrer Josep de Zuleta
Tel: 973-35-21-95
No restaurant.

Parador de la Seo de Urgell III
carrer Santo Domingo
Tel: 973-35-20-00

Sevignac-Meyracq
Les Bains de Secours I
Tel: 59-05-62-11
Good value restaurant—best in the Ossau valley.

Tarbes
Hôtel Henri IV I
7 avenue Bertrand-Barère
Tel: 62-34-01-68
24 rooms. No restaurant.

Hôtel de la Marne I
4 avenue de la Marne
Tel: 62-93-03-64
25 rooms. No restaurant.

Hôtel Président I
rue A Briand
Tel: 62-93-98-40
57 rooms. Restaurant. Best hotel in Tarbes.

Torla
Edelweiss I
carretera de Ordesa
Tel: 974-48-61-73
57 rooms.

Ordesa I
carretera de Ordesa
Tel: 974-48-61-25
69-room modern hotel in own grounds 3km (2 miles) from village.

Viñamala I
Fatas, 5
Tel: 974-48-61-56
In the main part of the village. Several rooms have large sunny terraces with good views.

Vernet les Bains
Hostellerie Compte II
Guifred
6 avenue des Thermes
Tel: 68-05-51-37
10 rooms. Restaurant.

Hôtel le Mas Fleuri II
25 boulevard Clemenceau
Tel: 68-05-51-94
35 rooms. No restaurant.

Hôtel Princess I
rue des Lavandières
Tel: 68-05-56-22
40 rooms. Restaurant.

Villefranche-de-Conflent
Le Vauban I
5 place de l'Eglise
Tel: 68-96-18-03
16 rooms. No restaurant.

Restaurants

Here is a selection of some of the best restaurants in the Pyrenees, many specializing in local cuisine. Note also that many of the hotels listed in the previous section have their own restaurants.

Andorra la Vella
Celler d'En Toni
4 Verge del Pilar
Tel: 21-2-52
One of the best restaurants in Andorra la Vella.

Moli dels Fanals
carrer Dr Vilanova
Tel: 21-3-81

La Truita
58 avenue Meritxell
Tel: 20-7-73

Argelès-Gazost
Le Viscos
St Savin
Tel: 62-97-02-28
Finest restaurant in the area. One and a half kilometres (1 mile) south of the town.

Argelès sur Mer
Al Pescadou
blvd des Albères
Tel: 68-81-38-12
Specializes in fish.

Solarium
avenue Vallespir
Tel: 68-81-10-74

Ax-les-Thermes
Le Castelet
Perles et Castelet
Tel: 61-64-24-52
Rural restaurant 3 km (2 miles) north-west of Ax. Terrace.

Bagnères de Bigorre
Le Bigourdan
rue Victor Hugo
Tel: 62-95-20-20

Le Trianon
place de Thermes
Tel: 62-95-09-34

Bagnères de Luchon
Les Jardins des Cascades
Montauban de Luchon
Tel: 61-79-83-09
Leading restaurant in the area.

Le Pailhet
12 avenue Maréchal Foch
Tel: 61-79-09-60

Banyuls
Sardinal
place Paul Reig
Tel: 68-88-30-07
Attractive restaurant with terrace. Catalan fish dishes.

Bayonne
Auberge Cheval Blanc
rue Bourg-Neuf
Tel: 59-59-01-33
Family-run restaurant in old building. Traditional recipes.

François Miura
24 rue Marengo
Tel: 59-59-49-89
In the heart of the old town. Features local produce.

Restaurant Tanière
avenue Cap Resplandy
Tel: 59-25-53-42
By the River Adour. Excellent for fish and vegetarian dishes.

Besalú
Cúria Reial
placa Major
Tel: 972-59-02-63
In medieval cellars.

Pont Vell
Pont Vell
Tel: 972-59-10-27
Lovely setting on bridge over River Fluvia. Unusual dishes. Good service.

Cadaqués
Galiota
carrer Narciso Montariol
Tel: 972-25-81-87
Michelin rosette.

Cauterets
Pont d'Espagne
Pont d'Espagne
Tel: 62-92-54-10
6.5 km (4 miles) from Cauterets in an attractive situation.

Céret
Les Feuillants
1 boulevard La Fayette
Tel: 68-87-37-88
One Michelin rosette.

La Terrasse au Soleil
route de Fontfrède
Tel: 68-87-01-94
Terrace restaurant.

Collioure
La Balette
route de Port Vendres
Tel: 68-82-06-07
Near harbour. Good fish restaurant.

La Frégate
24 boulevard Canulle Pelletan
Quayside
Tel: 68-82-06-05
Good fish restaurant.

Eus
Grangousier
Tel: 68-96-28-32
Stylish. Swimming pool. Heliport.

Figueres
Ampurdén
N11
Tel: 972-50-05-62
One and a half kilometres (1 mile) north of town. Regional cuisine. Michelin rosette.

Foix
Au Camp du Drap d'Or
rue Noel-Peyrevidal
Tel: 61-02-87-87
Close to Castle. Traditional cuisine but fashionably light.

Médiéval
rue des Chapeliers
Tel: 61-02-81-50
Restaurant on two floors—one rustic, one modern.

Fuenterrabía
Ramon Roteta
calle Irún
Tel: 972-64-16-93
Elegant surroundings and garden for al fresco dining.

Gavarnie
Vignemale
Tel: 62-92-40-00
Reopened in 1988 after refurbishment. Best restaurant in Gavarnie.

Girona
Albereda
carrer Alberada 7
Tel: 972-22-60-02

Selva Mar
carrer Santa Eugenia
Tel: 972-23-63-29
Speciality is seafood.

Jaca
La Cocina Aragonesa
carrer Cervantes 5
Tel: 974-36-10-50
Part of Hotel Condé Aznar. Basque Cuisine.

Restaurant Oreol
Aparthotel Oreol
avenue Francia 37
Tel: 974-36-24-11
Fish specialities. Also self-service budget meals.

El Parque
paseo de la Constitucion
Tel: 974-36-09-00
Part of the Gran Hotel. Emphasizes fresh food from the local market.

Jurançon
Castel du Pont d'Oly
2 avenue Bansky
Tel: 59-06-13-40
Quiet terrace restaurant.

Ruffet
3 avenue Charles Touzet
Tel: 59-06-25-13
Béarnaise cuisine in restaurant.

Lló
Auberge Atalaya
Tel: 68-04-70-04
One of the really good restaurants of the region.

Lourdes
Auberge Maurice Prat
22 avenue Antoine Béguère
Tel: 62-94-01-53

L'Ermitage
place Monseigneur Laurence
Tel: 62-94-08-42
Recommended restaurant.

Mantet
Bouf' Tic
Tel: 68-05-51-76
Auberge with rooms.

Chez Richard
Tel: 68-05-60-99
Catalan Cuisine

El Tupi
Tel: 68-05-61-27
Pizzas and à la carte with rooms.

La Molina
Adsera
Tel: 972-89-20-01
Renowned restaurant El Tirol.

Molitg les Bains
Château de Riell
Tel: 68-05-04-40
Restaurant with Michelin rosette.

Oloron
Hôtel Darroze
place de la Mairie
Tel: 59-39-00-99
Good restaurant.

Pamplona
Hartza
calle Juan de Labrit
Tel: 948-22-45-68
Low-fat meals. One Michelin rosette.

Josetxo
plaça Principe de Viana
Tel: 948-22-20-97
Traditional Navarrese or French cuisine. One Michelin rosette.

Rodero
calle Arrieta 3
Tel: 948-22-80-35

Pau
Au Fin Gourmet
24 avenue Gaston Lacoste
Tel: 59-27-47-71

Chez Pierre
16 rue L Barthou
Tel: 59-27-76-86
One Michelin rosette.

Le Viking
33 boulevard Tourasse
Tel: 59-84-02-91
One Michelin rosette.

Perpignan
Le Bourgogne
63 avenue Général Leclerc
Tel: 68-34-96-05

Chapon Fin
Park Hotel, blvd Jean Bourrat
Tel: 68-35-14-14
Michelin rosette. Menu features fresh local produce.

Le Festin de Pierre
7 rue du Théâtre
Tel: 68-51-28-74
15th-century building in the old quarter.

El Port de la Selva
Hostal Comercio
Fish Market
Tel: 972-38-70-14
Fish restaurant and Catalan dishes.

Quillan
La Chaumière
blvd Charles de Gaulle
Tel: 68-20-17-90
Recommended restaurant.

Hôtel Pierre-Lys
avenue. Carcassonne
Tel: 68-20-08-65
Recommended restaurant.

Roses
El Bulli
calla Montjoi
Tel: 972-25-76-51
Michelin rosette restaurant with breathtaking views.

St Etienne de Baïgorry
Hôtel Arcé
Centre Ville
Tel: 59-37-40-14
Local produce and regional specialities. Terrace and gardens on the river.

St Girons
Eychenne
avenue Laffont
place du Centre
Tel: 61-66-20-55
Restaurant with Michelin rosette.

St Jean Pied-de-Port
Central
place Général de Gaulle
Tel: 59-37-00-22
Restaurant highly recommended.

Etche Ona
15 pl Floquet
Tel: 59-37-01-14
Recommended restaurant.

Pyrénées
place Général de Gaulle
Tel: 59-37-01-01
Situated opposite the old walls. One of the best hotels and restaurants in the Pyrenees. Two Michelin rosettes.

San Sebastián
Akelare
Monte Igueldo
Tel: 943-21-20-52
Marvellous views. Two Michelin rosettes.

Restaurant Alejandro
calle Fermin Calbetón
Tel: 943-42-71-58
In the heart of the old town. One Michelin rosette.

Arzak
Alto de Miracruz
Tel: 943-27-84-65
Three Michelin rosettes for delicacy, originality and daring.

Rekondo
Monte Igueldo
Tel: 943-21-29-07
Grilled fresh fish.

Sevignac-Meyracq
Les Bains de Secours
Tel: 59-05-62-11
Good value restaurant—best in the Ossau valley.

Tarbes
L'Ambroisie
38 rue Larrey
Tel: 62-93-09-34

Caravelle
Airport of Tarbes-Ossun-Lourdes
Tel: 62-32-99-96
Marvellous views over Pyrenees. Highly praised.

Le Petit Gourmand
avenue Bertrand-Barère
Tel: 62-34-26-86
Friendly and relaxed.

Index

Page references in *italic* refer to illustrations, those in **bold** refer to main entries.